Free College Money and Training for Women

by

Matthew Lesko

and

Mary Ann Martello

Researchers
Laura Difore, Allison Mays, Marcelle McCarthy
Cindy Owens, Bradley Sowash, Emily Subler

Production
Cynthia D. Wade

Marketing
Kim McCoy

Support
Mercedes Sundeen

Cover
Steve Bonham

FREE COLLEGE MONEY AND TRAINING FOR WOMEN, Copyright 2000 by Matthew Lesko and Mary Ann Martello. All rights reserved. Printed in the United States of America. Published by Information USA, Inc., P.O. Box E, Kensington, MD 20895.

Clip art used in this publication © Dynamic Graphics, Inc.; Totem Graphics; One Mile Up; Tech Pool; Image Club Graphics, Inc.; and Corel Corp.

FIRST EDITION

Library of Congress Cataloging-in-Publication date
Lesko, Matthew
Martello, Mary Ann

Free College Money and Training for Women

ISBN # 1-878346-52-0

Most books by Matthew Lesko are available at special quantity discounts for bulk purchases for sales promotions, premiums, fund-raising or educational use. Special books or book excerpts also can be created to fit specific needs.

For details, write Information USA, Special Markets, Attention: Kim McCoy, P.O. Box E, Kensington, MD 20895; or 1-800-797-7811, Marketing; {www.lesko.com}.

Table of Contents

Table of Contents

Table of Contents

Table of Contents

Table of Contents

Women Are Smarter Than Men

You can argue until you're blue in face about who is smarter, man or woman. But it is clear from the statistics that women know better than men that adult training and higher education are the keys to living a successful life in the 21st Century.

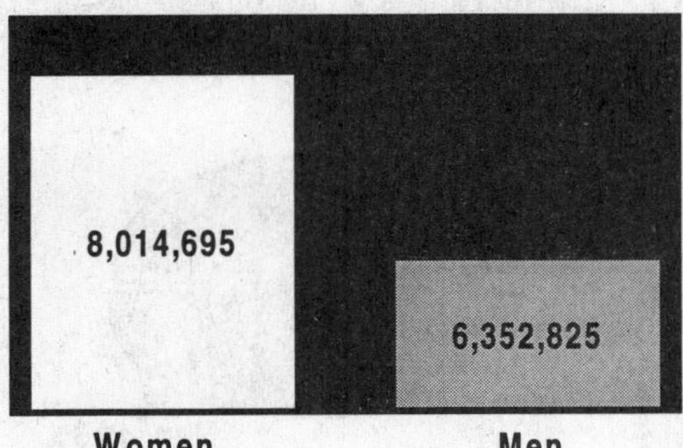

Source: 1998 Digest of Education Statistics

More Women Over Age 35 Are In College Than Men Over Age 35

1996 Enrolled College Students Over 35

Women 1,753,000

Men 1,039,000

Source: 1998 Digest of Education Statistics

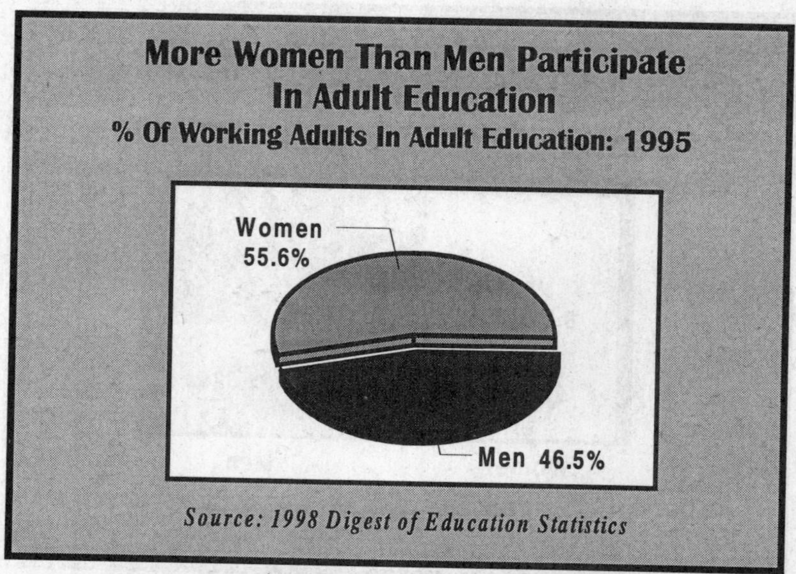

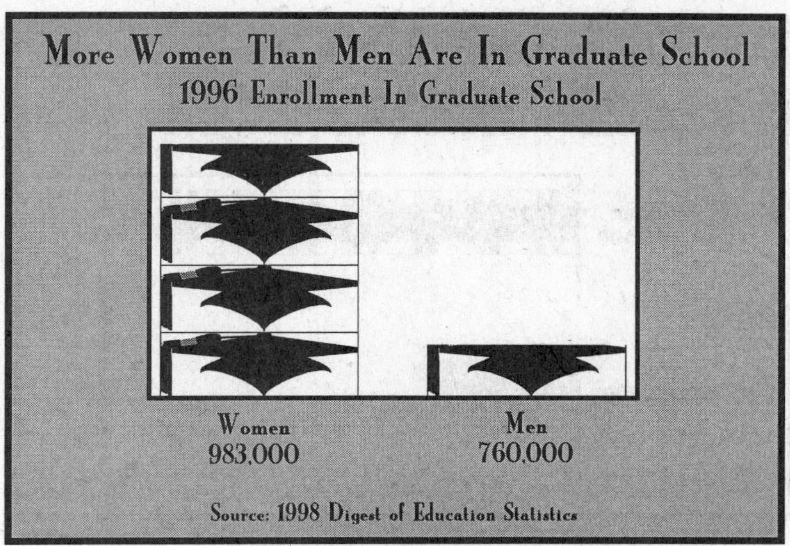
More Women Than Men Are In Graduate School
1996 Enrollment In Graduate School
Women
983,000
Men
760,000
Source: 1998 Digest of Education Statistics

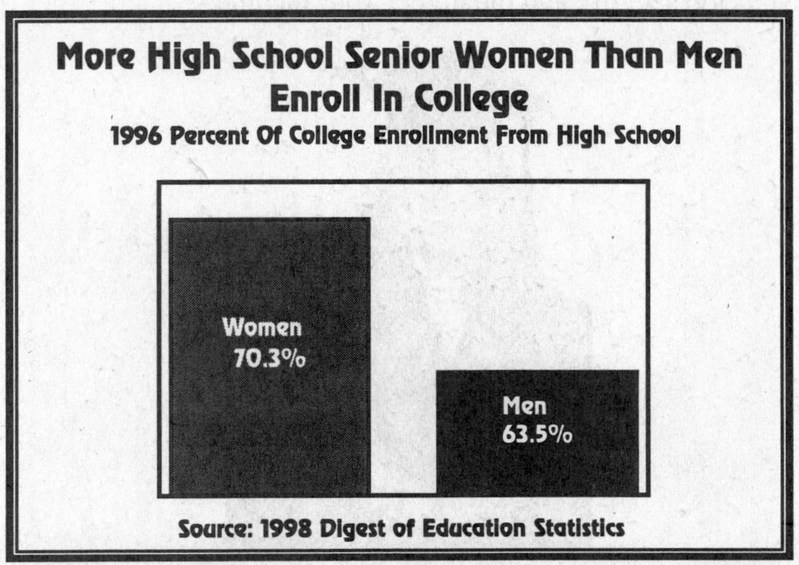
More High School Senior Women Than Men Enroll In College
1996 Percent Of College Enrollment From High School
Women
70.3%
Men
63.5%
Source: 1998 Digest of Education Statistics

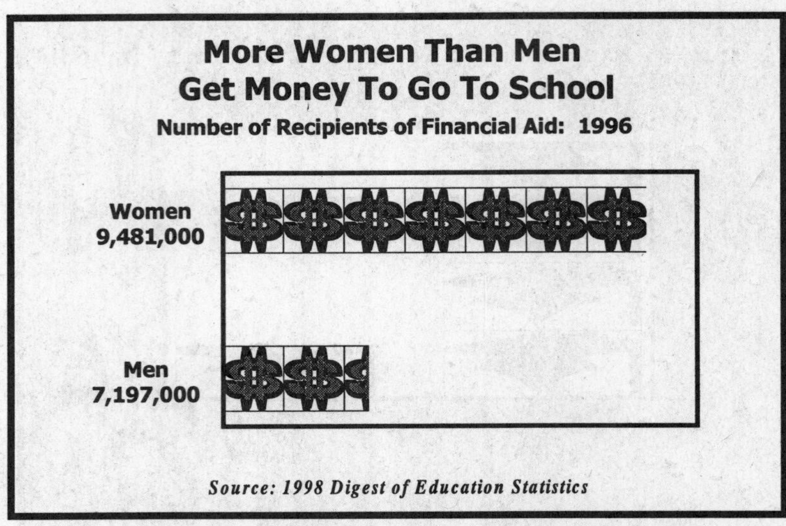

The more education and training you receive the higher your job security and the higher your income.

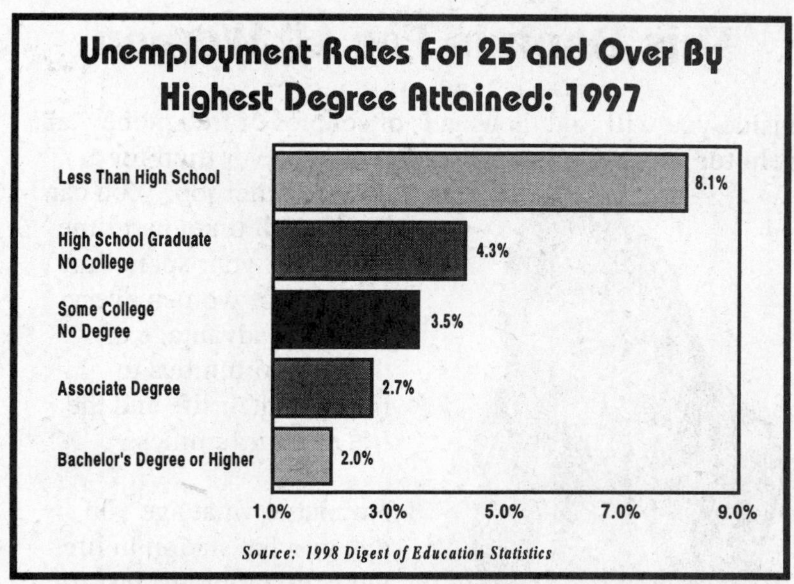
Unemployment Rates For 25 and Over By Highest Degree Attained: 1997
Less Than High School
8.1%
High School Graduate No College
4.3%
Some College No Degree
3.5%
Associate Degree
2.7%
Bachelor's Degree or Higher
2.0%
1.0%
3.0%
5.0%
7.0%
9.0%
Source: 1998 Digest of Education Statistics

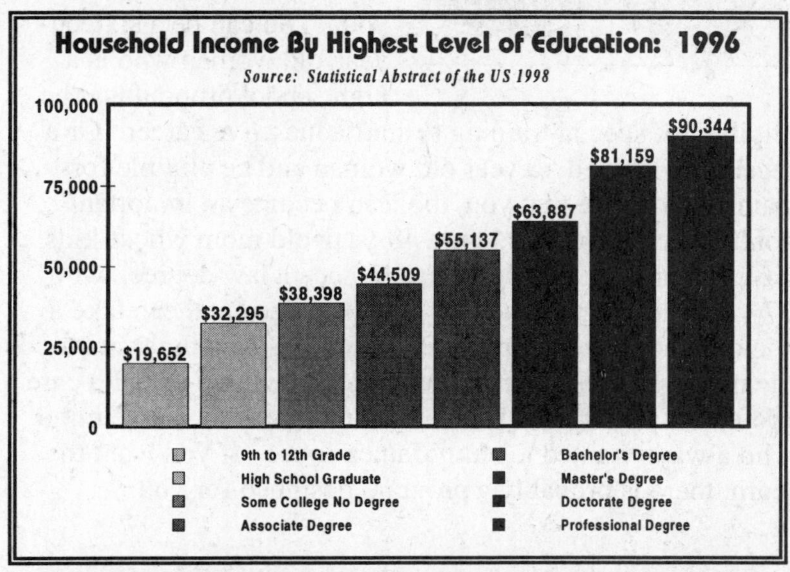
Household Income By Highest Level of Education: 1996
Source: Statistical Abstract of the US 1998
100,000
75,000
50,000
25,000
0
$19,652
$32,295
$38,398
$44,509
$55,137
$63,887
$81,159
$90,344
9th to 12th Grade
High School Graduate
Some College No Degree
Associate Degree
Bachelor's Degree
Master's Degree
Doctorate Degree
Professional Degree

This Book Is For All Women

Inside you will find thousands of sources of free money and help for women who want to go to college or train for a new or better job. You can do this full time, part time or even in your spare time. Millions of women every year take advantage of these opportunities to improve their life and the life of their families.

No matter what age you are, or what station in life, there are programs just for you. You can be a sixteen-year-old woman who is a high school dropout and be eligible for special training to start a lucrative career. Or a recently widowed 60 year old woman and be eligible for training to insure that you, too, can become an important contribution to society. Or a 48-year-old mom whose kids have left and who is eligible to finance a law degree. Or a 27-year-old yuppie who just got downsized and can take a 4-month computer course. Or a 35-year-old woman with the mid-career blues and be eligible to become a health care professional. Or a 90-year-old woman with an active mind who always wanted to study James Joyce. If you want to learn, there is probably a program designed for you.

The Money Goes Begging

I'm sure I'd sell a lot more books if I could make everyone believe that all this money goes begging. But the truth is that some of it does and some of it doesn't.

A recent article in the Washington Post described a Maryland scholarship program that expected to give out 2,000 awards at $3,000 each but only 700 people applied. That's only 35% of what was available to be given out. Another program in Ohio, that offered four scholarships of up to $2,000 to students who wanted to study family and consumer science, could only find three people to apply. Another waste.

There are people out there with needs and there are programs offered by government and non-profit organizations that provide money to meet those needs. The problem is that these organizations do not have advertising money to tell you about them. They are not going to come to your door and tell you about it. It's up to you to go get it. This book gives you the tools to get the money you need. So go get it.... it's over $80 Billion. Someone has to get this money and it might as well be YOU.

This Book Is Incomplete

No matter how hard we do our research for a book, it is impossible to include every possible money program known to mankind — whoops.... Womankind. What's in this book are only those programs that were found by our researchers at the time the book was printed. Every day, existing programs go out of business and new ones crop up.

It is important, if you are looking for money, that you do not give up if all your needs are not met after reading this book. No one person knows everything, not even me. It's important that you keep looking to discover those new sources of money that will be in our next edition.

Matthew Lesko

66 Federal Money Programs Worth $30 Billion

Most people have heard of the federal government's largest money programs for students like the Pell Grant Program and the Guaranteed Student Loan program. But did you know that the federal government is the single largest source of money for students — whether they show financial need or not? It's true, but very few people are aware of the many grant programs in place and just waiting to give money to those students smart enough to find out about them. These little known programs provide students with:

- $15,000 to do graduate studies in housing related topics for the Department of Housing and Urban Development
- Money to finance a graduate degree in criminal justice from the Department of Justice
- $14,000 to get a graduate degree in foreign languages from the Department of Education
- $8,800 plus tuition and expenses to be a nurse from the Department of Health and Human Services

How To Apply

Requirements and application procedures vary widely from program to program. Some programs accept applications once a year, while others award money on a year round basis. Some programs require you to apply directly to the main funding office in Washington, DC, while other programs distribute the money to local organizations, which then distribute funds to individuals. Many of the programs give the money directly to the schools, and then the schools distribute it. For those, you need to request a listing of the schools that receive the funds.

All these federal programs are listed in the Catalogue of Federal Domestic Assistance, which is available in most libraries. This catalogue lists all the government grant and loan programs available. The program name and number in parenthesis refer to this publication.

Get Loans Directly From Your School

(Federal Direct Loan 84.268)

The Direct Loan Program was begun to provide loans directly to students through schools, rather than through private lenders. Borrowers complete an application, the Free Application for Federal Student Aid (FAFSA), for all Department student financial aid programs. Schools receive the funds and then disburse them to students.

There are four different direct loans: Federal Direct Stafford/Ford Loans are for students who demonstrate financial need; Federal Direct Unsubsidized Stafford/Ford Loans are for students regardless of financial need; Federal Direct PLUS Loans are for parents to pay for their children's education; and Federal Direct Consolidation Loans help combine one or more federal education loans into one loan. The amount one can borrow depends upon dependent/independent status of student and year in school. There are several different repayment options including income contingent repayment plan. Interest rates for loans vary each year.

For your Free Application for Federal Student Aid, contact Federal Student Aid Information Center, P.O. Box 84, Washington, DC 20044; 800-433-3243. Contact: U.S. Department of Education, Direct Loan Payment Center, P.O. Box 746000, Atlanta, GA 30374; 800-557-7394; {www.ed.gov/DirectLoan/fact.html}.

$15,000 For Graduate Students To Study Overseas

(Educational Exchange - Graduate Students 82.001)

Graduate students who would like to spend a year studying overseas can apply for the Fulbright Program, where if accepted, they will receive round trip transportation, tuition, books, maintenance for one academic year in one country, and health insurance. Students apply through the Fulbright program adviser located at their college or university, or they can apply as an at-large applicant by contacting the New York office of the Institute of International Education. Money available: $14,500,000. The average award per student is $21,000, but awards can range anywhere from $1,200 to $40,000.

Contact Institute of International Education, 809 United Nations Plaza, New York, NY 10017; 212-984-5330; {www.iie.org}.

$4,000 Grants For Students Having Trouble Paying Tuition

(Federal Supplemental Education Opportunity Grants 84.007)

If you are working towards your first undergraduate baccalaureate degree and are having trouble paying the bills, you may qualify for money through the Federal Supplemental Educational Opportunity Grants (FSEOG) program. Grants are for undergraduate study and range from $100 to $4000 per academic year, with the student eligible to receive a FSEOG for the time it takes to complete their first degree.

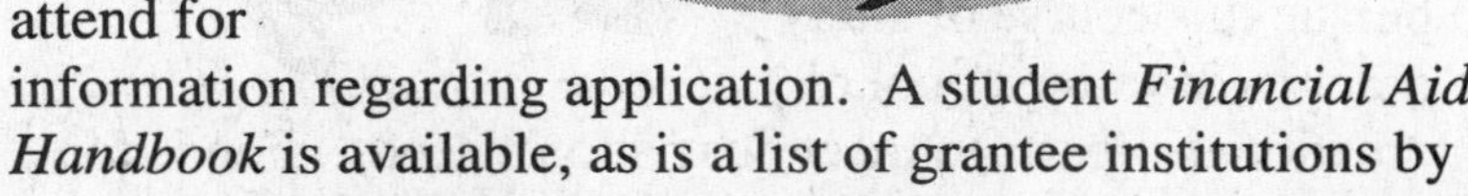

Students should contact the Financial Aid office of the school they attend or plan to attend for information regarding application. A student *Financial Aid Handbook* is available, as is a list of grantee institutions by contacting the Federal Student Aid Information Center, P.O. Box 84, Washington, DC 20044; 800-433-3243. Money available: $619,000,0900. Estimated average award is $745. Contact Student Financial Assistance Program, Office of the Assistant Secretary for Post-Secondary Education, U.S. Department of Education, 400 Maryland Ave., SW, Washington, DC 20202; 202-7081-8242; {www.ed.gov}.

Money For a Foreign Language Degree

(National Resource Centers and Fellowships Program for Language and Area or Language and International Studies 84.015)

In this global world, foreign languages and international studies are becoming increasingly important. The Department of Education has funds to support centers which promote instruction in foreign language and international studies at colleges and universities. In addition, there are graduate fellowships to pursue this course of study in order to develop a pool of international experts to meet our nation's needs. Funds for

centers may be used for instructional costs of language and area and international studies programs, administration, lectures and conferences, library resources and staff, and travel. Grants for fellowships include tuition, fees, and a basic subsistence allowance. Students must apply to those institutions that received the money. For a listing of institutions that received money, contact the office listed below. Students can contact these institutions directly. Money available: Grants: $13,719,000.

Contact International Studies Branch, Center for International Education, Office of Postsecondary Education, U.S. Department of Education, Seventh and D Sts., SW, Washington, DC 20202; 202-401-9783; {www.ed.gov/office/OPE/OHEP/iegps/flas.html}

Money For Students And Teachers To Travel Overseas

(Fulbright-Hays Training Grants - Group Projects Abroad 84.021)

The program objective is to help educational institutions improve their programs in modern foreign language and area studies through overseas study/travel seminar group research, advanced foreign language training, and curriculum development. Funds are available to support overseas study/travel seminar group research and advanced foreign language training. Grant funds may be used for international travel, maintenance allowances, rental of instructional facilities in the country of study, and more. Money available: $2,326,000.

Contact Office of Assistant Secretary for Postsecondary Education, U.S. Department of Education, 600 Independence Ave., SW, Washington, DC 20202; 202-708-7283; {www.ed.gov/offices/OPE/OHEP/iegps/index.htm}.

Money For Ph.D. Students To Do Research Overseas

(Fulbright-Hays Training Grants - Doctoral Dissertation Research Abroad 84.022)

Graduate students now have the opportunity to engage in full time dissertation research abroad in modern foreign language and area studies. This program is designed to develop research knowledge and capability in world areas not widely included in American curricula. The grant includes a basic stipend, round trip airfare, baggage allowance, tuition payments, local travel, and more. Candidates apply directly to the institutions at which they are enrolled. Money available: $2,072,000.

Contact Karla Ver Bryck Block, Advanced Training and Research Branch, Center for International Education, Office of Assistant Secretary for Postsecondary Education, U.S. Department of Education, 600 Independence Ave., SW, Washington, DC 20202, 202-401-9774, {www.ed.gov/offices/OPE/OHEP/iegps/index.htm}

Loans To Go To School

(Federal Family Education Loans 84.032)

Guaranteed loans for educational expenses are available from eligible lenders such as banks, credit unions, savings and loan association, pension funds, insurance companies, and schools to vocational, undergraduate, and graduate students enrolled at eligible institutions. Loans can be used to pay the costs associated with obtaining a college education. The PLUS program is also available, which allows parents to borrow for their dependent student. More information is available by contacting the lending institution regarding the loans available and the application procedure. Money available: $21,032,000,000.

Contact Division of Policy Development, Policy, Training and Analysis Service Office of Assistant Secretary for Postsecondary Education, U.S. Department of Education, Washington, DC 20202; 202-708-8242; {www.ed.gov/offices/OPE}.

Work-Study Program Pays For School

(Federal Work-Study Program 84.033)

Part-time employment is available to students to help meet education expenses. This program pays an hourly wage to undergraduates. Graduate students may be paid by the hour or may receive a salary. There are Federal Work-Study jobs both on and off campus. Money can be used to help defray the costs of higher education.

Students should contact the educational institution they attend or plan to attend to find out about application procedures. A Student Financial Aid Handbook is available, as is a list of grantee institutions, by contacting Federal Student Aid Information Center, P.O. Box 84, Washington, DC 20044; 800-433-3243. Money available: $900,000,000.

Contact Division of Policy Development, Student Financial Assistance Programs, Office of Assistant Secretary for Postsecondary Education, 400 Maryland Ave., SW, Washington, DC 20202; 202-708-9167; {www.ed.gov/offices/OPE}.

Low-Interest Student Loans

(Federal Perkins Loan Program 84.038)

Low-interest loans are available to eligible post-secondary students with demonstrated financial need to help meet educational expenses. Students can borrow money to meet the costs of school.

These loans are for students with exceptional financial need. To apply, contact the Financial Aid office of the school you attend or plan to attend. A student Financial Aid Handbook is available, as well as a list of grantee institutions by contacting the Federal Student Aid Information Center, P.O. Box 84, Washington, DC 20044; 800-433-3242. Money available: $60,000,000.

Contact Division of Policy Development Student Financial Assistance Programs, Office of Assistant Secretary for Postsecondary Education, U.S. Department of Education, 600 Independence Ave., SW, Washington, DC 20202; 202-708-8242; {www.ed.gov/offices/OPE}.

Get Help To Study

(TRIO Upward Bound 84.047)

This program generates skills and motivation necessary for success in education beyond high school among low income and potential first-generation college students and veterans. The goal of the program is to increase the academic performance and motivational levels of eligible enrollees so that they have a better chance of completing secondary school and successfully pursuing postsecondary educational programs.

Eligible students must have completed the eighth grade and be between the ages of 13 and 19, enrolled in high school, and need such services to achieve their goal of college. The program provides instruction in reading, writing, study skills, and mathematics. They can provide academic, financial, or personal counseling, tutorial services, information on student financial assistance, assistance with college and financial aid applications, and more.

Contact your local Upward Bound project to find out more about this program. For a listing of institutions that received money contact the office listed below. Money available: $243,000,000.

Contact Division of Student Services, Education Outreach Branch, Office of Postsecondary Education, U.S. Department of Education, 600 Independence Ave., SW, Room 5065, Washington, DC 20202; 202-708-4804; {www.ed.gov/offices/ OPE}.

$2,700 Grants To Go To School

(Federal Pell Grant Program 84.063)

Grants are available to students with financial need to help meet education expenses. Grants may not exceed $2,700 per year, and must be used for student's first bachelor's or other professional degree. Once an application is completed, the student's financial eligibility for assistance is calculated and the agency then notifies the student of eligibility. A Free Application for Federal Student Aid is available from the Federal Student Aid Information Center, P.O. Box 84, Washington, DC 20044; 800-433-3243. Money available: $7,594,000,000.

Contact Division of Policy Development, Student Financial Assistance Programs, Office of Postsecondary Education, U.S. Department of Education, 600 Independence Ave., SW, Washington, DC 20202; 202-708-8242; {www.ed.gov/offices/OPE}.

Aid For Students Who Want To Help The Deaf

(Training Interpreters For Individuals Who Are Deaf and Individuals Who Are Deaf-Blind 84.160)

This program supports projects that train new interpreters and improve the skills of manual, oral, and cued speech interpreters already providing services to individuals who are deaf and individuals who are deaf-blind. Grants are awarded for training, classroom instruction, workshops, seminars, and field placements. Ten grants are awarded to colleges and universities that have ongoing sign language/oral interpreter training programs of proven merit.

Programs include training courses connected to degree programs in interpreting; short term practical training leading to interpreter certification; and workshops, seminars, and practices. Students must apply to those institutions that have received the program money. For a listing of institutions that received money contact the office listed below. Money available: $2,100,000.

Contact Deafness and Communicative Disorders Branch, Rehabilitation Services Administration, U.S. Department of Education, 600 Independence Ave., SW, Washington, DC 20202; 202-205-9152; 202-205-8352 TTY; {www.ed.gov/offices/OSERS/RSA/PGMS/RT/scholrsp.html}.

Money For Students Interested In Helping People With Disabilities

(Rehabilitation Training 84.129)

This program supports projects that provide new personnel and improve the skills of existing personnel trained in providing vocational rehabilitation services to individuals with disabilities in areas targeted as having personnel shortages.

Training grants are provided in fields directly related to the vocational and independent living rehabilitation of individuals with disabilities, such as rehabilitation counseling, independent living, rehabilitation medicine, physical and occupational therapy, speech-language, pathology and audiology, and more. Projects include residency scholarships in physical medicine and rehabilitation; teaching and graduate scholarships in rehabilitation counseling; and more.

Students must apply to those institutions that have received the program money. A catalogue of projects is available that provides address, phone number, contact person, and an abstract for each grant awarded. Money available: $17,200,000. Contact Rehabilitation Services Administration, Office of Special Education and Rehabilitation Services, U.S. Department of Education, Washington, DC 20202; 202-205-8926; {www.ed.gov/offices/OSERS/RSA/PGMS/RT/scholrsp.html}.

$25,400 Per Year For Graduate Study

(Jacob K. Javits Fellowships 84.170)

This program provides fellowships to individuals of superior ability for graduate study in the fields within the arts, humanities, and social sciences. Money can be used to support a student while he or she attends an institution of higher education.

To apply for these fellowships contact the Federal Student Aid Information Center, P.O. Box 84, Washington, DC 20044; 800-4-FED-AID. Money available: $5,931,000.

Contact Higher Education Programs, Office of Postsecondary Education, U.S. Department of Education, Washington, DC 20202; 202-260-3574; {www.ed.gov/offices/OPE/OHEP/iegps/javits.htm}.

$1,500 Per Year For College

(Robert C. Byrd Honors Scholarships 84.185)

Scholarships are available to exceptionally able students who show promise of continued academic achievement. Scholarships for up to four years to study at any institution of higher education are available through grants to the states. The scholarships are awarded on the basis of merit and are renewable.

To apply for this grant award, interested applicants must contact their state educational agency, which administers this program. Money available: $39,288,000.

Contact U.S. Department of Education, Office of Student Financial Assistance, Office of the Assistant Secretary for Postsecondary Education, Division of Higher Education Incentive Programs, The Portals, Suite C-80, Washington, DC 20024; 202-260-3394; {www.ed.gov}.

Money For Graduate Study

(Graduate Assistance In Areas Of National Need 84.200)

Fellowships are available through graduate academic departments to graduate students of superior ability who demonstrate financial need and are able to enhance the capacity to teach and conduct research in areas of national need.

Designated academic areas change each year and are currently biology, chemistry, engineering, foreign languages, mathematics, and physics. Money can be used to support a student completing a graduate degree program. Students must apply to those institutions that have received the money. For a listing of institutions that received money contact the office listed below. Money available: $26,800,000.

Contact International Education and Graduate Programs Service, Office of Postsecondary Education, U.S. Department of Education, 600 Independence Ave., SW, Washington, DC 20202; 202-260-3608; {www.ed.gov/offices/OPE/OHEP/ iegps/gaann.htm}.

Grants For Those Who Have Trouble Paying Tuition

(Ronald E. McNair Post Baccalaureate Achievement 84.217)

This program provides grants to institutions of higher education to prepare low income, first-generation college students and students underrepresented in graduate education for graduate study. Money can be used to pay the costs for research and other scholarly activities, summer internships, seminars, tutoring, academic counseling, and securing admission and financial assistance for graduate study.

Students must apply to those institutions that have received the money. For a listing of institutions that received money contact the office listed below. Money available: $23,540,000.

Contact U.S. Department of Education, Division of Student Services, Office of Postsecondary Education, 600 Independence Ave., SW, Washington, DC 20202; 202-708-4804; {www.ed.gov/offices/OPE/OHEP/hepss/mcnair.html}.

Money For Public Service Students

(Harry S. Truman Scholarship Program 85.001)

A special scholarship program for college juniors has been established to encourage students to pursue careers in public service. Money can be used to support a student completing his or her undergraduate and graduate studies.

A faculty representative is appointed for each school and is responsible for publicizing the scholarship program; soliciting recommendations on students with significant potential for leadership; conducting a competition on campus; and forwarding the institution's official nomination to the Truman Scholarship Review committee. For more information write to the Foundation listed above. Money available: $3,187,000.

Contact Louis Blair, Executive Secretary Truman Scholarship Foundation, 712 Jackson Place, NW, Washington, DC 20006; 202-395-4831; {www.truman.gov}.

Spend A Semester In A Department Of Energy Lab

(Science and Engineering Research Semester 81.097)

The program objective is to give undergraduate students the opportunity to participate in hands-on research at the cutting edge of science at the Department of Energy laboratories, and to provide training and experience in the operation of sophisticated state-of-the-art equipment and instruments.

Those students majoring in energy related fields can spend a semester at many of the Department of Energy's labs. The energy research must be concentrated in an area of the laboratory's ongoing research. Applications may be obtained by writing to ERULF, ORISE 36, P.O. Box 117, Oak Ridge, TN 37831; 423-576-2478; {www.orau.gov/ doe_erulf}. Money available: $2,500,000. Students receive a weekly stipend of $350.

Contact Sue Ellen Walbridge, Office of Laboratory Management, U.S. Department of Energy, Washington, DC 20585; 202-586-7231.

Money For Minority Students At Junior Colleges Who Are Energy Majors

(Minority Technical Education Program 81.082)

The program objective is to provide scholarship funding to financially needy minority honor students pursuing training in energy related technologies and to develop linkages with energy industries. Scholarship funds are available to defray costs of tuition, books, tools, transportation, and laboratory fees for minority students attending junior colleges and majoring in energy related field. The students must apply to those institutions that received the money. For a listing of those institutions contact the office listed below. Money available: $382,000.

Contact The Minority Energy Information Clearinghouse, Minority Economic IMPACT, Office of Economic Impact and Diversity, U.S. Department of Energy, Forrestal Building, Washington, DC 20585; 202-586-5876; {www.hr.doe.gov/ed/omei/MTEP.HTM}.

Part-Time Jobs In The Government

(Student Temporary Employment Program 27.003)

The program gives students 16 years of age and older an opportunity for part time temporary employment with federal agencies in order to allow them to continue their education without interruptions caused by financial pressures. The money can be used to pay expenses while attending school. Apply for this program through the youth division of the local office of the State Employment Service.

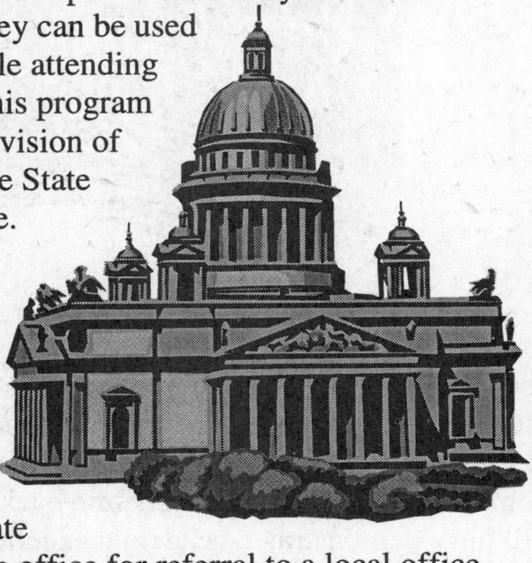

Look in the government section of your phone book to find an office near you, or contact the Main State Employment Service office for referral to a local office. Contact Employment Service, Office of Personnel Management, 1900 E St., NW, Washington, DC 20415; 202-606-0830; {www.usajobs.opm.gov}.

INTERNSHIPS FOR GRADUATE STUDENTS TO WORK AT 54 GOVERNMENT AGENCIES

(Presidential Management Intern Program 27.013)

The PMI Program is a two-year entry-level employment and career development program designed to attract to the federal civil service men and women with graduate degrees from diverse cultural and academic backgrounds. Interns will have demonstrated academic excellence, possess management and leadership potential, and have a commitment to and a clear interest in a public service career. Nominees for the PMI Program undergo a rigorous, competitive screening process.

Being selected as a PMI Finalist is a first step, guarantee a job. Agencies designate positions for and each establishes its own procedures for considering hiring PMIs. Once hired by agencies, PMIs are encourage to work with their agencies to establish an "individual development plan." PMIs participate in training conferences, seminars, and congressional briefings. Money can be used to pay for expenses.

An application form and more information can be requested by contacting the Career America Hotline at 912-757-3000. Contact Office of Personnel Management, Philadelphia Service Center, Federal Building, 600 Arch St., Philadelphia, PA 19106; 215-597-7136; {www.usajobs.opm.gov}.

Money for Health Profession Students

(Health Professions Student Loans 93.342)

The Health Professions Student Loan Program provides long-term, low interest rate loans to full-time financially needy students pursuing a degree in dentistry, optometry, pharmacy, pediatric medicine, or veterinary medicine. Under this program, funds are made available to schools for the establishment of revolving student loan funds.

To apply for this loan, contact the student financial aid office at the school where you intend to apply for admission or where you are enrolled. Loans can not exceed tuition. The interest rate is 5%. A Health Professions Student Loan Fact Sheet is available from the office listed above. Money available: $5,000,000.

Contact Health Professions Student Loan Program, Division of Student Assistance, Bureau of Health Professions, Health Resources and Services Administration, Public Health Service, U.S. Department of Health and Human Services Administration, Parklawn Building, Room 8-34, 5600 Fishers Lane, Rockville, MD 20857; 301-443-4776; {www.hrsa.dhhs.gov/bhpr}.

Money For Primary Care Students

(Health Professions Student Loans, Including Primary Care Loans 93.342)

The Primary Care Loan Program provides long-term low interest rate loans to full-time financially needy students pursuing a degree in allopathic or osteopathic medicine. Under this program, funds are made to schools to establish revolving student loan funds. Students must agree to enter and complete residency training in primary care and to practice in primary care until the loan is paid in full.

To apply for this loan, contact the student financial aid office at the school where you intend to apply for admission or where you are enrolled. Loans cannot exceed tuition. Money available: $5,000,000. Contact Division of Student Assistance, Bureau of Health Professions, Health Resources and Services Administration, Public Health Service, U.S. Department of Health and Human Services Administration, Parklawn Building, Room 8-34, 5600 Fishers Lane, Rockville, MD 20857; 301-443-4776; {www.hrsa.dhhs.gov/bhpr}.

LOANS FOR DISADVANTAGED HEALTH PROFESSION STUDENTS

(Loans for Disadvantaged Students 93.342)

Loans for Disadvantaged Students Program provides funding to eligible health professions schools for the purpose of providing long-term, low-interest loans to assist full-time, financially needy, disadvantaged students to pursue a career in allopathic or osteopathic medicine, dentistry, optometry, podiatry, pharmacy, or veterinary medicine. To apply for this loan, contact the student financial aid office at the school where you intend to apply for admission or where you are enrolled. Loans For Disadvantaged Students Fact Sheet is available from the office listed above. Money available: $5,000,000.

Contact Division of Student Assistance, Bureau of Health Professions' Health Resources and Services Administration, Public Health Service, U.S. Department of Health and Human Services Administration, Parklawn Building, Room 8-34, 5600 Fishers Lane, Rockville, MD 20857; 301-443-4776; {www.hrsa.dhhs.gov/bhpr}.

Money For Nursing Students

(Nursing Student Loans 93.364)

The Nursing Student Loan program provides for long-term, low-interest loans to full-time and half-time financially needy students pursuing a course of study leading to a diploma, associate, baccalaureate or graduate degree in nursing. Federal funds for this program are allocated to accredited public or nonprofit nursing schools. These schools are responsible for selecting the recipients of loans and for determining the amount of assistance a student requires.

To apply for this loan, contact the student financial aid office at the school where you intend to apply for admission or where you are enrolled. Interest rate is 5%. Money available: $3,000,000. Contact Division of Student Assistance, Bureau of Health Professions, Health

Resources and Services Administration, Public Health Service, U.S. Department of Health and Human Services Administration, Parklawn Building, Room 8-34, 5600 Fishers Lane, Rockville, MD 20857; 301-443-4776; {www.hrsa.dhhs.gov/bhpr}.

Money For Faculty Loan Repayments

(Disadvantaged Health Professions Faculty Loan Repayment Program 93.923)

The Faculty Loan Repayment Program provides a financial incentive for degree-trained health professionals from disadvantaged backgrounds to pursue an academic career. The health professional must agree to serve as a member of a faculty of a health professions school, providing teaching services for a minimum of two years, faculty for schools of medicine, nursing, osteopathic medicine, dentistry, pharmacy, pediatric medicine, optometry, veterinary medicine, public health, or a school that offers a graduate program in clinical psychology. The federal government, in turn, agrees to pay as much as $20,000 of the outstanding principal and interest on the individual's educational loans.

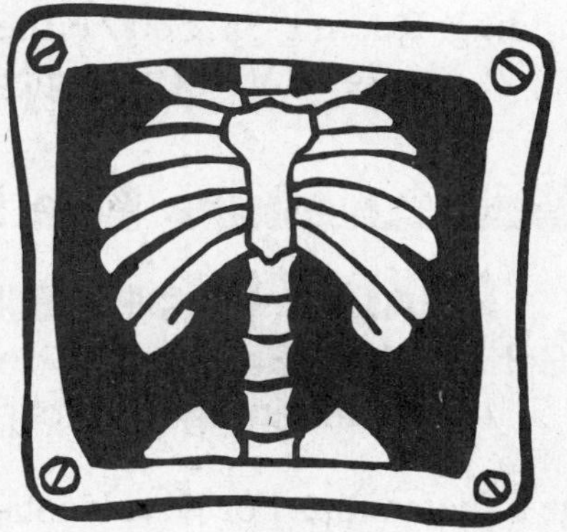

To participate in the program, an individual must be from a disadvantaged background, must not have been a member of a faculty of any school at any time during the 18 month period preceding the date on which the program application is received, must have a degree or be enrolled as a full-time student in the final year of training leading to a degree in one of the eligible disciplines, and must have entered into a contract with an eligible health professions school to serve as a full-time faculty member for a minimum of two years. Money available: $1,061,000.

Contact Division of Student Assistance, Bureau of Health Professions, Health Resources and Services Administration, Public Health Service, U.S. Department of Health and Human Services Administration, Parklawn Building, Room 8-34, 5600 Fishers Lane, Rockville, MD 20857; 301-443-1503; {www.hrsa.dhhs.gov/bhpr}.

Scholarships For Disadvantaged Health Profession Students

(Scholarships For Health Profession Students From Disadvantaged Backgrounds 93.925)

The Scholarships For Disadvantaged Students program provides funds to eligible schools for the purpose of providing scholarships to full-time financially needy students from disadvantaged backgrounds enrolled in health professions and nursing programs. Under this program, funds are awarded to accredited schools of medicine, osteopathic medicine, dentistry, optometry, pharmacy, podiatric medicine, veterinary medicine, nursing (diploma, associate, baccalaureate, and graduate degree), public health, allied health (baccalaureate and graduate degree programs of dental hygiene, medical laboratory technology, occupational therapy, physical therapy, radiologic technology), and graduate programs in clinical psychology.

The schools are responsible for selecting recipients, making reasonable determinations of need and disadvantaged student status, and providing scholarships that cannot exceed the student's financial need. To apply for this scholarship, contact the student financial aid office at the school where you intend to apply for admission or where you are enrolled. Money available: $18,000,000.

Contact Division of Student Assistance, Bureau of Health Professions, Health Resources and Services Administration, Public Health Service, U.S. Department of Health and Human Services Administration, Parklawn Building, Room 8-34, 5600 Fishers Lane, Rockville, MD 20857; 301-443-4776; {www.hrsa.dhhs.gov/bhpr}.

Money For American Indians Who Want To Be Health Care Professionals

(Health Professions Recruitment Program For Indians 93.970)

The program objective is to increase the number of American Indians and Alaskan Natives who become health professionals and money has been set aside to help identify students interested in the field and to assist them in enrolling schools. Some of the projects funded include the recruitment of American Indians into health care programs, a variety of retention services once students have enrolled, and scholarship support.

Students should contact their school directly for assistance. Money available: $2,870,700. Contact Indian Health Service, Division of Health Professions Support, 12300 Twinbrook Parkway, Suite 100, Rockville, MD 20852; 301-443-4242; {www.ihs.gov}.

Health Professions Scholarships For American Indians

(Health Professions Pregraduate Scholarship Program for Indians 93.123)

The program objective is to provide scholarships to American Indians and Alaskan Natives for the purpose of completing pregraduate education leading to baccalaureate degree in the areas of pre-medicine or pre-dentistry. Money can be used to support a student while completing their degree.

Contact the Indian Health Service for application information. Money available: $1,702,569. Awards range from $12,283 to $27,217. Contact Indian Health Service, Scholarship Program, 12300 Twinbrook Parkway, Suite 100, Rockville, MD 20852; 301-443-6197; {www.ihs.gov}.

Opportunity To Receive College Tuition From NSA

(Mathematical Sciences Grants Program 12.901)

National Security Agency (NSA) will consider any student who meets the requirements below and who chooses a full-time college major in either computer science, electrical or computer engineering, languages or mathematics. Requirements consist of having a minimum SAT score of 1100 and a minimum composite ACT score of 25. Chosen

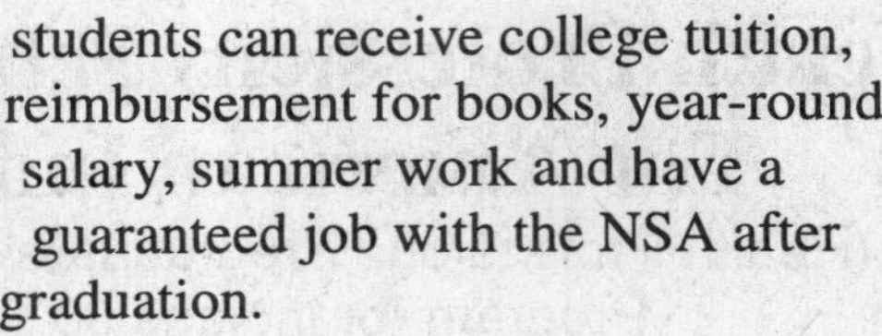

students can receive college tuition, reimbursement for books, year-round salary, summer work and have a guaranteed job with the NSA after graduation.

Students must work for NSA for one and a half times their length of study, which is usually about five years. Money available: $2,600,000. Contact National Security Agency, Manager, Undergraduate Training Program, Attn: S232R (UTP), 9800 Savage Rd., Suite 6840, Ft. Meade, MD 20755-6840; 800-669-0703; {www.nsa.gov}.

Money For American Indians Who Need Extra Studies For Health Care Program

(Health Professions Preparatory Scholarship Program for Indians 93.971)

The program objective is to make scholarship available to American Indians and Alaskan Natives who need to take some extra courses in order to qualify for enrollment or re-enrollment in a health profession school. Money can be used for up to two years of scholarship support, and the funds can cover tuition, stipends, and books.

Students must apply to the Indian Health Service Office for application information. Money available: $2,000,000. Grants range from $13,182 to $26,019. Contact Indian Health Service, Scholarship Program, 12300 Twinbrook Parkway, Suite 100, Rockville, MD 20852; 301-443-6197; {www.ihs.gov}.

Scholarships For Health Care Professionals

(Health Professions Scholarship Program 93.972)

This program objective is to provide scholarships to American Indians and Alaskan natives attending health professions schools and who are interested in serving other Indians. Upon completion, scholarship recipients are obligated to serve in the Indian Health Service one year for each year of scholarship support, with a minimum of two years.

The health professions needed are listed annually in the Federal Register. The money can be used to support a student completing a health profession degree. Money available: $7,300,000. Grants range from $12,136 to $38,222.

Contact Indian Health Service, Scholarship Program, 12300 Twinbrook Parkway, Suite 100, Rockville, MD 20852; 301-443-6197; {www.ihs.gov}.

Grants For Nurse Anesthetists

(Grants For Nurse Anesthetist Faculty Fellowships 93.907)

The program objective is to provide financial assistance and support through fellowships to certified registered nurse anesthetists (CRNAs) who are faculty members of accredited nurse anesthetist programs to enable them to obtain advanced education relevant to their teaching functions.

Money can be used to support faculty members while on fellowship. Faculty members need to apply to those institutions that have received the grants. Money available: $223,997. Grants range from $1542 to $24,308.

Contact Bureau of Health Professions, Health Resources and Services Administration, Public Health Service, Room 9-36, Parklawn Building, 5600 Fishers Lane, Rockville, MD 20857; 301-443-6193; {www.hrsa.dhhs.gov/bhpr}.

Money For Dental Students For Advanced Residency Training

(Residency Training And Advanced Education in General Practice Of Dentistry 93.897)

The program objective is to assist schools of dentistry or dental training to institute residency training and advanced educational programs in the general practice of dentistry. The grant can be used to support personnel, residents or trainees who are in need of financial assistance, to purchase equipment, and for other expenses necessary to conduct the program. Money can be used to support a student while he or she completes a dental training program or residency. Students must apply to those institutions that have received the money.

For a listing of institutions that received money contact the office listed below. Money available: $3,500,000. Contact Public Health and Dental Education Branch, Division of Associated Dental and, Public Health Professions, Bureau of Health Professions, Health Resources and Services Administration, Public Health Service, U.S. Department of

Health and Human Services, 5600 Fishers Lane, Rockville, MD 20857; 301-443-4832; {www.bphc.hrsa.dhhs.gov}.

Health Careers Opportunity Program

(Health Careers Opportunity Program 93.822)

The Health Careers Opportunity Program provides assistance to individuals from disadvantaged backgrounds to obtain a health or allied health profession degree. Grants can be used to identify, recruit, and select individuals from minority and disadvantaged backgrounds for education and training in a health or allied health professions school; facilitate entry of eligible students into such schools; provide counseling or other services designed to assist such individuals in successfully completing their education and training; provide preliminary education for a period prior to entry into the regular course of health or allied health professions education, designed to assist students in successfully completing regular courses of education, or refer the appropriate individuals to institutions providing preliminary education; and provide disadvantaged students with information on financial aid resources.

For a listing of institutions that received money contact the office listed below. Money available: $26,870,000. Contact Division of Disadvantaged Assistance, Bureau of Health Professions, Health Resources and Services Administration, Public Health Services, U.S. Department of Health and Human Services, Room 8A-09, 5600 Fishers Lane, Rockville, MD 20857; 301-443-4493; {www.hrsa.dhhs.gov/bhpr}.

Money For Nursing Students To Repay Their Loans

(Nursing Education Loan Repayment Agreements For Registered Nurses Entering Employment At Eligible Health Facilities 93.908)

As an incentive for registered nurses to enter into full time employment at health facilities with nursing shortages, this program assists in the repayment of their nursing education loans. The program is designed to increase the number of registered nurses serving designated nurse shortage areas. Nurses can use the money to pay off nursing student loans. An Applicant Information Bulletin For Registered Nurses is available at the address listed below. Money available: $2,183,000.

Contact Loan Repayment Programs Branch, Division of Scholarships and Loan Repayment, Bureau of Primary Health Care, Health Resources and Services Administration, 4350 East-West Highway, Rockville, MD 20857; 301-594-4400; 800-435-6464; {www.bphc.hrsa.dhhs.gov}.

Money For Health Professionals Who Want To Be In Public Health

(Public Health Traineeships 93.964)

The program objective is to help support graduate students who are studying in the field of public health. Grants are given to colleges and universities offering graduate or specialized training in the public health field. Support is limited to the fields of biostatistics, epidemiology, environmental health, toxicology, public health nutrition, and maternal and child health. Money can be used to support a student completing a public health degree, and includes a stipend, tuition, and fees, and a transportation allowance. Students must apply to those institutions that have received the money.

For a listing of institutions that received money contact the office listed below. Money available: $2,326,000. Contact Division of Associated, Dental, and Public Health Professions, Bureau of Health Professions, Health Resources and Services Administration, Public Health

Service, Parklawn Bldg., Room 8C-09, 5600 Fishers Lane, Rockville, MD 20857; 301-443-6041; {www.hrsa.dhhs.gov/bhpr}.

Scholarships For National Health Service Corps

(National Health Service Corps Scholarship Program 93.288)

The program objective is to provide service-conditioned scholarships to health professions students to assure an adequate supply of physicians, dentists, certified nurse midwives, certified nurse practitioners, and physician assistants in Health Professional Shortage Areas. The scholarship pays for tuition and required fees, books, supplies, and equipment for the year, plus a monthly stipend to students ($935 per month), and a single annual payment to cover the cost of all other reasonable educational expenses.

Each year of support incurs one year of service, with a two-year minimum service obligation required. Service sites are selected from those listed by the National Health Service Corps one year prior to service in federally designated Health Professional Shortage Areas. Money available: $30,066,400. Contact National Health Service Corps Scholarships, Division of Scholarships and Loan Repayments, Bureau of Primary Health Care, Health Resources and Services Administration, Public Health Service, U.S. Department of Health and Human Services, 4350 East-West Hwy., 10th Floor, Bethesda, MD 20814; 301-594-4410; 800-638-0824; {www.bphc.hrsa.dhhs.gov/nhsc}.

$30,000 TO STUDY THE HUMANITIES

(Promotion of the Humanities - Fellowships and Stipends 45.160)

Fellowships and Summer Stipends provide support for scholars to undertake full-time independent research and writing in the humanities. Grants are available for 6 to 12 month fellowships and two months of summer study. Projects may contribute to scholarly knowledge or to the general public's understanding of the humanities. The proposed study or research may be completed during the grant period or it may be part of a longer project.

Contact the office listed below for application information. Money available: $6,100,000. Stipends are $4,000 for summer; $24,000 for 6-8 months; and $30,000 for 9-12 months. Contact Fellowships and Stipends, Division of Research and Education, National Endowment for the Humanities, Room 318, Washington, DC 20506; 202-606-8466; {www.neh.gov}.

Grants For Graduate Training In Family Medicine

(Grants For Graduate Training In Family Medicine 93.379)

The program objective is to increase the number of physicians practicing family medicine, particularly to those willing to work in medically under-served communities. Grants are available to cover the cost of developing and operating residency-training programs, and to provide financial assistance to participants in the programs. A grant may be made to a residency program in family practice; an internship program in osteopathic medicine which emphasizes family medicine; or a residency program in osteopathic general practice.

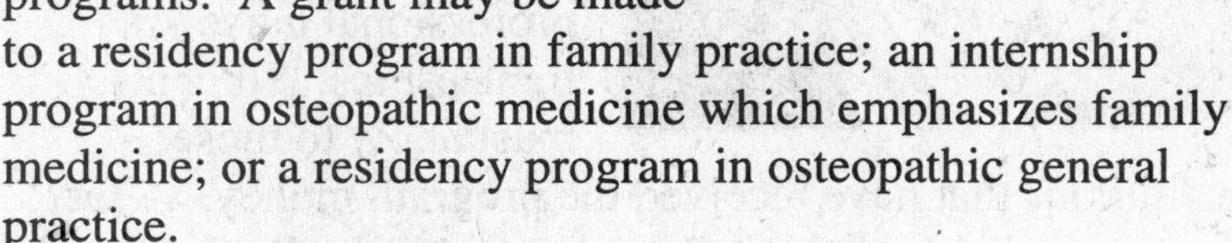

Money can be used to support a student while he or she completes a residency or internship program. Residents must apply to those institutions that have received the money. For a listing of institutions that received money contact the office listed below. Money available: $13,616,136. Contact Division of Medicine, Bureau of

Health Professions, Health Resources and Services Administration, Public Health Service, U.S. Department of Health and Human Services, Room 9A27, 5600 Fishers Lane, Rockville, MD 20857; 301-443-1467; {www.hrsa.dhhs.gov/bhpr}.

Money To Train To Be A Professional Nurse

(Professional Nurse Traineeships 93.358)

The program objective is to prepare individuals who have completed basic nursing preparation as nurse educators, public health nurses, nurse midwives, and nurse practitioners, or as other clinical nursing specialists. Money can be used to support a student while they complete the professional nurse traineeships. Students must apply to those institutions that have received the program money. A fact sheet is available entitled *Program Guide for Professional Nurse Traineeship Program.*

For a listing of institutions that received money contact the office listed below. Money available: $15,666,000. Students may receive stipends up to $8,800 plus tuition and other expenses. Contact Division of Nursing, Bureau of Health Professions, Health Resources and Services

Administration, Public Health Service, U.S. Department of Health and Human Services, 5600 Fishers Lane, Rockville, MD 20857; 301-443-6193; {www.hrsa.dhhs.gov/bhpr}.

Money For Job Safety and Health Training

(Occupational Safety and Health - Training Grants 93.263)

The program objective is to develop specialized professional and paraprofessional personnel in the occupational safety and health field with training in occupational medicine, occupational health nursing, industrial hygiene, and occupational safety. Money can be used to pay for long and short-term training and educational resource centers. Students must apply to those institutions that have received the money.

For a listing of institutions that received money contact the office listed below. Money available: $11,092,000. Contact National Institute for Occupational Safety and Health (NIOSH), Centers for Disease Control and

Prevention, Public Health Service, U.S. Department of Health and Human Services, 1600 Clifton Rd., Atlanta, GA 30333; 404-639-3525; {www.cdc.gov/niosh}.

MONEY FOR HEALTH CARE TRAINING IN RURAL AREAS

(Interdisciplinary Training For Health Care For Rural Areas 93.192)

This program is designed to help fulfill the health care needs of people living in rural areas. Money is set aside to recruit and retain health care professionals in rural health care settings. Funds can be used for student stipends, postdoctoral fellowships, faculty training, and the purchase or rental of necessary transportation and telecommunication equipment. Money can be used to support health profession students while they complete their degree or training. Students must apply to those institutions that have received the money.

For a listing of institutions that received money contact the office listed below. Money available: $3,926,000. Contact Division of Associated, Dental and Public Health Professions, Bureau of Health Professions, Health Resources and Services Administration, Room 8C-26, Parklawn Building, 5600 Fishers Lane, Rockville, MD 20857; 301-443-6867; {www.hrsa.dhhs.gov/bhpr}.

GRANTS FOR PEDIATRIC TRAINING

(Grants For Pediatric Primary Care Residency Training 93.181)

Hospitals and schools of pediatric medicine can receive money to support residency programs for primary care pediatric practice. Funds can be used to cover the development and establishment of Pediatric Primary Care Residency programs and to provide resident stipends for those planning to specialize in pediatric primary care. Money can be used to support a resident while he or she completes his or her pediatric primary care residency. Students must apply to those institutions that have received the money.

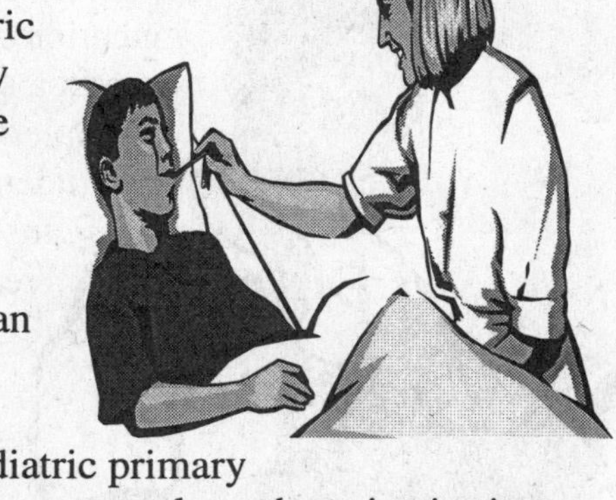

For a listing of institutions that received money contact the office listed below. Money available: $624,440. Contact Division of Medicine, Bureau of Health Professions, Health Resources and Services Administration, Public Health Service, U.S. Department of Health and Human Services, Room 8C-26, Parklawn Building, 5600 Fishers Lane, Rockville, MD 20857; 301-443-6880.

Money For Disadvantaged Students To Study Nursing

(Nursing Education Opportunities For Individuals From Disadvantaged Backgrounds 93.178)

Schools of nursing can receive financial assistance to meet the costs of projects that increase nursing education opportunities for individuals from disadvantaged backgrounds. Money can be used for counseling, preliminary education of students, and to support a student while completing a nursing degree. Students must apply to those institutions that have received the money.

For a listing of institutions that received money contact the office listed below. Money available: $3,779,000. Contact Division of Nursing, Bureau of Health Professions, Health Resources and Services Administration, Public Health Services, U.S. Department of Health and Human Services, Room 8C-26, Parklawn Building, 5600 Fishers Lane, Rockville, MD 20857; 301-443-6880; {www.hrsa.dhhs.gov/bhpr}.

Get Your Loans Paid Through Indian Health Service

(Indian Health Service Loan Repayment Program 93.64)

To ensure that there are enough trained health professionals, the Indian Health Service provides for the repayment of loans to those professionals who agree to serve in an Indian Health Service Facility. Money can be used for the repayment of student loans. An application is available by contacting the office listed above. Money available: $11,233,900. The minimum period of participation is two years, and the maximum loan payment is $30,000 per year. Contact Indian Health Service, Loan Repayment Program, 12300 Twinbrook Parkway, Suite 100, Rockville, MD 20852; 301-443-3369; {www.ihs.gov}.

Money To Repay Loans

(National Health Service Corps Loan Repayment 93.162)

The National Health Service Corps provides for the repayment of educational loans for health professionals who agree to serve in a health manpower shortage area. Priority is given to primary care physicians, dentists, certified nurse midwives, certified nurse practitioners, and physicians' assistants. Money can be used to repay student loans. The amount of money available per professional is up to $25,000 a year during the first two years of practice and $35,000 for each year after that. Health professionals also receive a very competitive salary and benefits package. Money available: $36,000,000.

Contact National Health Service Corps Scholarships, Division of Scholarships and Loan Repayments, Bureau of Primary Health Care, Health Resources and Services Administration, Public Health Service, U.S. Department of Health and Human Services, 4350 East-West Hwy., 10th Floor, Bethesda, MD 20814; 301-594-4410; 800-435-6464; {www.bphc.hrsa.dhhs.gov/nhsc}.

Money For Minorities Pursuing a Health Professions Education

(Programs of Excellence In Health Professions Education For Minorities 93.157)

The program helps health professions schools train minority health professionals. These funds can be used to recruit and retain faculty, improve the facilities and information resources, and improve student performance, student recruitment, and student research. Students must apply to those institutions that have received the money.

For a listing of institutions that received money contact the office listed below. Money available: $22,800,000.

Contact Division of Disadvantaged Assistance, Bureau of Health Professions, Health Resources and Services Administration, Public Health Service, U.S. Department of Health and Human Services, Room 8A-09, Parklawn Building, 55600 Fishers Lane, Rockville, MD 20857; 301-443-4493; {www.hrsa.dhhs.gov/bhpr}.

Financial Assistance For Disadvantaged Health Professions Students

(Financial Assistance For Disadvantaged Health Professions Students 93.139)

Health profession students who are of exceptional financial need and are studying for a degree in medicine, osteopathic medicine, or dentistry can receive financial support. Money can be used to support a student while in school. Funds are awarded to accredited schools of medicine, osteopathic medicine, or dentistry. Students should apply to their school for these scholarships. Money available: $6,741,000. The maximum amount available per student is $18,000.

Contact Division of Student Assistance, Bureau of Health Professions, Health Resources and Services Administration, Public Health Service, U.S. Department of Health and Human Services, Room 8-34, 5600 Fishers

Lane, Rockville, MD 20857; 301-443-4776; {www.hrsa.dhhs.gov/bhpr}.

Money To Train To Become A Nurse Anesthetist

(Nurse Anesthetist Traineeships 93.124)

Registered nurses can receive money to become nurse anesthetists through this program that provides funds for a maximum 18-month period of full-time study. Nurses must complete 12 months of study in a nurse anesthetist program. Money can be used to support a student while completing the training program. Students need to apply to those institutions that have received the money.

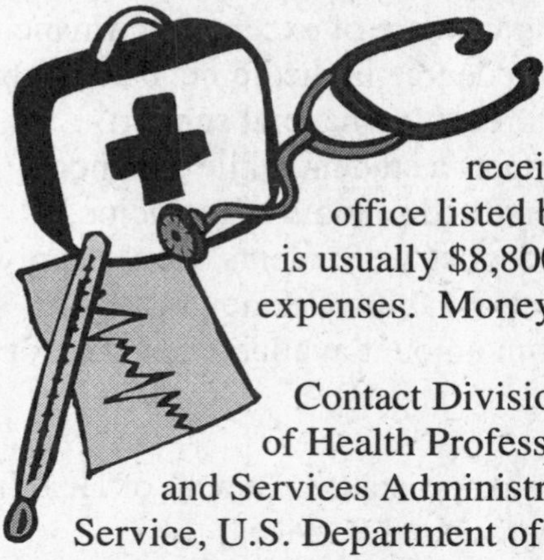

For a listing of institutions that received money contact the office listed below. Student stipend is usually $8,800 plus tuition and other expenses. Money available: $2,717,000.

Contact Division of Nursing, Bureau of Health Professions, Health Resources and Services Administration, Public Health Service, U.S. Department of Health and Human Services, Room 9-36, 5600 Fishers Lane, Rockville, MD 20857; 301-443-5763; {www.hrsa.dhhs.gov/bhpr}.

Money To Study Food

(Food and Agricultural Science National Needs Graduate Fellowship Grants 10.210)

The program awards grants to colleges and universities that have superior teaching and research competencies in the food and agricultural sciences. These grants are to be used to encourage outstanding students to pursue and complete a graduate degree in an area of the food and agricultural sciences for which there is a national need for development of scientific expertise.

Money can be used to support a student completing a graduate, masters, or doctorate degree. Students must apply to those institutions that received the money. For a listing of institutions that received money contact the office listed below. Money available: $2,910,000.

Contact Grants Program Manager, Office of Higher Education Programs, CSREES, U.S. Department of Agriculture, Administrative Building, Room 338A, 14th and Independence Ave., SW, Washington, DC 20250; 202-720-1973; {www.reeusda.gov/serd/hep/ index.htm}.

Money To Help Math Students and Summer Scientists

(Independent Education and Science Projects and Programs 11.449)

This program objective is to increase the number of minority students enrolling in college and majoring in math, science and engineering. Another objective is to recruit scientists and engineers from the Boulder county area to serve as science/math tutors. Money can be used to help high school and middle school students who are part of the Math, Engineering, Science Achievement (MESA) Program in Colorado. It is also for students pursuing a course of study related to oceanic and atmospheric sciences and who are interested in a summer hands-on experience in a laboratory setting. Money can be used for transportation, housing and stipends for students during the summer months where students learn about the laboratories mission and perform hands-on assignments. Money available: $75,000.

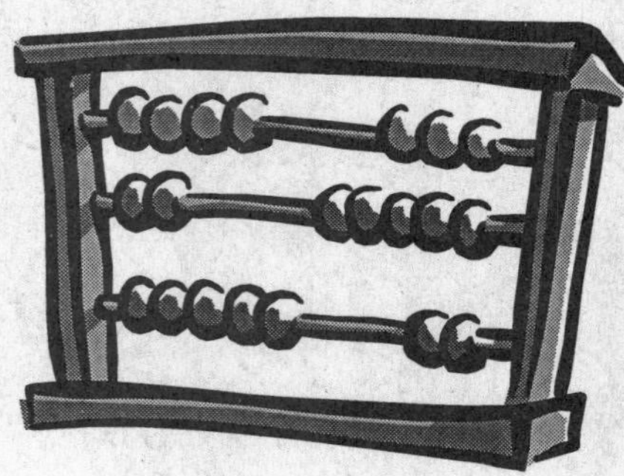

Contact Tony Tafoya, NOAA/Environmental Research Laboratories, R/Ex-4, 325 Broadway, Boulder, CO 80303; 303-497-6731; {www.etl.noaa.gov}.

Money To Study Community Planning and Development

(Community Development Work-Study Program 14.512)

The Community Development Work-Study Program makes grants to institutions of higher education to provide assistance to economically disadvantaged and minority students. Students take part in community development work-study programs while they are enrolled full-time in graduate or undergraduate programs with that major. Grants are given to encourage minority and economically disadvantaged students to develop careers in community and economic development, community planning, and community management. Related fields include public administration, urban management, and urban planning.

Student assistance is in the form of work stipends, tuition support, and additional support to cover books and travel related to conferences and seminars. Students must apply to those institutions that received the money. For a listing of institutions that received money contact the office listed below. Money available: $3,000,000. Average grant per student is $30,000. Contact U.S. Department of Housing and Urban Development, Community Planning and Development, Office of University Partnerships, 451 7th St., SW, Room 8130, Washington, DC 20410; 202-708-1537, ext. 218; {www.huduser.org}.

Money To Study Housing Issues

(Doctoral Dissertation Research Grant Program)

The program objective is to encourage doctoral candidates to engage in policy related housing and urban development research and to assist them in its timely completion. Money can used to support Ph.D candidates while they complete work towards their degree. Students must have a fully developed and approved dissertation proposal that addresses the purpose of this program. Students can request an application package from the address listed below or by calling HUD USER at 800-245-2691. Each student is eligible for up to $15,000 per year.

Contact Division of Budget, Contracts, and Program Control, Office of Policy Development and Research, U.S. Department of Housing and Urban Development, 451 7th St., SW, Room 8230, Washington, DC 20410; 202-708-0544; {www.huduser.org}.

Money For Members Of Indian Tribes To Go To College

(Indian Education-Higher Education Grant Program 15.114)

The program objective is to provide financial aid to eligible Indian students to enable them to attend accredited institutions of higher education. Members of an Indian tribe may be eligible for these grants to supplement the total financial aid package prepared by their college financial aid officer. Once you have been accepted by a college and have completed their financial aid application, you may request a grant application form from your tribal group. Money available: $20,290,000. The amount of assistance per student ranges from $300-$5000 per year. Contact Bureau of

Indian Affairs, Office of Indian Education Programs, Code 522, Room S 3512-MIB, U.S. Department of the Interior, 1849 C St., NW, Washington, DC 20240; 202-219-1127; {http://shaman.unm.edu/oiep/home.htm}.

Money For Criminal Justice Majors

(Criminal Justice Research and Development - Grant Research Fellowships 16.562)

The program objective is to improve the quality and quantity of knowledge about crime and the criminal justice system. Additionally, the program seeks to increase the number of persons who are qualified to teach in collegiate criminal justice programs, to conduct research related to criminal justice issues, and to perform more effectively within the criminal justice system. Students can receive a fellowship for a year, plus, tow to three months to visit the National Institute of Justice to work with staff as an intern.

This competitive program provides fellowship stipends, major project costs and certain university fees, round trip travel expenses to the Institute, and housing costs. Detailed information can be received by requesting the NIJ Research Plan from the National Criminal Justice Reference Service, Box 6000, Rockville, MD 20850; 800-851-3420. Money available: $150,000. Maximum grant per student $15,000.

Contact National Institute of Justice, 633 Indiana Ave., SW, Washington, DC 20531; 202-307-2942; {www.ncjrs.org}.

Money To Study The Break Up Of The USSR

(Russian, Eurasian, and East European Research and Training 19.300)

The program is designed to sustain and strengthen American expertise on the Commonwealth of Independent States, Georgia, the Baltic countries, and countries of Eastern Europe by supporting graduate training; advanced research; public dissemination of research data, methods, and findings; contact and collaboration among government and private specialists; and first hand experience of the (former) Soviet Union and Eastern European countries by American specialists, including on site conduct of advanced training and research. Graduate students interested in conducting research on the Commonwealth of Independent States, Georgia, the Baltic countries, and the countries of Eastern Europe can receive fellowships which can support a student while conducting research or training.

Funds are given to nonprofit organizations and institutions of higher learning who act as intermediaries for the federal funds by conducting their own competitions to make the awards. Grants in the past include grants for onsite independent short term research; individual exchange fellowships for American graduate students to pursue research in the region; and advanced in-country language training fellowships in Russian, Ukrainian, Hungarian, Polish, and more. Students must apply to those institutions that received the money. For a listing of institutions that received money contact the office listed below. Money available: $4,800,000. Contact Eurasian and East European Research and Training Program, INR/RES, U.S. Department of State, 2201 C St., NW, Room 6841, Washington, DC 20520; 202-736-4572; {www.state.gov/www/regions/mis/ grants}.

$3,000 A Year To Be A Merchant Marine

(State Marine Schools 20.806)

The program objective is to train merchant marine officers in State Marine Schools. You can receive $3,000 per year to train to be a merchant marine officer at a designated State Marine School. In exchange for this incentive payment program, you must commit yourself to a minimum of five years duty to the Maritime Administration, which can be satisfied by: serving as a merchant marine officer aboard vessels; as an employee in a U.S. maritime related industry, profession or marine science; or as a commissioned officer on active duty in an armed force of the U.S. or in the National Oceanic and Atmospheric Administration. You must also remain in a reserve unit of an armed force for a minimum of eight years.

Students need to apply to one of the State Marine Schools. Money available: $6,750,000. Contact Office of Maritime Labor and Training, Maritime Administration, U.S. Department of Transportation, 400 7th St., SW, Washington, DC 20590; 202-366-5755; {http://marad.dot.gov}.

All Expenses Plus $558 A Month To Be A Merchant Marine

This program trains merchant marine officers while they attend the Merchant Marine Academy in Kings Point, NY. Students receive training, subsistence, books, quarters, uniforms, medical care, and program travel without cost. In addition, the student will receive a monthly wage from their steamship company employer. Money available: $33,250,000. An allowance is prescribed for all personnel for uniforms and textbooks. During the sea year a midshipman will earn $558.04 per month from the steamship employer.

Contact Office of Maritime Labor and Training, Maritime Administration, U.S. Department of Transportation, 400 Seventh St., SW, Washington, DC 20590; 202-366-5755; {http://marad.dot.gov}.

Money For Social, Behavioral, And Economic Sciences Students

(Social, Behavioral, and Economic Sciences 47.075)

The program objective is to promote the progress of the social, behavioral, and economic science; to facilitate cooperative research activities with foreign scientists, engineers, and institutions and to support understanding of the resources invested in science and engineering in the U.S. Funds are provided for U.S. scientists and engineers to carry out studies abroad, to conduct research, to engage in joint research projects with foreign counterpart organizations, and to support international scientific workshops in the U.S. and abroad.

Money can be used for paying associated costs necessary to conduct research or studies for doctorate students; and more. Students must contact the office listed below for application information. Money available: $150,260,000. Contact Assistant Director, Social, Behavioral, and Economic Research, National Science Foundation, 4201 Wilson Blvd., Arlington, VA 22230; 703-306-1710; {www.nsf.gov}.

Money For Disabled Veterans To Go To College

(Vocational Rehabilitation For Disabled Veterans 64.116)

The program objective is to provide all services and assistance necessary to enable service-disabled veterans and service persons hospitalized pending discharge to achieve maximum independence in daily living and, to the maximum extent possible, to become employable and to obtain and maintain suitable employment.

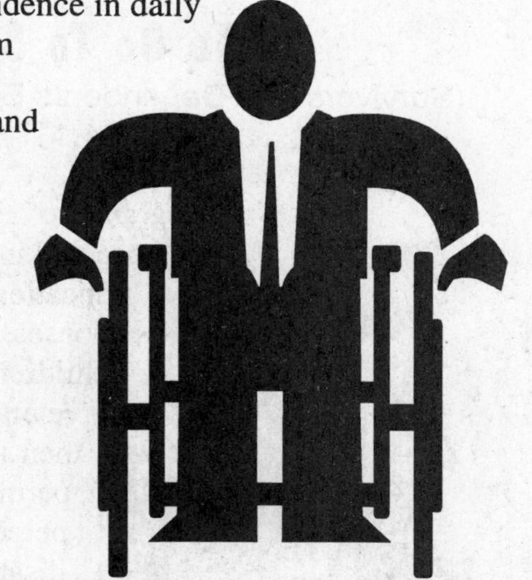

The fund provides for the entire cost of tuition, books, fees, supplies, and other services to help the veteran live with a reduced dependency on others while staying in their homes and communities. The veteran also receives a monthly allowance, a work-study allowance, and more. Enrollment can be in a trade, business, or technical schools, colleges, apprenticeship programs, cooperative farming, special rehabilitation facilities, or at home when necessary. Students must obtain an application from any Veterans Affairs office or regional office. Money available: Direct payments: $402,907,0000; Loan advances: $2,401,000. Monthly full time allowances per student range from $413 for a single veteran to $604 for a veteran with two dependents, plus $44 for each dependent in excess of two. Contact Department of Veterans Affairs, Central Office, Washington, DC 20420; 800-827-1000; {www.va.gov}.

Money For Spouses And Children Of Deceased Or Disabled Veterans To Go To School

(Survivors and Dependents Educational Assistance 64.117)

The program provides partial support to those seeking to advance their education who are qualifying spouses, surviving spouses, or children of deceased or disabled veterans who, as a result of their military service, have a permanent and total (100 percent) service connected disability, or a service personnel who have been listed for a total of more than 90 days as currently Missing in Action, or as Prisoners of War. Spouse, surviving spouse, or child of a deceased or disabled veteran can receive monthly payments to be used for tuition, books, subsistence, for courses, training, or college. Financial assistance is $485 per month, and there is tutorial assistance, vocational counseling and testing, and a work-study allowance. Benefits may be awarded for pursuit of associate, bachelor, or graduate degrees at colleges and universities, as well as study at business, technical, or vocational schools.

Information on the program and application forms are available from your local or regional Veterans Affairs office. Money available: $108,530,000. Contact Department of Veterans Affairs, Central Office, Washington, DC 20420; 800-827-1000; {www.va.gov}.

Money For Vietnam Veterans To Go To School

(Post-Vietnam Era Veterans' Educational Assistance 64.120)

Post-Vietnam veterans who entered the Armed Services between 1977 and 1985 may be eligible for funds to obtain a college degree or vocational training. Through this program, the government matches $2 for every $1 the serviceman contributes. Some contribution to the fund must have been made prior to April 1, 1987. Contact your local or regional Veterans Affairs office for additional information or application materials. Money available: $54,614,000.

Up to a maximum of $8,100 of basic benefits is available per student, as well as a work-study allowance of minimum wage and tutorial assistance up to a maximum of $1,200. Contact Department of Veterans Affairs, Central Office, Washington, DC 20420; 800-827-1000; {www.va.gov}.

Money For Retired Veterans To Go To School

(All-Volunteer Force Educational Assistance 64.124)

This program helps servicemen readjust to civilian life after their separation from military service, assists in the recruitment and retention of highly qualified personnel in the active and reserve components in the Armed Forces, and extends the benefits of a higher education to those who may not otherwise be able to afford it. Honorably discharged veterans can take advantage of the Montgomery GI Bill Active Duty benefits, which provides funds to pursue professional or vocational education, and even covers correspondence courses.

Veterans can receive a monthly stipend while attending school, with the amount varying depending upon date of entry into the service and length of service. Additional information and application materials are available through any regional Veterans Affairs office. Money available: $816,798,000. A maximum allowance of $19,008 as basic assistance is available per student, as well as a work-study allowance, and up to $1,200 in tutorial assistance. Contact Department of Veterans Affairs, Central Office, Washington, DC 20420; 800-827-1000; {www.va.gov}.

Volunteer And Earn Money To Pay For School

(AmeriCorps 94.006)

AmericCorps is an initiative designed to achieve direct results in addressing the nation's critical education, human, public safety, and environmental needs at the community level. The program provides meaningful opportunities for people to serve their country in organized efforts, fostering citizen responsibility, building their community, and providing education opportunities for those who make a serious commitment to service.

Stipends can be used to support the person while they volunteer. Health care and childcare benefits may also be provided. Participants will also receive an education award, which may be used to pay for higher education or for vocational training, and may also be used to repay any existing student loans. Contact the Corporation for National Service to locate programs in your area or to apply for programs at the national level. Money available: $256,816,000.

Contact Corporation for National Service, 1201 New York Ave., NW, Washington, DC 20525 202-606-5000, ext. 474; {www.americorps.org}.

State College Money

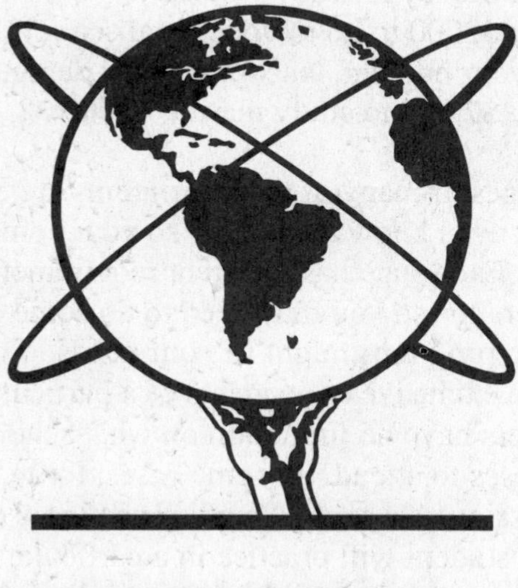

After checking out what money programs are available from the federal government, your next task is to find out what's available at the state level. There are close to 400 programs worth almost $3 billion dollars in financial aid available thru all 50 states. Just because you or your parents don't have the money to pay for college, that doesn't mean your dream of a college degree will never happen. Even if you do have the money, financial assistance from one of these programs could make things a little easier for all concerned.

Did you know that there are state money program which:

- Pay for a singing degree?
- Give you money to study wildlife?
- Give you $2000 to go to vocational school?
- Pay for your nursing, teaching or law degree?
- Give you $7,000 to study marine sciences?

The advantages of many of these programs are that most people don't even know they exist, so your competition will be less. Each state has different requirements for their various programs, so you may need to do some checking on what specific programs might fit your needs. Some programs are exclusive to residents of a particular state, whereas others have no limitation on what school the student chooses to attend. In some cases, for teachers or health professionals a service requirement may exist which says that the student will practice in a particular state after graduation for a certain period of time.

What follows is a concise and comprehensive state-by-state listing of available programs. It will allow you to shop around for the best program to suit your individual needs. By remaining flexible and adjusting your educational goals to fit the program that most appeals to you, chances are you might find yourself pursuing the college education that you always thought was beyond your reach. Using this information might be an important first step in building a successful future for yourself.

STATE AID

ALABAMA

Alabama Commission on Higher Education
P.O. Box 30200
Montgomery, AL 36130-2000
334-242-2271
Fax: 334-242-0268
www.ache.state.al.us

General requirements: Residents of Alabama and attending an in-state school.

Programs Available:

Grants To Students Who Can't Afford Tuition
(Alabama Student Assistance Program)

Grants To Students Attending Private Colleges
(Alabama Student Grant Program)

Join The National Guard And Get $1,000 A Year For College
(Alabama National Guard Assistance Program)

Scholarships and Loans To Nursing Students
(Alabama Nursing Scholarships)

Tuition, Fees, And Books To Spouses and Children Of Veterans (Alabama GI Dependents Educational Benefit Program)
Grants To Children And Grandchildren Of Veterans (American Legion Scholarship and American Legion Auxiliary Scholarship Programs)
Free Tuition If You're Over 60 (Senior Adult Scholarships)
Money For Jocks Going To Junior College (Junior And Community College Athletic Scholarships)
Money For Dancers, Singers, and Actors Attending Junior College (Junior and Community College Performing Arts Scholarships)
Grants To Children Of The Blind (Alabama Scholarships For Dependents of Blind Parents)
Grants For Dependents Of Fire Fighters And Police Officers Killed In The Line Of Duty (Police Officers and Fire Fighters Survivor's Educational Assistance Program)
Loans That Guarantee The Price Of Your Future Tuition (Prepaid College Tuition Program)
Tuition And Fees, For Teachers To Take Technology Classes (Technology Scholarship Program For Alabama)
Money For Tuition And Books To Smart Students Attending A Two-Year College (Two-Year College Academic Scholarship)

ALASKA

Alaska Commission on Postsecondary Education
3030 Vintage Boulevard
Juneau, AK 99801-7109
907-465-2962
800-441-2962
Fax: 907-465-5316
www.state.ak.us/acpe/home.html

General requirements: Alaska resident and attending an in-state or out-of-state school.

Programs Available:
Free Money To Go To School If You Work In Law Enforcement (Michael Murphy Memorial Scholarship Loan)
Money For 8 Years Of College If You Study Food Or Wildlife (A.W. "Winn" Brindle Memorial Scholarship Loan)
$7,500 A Year and Travel Money If You Study To Be A Teacher In A Small Town (Teacher Scholarship Loan Program)
Alaska Residents Get Special Tuition Rate At Select Out-Of-State Colleges (Western Undergraduate Exchange Program)
Reduced Tuition Rates In Select Masters and Doctoral Programs At Colleges In 14 Western States (Western Regional Graduate Program)
Receive Residential Tuition Rate At University Of Washington School Of Medicine And Return To Alaska And Practice Medicine (WWAMI Medical Education Program)

ARIZONA

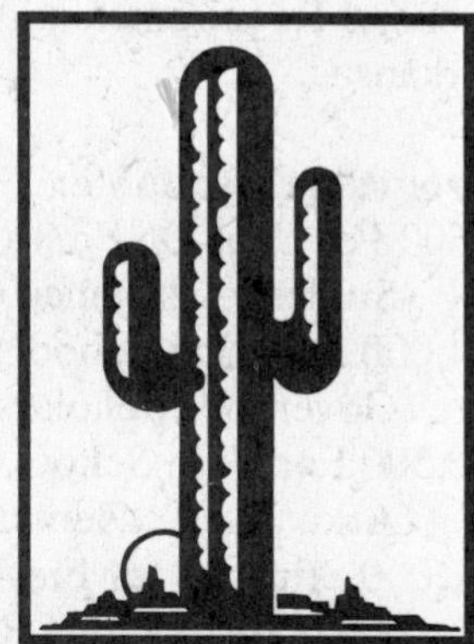

Arizona Commission for
Postsecondary Education
2020 North Central, Suite 275
Phoenix, AZ 85004-4503
602-229-2591
Fax: 602-229-2599
www.acpe.asu.edu

General requirements: Students should contact the financial aid office at the college they plan to attend for applicable scholarship, grant, and loan information. State residency is required for the programs listed.

Programs Available:

$2,500 Grants For Students Having Trouble Paying Tuition (Leveraging Education's Assistance Partnership (LEAP))

$1,500 A Year For Full-Time Study At A Private School In A Baccalaureate Degree-Granting Program (Arizona Private Postsecondary Education Student Financial Assistance Program (PFAP))

Money To Students Who Honored Their Pledge To The ASPIRE Program (ASPIRE)

ARKANSAS

Arkansas Department of Higher Education
114 East Capitol
Little Rock, AR 72201
501-371-2000
Fax: 501-371-2001
www.adhe.arknet.edu

General Requirements: Applicants must be current residents of Arkansas.

Programs Available:

$600 Per Year On First-Come, First-Served Basis (Student Assistance Grants)

$4,000 For High School Graduates With At Least 3.6 Averages (Governor's Scholars)

$2,500 For High School Graduates with At Least 2.5 Averages (Arkansas Academic Challenge Scholarship)

$1,000 Stipends for Freshman and Sophomore Minorities to Enroll in Teaching Programs (Freshman/Sophomore Minority Grant Program)

Tuition Reimbursement for Teachers and Administrators to Continue Their Education (Teacher and Administrator Grant Program)

Free Money For School If You Become a Math, Science, or Special Education Teacher, or a Guidance Counselor (Emergency Secondary Education Loan)

Up To $5,000 Per Year for African-American, Asian American, and Hispanic College Juniors and Seniors When They Agree to Teach in Arkansas (Minority Teacher Scholarship)

$1,000 To Top Ten GED Scorers (Second Effort Scholarship)

Up To $7,500 for Minorities to Enter a Master's Program in Mathematics, the Sciences, or Foreign Language (Minority Masters Fellows Program)

Grants To Dependents Of Law Enforcement Officers, Firemen, and Game Officers Killed Or Totally Disabled In The Line Of Duty (Law Enforcement Officer's Dependents Scholarship)

CALIFORNIA

California Student Aid Commission
P.O. Box 419026
Rancho Cordova, CA 95741-9026
916-526-7590
Fax: 916-526-8002
www.csac.ca.gov

General requirements: Applicants must be residents of California.

Programs Available:

Grants For Tuition, Living Expenses, and Vocational Training (Cal Grants A, B, and C)

Help To Work Your Way Through College (State Work-Study Program)

$8,000 To Become A Teacher (Assumption Program of Loans for Education (APLE))

Grants To Dependents Of Fire Fighters, Police Officers, and Correctional Officials Killed Or Totally Disabled In The Line Of Duty (Law Enforcement Personnel Dependents Scholarship)

Up To $6,000 Loan Assumption to Become a full-time Faculty Member (Graduate Assumption Program of Loans for Education)

Money for High School Graduates and Community College Transfer Students in Financial Need (California Student Opportunity and Access Program)

COLORADO

Colorado Commission on Higher Education
1300 Broadway, 2nd Floor
Denver, CO 80203
303-866-2723
www.state.co.us/cche_dir/hecche.html

General requirements: Applicants must be resident of Colorado.

Programs Available:

Grants To Students From Families Who Don't Normally Go To College (Colorado Diversity Grants)

Grants To Students Who Are Having Trouble Paying For Tuition (Colorado Student Incentive Grants (CSIG))

More Grants To Students Who Are Having Trouble Paying For Tuition (Colorado Student Grants (CSG))

Money For Students Going To College Part Time (Colorado Part Time Grants)

State Jobs For Students Having Trouble Paying Tuition (Colorado Work-Study)

Money For Smart Students Going To College In Colorado (Undergraduate Merit Awards)

Money For Graduates Who Have Trouble Paying Tuition (Colorado Graduate Grants)

Money For Smart Graduate Students (Colorado Graduate Fellowships)

Grants To Dependents Of POW/MIA's or Fire Fighters, Police Officers, and Correctional Officials Killed Or Totally Disabled In The Line Of Duty (Law Enforcement/POW-MIA Dependents Tuition Assistance)

Money To Be A Nurse And Practice In Colorado (Colorado Nursing Scholarship)

Receive Up To 75% of Tuition To Become A Colorado National Guard (Colorado National Guard Tuition Assistance)

CONNECTICUT

Department of Higher Education
61 Woodland Street
Hartford, CT 06105
860-947-1800
Fax: 860-947-1310
http://ctdhe.commnet.edu

General requirements: Applicants must be Connecticut residents for in-state and out-of-state schools programs.

Programs Available:

$2,000 A Year If You Are In Top 20% Of Your High School Class (Capitol Scholarship)

$7,777 A Year To Attend A Private College (Connecticut Independent College Student Grant)

Money For Students Who Need Help Paying Tuition At A Public University (Connecticut Aid for Public College Students)

Up To $5,000 A Year For Minority Juniors Or Seniors To Become Teachers In The Connecticut Public School System. (Connecticut Minority Teacher Incentive Program)

Money For Students Who Need Help Paying For College (Tuition Set Aside Aid)

DELAWARE

Commission on Higher Education
Carvel State Office Building
820 N. French St
Wilmington, DE 19801
800-292-7935
302-577-3240

Fax: 302-577-6765
www.doe.state.de.us/high-ed
General requirements: Applicants must be Delaware residents for in-state or out-of-state colleges.

Programs Available:

Money To Be A Teacher In Delaware (Christa McAuliffe Teacher Scholarship Loan)

$1250 A Year For Undergraduate Students (Diamond State Scholarship)

Full Tuition, Room and Board To Smart High School Seniors (B. Bradford Barnes Scholarship)

$3,000 A Year To Be A Registered Or Practical Nurse And Practice In A State-Owned Hospital (Delaware Nursing Incentive Scholarship Loan)

Money For Students From Delaware To Study Optometry In Pennsylvania (Delaware Optometric Institutional Aid)

Money Towards Education For Children Of Deceased Veterans Or State Officers, and Prisoners Of War or MIA's (Educational Benefits For Children Of Deceased Veterans)

Up To $1,000 Per Year For Part-Time Students Who Work Part-Time (Governor's Workforce Development Grant)

Money For Full-Time Students in Undergraduate Or Graduate Program in Financial Need (Scholarship Incentive Program)

Tuition, Fees, and Room and Board At Delaware State University For Smart High School Seniors in Financial Need (Holloway Scholarship)

$20,000 Per Year for Medical Training To Practice In Delaware (DIMER Loan Program)

Money For Smart and Needy Students To Become A Librarian In Delaware (Librarian Incentive Scholarship Program)

Money For A Master's in Speech/Language Pathology To Be Used For Service In Delaware Public Schools (Speech/Language Pathologist Incentive Program)

DISTRICT OF COLUMBIA

Office of Postsecondary Education
2100 Martin Luther Kings, Jr., Avenue, SE
Washington, DC 20020
202-727-3688
www.dhs.washington.dc.us/Prog_Cit_Service/OPERA/opera.htm

General requirements: Applicants must be District of Columbia.

Programs Available:

Money For Students In Great Need
(D.C. Leveraging Educational Assistance Program)

FLORIDA

Florida Office of Students Financial Assistance
255 Collins Building
325 West Gaines Street
Tallahassee, FL 32399-0400
850-488-4095
Fax: 850-488-3612
www.firn.edu/doe/bin00065/home0065.htm

General requirements: Applicants must be Florida residents for in-state or out-of-state school programs.

Programs Available:

Money For Excellent High School Graduates (Florida Bright Futures Scholarship Program)

Money For Students Who Have Trouble Paying Their Tuition (Florida Student Assistance Grants (FSAG))

Up To $4,000 To Study To Be An Occupational Therapist, A Physical Therapist, or An Assistant And Work In Florida Public Schools (Occupational Therapist And Physical Therapist Scholarship Loan Program)

$2,000 For Hispanic Americans Who Want To Go To College (Jose Marti Scholarship Challenge Grant Fund)

Up To $4,000 To Descendants Of African American Rosewood Families In Need (Rosewood Family Scholarship Fund)

Money For Dependents Of Deceased Or Disabled Veterans And POW/MIA's (Scholarships For Children Of Deceased Or Disabled Veterans)

Money For Smart High School Graduates Who Want To Be Teachers In Florida ("Chappie" James Most Promising Teacher Scholarship)

Free College Money If You Teach In Florida Public Schools (Critical Teacher Shortage (CTS) Forgivable Loans)

Grants For American Indians To Go To College
(Seminole/Miccosukee Indian Scholarship)
Money To Become A Nurse And Work In An Underserved Area Of Florida For One Year (Nursing Scholarship Program)
Tuition Assistance To Students At Private Non-Profit Colleges (William L. Boyd, IV, Florida Resident Access Grant)
50% Of Tuition A Year For Community College Graduates, Or State Student Transfers To Enroll In Limited Access Programs At A Private College (Limited Access Competitive Grant)
Money To Community College And Private College Students (Ethics In Business Scholarship Program)
Jobs Related To Educational Goals For Students In Financial Need (Florida Work Experience Program)
$3,000 A Year To Smart High School Graduates (Mary McLeod Bethune Scholarship)

GEORGIA

Student Finance Commission
2082 East Exchange Place
Tucker, GA 30084
800-776-6878
770-414-3000
Fax: 770-724-9089
www.gsfc.org

General requirements: Must be a resident for Georgia for in-state or out-of-state programs.

Programs Available:

$1,000 Per Year To Attend A Public In-State College Within 50 Miles Of The Border, Or An Independent Out-Of-State College (Tuition Equalization Grant)

Up To $1,575 Per Year For High School Valedictorian, Salutatorian or STAR Students (Governor's Scholarship Program)

$3,000 Per Year To Become An Engineer In Georgia (Scholarship for Engineering Education)

$2,000 Per Year For Children of Georgia Officers, Firefighters, and Prison Guards Permanently Disabled Or Killed In The Line Of Duty
(Law Enforcement Personnel Dependents)

Money To Children Of Officers, Firefighters, EMT's, Correction Officers and Prison Guards Permanently Disabled Or Killed In The Line Of Duty
(Public Safety Memorial Grant)

$1,500 Per Year To Participate In The ROTC Program At N.G.A. College and State University
(North Georgia College ROTC Grant)

Full Scholarship For Outstanding Students To N.G.A. College and State University and To Join Georgia's Army National Guard (North Georgia College Military Scholarship)

Smart Students Receive a Full Scholarship To Georgia Military College and Then Join the Georgia National Guard (Georgia Military College State Service Scholarship)

$10,000 Per Year To Become A Primary Care Physician And Practice In Underserved Areas of Georgia (Osteopathic Medical Loan)

Up To $5,000 per Year To Students Having Trouble Paying For College-Must Apply For The Federal Pell Grant Also (Student Incentive Grant)

Funds For College To Former Georgia Peach Corps Member (Georgia Peach CORPS Grant)

Get Financial Aid For College If You Work At Jobs On Campus (Work Incentive For Student Education)

HAWAII

Systems Group
641-18th Avenue, V201
Honolulu, HI 96816
808-733-9124

General requirements: Applicants must be Hawaii residents.

Programs Available:

Money To High School Graduates With A 3.5 GPA
(Regents Scholarship for Academic Excellence)

Money For Students Planning To Study Pacific/Asian Studies
(Pacific Asian Scholarships)

IDAHO

Office of the State Board of Education
P.O. Box 83720
Boise, ID 83720-0037
208-334-2270
www.sde.state.id.us/osbe/board.htm

General requirements: Applicants must be Idaho residents.

Programs Available:

$2,750 To Study In Idaho
(Idaho Scholarship Program)

Disadvantaged High School Students Can Get $3,000 To Go To College (Idaho Minority and "At-Risk"Student Scholarship)

Free Money For Students Studying To Be Teachers Or Nurses (Education Incentive Loan Forgiveness)

Up To $5,000 For Students In Need To Attend A Public Or Private School In Idaho (Idaho Student Incentive Grant)

ILLINOIS

Illinois Student Assistance Commission
1775 Lake Cook Drive
Deerfield, IL 60015
847-948-8550 ext. 3503
Fax: 847-831-8519
www.isac-online.org

General requirements: Applicants must be Illinois residents.

Programs Available:

Grants Up To $4,120 No Matter What Your Grades Are
(Monetary Award Program)

$1,000 For Students In The Top 5% Of Their Class (Illinois Merit Recognition Scholarship Program)

Join The National Guard For Free Tuition For Graduate Or Undergraduate Studies (National Guard Grant Program)

Veterans Living In Illinois Can Get Free Tuition and Fees (Illinois Veteran Grant Program)

Grants To Dependents Of Fire Fighters Or Police Officers Killed Or Permanently Disabled In The Line Of Duty (Grant Program For Dependents Of Police Officer Or Fire Officers)

Grants To Dependents Of Correctional Officers Killed Or Disabled In The Line Of Duty (Correctional Officer Grant Program)

Money For Freshman Students In Great Financial Need (Illinois Incentive For Access Program)

Money To Holders Of Illinois College Savings Bonds When They Mature (Bonus Incentive Grant)

Up To $5,000 Per Year For African-Americans, Hispanic-Americans, Asian-Americans, Or Native Americans To Become Teachers In Illinois (Minority Teachers Of Illinois Scholarship Program)

Up To $5,000 For Talented Minority Students To Teach In Designated Areas Of Illinois (David A. DeBolt Teacher Shortage Scholarship Program)

Talented Students Receive Free Tuition To Become Special Education Teachers (Illinois Special Education Teacher Tuition Waiver Program)

INDIANA

State Student Assistance Commission of Indiana
150 West Market Street, Suite 500
Indianapolis, IN 46204
317-232-2350
Fax: 317-232-3260

www.state.in.us/ssaci
General requirements: Applicants must be Indiana residents.

Programs Available:
Indiana College Students Who Have Trouble Paying Tuition (Indiana Higher Education Grant Program)
Four Years Of Tuition To 8th Graders Who Pledge Good Citizenship To The State Twenty-first Century Scholars Program)
Money To Nursing Students Who Will Work As A Nurse In Indiana For 2 Years (Nursing Scholarship)
Money to Black Or Hispanic Students To Become A Teacher, Special Education Teacher, Or Occupational or Physical Therapist And Work In Indiana (Minority Teacher/Special Education Scholarship)

IOWA

Iowa College Student Aid Commission
200 Tenth Street, 4th Floor
Des Moines, IA 50309-2036
515-281-3501
www.state.ia.us/collegeaid
General requirements: Applicants must be Iowa residents.

Programs Available:
Money For High School Graduates In The Top 15% Of Their Class (State of Iowa Scholarship Program)
Grants To Pay For Tuition At Private Colleges (Iowa Tuition Grants)
$600 To Take A Vocational Education Course (Iowa Vocational-Technical Tuition Grants)
Grants To Students Who Need Money For Education (Iowa Grants)

KANSAS

Kansas Board of Regents
700 SW Harrison, Suite 1410
Topeka, KS 66603
785-296-3421
Fax: 785-296-0983
www.ukans.edu/~kbor

General requirements: Applicants must be Kansas's residents.

Programs Available:

$1,500 A Year For Minority Students (Ethnic Minority Scholarships)

$500 To Take A Vocational training Course (Vocational Scholarship)

$5,000 A Year If You Study To Be A Teacher In Kansas (Kansas Teacher Scholarship)

$3,500 A Year To Be A Nurse (Kansas Nursing Scholarship)

$1,000 To High School Graduates Who Have Trouble Paying Tuition (Kansas State Scholarship)

Money For Students At Public Or Private School Who Need Financial Help (Kansas Comprehensive Grants)

Up To $15,000 Per Year At Osteopathy School To Practice In Kansas (Kansas Osteopathy Scholarship)

Get Residence Tuition Rate To Attend An Out-Of-State School Of Optometry And Practice In Kansas (Kansas Optometry Scholarship)

Pay In-State Tuition Rate At University Of Missouri-Kansas City To Study Dentistry (Kansas Dentistry Assistance)

Stipends From $1,000 To $ $8,000 To Study Abroad (James B Pearson Fellowship)

Tuition And Fee Reimbursement To Continue Graduate Studies At A Kansas Public University Kansas Distinguished Scholarship Program)

Up To $8,000 A Year To Ethnic Minority Students For Enrollment In Kansas Graduate Programs (Kansas Ethnic Minority Fellowship)

KENTUCKY

Kentucky Higher Education Assistance Authority
1050 U.S. 127 South
Suite 102
Frankfort, KY 40601-4323
800-928-8926
502-564-7990
www.kheaa.com

General requirements:
Applicants must be residents of Kentucky.

Programs Available:

Grants To Financially Needy Full-Time And Part-Time Students (College Access Program Grants (CAP))

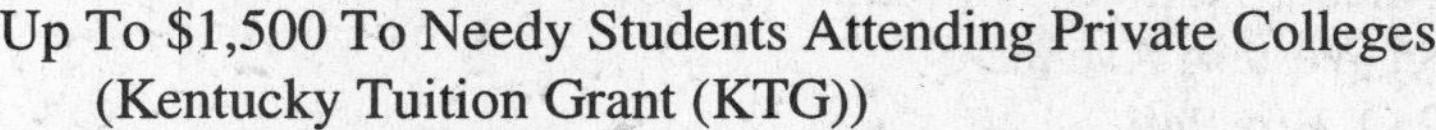

Up To $1,500 To Needy Students Attending Private Colleges (Kentucky Tuition Grant (KTG))

Money To Smart High School Graduates Going To College (Kentucky Educational Excellence Scholarship)

Money To Smart, Financially Needy Students Studying To Be A Teacher (KHEAA Teacher Scholarship)

Reduced Tuition Rate At Pikeville College School of Osteopathic Medicine (Osteopathic Medicine Scholarship)

Students Attending School At Least Half-Time Work AT Career Related Jobs (KHEAA Work-Study)

LOUISIANA

Office of Student Financial Assistance
P.O. Box 91202
Baton Rouge, LA 70821-9202
225-922-1011
Fax: 225-922-0790
www.osfa.state.la.us

General Requirements: Applicants must be Louisiana residents.

Programs Available:

Maximum $7,000 Grant To Study Forestry Or Marine Sciences (Louisiana Rockefeller State Wildlife Scholarship)

Free Tuition For Smart Students (Louisiana Tuition Opportunity Program (TOPS))

Up To $2,000 For High School Graduates Having Trouble Paying For College. Must Also Apply For The Federal Pell Grant (State Student Incentive Grant)

MAINE

Finance Authority of Maine (FAME)
83 Western Avenue
P.O. Box 949
TDD: 207-626-2717
Augusta, ME 04332-0949
207-632-3263
Fax: 207-623-0095
www.famemaine.com

General requirements: Applicants must be Maine residents.

Programs Available:

Money For Students From Maine To Study In New England States, Alaska, Delaware, DC, Maryland, and Pennsylvania (Maine Student Incentive Scholarship Program (MSISP))

Money For Students In The Upper 1/4 Of Their Class Who Want To Be Teachers (Teachers for Maine)

Money For Dependents Of Veterans Killed Or Disabled In Military Service (State Veterans Benefits)

Aid To Needy Students Studying In Fields Of Medicine, Dentistry, Optometry and Veterinary Science (Medical Education Program)

Access To Seats AT Out-Of-State Medical Schools (Maine Access To Medical Education Program)

MARYLAND

Maryland Higher Education Commission
State Scholarship Administration
The Jefferey Building
16 Francis Street, Suite 209
Annapolis, MD 21401-1781
410-974-5370
Fax: 410-974-5994
www.mhec.state.md.us

General requirements: Applicants must be Maryland residents, unless specified for in-state or out-of-state schools.

Programs Available:

$2,000 To Full- Or Part-Time Students (Senatorial Scholarship Program)

$200 To Full-Time Or Part-Time Students (Delegate Scholarship Program)

$1,500 To Take A Vocational Education Course (Tolbert Grant)

$3,000 A Year For Smart Students (Distinguished Scholar Program)

$4,800 To Get A Degree In Nursing (Maryland State Nursing Scholarship)

$3,000 A Year To Become A Teacher In Maryland (Teacher Education Distinguished Scholar Program)

Grants To Dependents of POW's, Fire Fighters, Police Officers, and Safety Personnel Killed Or Disabled In The Line OF Duty (Edward Conroy Grant)

Grants to Study Physical Therapy (Physical and Occupational Therapists and Assistants Scholarships)

$7,500 A Year To Study Family Practice Medicine (Family Practice Medical Scholarship)

Grants To Study Law, Dentistry, Medicine, Nursing, Or Pharmacy (Professional School Scholarship)

Tuition, Fees, Room and Board To Become A Teacher (Sharon Christa McAuliffe Critical Shortage Teacher Scholarship)

$2,000 To Study Child Care, Full Or Part-Time (Child Care Provider Scholarship)

Free Tuition To Fire Fighters, and Rescue Squad Members Who Want To Study Full Or Part-Time (Reimbursement of Fire Fighters, Ambulance, and Rescue Squad Members)

Student Loans If You Work For A Non-Profit (Loan Assistance Repayment Program (LARP))

Up To $8,300 Per Year To Students In Extreme Financial Need (Guaranteed Access Grant)

Up To $3,000 Per Year For Students From Low Or Moderate Income Families (Educational Assistance Grant)
Money Towards Tuition And Fees To Study And Practice To Be A Nurse In Maryland (State Nursing Scholarship and Living Expenses)
Tuition Reimbursement To Medical Residents and Physicians Specializing In Primary Care Who Work In Undeserved Areas of Maryland (Loan Assistance Repayment Program in Primary Care Services)
Non-resident Nursing Students Pay Resident Rate At Maryland Public Colleges (Health Manpower Shortage Program Tuition Reduction for Non-resident Nursing Student)

MASSACHUSETTS

Board of Higher Education
Office of Student Financial Assistance
330 Stuart Street, Suite 304
Boston, MA 02116
617-727-9420
Fax: 617-727-0667
www.osfa.mass.edu

General requirements: Applicants must be Massachusetts's residents.

Programs Available:
Maximum $2,500 For Full-Time Students (MASSGrant)
Money To MASSGrant Smart Students Who Are In Financial Need (Performance Bonus Grant)
Grants To Residents Attending An Independent School Full-Time (Gilbert Grant)
Money To Undergraduates Attending Public Colleges Or Universities (Tuition Waiver/Cash Grant)

Aid To Children And Spouses Of Deceased Fire, Police Or Corrections Officers, Or Children Of POW/MIA (Public Service Scholarship)

Money To Part-Time Students In Public Colleges Who Are In Financial Need (Part-Time Grant)

Up To 50% Of The Cost Of College For High School Students With Severe Personal Problems, Medical Problems, Or Have Overcome A Hardship (Christian A. Herter Memorial Scholarship)

No Interest Loan Program (NIL)

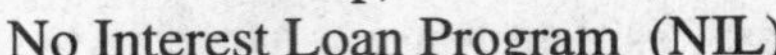

MICHIGAN

Michigan Department of Treasury
Higher Education Assistance Authority
1st Floor, Hannah Building
608 West Allegan
Lansing, MI 48901
888-447-2687
517-447-2687
www.treas.state.mi.us/college/mheaa.htm

General requirements: Applicants must be Michigan residents.

Programs Available:

Money For Smart Kids Who Have Trouble Paying Tuition (Competitive Scholarships)

Money For Students Attending Private Colleges (Tuition Grants)

MINNESOTA

Minnesota Higher Education Programs
Capitol Square Building
Suite 400
550 Cedar Street
St. Paul, MN 55101
800-657-3866
612-296-3974
www.heso.state.mn.us

General requirements: Applicants must be residents of Minnesota, unless otherwise specified.

Programs Available:

Money To Pay Half Your College Expenses (State Grant Program)

Money To Help Pay For Child Care While You Go To School (Child Care Grant Program)

Money To High School Students Who High On The Advanced Placement or International Baccalaureate Tests (Advanced Placement and International Baccalaureate Scholarships)

Up To $4,000 Per Year For Minority Students To Become A RN (Nursing Grants For Persons Of Color)

Up To $1,850 For Indian Students In Financial Need That Will Benefit From College (Minnesota Indian Scholarship Program)

$1,000 For High School Students To Take Summer Courses At A College (Summer Scholarships For Academic Enrichment)

Part or Full-Time Work On Or Off Campus For Students With A Financial Need (State Work-Study Program)
Money To Dependents of POW's And MIA's (State Veterans' Dependents Assistance Program)
Tuition And/Or Stipends To Veterans And Children Of Deceased Veterans (Educational assistance For War Orphans And Veterans)
Tuition And Fees For Children And Spouses Of Public Safety Officers Killed In The Line Of Duty After 1973 (Safety Officers' Program)
Minnesota Students Pay Reduced Tuition Rate At Selected Out Of State Colleges (Reciprocity Programs)
Aid To Dislocated Workers For Training Programs (Grants For Dislocated Workers)
Tuition To High School Students That Have Excelled At English/Creative Writing, Fine Arts, Foreign Language, Math Science Or Social Science (Minnesota Academic Excellence Scholarship)
Tuition Assistance To High School Students That Graduated In The Top 10% Of Their Class That Are Attending The College of Agriculture, Food and Environmental Sciences (Farm Families Scholarships)

MISSISSIPPI

Mississippi Institution of Higher Learning
Office of State Student Financial Aid
3825 Ridgewood Road
Jackson, MS 39211-6453
601-982-6663

General requirements: Applicants must be residents of Mississippi.

Programs Available:

Stipend/Apprenticeship Program To Study Psychology During The Summer (Apprenticeship Program)

Money To Students In A Speech Pathology, Psychology or Occupation Therapy Program Who Will Serve

In A State-Operated Health Hospital (Health Education Programs)

Money To Registered Nurses Who Want To Become Nursing Teachers In Mississippi (Nursing Teacher Stipend Program)

$4,000 A Year To Attend The University of Mississippi School of Dentistry And Practice In A Needed Area (State Dental education Loan/Scholarship Program)

$6,000 A Year To Study Family Medicine, Internal Medicine, Pediatrics or Obstetrics/Gynecology At The University of Mississippi School of Medicine (State medical Education Loan/Scholarship Program)

$6,000 A Year For Minority Students To Study At The Mississippi State University College of Veterinary Medicine (Veterinary Medicine Minority Loan/Scholarship Program)

Full Tuition For Financially Needy Students To Pursue A Baccalaureate Or First Associate Undergraduate Degree (Higher Education Legislative Plan For Needy Students (HELP))

Up To $2,500 To Smart First-Time Freshmen (Mississippi Eminent Scholars Grant (MESG))

Money To Residents To Attend Public or Private Schools In Mississippi (Mississippi Resident Tuition Assistance Grant (MTAG))

Grants To Minority Students To Study At The Gulf Coast Research Laboratory During The Summer (Gulf Coast Research Laboratory Minority Summer Grant Program)

Tuition, Room And Fees To Spouses and Children Of Firefighters And Law Enforcement Officers That Were Totally Disabled Or Killed (Mississippi Law Enforcement Officers and Firemen Scholarship Program)

Grants To Full-Time Students Who Have Trouble Paying For Tuition (State Student Incentive Grant)

Tuition, Room And Meals, Books And Fees To Students Studying For A Class "A" Standard Teacher Education License Who Will Teach In Mississippi (Critical Needs Teacher Loan/Scholarship Program (CNTP))

Up To $8,000 To Smart Students Who Get A Class "A" Standard Teacher Educator License And Teach In Mississippi Public Schools (William Winter Teacher Scholar Loan Program (WWTS))

Aid To Teachers To Pursue A First Master's Degree And A Class "AA" Standard Teacher Education License (Graduate Teacher Summer Loan/Scholarship (GTS))

Financial Aid To Teachers From An Area With A Shortage Of Teachers To Study For A Masters Or Educational Specialist Degree (Mississippi Teacher Fellowship)

Money To Minority Students To Study For A Ph.D Degree In Science, Math, Math or Science Education, And Engineering. (Southern Regional Education Board (STEB) Doctoral Scholars)

Students Studying For A Graduate Degree In Criminal Justice, Public Administration, or Public Policy Can Work For State Or Local Agencies And Offices (Mississippi Public Management Graduate Intern Program)

Money To Pursue Health Related Degrees In Another State That Are Not Offered In Mississippi (Out Of State Programs)

Assistance To Residents To Attend Designated Out Of State Schools of Optometry or Osteopathic Medicine (Southern Regional Education Bard (SREB) Loan/Scholarship Program)

Nursing Education Loans/Scholarship Program:

$1,500 A Year For RN's Going To School To Get A BSN Degree Who Will Be A Nurse In Mississippi (RN To BSN Program)

Up To $4,000 For Nursing Students To Get A BSN Degree (BSN Program)

$3,000 Per Year To Study Full-Time For A MSN Degree (MSN Program)

$5,000 Per Year For To Get A DSN Degree And Work In Mississippi For One Year (DSN Program)

MISSOURI

Missouri Department of Higher Education
P.O. Box 1438
3515 Amazonas Drive
Jefferson City, MO 65109-5717
573-751-2361
Fax: 573-751-6635
www.mocbhe.gov

General requirements: Applicants must be Missouri residents.

Programs Available:

$2,000 A Year To Students With ACT Scores In The Top 3% (Missouri Higher Education Academic Scholarship Program)

Grants To Full-Time Students In Financial Need (Charles Gallagher Student Financial Assistance Program)

Tuition For Dependents Of Public Safety Officers Or Department Of Highway Officers Who Were Killed In The

Line Of Duty (Public Service Officer or Employee's Child Survivor Grant Program)

Help Paying Tuition For Part-Time Students Who Work (Marguerite Ross Barnett Memorial Scholarship)

Tuition For Child Or Spouse of Deceased Vietnam Veteran (Vietnam Veterans Survivors Grant Program)

Money For College For Top Undergraduates and Graduates (Higher Education Scholarship Program

Reduced Tuition For Designated Programs At A College In Kansas, Michigan, Minnesota or Nebraska (Midwest Student Exchange Program)

MONTANA

Office of the Commissioner of Higher Education
P.O. Box 203101
Helena, MT 59620-3101
406-444-6570
Fax: 406-444-1469
www.montana.edu/wwwoche

General requirements: Applicants must be Montana residents.

Programs Available:

Grants To Students Who Can't Afford Tuition (Leveraging Education Assistance Partnership Program)

Money For Students Who Are Semifinalists In The National Merit Scholarship Competition (Honor Scholarship for National Merit Scholarship Semifinalists)

$1350 To Top Ranking High School Seniors (High School and Community College Honor Scholarships)

Free Tuition For Senior Citizens, Veterans, War Orphans, Etc. (Fee Waivers)

Money For Students Who Work To Help Pay For College (Montana Tuition Assistance Program)

NEBRASKA

Nebraska Coordinating Commission
For Postsecondary Education
140 North Eighth Street, Suite 300
P.O. Box 95005
Lincoln, NE 68509-5005
402-471-2847
Fax: 402-471-2886
http://nol.org/NEpostsecondaryed

General requirements: Nebraska has a de-centralized grant program. Students should apply for grants through the financial aid office of the college or university that they plan to attend. The school distributes the aid to the specific student. State residency is required.

NEVADA

Nevada Department of Education
Student Incentive Grant Program
700 East 5th Street
Carson City, NV 89701-9050
775-687-9200

General requirements: Nevada has no state scholarships. Students should contact the financial aid office at the college they plan to attend for further information. State residency is required.

Programs Available:
Up To $2,500 For Undergraduate and Graduate Students In Financial Need (Access Grant)
Up To $5,200 A Year To Students That Offer Leadership And Service To Their School (Grants-in-Aid)
Grants To Students Who Need Help Paying For School (Leveraging Educational Assistance Program)

NEW HAMPSHIRE

New Hampshire Postsecondary Education Commission
2 Industrial Park Drive
Concord, NH 03301-8512
603-271-2555
TDD:800-735-2964
Fax: 603-271-2696
www.state.nh.us/postsecondary

General requirements: Applicants must be New Hampshire residents for programs involving colleges in and out of state.

Programs Available:
Grants To Attend Colleges In The New England States (New Hampshire Incentive Program)
Money For Dependents Of Veterans Who Died In Service (War Orphans Scholarship)
Grants For Nurses Who Agree To Practice In New Hampshire (New Hampshire Nursing Scholarship Program)
Aid For Students Who Enroll In Programs That Are In Need Of Trained Employees (Career Incentive Program)

NEW JERSEY

New Jersey Department of Higher Education
Office of Student Assistance
4 Quakerbridge Plaza, CN 540
Trenton, NJ 08625
609-588-3288
www.state.nj.us/treasury/osa

General requirements: Applicant must be a New Jersey resident.

Programs Available:

$6050 A Year In Grants To Full-Time Students (Tuition Aid Grants)

Grants, Tutoring, and Counseling To Students On Limited Income (Educational Opportunity Fund Grants (EOF))

Grants To Students With High SAT Scores (Edward J. Bloustein Distinguished Scholar Program)

Grants To Smart High School Juniors (Garden State Scholars Program)

Tuition to Disadvantaged/Minority Students In A Program Leading Toward A Medical Degree At University of Medicine and Dentistry of New Jersey (Martin Luther King Jr. Physician-Dentist Scholarship)

Tuition, Fees, Room and Board To Disadvantaged/ Ethnic Minority Students In The Minority Student Program at Rutgers University School for Law (C.Clyde Ferguson Law Scholarship)

$1,000 Per Year To Top 10% Of Class From An Urban Area (Urban Scholars)

Tuition For Spouses And Children Of Emergency Service Personnel And Law Enforcement Officers Killed In The Line Of Duty (Public Tuition Benefits Program)

Up To $70,000 Student Loan Redemption For Physicians and Dentist Located In Needy Areas Of New Jersey (Physician and Dentist Loan Redemption Program)

Attend A Veterinarian School Out-Of-State (Veterinary Medicine Scholarship)

NEW MEXICO

New Mexico Commission On Higher Education
1068 Cerrillos Road
Santa Fe, NM 87501
505-827-7383
Fax: 505-827-7392
www.nmche.org

General requirements: Applicants must be New Mexico residents, unless otherwise stated.

Programs Available:

Free Tuition To Students with "Good Moral Character" (Three Percent Scholarship Program)

Tuition, Books, and Fees For High School Students In Top 5% Of Class (New Mexico Scholars Program)

Part-Time Jobs To Undergraduate and Graduate Students (New Mexico Work-Study Program)

Money For Osteopathic Students Willing To Practice In New Mexico (Osteopathic Medical Student Loan Program)

Grants To Half-Time and Full-Time Students In Financial Need (New Mexico Student Incentive Grant)

Tuition, Books, And Fees To Vietnam Veterans (Vietnam Veterans' Scholarship Program)

Money For Students Attending Private Colleges (Student Choice)

Money Applied Towards Tuition and Fees For Athletes (Athletic Scholarships)

Financial Aid To Students With Children (Child Care Grants)

Children Of Military Personnel, Members Of New Mexico National Guard, and New Mexico State Police Killed On Active Duty (Children Of Deceased Military and State Police Personnel Scholarship)

Smart Out-Of-State Students Pay Resident Rate At A Public New Mexico College (Competitive Scholarships)

Money To High School Seniors Going Directly Into College Full-Time (Lottery Success Scholarships)

Up To $2,500 For Students In Financial Need To Attend College Full-Time (Legislative Endowment Scholarships)

Reduced Tuition For New Mexico's Senior Citizens (Senior Citizens Reduced Tuition Act)

Money For Osteopathic Students Willing To Practice In New Mexico (Osteopathic Medical Student Loan For Service Program)

$12,000 For Nursing Students Willing To Practice In New Mexico (Nursing Student Loan For Service Program)

Money For Medical Students Willing To Practice In New Mexico (Medical Student Loan for Service Program)

Money For Women And Minority Ph.D. Students (Minority Doctoral Assistance Loan for Service Program)

Students Of Allied Health Programs That Will Practice In Designated Areas Of New Mexico (Allied Health Professional Loan For Service Program)

Loan Reimbursement To Health Professionals That Practice In Specified Areas of New Mexico (Health Professional Loan Repayment Program)

NEW YORK

New York Higher Education Services Corporation
Grants and Scholarship Information
99 Washington Avenue
Albany, NY 12255
888-NYSHESC
518-474-1137
www.hesc.com

General requirements; Applicants must be residents of New York. Amounts awarded are determined by the type of school your are planning to attend, your financial state (net taxable income), year in which the award is received, and amount of tuition.

Programs Available:

Grants For Full-Time Students (Tuition Assistance Program (TAP))

Grants For Part-Time Students (Aid For Part-Time Study (APTS)

Money For Accounting, Veterinary, and Students Pursuing 19 Other Professional Careers (New York Regents Professional Opportunity Scholarships)

Money For Students Studying Medicine Or Dentistry (New York Regents Health Care Opportunity Scholarships)

Money For Native Americans To Attend College (State Aid To Native Americans)

Grants To Dependents Of Deceased Or Disabled Veterans (Regents Award For Child Of Veteran)

Grants To Dependents Of Deceased Correction Officer (Child Of Correction Officer)

Tuition And Fees For Dependents Of Deceased Police Officers And Fire Fighters (Memorial Scholarships For Children Of Deceased Police Officers And Fire Fighters)

$1,000 Per Semester For Vietnam Veterans (Vietnam Veterans Tuition Awards)

Outstanding High School Seniors Receive Up To $1,500 A Year (Scholarships For Academic Excellence)

Up To $15,000 For A Career As A Midwife, Nurse Practitioner, Or Physician Assistant (New York State Primary Care Service Corps)

Up To $1,000 Per Semester For Persian Gulf Veterans (Persian Gulf Veterans Tuition Awards)

$4,725 For Full-Time AmeriCorp Members (AmeriCorps Education Award)

Up To $3,400 A Year In Tuition For Members Of State Military Forces (National Guard-NYS Educational Incentive Program)

NORTH CAROLINA

North Carolina State Education Assistance Authority
P.O. Box 2688
Chapel Hill, NC 27515-2688
919-549-8614
Fax: 919-549-8481
www.ncseaa.edu

General requirements: Applicants must be residents of North Carolina.

Programs Available:

Grants For Full-Time And Part-Time Students (Appropriated Grants)
$3,000 For Smart High School Students Active In Public Service (Incentive Scholarship Program)
Grants For Minorities Studying Part Time Or Full Time (Minority Presence Grant Program)
Grants For Minorities Studying Law, Veterinary Medicine, Or Working On A Ph.D. (Minority Presence Grant Program: Doctoral/Law/Veterinary Medicine Program)
Grants For Students Going Part Time To Junior Colleges (North Carolina Community College Scholarship Program)
Grants Given By State Legislators To Students Who Don't Even Need The Money (North Carolina Legislative Tuition Grant Program, Private College)
$8,500 A Year For Undergraduate Or Graduate Students In Health, Science, Or Mathematics (North Carolina Student Loan Program For Health, Science, and Mathematics)
$5,000 A Year To Students Who Want To Be Teachers (North Carolina Teaching Fellows Scholarship Program)
Grants To Dependents Of Deceased Or Disabled Veterans Or POW/MIA's (North Carolina Veteran Scholarship)
Grants To Full-Time Or Part--Time Native American Students (Incentive Scholarship and Grant Program)

Money For Students In 2-Year Or 4-Year Nursing Programs (Nurse Education Scholarship Loan Program)

$5,000 A Year For Nursing Students Willing To Practice In North Carolina (Nurse Scholars Program)

$5,000 Plus Tuition And Fees For Dental Students (Board of Governors Dental Scholarship)

$5,000 Plus Tuition And Fees For Medical Students (Board of Governors Medical Scholarship Program)

Free Loans For Studying Psychology, Counseling, Or Speech (Prospective Teacher Scholarship Loans)

Grants To Part-Time Or Full-Time Students Attending Private Colleges (State Contractual Scholarship Program, Private Colleges)

Tuition, Fees, And Day Care For The Physically Or Mentally Disabled (Vocational Rehabilitation Program)

$6,000 A Year Towards A Master's Degree For Nurses Who Will Teach In North Carolina (North Carolina Master's Nurse Scholar Program)

Up To $4,000 A Year For Active Members Of The North Carolina Army Or Air National Guard To Attend School (North Carolina National Guard Tuition Assistance Program (TAP))

Money For College To Vietnam Veterans Or Their Families

Four-Year Scholarships To Students Who Are Going To Enroll In The ROTC Program (Reserve Officer's Training Corps Scholarships (ROTC))

Tuition, Fees, And Books For The Freshman Year Of College At Select Universities In North Carolina (Freshman Scholars Program)

$3,000 To Native American Freshmen Who Graduated In The Top 1/2 Of Their Class And Active In Public Service (AMBUCS Scholarships For Therapists Merit Based Scholarship)

$2,500 A Year For Students In Academic Health Science Programs To Study Substance Abuse (North Carolina Governor's Institute On Alcohol And Substance Abuse Public Policy Scholars Program)

$20,000 A Year For Full-Time Study To Become Part of The Administration In Public Schools (Principal Fellows Program)

$1,200 A Year For Teacher Assistants To Attend Community College (Teacher Assistant Scholarship Loan Two-Year Program)

Tuition, Fees, Books and Supplies, and Reader Services To Full-Time Visually Impaired Students With Financial Need (Rehabilitation Assistance For Visually Handicapped)

NORTH DAKOTA

University Systems
600 East Boulevard
Bismarck, ND 58505-0230
701-328-4114

General requirements: Applicants must be residents of North Dakota.

Programs Available:

Money for Students In Financial Need (State Grant Student Incentive Program)

Tuition Aid For Students In The Upper 5% Of Their Class (North Dakota Scholars Program)

OHIO

Ohio Board of Regents
State Grants and Scholarship Department
P.O. Box 182452
Columbus, OH 43218-2452
888-833-1133

614-466-7420
Fax: 614-752-5903
www.regents.state.oh.us
General requirements: Applicants must be residents of Ohio.

Programs Available:
Grants For Low To Moderate Income Families To Pay Tuition (Ohio Instructional Grants)
Grants To Pay Tuition At Private Colleges (Ohio Student Choice Grant Program)
Grants To Dependents Of Deceased Or Disabled Veterans (Ohio War Orphans Scholarship Program)
$2,000 A Year To Smart High School Students Who Attend Ohio Colleges
(Ohio Academic Scholarship Program)
$3,500 A Year For Smart Graduate Students (Regents Graduate/Professional Fellowship Program)
Tuition Assistance To Dependents Of Fire Fighters And Police Officers Killed In The Line Of Duty
(Ohio Safety Officers College Memorial Fund)
Money For Students Who Need Financial Help To Attend School Part-Time
(Part-Time Student Instructional Grant Program)
$3,000 Per Year For Students Enrolled in A Nurse Education Program (Nurse Education Assistance Loan Program)

OKLAHOMA

Oklahoma State Regents for Higher Education
500 Education Building
State Capitol Complex
Oklahoma City, OK 73105
405-524-9100
Fax: 405-524-9230

www.okhighered.org
General requirements: Applicants must be Oklahoma residents.

Programs Available:

Money For Students Having Trouble Paying Tuition (Oklahoma Tuition Aid Grant Program)

Grants To Top 15% High School Students Who want To Be Teachers (Future Teachers Scholarship Program)

Money To Smart Students Going To Public Or Private Colleges (Academic Scholars Program)

Money For Members And Enlistees Of The National Guard Going To School To Earn A Bachelor's Degree (National Guard Tuition Waiver)

Aid For Smart, Well Behaved High School Students With Financial Need (Must Apply During 9th and 10th Grade) (Oklahoma Higher Learning Access Program)

Tuition, Fees, Room and Board, and Required Books For Smart Students At 10 Participating Universities In Oklahoma (Regional University Baccalaureate Scholarship)

Money For Full-Time Undergraduates Who Need Help To Pay For School (William P. Willis Scholarship)

Money To Minority Graduate Students Who Agree To Teach At Oklahoma Colleges Or Universities After Graduating With A Doctor's Degree (Doctoral Study Grant Program)

$4,000 A Year And A Fee Waiver To Minorities To Study In The Field Of Medicine, Dentistry, Law, Optometry, Pharmacy, And Veterinary Medicine (Professional Study Grant)

Tuition, Special Fees, Books, and Room And Board To Dependent Children Of Victims Of The Bombing Of The Alfred P. Murrah Federal Building (Heartland Scholarship Fund)

Money To Study In A Specialized Field Of Chiropractic Medicine (Chiropractic Education Assistance Program)

OREGON

Oregon State Scholarship Commission
1500 Valley River Drive, Suite 100
Eugene, OR 97401
800-452-8807
503-687-7400
www.ossc.state.or.us

General requirements: Applicants must be residents of Oregon.

Programs Available:

Grants To College Students In Financial Need; Must Apply For FASA Too (Need Grants)

Tuition And Fees For Children Of Firefighters, Police Officers, Correction and Investigators That Are In Financial Need (Deceased Or Disabled Public Safety Officer)

$600 For Full-Time Attendance At Hair Stylist, Cosmetology Or Manicure School; Must Also Apply For FASA (Oregon Barbers And Hairdressers Grant Program

Student Loans Forgiven If You Become A Nurse In A Needed Area Of Oregon (Oregon Nursing Loan Program)

PENNSYLVANIA

Pennsylvania Higher Education Assistance Agency
1200 North 7th Street
Harrisburg, PA 17102
TTY: 800-654-5988
717-720-2850
Fax: 717-720-3907
www.pheaa.org

General requirements: Applicants must be Pennsylvania residents for in-state schools, unless otherwise specified.

Programs Available:

80% Of Tuition And Fees For Financially Needy Students (Pennsylvania State Grants)

Students Provided With Employment Opportunities In High-Technology And Community Service Positions (Pennsylvania State Work-Study Program)

$2,900 For Veterans Who Want To Go To School (Financial Aid For Veterans)

Tuition, Fees and Room And Board Waiver For The Children Of Police Officers, Firefighters, Rescue And Ambulance Squad Members, Correction Employees and National Guard Members Who Died In The Line Of Duty (The Postsecondary Educational Gratuity Program)

RHODE ISLAND

Rhode Island Higher Education Assistance Authority
560 Jefferson Boulevard
Warwick, RI 02886
401-736-1100
Fax: 401-732-3541
TDD: 401-222-6195
www.riheaa.org

General requirements: Applicants must be residents of Rhode Island.

Programs Available:

Money For Students Who Need Help Paying For College (State Grant Program)

Students In Financial Need Can Get Work At Non-Profit Agencies In Rhode Island; Must Be Receiving The Rhode Island State Grant Program (Community Service Initiative)

Work-Study Awards To Students That Work For Specific Rhode Island Employers (College Allocation Program (CAP))

SOUTH CAROLINA

South Carolina Commission on Higher Education
1333 Main Street, Suite 200
Columbia, SC 29201
803-737-2260
Fax: 803-737-1426
www.state.sc.us/tuitiongrants

General requirements: Applicants must be residents of South Carolina.

Programs Available:

$3,320 For Students In Financial Need (South Carolina Tuition Grants)

$5,000 For High School Seniors With High Test Scores (Palmetto Fellows Scholarship)

Up To $2,500 To Students In Extreme Financial Need (Need Based Grant)

$2,000 A Year For Smart Students (Legislative Incentive For Future Excellence (LIFE))

Money To High School Students Who Graduated With A STAR Diploma (Superior Scholars For Today and Tomorrow (STAR) Scholarship)

SOUTH DAKOTA

South Dakota Department of Education And Cultural Affairs
Office of the Secretary
7000 Governors Drive
Pierre, SD 57051
605-773-3134

Currently, there are no state aided financial aid programs available. South Dakota assigns state general funds to support public higher education schools. General state funds are rarely awarded directly to student aid.

TENNESSEE

Tennessee Student Assistance Corporation
404 James Robertson Parkway, Suite 1950
Nashville, TN 37243-0820
615-741-6101
Fax: 615-741-6101
www.state.tn.us/tsac

General requirements: Applicants must be residents of Tennessee.

Programs Available:

$5,000 A Year For Minorities In The Top 25% Of Class To Become Teachers (Minority Teaching Fellows Program)

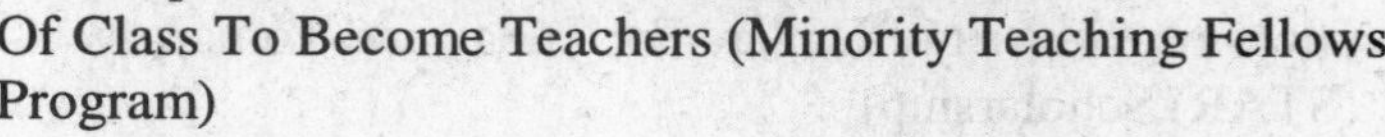

$1,626 For Financially Needy Students (Tennessee Student Assistance Award Program (TSAA))

$6,000 A Year For Very Smart High School Graduates Entering College (Ned McWherter Scholars Program)

Up To $3,000 Of Student Loan Forgiven For College Juniors, Seniors And Post Baccalaureate Students Who Will Teach In Tennessee Public Schools (Tennessee teaching Scholars program)

Money To Smart Full-Time Students In A Teacher Education Program (Christa McAuliffe Scholarship Program)

Financial Aid For Children Of Law Enforcement Officers, Firemen, Or Emergency Medical Technicians Killed In The Line Of Duty (Dependent Children's Scholarship Program)

Grants To Tennessee Residents With A Physical, Mental or Emotional Disability (Vocational Rehabilitation Grants)

TEXAS

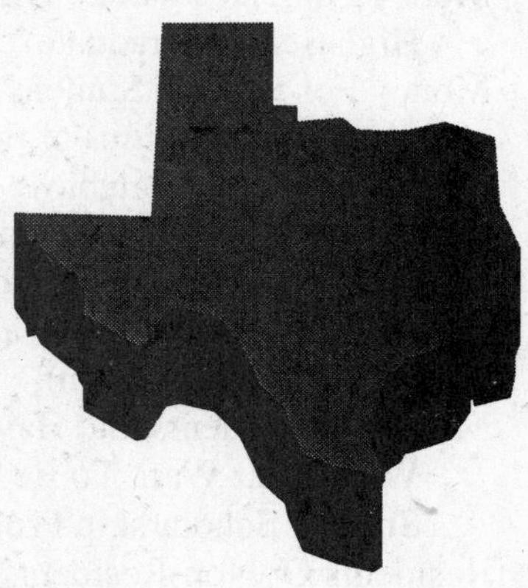

Texas Higher Education
Coordinating Board
Box 12788, Capitol Station
Austin, TX 78711-2788
512-483-6100
www.thecb.state.tx.us/start/stu

General requirements: Applicants must be residents of Texas, unless otherwise specified.

Programs Available:

Money To Attend Public Colleges In Texas (Texas Public Education Grant)

Money To Attend Private Colleges In Texas (Tuition Equalization Grant)

$1,250 For Half Time Or Full Time Students
(Student Incentive Grant)

Grants to Financially Needy Students
(Texas Tuition Assistance Grant)

Money To Study To Be A Nurse

Tuition And Fees For Blind Or Deaf Students

Money For Dependents Of Disabled Or Deceased Firemen, Peace Officers, Custodial Employees of the Department Of Corrections, Or Game Wardens

Money For Dependents Of POW/MIAs (Children Of Prisoners Of War Or Persons Missing In Action)

Tuition And Fees For Fire Fighters To Take Science Courses (Fire Fighters Enrolled in Fire Science Courses)

Free Tuition And Fees For Veterans (Veterans and Dependents (The Hazelwood Act))

Money For The smartest High School Students (High Ranking High School Graduate)

Money For Foreign Students From Central America (Students from Other Nations of the American Hemisphere (Good Neighbor Scholarship))

Aid To Students Who Graduate In No More Than 36 Months (Early High School Graduation Scholarship)

Tuition and Fees For At Least Half-Time (Texas New Horizons Scholarship Program)

Money To Students that Have Completed 120 Hours Of College Work That Want To Be Accountants (Fifth-Year Accounting Student Scholarship Program)

Residents Or Non-Residents With Financial Need (License Plate Insignia Scholarship)

Aid To Students Who Practice Primary Health Care In Designated Communities After Graduation (Community Scholarship program)

Stipends Of Up To $15,000 A Year To Primary Care Residents To Practice In Medically Under-Served Areas (Texas Health Service Corps Repayment Program)

Money To Students Who Are Studying For A Degree In Specified Primary Care Areas And Agree To Serve In Areas With Severe Shortages
(Texas Health Service Corps Scholarship Program)

Forgiveness Loans For Top Students To Work In Their Community After Graduation (Outstanding Rural Scholarship Program)

Up To 5 Years Of Loan Repayment for Physicians In Specialized Areas
(Physician Education Loan Repayment Program)

Up To $5,000 In Loan Repayment For Physician Assistants Who Have Practiced In Specified Area (Rural Physician Assistant Loan Reimbursement)

Hours Of Part-time Work For Students In Financial Need
(Texas College Work-Study Program)

Fees and Tuition For Disabled Peace Officers
(Disabled Peace Officers)

Tuition and Fees For Students That Have Been In Foster Care
(Foster Care Students)

Exemption From Tuition For Up To 6 Semester Credit Hours Per Semester
(Senior Citizens)

Exemption From Fees and Tuition For Up To 1 Year For High School Seniors That Received Financial Assistance.
(Assistance For Needy Families)

ROTC Students receive Tuition, Fees And Partial Exemption From Room and Board
(Reserve Officer's Training Corps/National Guard Students)

Money To Currently Employed Certified Educational Aides In Financial Need
(Certified Educational Aides)

Special Tuition Rate For Graduate Students To Out-Of-State College When The Degree Is Not Offered In Texas
(Academic Common Market)

UTAH

Utah System of Higher Education
3 Triad Center, Suite 550
Salt Lake City, UT 84180-1205
801-321-7101
www.state.ut.us/html/education.htm
General requirements: Applicants must be residents of Utah.

Programs Available:

Grants For Students In Financial Need (State Student Incentive Grant Program)

Money To Go To School In Utah (Utah Centennial Opportunity Program For Education Grant)

Tuition and General Fees For Outstanding Students To Teach In Utah (Terrel H. Bell Teaching Incentive Loan)

VERMONT

Vermont Student Assistance Corporation
P.O. Box 2000
Champlain Mill- 4th Floor
Winooski, VT 05404
800-798-8722
802-655-4050
www.vsac.org

General requirements: Applicants must be Vermont residents, unless otherwise stated.

Programs Available:

Grants For Students In Financial Need (Vermont Incentive Grants)

Grants For Part Time Students (Vermont Part Time Student Grants)

$500 Per Course If You're NOT Working Toward A Degree (Vermont Non-Degree Student Grant Program)

VIRGINIA

Virginia State Council of Higher Education
Office of Financial Aid
James Monroe Building
101 North 14th Street, 9th Floor
Richmond, VA 23219
804-225-2137
TDD: 804-371-8017
Fax: 804-225-2604
www.schev.edu

General requirements: Applicants must be Virginia residents.

Programs Available:

$3,000 For Students In Financial Need (Virginia College Assistance Program (CSAP))

Grants For Students Even Though They Don't NEED The Money (Virginia Tuition Assistance Grant Program (TAG))

Free Tuition For White Students To Attend Black Colleges (Virginia Transfer Grant Program (VTGP))
Grants To Black Undergraduate Students (Last Dollar Program)
Nursing Students Receive $100 A Month For Every Month They Agree To Work In Virginia (Medical Scholarship Program)
$2,500 To Dental Students Who Agree To Work In Small Virginia Towns (Rural Dental Scholarships)
$3,000 A Year For Teaching Students For Every Year They Agree To Work In Virginia (Virginia Teaching Scholarship)
Free Tuition, Fees, And Room and Board For State Cadets (State Cadetships)
Free Tuition For Dependents Of Disabled Veterans (Virginia War Orphan Education Act)
Free Tuition And Fees For Students Who Want To Study Soil Science (Soil Scientist Program)
Free Tuition For Students Over 60 (Senior Citizens Tuition Waiver)
Money To Needy Students Attending AT Least Half Time (Commonwealth Awards)
Money For Smart Students Going To School Full Time (Graduate and Undergraduate Assistance Program)
Money To High School Graduates Who Need Help Paying For College (Virginia Guaranteed Assistance Program (VGAP))
Virginia Army National Guard Members Receive Tuition Assistance (Virginia National Guard)
Financial Aid For Visually Handicapped Students; Must Also Apply For Additional Funding (Virginia Assistance For The Visually Handicapped)
Vocational Rehabilitation To Residents With A Disability; Must Also Apply for Additional Aid Virginia Department of Rehabilitative Services College Program)
In-State Tuition Rate For Students Who Study A Selected Program At One Of 13 Southern State Schools (Academic Common Market)

Aid To Northhampton Or Accomack Juniors And Seniors Who Commute To The University of Maryland-Eastern Shore or Salisbury State University (Eastern Shore Tuition Assistance Program)

Tuition Assistance To Study Library Science, Optometry, Forensic Science and Paper and Pulp Technology At Specified Out-Of-State Schools (Regional Contract Programs)

WASHINGTON

Higher Education Coordinating Board
917 Lakeridge Way
P.O. Box 43430
Olympia, WA 98504-3430
360-753-7809
TTY: 360-753-7809
Fax: 360-753-7808
www.hecb.wa.gov

General requirements: Applicants must be Washington residents for in-state or out-of-state programs, when specified.

Programs Available:

College Students Who Have Trouble Paying For Tuition (Washington State Need Grant Program)

Part-Time Employment To Students Who Need Money (Washington State Work Study Program)

Grants To Financially Needy Placebound Students To Finish Their Education (Educational Opportunity Grant)

Money To Students Who Will Practice Primary Care In Needed Areas After Graduating (Health Professional Scholarship)

Grants To Teachers, Principals, and School District Administrators For Part-Time Study At University of Washington (Christa Mc Auliffe Award For Excellence)

Money To High School Students In The Top 1% (Washington Scholars Program)
Money To Outstanding Vocational-Technical Students (Washington Award For Vocational Excellence (WAVE))
Financial Aid For American Indian Students In Need (American Indian Endowed Scholarship)
Up To $200 To Blind Students For Reimbursement Of Special Equipment, Services And Supplies (Aid To Blind Students)
Money To Study Optometry In Other States And Practice In Washington (Western Interstate Commission
For Higher Education (WICHE) Professional Student Exchange Program)
Money To Get A Master's Or Ph.D. In Out-Of-State Schools (Western Interstate Commission For Higher Education(WICHE) Regional Graduate Program)
Free Tuition And Fees To Financially Needy Students (Tuition Waiver Program)

WEST VIRGINIA

State College and University Systems
1018 Kanawha Boulevard, East
Suite 700
Charleston, WV 25301
304-558-2101
Fax: 304-558-0259
www.scusco.wvnet.edu

General requirements: Applicants must be residents of West Virginia.

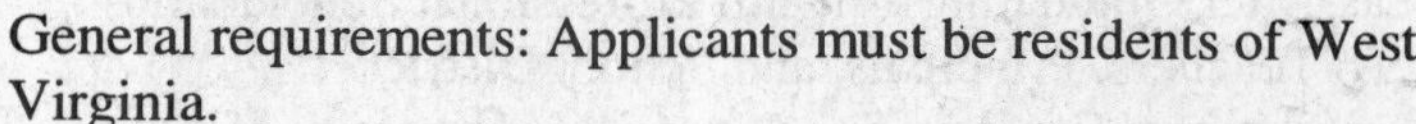

Programs Available:
Money For Financially Needy Students (West Virginia Higher Education Grant)
Money To Study Teaching At The Graduate Or Undergraduate Level (Underwood-Smith Teacher Scholarship Program
Money For Medical Students To Practice In West Virginia For A Time (Medical Student Loan Program)

WISCONSIN

State of Wisconsin Higher Education Aids Board
P.O. Box 7885
Madison, WI 53707-7885
608-267-2206
Fax: 608-267-2808
http://heab.state.wi.us

General requirements: Applicants must be residents of Wisconsin. Students should contact the Financial Aid Office of the College they plan on attending for applications.

Programs Available:
Grants To College Or Vocational Students (Wisconsin Higher Education Grant)
Grants To Students Attending Private Colleges In Wisconsin (Wisconsin Tuition Grant)

Grants To Blacks, Hispanics, Native Americans, And Former Citizens Of Laos, Vietnam, and Cambodia (Minority Retention Grant)
Grants To Non-Traditional Students (Talent Incentive Program)
Cheap Tuition For Attending Minnesota University (Minnesota-Wisconsin Reciprocity Program)
$2,250 A Year To High School Seniors Who Have The Highest GPA In Their School (Academic Excellence Scholarships)
Up To $1,800 A Year To Severely Visually Or Hearing Impaired Students To Go To College In Or Out-Of-State (Handicapped Student Grant)
$2,500 Per Year For Minority College Juniors Or Seniors Who Become Teachers In Wisconsin (Minority Teacher Loan Program)
$2,000 For Students In Programs At The Milwaukee Teacher Education Center Who Agree To Teach In Wisconsin (Teacher Education Loan Program)

WYOMING

Wyoming Department of
Higher Education
Hathaway Building
2300 Capitol Avenue
Cheyenne, WY 82002
307-777-6213

General Requirements: Wyoming offers the Leveraging Educational Assistance Program (LEAP). Applicants must be Wyoming residents and college freshmen and sophomores in financial need. The individual schools handle these programs and should be contacted for information and applications.

Free Scholarships

Organizations are continuously initiating, ending or changing scholarship programs. We have attempted to gather information on some scholarships available, but because of the perpetual changes you will want to check directly with the organization for details and the most up-to-date information. When possible, we have included the website of the organization offering the scholarship for your convenience.

Using the Internet!

Half the battle of scholarships is FINDING them! Thanks to the advent of the Internet, it has become increasingly easy to find scholarships and financial aid information. If you have Internet access, you will want to consider exploring the following websites first. All allow free searches of their databases. Some allow you to "save" your search results, others automatically notify you of new or updated scholarship offerings, and some provide excellent advice on how to improve your odds of winning scholarships. To maximize your information, it is recommended to try all of them because each database offers different information and services.

FreSch! The Free Scholarship Information Service
www.freschinfo.com

FastWeb: Financial Aid Search through The Web
www.fastweb.com

FastAid
www.fastaid.com

SallieMae
scholarships.salliemae.com

CollegeEdge
www.CollegeEdge.com/FA/

GoCollege
www.gocollege.com

SRN Express Search
www.rams.com/srn/search.html

ExPan Online
www.collegeboard.org/fundfinder/bin/fundfind01.pl

CollegeNet
www.collegenet.com

Molis Scholarship Search for Minority Students
www.fie.com/molis/scholar.htm

OSAD Scholarship Search for Study Abroad
www.istc.umn.edu/osad/scholarship-search.html

IUPUI Scholarship Database
www.iupui.edu/~creation/scentral.html

For those of you with AOL access, try RSP Funding by going to **KEYWORD: RSP.**

General Financial Aid Information Websites

FinAid
www.finaid.org

The Financial Aid Resource Network
www.theoldschool.org

Employers

If you have a job, ask your own human resources department if they offer scholarships or tuition reimbursement programs. If you are still in high school, have your parents ask their employers.

Professional or Social Organizations

What professional or social organizations are you or your parents involved with? 4H, JayCees, Lions Club? Association for Internet Addiction? If you or your parents are a member of an organization, ask them and see if they offer any kind of scholarships. If you are NOT a member of any organizations, the next thing to check with is organizations that represent what you are planning on studying. Many such organizations offer scholarships to students who are studying what they support, even if you are not a member. For example, the American Medical Record Association offers several scholarships for those planning on making a career in medical record administration, but there is no requirement that you be a member. Many organizations that do permit non-members to apply for scholarships, however, do expect you to join the organization after receiving the scholarship.

Labor Unions

Are you or your parents a member of a union? All the major labor unions offer scholarships for members and their dependent children (AFL-CIO, Teamsters, etc.)

Church

Check with your church. Your local parish may or may not have any scholarships for their members, but the diocese or headquarters may have some available. And if you have been very active in your local church, they may be able to help you in other ways.

High School

If you are still in high school, it is very important that you speak with your guidance counselor or administration office and ask about scholarships that are available to students at your school.

College

If you are already attending college, or are planning on attending, the financial aid office at your college can be an excellent resource for scholarships and financial aid. You will also find applications for most of the state and federal level aid programs available at your financial aid office.

Scholarships

$1,000 + Job From Microsoft

Women or minorities studying computers can receive $1,000 scholarships and paid summer internships that allow you to help develop products for Bill Gates. Contact Mary Blain, National Women's Technical Scholarship Application or National Technical Scholarship Application, Microsoft Corporation, One Microsoft Way, Redmond, WA 98052; {www.microsoft.com/college/scholarship.htm}.

$5,000 FOR MINORITIES IN SCIENCE AND ENGINEERING

Xerox Technical Minority Scholarship Program provides funding to minorities enrolled in technical science or engineering majors including computer and software engineering, and information management. $4,000 for undergraduates and $5,000 for graduate students. Contact: Xerox Corp.,

Corporate Employment and College Relations, Technical Minority Scholarship Program, 800 Phillips Rd., Webster, NY 14580; {www.xerox.com/employment/scholar.htm}.

Women In Science and Engineering Scholarship

Program Intel offers a Minority Engineering Scholarship Program for undergraduates interested in computer science or engineering and a Women in Science and Engineering Scholarship Program. They also provide internships and mentors to scholarship recipients. Scholarships are only available at selected colleges and universities, and Intel does not accept applications directly from students. Students must be nominated by their school for a scholarship. For more information, contact {www.intel.com/intel/community/scholars.htm}.

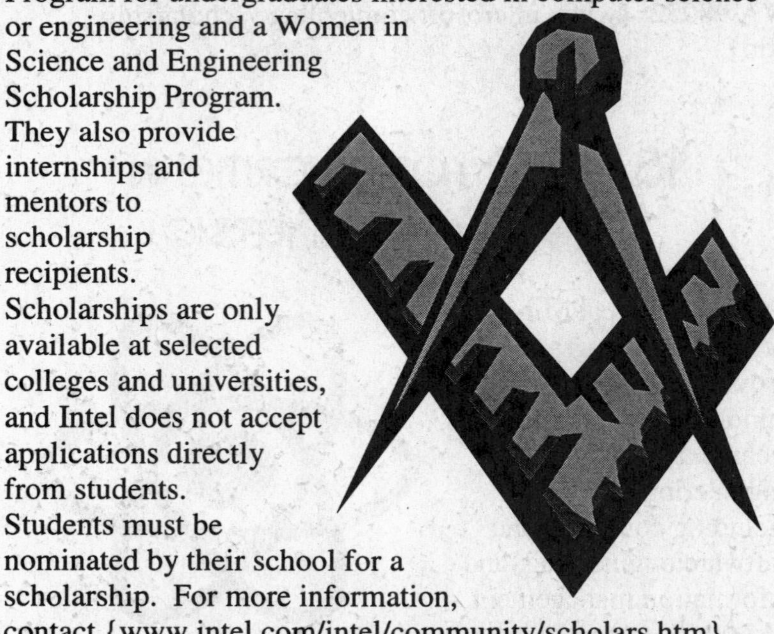

Scholarships For Mature Women

The Women's Opportunity Award's intent is to assist mature women who need additional skills, training and education to upgrade their employment status in order to enter or return to the job market. Applicant should be the head of her household with financial responsibility for her dependents, indicate that specific training is necessary to enter or re-enter the job market, demonstrate financial need and be entering vocational or technical training, or be completing an undergraduate degree. Contact Women's Opportunity Award Soroptimist International of the Americas, Two Penn Center Plaza, Suite 1000, Philadelphia, PA 19102.

Scholarships for Smart Business Majors

Fifty Exceptional Student Fellowships, consisting of $3000 each to be used for educational expenses during the academic year following the competition, are given each year. Applicants must be full time junior or senior college students majoring in a business-related field, demonstrate significant leadership in extra-curricular activities, have a minimum 3.6 GPA, be nominated by a dean, department head, professor or academic advisor, currently attend an accredited college or university in the U.S. and be of U.S.

citizenship. Contact the Foundation for current application deadlines. Contact State Farm Companies Foundation, One State Farm Plaza, SC-3, Bloomington, IL 61710; 309-766-2039/2161; Nancy.Lynn.gr3o@statefarm.com; {www.statefarm.com}.

Scholarships for Composers

Young composers and musicians may apply for a variety of different awards, some which include the John Lennon Scholarship which is awarded for excellence in vocal/instrumental composition and has been established by Yoko Ono Lennon; the Annual Student Composer Awards ($500-$2,500) for which young composers of concert music may compete; and the Jerry Harrington Jazz Composition Award to encourage composition of new large-ensemble jazz works. Contact BMI Foundation, 320 West 57th Street, New York, NY 10019; 212-586-2000.

Scholarships Available For Family Of Fleet Reserve

This association offers four different scholarships. In order to be eligible, the applicant must either be a daughter/granddaughter of Naval, Marine Corps, and Coast Guard personnel, active Fleet Reserve, Fleet Marine Corps Reserve, and Coast Guard Reserve, retired with pay or deceased. Children/grandchildren of deceased FRA members or persons who had eligibility for FRA membership at the time of death, plus children/grandchildren of members of LA FRA are also eligible for these scholarships. Awarding of scholarships is based on financial need, scholarship proficiency and character.

Contact Fleet Reserve Association, Ladies Auxiliary, LA FRA Scholarship Administrator, c/o Fleet Reserve Association, 125 N. West Street, Alexandria, VA 22314-2754; 703-683-1400; 800-FRA-1924.

$1000 Scholarships For Smart Women Pursuing Science Majors

The Dr. Vicki L. Schechtman Scholarship awards $1000 to an undergraduate woman pursuing scientific studies. Preference is given to applicants pursuing research. Applicant must have a minimum GPA of 3.0 and be a U.S. citizen.

Graduate opportunities include four awards: Amy Lutz Rechel Award for plant biology students; Luise Meyer-Schutzmeister Award for women students in physics; Ruth Satter Memorial Award for women who have had to interrupt their education for 3 or more years in order to raise a family; The Diane H. Russel Award for graduate students in the biochemistry of pharmacology fields. Additionally, there are approximately 10 Citations of Merit given each year ranging from $250-$500.

Contact Association For Women In Science (AWIS), AWIS National Headquarters, 1200 New York Ave., NW, Suite 650, Washington, DC 20005; 202-326-8940; 800-886-AWIS; {e-mail: awis@awis.org}.

$1500 Scholarships For Children Of Air Force Members

This successful program has been awarding grants since 1988. The AFAS provides $1500 grants for undergraduate study to selected daughters and sons of active duty, retired or deceased Air Force members, stateside spouses of active duty members and surviving spouses of deceased personnel. The Society considers family income and education cost factors for its awards. Contact the AFAS for the current deadline.

Contact Air Force Aid Society (AFAS), Education Assistance Department, 1745 Jefferson Davis Hwy., Suite 202, Arlington, VA 22202-3410; 202-692-9313.

$2000 For Library Science Graduate Students

This association offers a variety of scholarships and grants, most in the amount of $2000. Each year the MLA awards money to qualified students in graduate library science programs. Money is also available to practicing health science librarians in order to enable them to continue to develop professionally. Contact Medical Library Association (MLA), 6 North Michigan Ave., Suite 300, Chicago, IL 60602-4805; 312-419-9094.

Garden Club Awards Up To $4000/Year

In order to stimulate knowledge of gardening and to restore, protect and improve the environment, this club offers a variety of scholarships and fellowships. Undergraduate and graduate students are eligible for awards up to $4000/year. Each scholarship varies in its focus and student eligibility. Contact the GCA for details and deadlines. Over $24,000 is available each year. Contact The Garden Club Of America (GCA), 14 East 60th Street, New York, NY 10022; 212-753-8287; {www.gcamerica.org}.

Money For Physical Therapy Doctoral Students

Physical therapist doctoral students pursuing scientific and clinical research are eligible for scholarships from this organization. Awards are based on the distinct phases of education and funding may vary from year to year depending on available resources. Contact the Foundation for details and deadlines. Contact Foundation For Physical Therapy, 1111 North Fairfax Street, Alexandria, VA 22314-1488; 706-684-5984; 800-875-1378; {e-mail: foundation@apta.org}.

Up To $1500 For Federal Employees And Dependents

Civilian federal and postal employees, with a minimum of three years of federal service, and their dependent family members are eligible for scholarships from FEEA. Applicants may be high school seniors or students who are continuing their college education and have a minimum GPA of 3.0. Awards range from $500-$1500 and are based on merit. Academic achievement, community service, a recommendation and a two-page essay are included in criteria for selection of recipients. A total of $250,000 is given out annually in scholarships. Contact Federal Employee Education And Assistance Fund, 8441 W. Bowles Ave., Suite 200, Littleton, CO 80123-3245; 303-933-7580; 800-323-4140; {www.fpmi.com/FEEA/FEEAhome.html}.

Up To $4000 For A Health And Nutrition Major

Odwalla's Femme Vitale Scholarship awards are granted annually to women in pursuance of a degree in health and

nutrition. Full time women students in a qualified field of study are eligible to apply for the scholarship. Up to $4000 may be awarded and may be used at any institution of higher learning that offers accredited undergraduate or graduate courses. The applicant must be a resident of or studying in one of the states where Odwalla juice products are sold. Products are sold in California, Washington, Utah, New Mexico, Arizona, Oregon, Texas, Colorado, Nevada, Illinois, Wisconsin, Michigan, Minnesota, Louisiana, New Jersey, Virginia, Maryland, Pennsylvania and Washington,

DC. Contact ODWALLA, 120 Stone Pine Road, Half Moon Bay, CA 94019; 650-726-1888; {www.Odwalla.com}.

$1500 For Women Over 35 Years Of Age Pursuing Below Graduate Level Education

The Foundation offers twenty-five awards at $1500 each to U.S. female citizens over the age of thirty-five years of age who are enrolled or accepted in either a certified program of technical/vocational training or an undergraduate program. This is not for graduate work or to pursue a second degree. Send a self-addressed stamped business envelope with your sex, age, level and/or year of study written on the envelope. Contact Jeanette Rankin Foundation, PO Box 6653, Athens, GA 30604; 404-543-8733; {www.wmst.unt.edu/jrf/}.

Up To $5000 For Health Information Management

AHIMA offers a variety of scholarships ranging from $1000-$5000 to members. Field of study must be in health information management or health information technology. Applicant must be a full time student in a program accredited by the Commission on Accreditation of Allied Health Education Programs (CAAHEP). Scholarships are available for undergraduate and graduate study. Contact American Health Information Management Association (AHIMA), 919 N. Michigan Ave., Suite 1400, Chicago, IL 60611-1683; 312-787-2672, ext. 302.

Money For Female Artists And Writers

This organization gives small grants that are designed to support feminists who are active in art, fiction, non-fiction and poetry. For more information, contact the organization. Grants range from $250-$1000. Contact Money For Women, P.O. Box 630125, Bronx, NY 10463.

Up To $10,000 For RN's To Pursue Graduate Nursing Education

Scholarships ranging from $2500-$10,000, with the amount

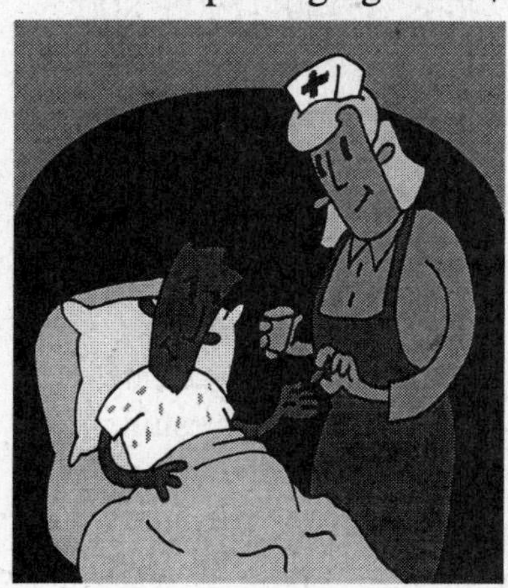

varying each year depending on contributions to the organization, are available to U.S. registered nurses. The RN must be a member of a national, professional nursing association, enrolled in or applying to a National League for Nursing accredited masters program in nursing, or at the doctoral level. The applicant must also be either a full time master's student or full or part time doctoral level student. The first criteria considered is academic excellence. Contact Nurses Educational Fund, Inc., 555 West 57th Street, New York, NY 10019; 212-399-1428.

$1000 For Students Interested In Medical Assisting

The AAMA offers the Maxine Williams Scholarship of $1000 for one school year. High school graduates who are enrolled in or soon to be enrolled in a post-secondary medical assisting program which is accredited by the Commission on Accreditation of Allied Health Education Programs are eligible. Scholarships are awarded based on interest, need, and aptitude. Contact American Association Of Medical Assistants (AAMA), 20 North Wacker Drive, Suite 1575, Chicago, IL 60606-2903; 312-899-1500; 800-228-2262.

Scholarships For Medical And Dental Assistant Studies

High school graduates interested in pursuing studies in medical technology, medical laboratory technician, medical assisting, dental assisting, phlebotomy or office laboratory technician may apply for a scholarship with this organization. Applicants must plan on studying at an accredited college or university in the United States. There is an April 1 deadline for submitting applications. Call for an application. Contact American Medical Technologists, 710 Higgins Road, Park Ridge, IL 60068-5765; 847-823-5169.

$1000 For A Woman In Surveying And Mapping

The Porter McDonnell Memorial Award of $1000 is given annually to a woman displaying potential leadership in surveying and mapping. This award is intended to assist with educational expenses of the Bachelor's degree. The Caddy McDonnell Memorial Scholarship Award of $1000 recognizes a woman enrolled in the surveying field who is a legal resident of one of the following western states: Montana, Idaho, Washington, Oregon, Wyoming, Colorado, Utah, Nevada, California, Arizona, New Mexico, Alaska, and Hawaii. This organization also offers a variety of other awards ranging from $500-$2000 and according to level of education.

Contact American Congress On Surveying And Mapping, 5410 Grosvenor Lane, Suite 100, Bethesda, MD 20814; 301-493-0200; {e-mail: lillym@mindspring.com}.

$500 Available For Masters And Doctoral Level Health Education

The AAHE has scholarships available in the amount of $500. There are separate awards for doctoral and masters level students who are currently enrolled in a health education programs. Applicants must have a minimum 3.0 GPA on a 4.0 scale and prior AAHE scholarship recipients may not apply. Contact American Association For Health

Education (AAHE), 1900 Association Drive, Reston, VA 20191-1599; 703-476-3437.

Money For Women Builders

This foundation awarded over $75,000 to worthy recipients in 1998! Applicants must be in a construction related degree program for a bachelor's or associate degree. You must have at least a 3.0 grade point average and be enrolled full-time in school. Application forms are available through www.fastweb.com or you can send a self-addressed stamped envelope to the address listed below.

Contact National Association Of Women In Construction (NAWIC), 327 South Adams, Fort Worth, TX 76104; 817-877-3943; {www.nawic.org}.

Creative Mothers Can Win Money!

This organization's goal is to assist mothers in educating their children. The American Mothers Cultural and Creative Arts Awards program grants monetary prizes to mothers in three different categories: arts and crafts, literature and vocal music. The intent of the program is to encourage mothers to develop talents that will uplift, teach and share with children. Financial awards are given to the winners in the contests.

Contact American Mothers Inc., The Waldorf Astoria, 301 Park Avenue, New York, NY 10022; 212-755-2539; {www.americanmothers.org}.

$1500-$5000 Available For Civil Engineers

The ASCE has many different scholarships available. Undergraduate freshmen, sophomores, or juniors who are National ASCE Student members are eligible for the Samuel Fletcher Tapman Scholarship, 12 awards of $1500 given annually, or are also eligible for the Charles Tiney Memorial Student Scholarship where $2000 is awarded annually.

The Arthur S. Tuttle Scholarship is for undergraduates in their senior year. $3000-$5000 is awarded to the recipient for the first year of formal graduate civil engineering education tuition. Membership applications may be submitted with scholarship application.

Contact American Society Of Civil Engineers (ASCE), Member Scholarships and Awards, 1801 Alexander Bell Drive, Reston, VA 20191-4400; 800-548-2723; {www.asce.org/peta/ed/cssf_hm.html}.

$500 For Full Time Food Majors

The Worthy Goal Scholarship Fund awards $500 scholarships for those interested in food service. Applicant must be a full time student who is either enrolled in or accepted in a food service related major or vocational training program for the fall following the award. In addition, local scholarships are available through IFSEA Senior branches.

Information regarding Senior branches may be obtained by calling IFSEA headquarters. A total of $100,000 in scholarships is available. Contact International Food Service Executives Association, OFSEA Headquarters, 1100 S. State Road 7, Suite #103, Margate, FL 33368-4033; 954-977-0767.

Creative Women Over 35 Are Eligible For $1000 Award

Women artists, photographers, writers and composers who are 35 years or older are eligible for scholarships of $1000. The intent of the scholarship is to support professional development. A portfolio of work is required with entry.

Contact The National League Of American Pen Women, Scholarship Chairman-Mrs. Mary Jane Hillery, 66 Willow Road, Sudbury, MA 01776-2663.

Bright Broadcasters Eligible For $1250-$5000 In Scholarships

College juniors, seniors and graduate students attending a BEA Member university and preparing for a career in broadcasting are eligible for a variety of awards offered by BEA. Fifteen scholarship awards, which range from $1250-$5000, are awarded to full time students to be used exclusively for tuition, student fees, books, and university dorm room and board. Applicants must possess evidence of high integrity and have a strong academic record.

Contact Broadcast Education Association, 1771 N St., NW, Washington, DC 20036-2891; 202-429-5354; {www.beaweb.org} or {e-mail: fweaver@nab.org}.

$1000 For Women In Advanced Agriculture Or Horticulture Study

The Association offers the Sarah Bradley Tyson Memorial Fellowship to properly qualified women for advanced study in agriculture, horticulture, and allied subjects. The $1000 award is to be used for advanced study at an educational institution of recognized standing within the U.S.A. A letter of application should be sent to the chairman, Mrs. Elmer Braun. Contact Women's National Farm And Garden Association, Inc., Mrs. Elmer Braun, 13 Davis Drive, Saginaw, MI 48603; 517-793-1714.

Up To $1500 For Veterinarian Students

The AAEP has two scholarships available. Fourth-year veterinary students are eligible for The AAEP/American Livestock Insurance Company Scholarship, which awards six $1500 scholarships each year. AAEP student members attending colleges of veterinary medicine either in the US or Canada are eligible. The second scholarship, The AAEP/United States Pony Club Scholarship, awards one $1000 to a current or graduate Pony Club member who is entering veterinary school. Contact American Association Of Equine Practitioners, 4075 Iron Works Pike, Lexington, KY 40511; 606-233-0147.

$2500 AVAILABLE FOR TECHNICAL COMMUNICATION STUDENTS

STC awards fourteen $2500 scholarships each year toward school tuition and expenses. Applicants must be full time students, either graduate students pursuing a master's or doctor's degree or undergraduate students pursuing a bachelor's degree. They should be studying communication or information about technical subjects such as technical writing, editing, graphical design, interface design, and web design. Awards are made to the school for the benefit of the selected student.

Contact Society For Technical Communication (STC), 901 N. Stuart Street, Suite 904, Arlington, VA 22203-1854; 703-522-4114; {www.stc-va.org}.

Money Available For Business Majors

The Kemper Foundation offers its scholarships to students enrolled in one of seventeen different colleges and universities. Contact the Foundation for a list of participating schools, as you apply for the scholarships through the schools. Eligibility consists of students interested in pursuing a career in business and is based on financial need.

The Foundation also awards a limited number of merit scholarships, $1500 per academic year, to scholars who show no financial need. The current maximum annual scholarship awarded is $7000. Those who obtain scholarships agree to work for pay during their summers for Kemper Insurance Companies in a variety of capacities and offices. Sixty to seventy scholarships are awarded each year. Contact Kemper Foundation, 1 Kemper Drive, Long Grove, IL 60049-0001.

Scholarships Starting At $2000 For Physician Assistants Students

The Foundation has awarded over 290 scholarships in the past nine years, totaling over $720,000. Student members of the AAPA who are currently enrolled in an accredited PA program are eligible to apply. Awards, which start at $2000, are intended to help students complete their education. Contact American Academy Of Physician Assistants, 950 N. Washington St., Alexandria, VA 22314-1552; 703-836-2272; {e-mail:aapa@aapa.org}.

Creative Kids Can Win Up To $20,000 In U.S. Savings Bonds

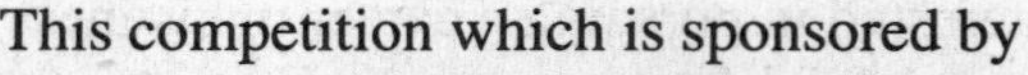

This competition which is sponsored by Duracell North Atlantic Group and administered by the National Science Teachers Association is offered to 6th through 12th grade students. The entrants are divided into two groups; grades 6-9 and grades 10-12 with many awards granted. Each group has one first place winner receiving a $20,000 U.S. Savings bond, two second place prizes of $10,000 savings bond, five third place prizes of $3000 savings bond, 12 fourth place prizes of

$1000 savings bond and 30 fifth place prizes of $500 savings bond. Students entering must create and build a working device that is powered by Duracell batteries. Contact DURACELL/NSTA Scholarship Competition, 1840 Wilson Boulevard, 3rd Floor, Arlington, VA 22201-3000; 888-255-4242; {e-mail: duracell@nsta.org}.

$500-$2500 Available For Architectural Students

A variety of scholarships, ranging from $500-$2500, are available to architectural students who are pursuing a professional degree in architecture. The scholarship applied for depends upon the student's level of education, starting from those just entering and proceeding to postgraduates and professionals.

The AIA/AAF Minority/Disadvantaged Scholarship program offers college freshmen and others twenty-five scholarships of $500-$2,500 based on financial need for bachelor or master of architecture majors. The AIA/AAF Scholarship Program for First Professional Degree Candidates awards $500-$2,500 for the final two years of a professional architecture degree program. The RTKL Traveling Fellowship offers one $2,500 award to a student who is almost finished with their program to encourage foreign travel to further their education.

Contact The American Institute Of Architects and The American Architectural Foundation, 1735 New York Ave., NW, Washington, DC 20006-5292; 202-626-7511.

Many Opportunities For Orthopedic Nurses

NAON offers a variety of grant and scholarship opportunities to NAON members, ranging from $1000-$5000 in value. Scholarships support attendance at NAON

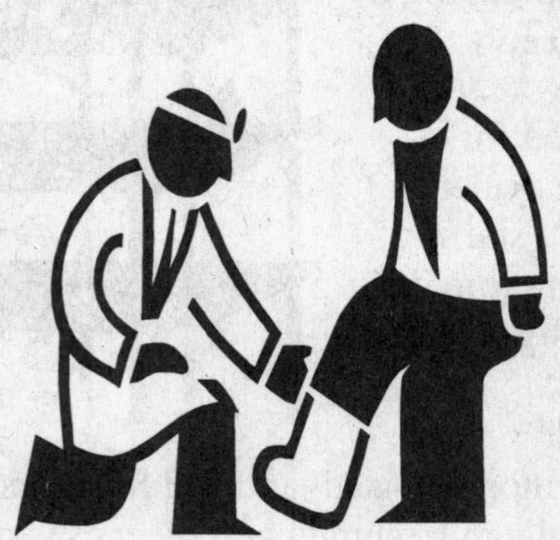

programs and continuing college education in the field of orthopedic nursing. Contact National Association Of Orthopedic Nurses (NAON), NAON Foundation, East Holly Avenue, Box 56, Pitman, NJ 08071-0056; 609-256-2310.

Beta Sigma Phi Members And Family Members Eligible For Scholarships

Scholarships are available to Beta Sigma Phi members, or the child or grandchild of a member in good standing. If you meet that eligibility, please contact to request one of the scholarship applications. Contact BETA SIGMA PHI, 1800 West 91st Place, Kansas City, MO 64114; 816-444-6800; {e-mail: bspintl@aol.com}.

$1500 Available For Students Pursuing Critical Care

The American Association of Critical Care Nurses offers scholarships of $1500 to promote nursing professionalism and to advance the science of critical care nursing. Students completing a generic baccalaureate-nursing program, as well as AACN members who are registered nurses completing a baccalaureate or graduate degree program in nursing, are eligible. The funds may be used for tuition, books, supplies and or fees while the student is enrolled in a baccalaureate program accredited by the National League for Nursing or a graduate program.

Contact American Association Of Critical Care Nurses, Educational Advancement Scholarship, AACN, 101 Columbia, Aliso Viejo, CA 92656-1491; 800-899-2226; {www.aacn.org}.

$500-$1500 Scholarships Available To Court Reporting Students

The NCRA has three scholarships available to students attending an NCRA approved court reporter education program. Lists of schools are available from NCRA on request. Applicants must be nominated by their program and are required to submit an essay on a predetermined subject. The awards range from $500-$1500.

The NCRA also awards six $500 tuition grants to student members of the Association who are chosen by a drawing. Contact National Court Reporters Association (NCRA), 8224 Old Courthouse Road, Vienna, VA 22182-3808; 703-556-6272; 800-272-6272.

Up To $5000 In Grants Available For English Teachers

Grants up to $5000 are awarded by the Research Foundation for pre-K-12 classroom teachers. Grants are intended for teachers to explore questions related to teaching English/Language Arts. Research questions should be related to work, and have arisen due to questions, concerns or ideas in the classroom. Members of NCTE may apply.

Contact National Council Of Teachers Of English (NCTE), 1111 W. Kenyon Road, Urbana, IL 61801-1096; 217-328-3870.

Opportunity For An RN To Win $3000 Toward Occupational Health Education

The AAOHN offers a $3000 award. Applicant must be a registered nurse who is either a full-time or part-time student in a nationally accredited school of nursing baccalaureate program and demonstrate an interest in occupational and environmental health. The Association also offers a variety of research grants for environmental and health registered nurses. Contact the Association for details.

Contact American Association Of Occupational Health Nurses (AAOHN), AAOHN Foundation, Suite 100, 2920 Brandywine Road, Atlanta, GA 30341-4146; 770-455-7757; {www.aaohn.org}.

Opportunity To Receive College Tuition From NSA

NSA will consider any student who meets the requirements below and who chooses a full-time college major in either computer science, electrical or computer engineering, languages or mathematics. Requirements consist of having a minimum SAT score of 1100 and a minimum composite ACT score of 25. Chosen students can receive college tuition, reimbursement for books, year-round salary, summer work and have a guaranteed job with the NSA after graduation. Students must work for NSA for one and a half times their length of study, which is usually about five years. Contact National Security Agency, Manager, Undergraduate Training Program, Attn: S232R (UTP), 9800 Savage Rd., Suite 6840, Ft. Meade, MD 20755-6840; 800-669-0703; {www.nsa.gov}.

Opportunity For $600-$12,000 For Manufacturing Engineering Students

The SME Education Foundation offers scholarships based on degree of education. High school students in their senior year are eligible to apply for scholarships ranging from $600-$2500 if they are planning to enroll full-time in a manufacturing engineering or manufacturing engineering technology program. Full-time college students with 30 completed hours and a minimum GPA of 3.5 who are pursuing a career in manufacturing engineering, manufacturing engineering technology, automated systems or robotics may apply for scholarships ranging from $900-$3500. Graduate fellowships are available to eligible applicants accepted in a manufacturing engineering or industrial engineering graduate program with a minimum GPA of 3.5. New this year is a program offered by SME for grandchildren and children of SME members providing up to $20,000 annually for graduating high school seniors. Contact Society Of Manufacturing Engineers (SME), Education Foundation, One SME Drive, PO Box 930, Dearborn, MI 48121-0930; 313-271-1500; {www.sme.org/foundation}.

Money Available For Therapists

AMBUCS offers scholarships ranging from $500-$1500 annually to students in their junior/senior year in a bachelor's degree program, or a graduate program leading to a master's or doctoral degree. There is also one two-year award in the amount of $6000 offered. Applicants must be accepted in an accredited program in physical therapy, occupational therapy, speech language pathology, and hearing audiology. Applications available through www.fastweb.com. Contact AMBUCS Scholarship Committee, P.O. Box 5127, High Point, NC 27262; 336-869-2166; {www.ambucs.com}.

$200-$5000 Available For Smart Women Engineers

The SWE administers over 90 scholarships per year ranging from $200-$5000. Women majoring in engineering or computer science in a college or university with an ABET-accredited program or in a SWE approved school are eligible. There are a variety of scholarships available. Applicants for sophomore, junior, senior and graduate scholarships must have a minimum GPA of 3.5.

SWE also offers re-entry scholarships to assist women, who have been out of the engineering job market as well as out of school for a minimum of two years, in obtaining the credentials necessary to re-enter the job market as engineers.

Contact Society Of Women Engineers (SWE), 120 Wall Street, 11th Floor, New York, NY 10005-3902; 212-509-9577; {www.swe.org}; {e-mail: hq@swe.org}.

Funeral Service Scholarships Opportunities Available

The NFDA provides a list of State Funeral Directors Associations, National Funeral Service Organizations and Mortuary Colleges that offer scholarships to funeral service students. The list provided has over 60 associations, organizations and colleges listed and provides amounts of scholarships available. Contact National Funeral Directors Association (NFDA), 13625 Bishop's Drive, Brookfield, WI 53005-6607; 414-789-1880; {www.nfda.org}; {e-mail: nfda@nfda.org}.

Opportunity For Pharmacy Students To Get $250-$5000 Scholarships

The ASHP has compiled a listing of a variety of scholarships ranging from $250-$7500. Applicants must either be entry-level B.S. or Pharm.D. program student, in the last three years of a B.S. of Pharm.D. program and planning to pursue the Ph.D. in a college of pharmacy graduate program, or in the final year of a pharmacy college B.S. or Pharm.D. program or have completed a pharmacy degree, depending on the scholarship.

Each scholarship offered may have additional requirements. Contact ASHP for a listing. College loans and residencies information is also available. Contact American Society Of Health-System Pharmacists (AHSP), 7272 Wisconsin Ave., Bethesda, MD 20814; 301-657-3000; {www.ashp.org}.

$2500 Scholarship Opportunity For School Librarian Media

The AASL /School Librarian's Workshop Scholarship offers $2500 for the professional education of persons who are pursuing school library media specialist standing at the preschool through high school levels in public or private educational settings. Applicants are required to have received bachelor's degree with proven academic excellence and to have the intention to pursue full-time graduate level education in an ALA accredited library school program. Contact the Association for details.

Contact Graduate Education, American Library Association, AASL/Scholarship Recommendation, 50 E. Huron St., Chicago, IL 60611-2795; 312-280-4386.

$4000 Scholarship For Communication Science Graduate Student

The Foundation offers full-time graduate students in communication sciences and disorders programs who demonstrate outstanding academic achievement the opportunity to compete for $4,000 scholarships. Graduate students with disabilities and minority students, who are enrolled in a communication sciences or disorders program, can compete for a $2,000 scholarship. Contact the Foundation for application availability and due dates.

Contact American Speech-Language-Hearing Foundation, 10801 Rockville Pike, Rockville, MD 20852; 301-897-5700.

Women Music Majors Eligible For $300 Scholarship

WBDI offers five annual scholarships to women who are currently enrolled in a music education program and are pursuing a career as a band director. Each award is a non-renewable $300 scholarship. Contact Women Band Directors International (WBDI), Linda Moorhouse, Department of Bands, School of Music, Louisiana State University, Baton Rouge, LA 70803.

National Security Related Careers Eligible For Scholarship

The Horizon Foundation offers scholarships valued at no less than $500 to encourage women to pursue careers related to the national security interests of the U.S. Applicants must be currently enrolled at an accredited university/college either full or part-time. Undergraduate (at least junior level status) and graduate students are eligible. Applicants must also have a minimum GPA of 3.25 and be a U.S. citizen. Women in engineering, computer science, physics, mathematics, business, law, international relations, political science, operations research, and economics fields have preference.

Contact Horizons Foundation Scholarship Program, WID Horizons Foundation, c/o National Defense Industrial Association (NDIA), 2111 Wilson Boulevard, Suite 400, Arlington, VA 22201-3061; 703-247-2552; {www.ndia.org/wid/}; {e-mail: william_j_lee@raytheon.com}.

$1000 Scholarship Opportunity For Women In Business Or Economic Education

The Foundation generally grants three $1000 scholarships per year. Women students who are pursuing a career in the business and/or economics field of study are eligible to apply. Applicants must be a full-time student at an approved college/university in the U.S. in pursuit of a business and/or economics degree and must have completed at least one semester or two quarters of college level study. Selection is based on scholastic achievement, leadership potential, motivation and financial need. Contact Phi Chi Theta Foundation Scholarship Committee, 8656 Totempole Dr., Cincinnati, OH 45249.

Daughters Of A Career Officer Eligible For Scholarships

This program is for seniors in high school who are the daughters of a career officer commissioned in the regular Army, Navy, Air Force, Coast Guard, or Marine Corps (active, retired or deceased). Selection is based on merit and need. Awards are for up to four years and are granted at the college of the candidate's choice.

Contact Daughters Of The Cincinnati, Scholarship Program, 122 East 58th Street, New York, NY 10022; 212-319-6915.

$5000 Grant Opportunity For Midwifery Students

The MCA Foundation offers the Hazel Corbin Grant to provide financial assistance to an individual who demonstrates academic excellence, financial need and a commitment to a family-centered maternity care and who is enrolled in an ACNM accredited midwifery program. The grant is in the amount of $5000.

Contact Maternity Center Association (MCA), 281 Park Avenue South, 5th Floor, New York, NY 10010; 212-777-5000; {www.maternity.org}; {e-mail: macbirth@ AOL.com}.

Money To Study The Earth And Sky

The AMS offers an array of graduate fellowships and undergraduate scholarships to help further the education of outstanding graduate and undergraduate students. Students must plan to pursue careers in the atmospheric or related oceanic and hydrologic sciences. The amount of the award depends on education level, with a range from $300-$15,000. Contact American Meteorological Society (AMS), 45 Beacon Street, Boston, MA 02108; 617-227-2426 #235; {www.ametosoc.org/AMS}; {e-mail: armstrong@ametsoc.org}.

Scholarship Of $2500 Available To High School Seniors With Inter-Scholastic Sports

This program offered by ESPN is not an athletic scholarship program. ESPN presents awards to eight graduating seniors, one male and one female in each of the four regions of the U.S.A., each year. The one time $2,500 grants are made to defray the cost of tuition, room and board at an accredited college/university. Selection criteria includes academic achievement, service to school and community, and leadership in interscholastic sports. Applicants must be legal U.S. citizens. Employees of ESPN, Inc., Walt Disney Co., the Hearst Corp. or their respective subsidiaries are not eligible. Contact Sports Leadership, ESPN Sportsfigures Scholarship, P.O. Box 630, Hartford, CT 06142-0630.

Scholarships From Zeta Phi Beta Sorority, Inc.

The Foundation offers nine different scholarships, two of which only Zeta Phi Beta Sorority members are eligible for. The general graduate scholarship is available to graduate women working on a professional degree, masters, doctoral or enrolled in post-doctoral study and is not to exceed $2500 per year. The general undergraduate scholarship is available to high school seniors and undergraduate students and ranges from $500-$1000.

The Deborah Partridge Wolfe International Fellowship is available to graduate and undergraduate U.S. students studying abroad and/or foreign students studying in the U.S. Amount varies from $500-$1000. The S. Evelyn Lewis Memorial Scholarship in Medical Health Sciences is available to graduate or undergraduate women enrolled in a program leading to a medicine or health science degree. Amount $500-$1000. The Lullelia W. Harrison Scholarship in Counseling is available to graduate or undergraduate students enrolled in a counseling degree program and awards $500-$1000. The Isabel M. Herson Scholarship in Education is available to graduate or undergraduate level students enrolled in either an elementary or secondary education degree program. Amount of $500-$1000.

The Zora Neal Hurston Scholarship is available to graduate students pursuing a degree in anthropology or related fields. Amount $500-$1000. The Nancy B. Woolridge McGee Graduate Fellowship and the Mildred Cater Bradham Social Work Fellowship are available to Zeta Phi Beta Sorority members only and each offers $500-$1000. Contact Zeta Phi Beta Sorority, Inc., National Education Foundation, 1734 New Hampshire Avenue, NW, Washington, DC 20009.

Scholarships For Licensed Radio Amateurs, Females Preferred

The FAR will be administering 67 scholarships, ranging from $500-$2500, for the coming academic year. FAR offers 28 different scholarships, which may have different requirements. Unless otherwise specified, all licensed amateurs meeting the specific requirements may compete for the awards if they are now enrolled or have been accepted for enrollment in an accredited university, college or technical school to pursue a full-time course of studies. Contact Foundation For Amateur Radio (FAR), P.O. Box 831, Riverdale, MD 20738.

$500-$1000 Offered To AMVETS Auxiliary And Family

AMVETS Auxiliary provides aid to members and sons/daughters or grandchildren of members in order to recognize and reward need, academic achievement, and potential. Applicants of the Career Start Scholarship must be AMVETS Auxiliary members who have completed at least one semester at an accredited technical school, business school, college, or university. The AMVETS Auxiliary Scholarship applicants may either be members or a son/daughter, or grandchild of a member and be in at least his/her second year of undergraduate study at an accredited college or university. Scholarships range from $500-$1000. Contact AMVETS Auxiliary National Headquarters, 4647 Forbes Boulevard, Lanham, MD 20706; 301-459-6255.

$300 Available For Geographic Education

The National Council for Geographic Education Committee for Women in Geographic Education offers a $300 scholarship to an undergraduate or graduate woman enrolled in a program leading to a career in geographic education. Applicants must have an overall GPA of 3.0 and a geography GPA of 3.5 and submit a 200 word essay. Contact NCGE for details. Contact Women In Geographic Education Scholarships, NCGE Central Office, Indiana

University of Pennsylvania, Leonard Hall, Room 16A, 421 North Walk, Indiana, PA 15705; 724-357-6290.

$2,000 For High School Female Golfers

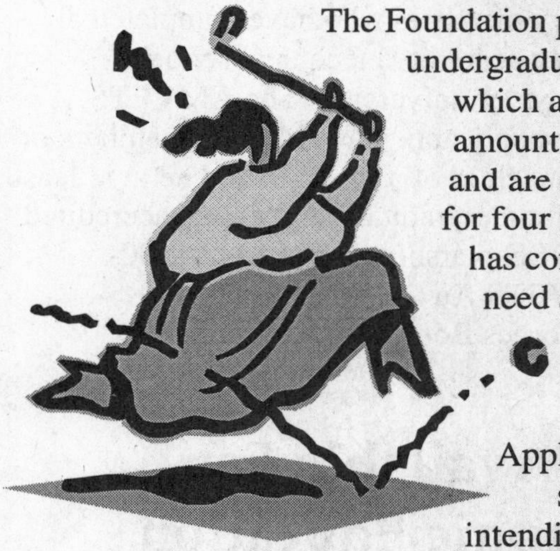

The Foundation provides undergraduate scholarships which awards grants in the amount of $2000 per year and are renewable each year for four years if the student has continued financial need and maintains a minimum GPA of 3.0.

Applicant must be a high school senior girl intending to graduate in the year of application, a U.S. citizen and meet the requirements of and plan to enroll at an accredited college/university. Selection is based on academic achievement, financial need, excellence of character and an involvement in the sport of golf, although skill or excellence in the sport of golf is not required. Contact Women's Western Golf Foundation, Director of Scholarship, Mrs. Richard W. Willis, 393 Ramsay Road, Deerfield, IL 60015.

$3000-$5000 For Family And Consumer Science Students

The AAFCS awards national and international fellowships annually to support graduate study in the family and consumer sciences field. The array of scholarships offered supports different aspects of the family and consumer sciences (formerly known as home economics) field and range from $300-$5000. Recipients of AAFCS fellowships, grants and awards must be current members of the Association. Membership must be applied for prior to applying for an award. Contact American Association Of Family And Consumer Sciences, 1555 King Street, Alexandria, VA 22314-2752; 703-706-4600; {www.aafcs.org}; {e-mail: staff@aafcs.org}.

Daughters Of The US Army Offers Scholarships

DUSA provides one-year, renewable awards of no more than $1000 for financial assistance for undergraduate education to daughters and granddaughters of active, retired or deceased Army officers. Applicants must be a daughter, stepdaughter, adopted daughter, or granddaughter of a career warrant officer or commissioned officer of the United States Army. Selection criteria includes personal record, financial need and a minimum GPA of 3.0 in academic work to date. Contact Society Of Daughters Of The United States Army, c/o Janet B. Otto, Chairman,

DUSA Memorial & Scholarship Funds, 7717 Rockledge Court, Springfield, VA 22151-3854.

Scholarships To Students Who Have Hearing Impairment Or Loss

The organization sponsors scholarships as prizes for contests. Enter contests through local Optimist Clubs. The International essay contest is for grades 10-12 (11-13 in Jamaica only) who attend school in the U.S., Canada or Jamaica. Topics change each year and prizes awarded range from medallions to a $5000 college scholarship. An all-expense paid Freedoms Foundation in Valley Forge, Pennsylvania trip is awarded to all district level winners. The Communication Contest for the Deaf and Hard of Hearing is for people up to the 12th grade in the U.S., Canada or Jamaica identified as having hearing loss/ impairment. Sign language, oral presentation or a combination of both may be used. Prizes range from medallions to a $1500 college scholarship. The Oratorical Contest is for U.S., Canadian or Jamaican students under the age of 16. Applicants are required to give a 4-5 minute speech. Topics vary every year. Each boy and girl winner progress to the next level. Prizes range from medallions to a $1500 college scholarship for each boy and girl district winner.

Contact Optimist International, 4494 Lindell Blvd., St. Louis, MO 63108; 314-371-6000.

SCHOLARSHIPS FOR YOUNG BLACK WOMEN

The Association provides financial assistance to young Black women interested in pursuing post-secondary education. Applicants must be graduating high school seniors or enrolled in an accredited college or university and have a minimum GPA of 2.5. All recipients must be full-time students and be either citizens of the U.S. or enrolled in an accredited college in the U.S.

Contact National Association Of Negro Business & Professional Women's Clubs, Inc., 1806 New Hampshire Avenue, Washington, DC 20009-3298; 202-483-4206.

$2000 Scholarships For Spouses And Children Of Blind Veterans

The Blinded Veterans Association offers its Kathern F. Gruber Scholarship Program to dependent children and spouses of blinded veterans of the U.S. Armed Forces. The veteran must be legally blind, but the blindness need not be service-connected. There are eight $2000 scholarships and eight $1000 scholarships available. Applicants must either be already enrolled in or accepted for admission, as a full-time student in an accredited institution of higher education, or business, secretarial or vocational school. Contact Blinded Veterans Association, 477 H Street, Northwest, Washington, DC 20001-2694; 202-371-8880.

Junior Miss Competition Rewards Winners With College Scholarships

This nationwide scholarship program's purpose is to recognize, reward and encourage excellence while promoting self-esteem in young women. Winners of local competition advance to state competition and all 50 state winners will travel to Mobile, AL to compete for the title of America's Junior Miss. The recipient of the America's Junior Miss title will receive a $30,000 college scholarship. State, local and national scholarships awarded annually total approximately $5 million. High school girls who are U.S. citizens are eligible to take part in the competition if they have never been married, however it is advisable to inquire during her sophomore year because the local competition may take place prior to her senior year. Contact America's Junior Miss, P.O. Box 2786, Mobile, AL 36652-2786; 334-438-3621.

$4000 Scholarship For Industrial Engineering

The Institute supports the advancement of engineering education and research through a variety of scholarships and awards. The United Parcels Service Scholarship for Female Students awards $4000 annually. Applicants must be undergraduate students pursuing an industrial engineering degree enrolled in any school in the U.S., Canada and Mexico which is accredited by an agency recognized by IIE. Applicants must be full-time students with an overall minimum 3.4 GPA who are active Institute members and have at least five full quarters or three full semesters of school remaining from the date of nomination. Please contact the Institute for details and other scholarship and award programs not limited to females only. Contact United Parcel Service Scholarship For Female Students, Institute of Industrial Engineers, 25 Technology Park/Atlanta, Norcross, GA 30092-2988; 770-449-0461; 800-494-0460.

$300-$1000 Scholarship For Chemistry Students

This National Honor Society for Women in Chemistry offers scholarships for women pursuing a chemistry degree in an accredited college or university. Scholarships vary depending on educational level and amounts awarded. The nominee may be, but need not be, a member of Iota Sigma Pi, depending on the scholarship. The Society also offers professional awards. Awards range from $300 to $1000. Please contact the address listed below for details. Contact Iota Sigma Pi, c/o Dr. Lily Ng, Chemistry Dept., Cleveland State University, Cleveland, OH 44115; {www-chem.ucsd.edu/Faculty/sawrey/ISP/}; {e-mail: I.ng@popmail.csuohio.edu}.

Legally Blind Eligible For $300-$10,000

The National Federation of the Blind is able to offer a broad array of scholarships to applicants who are legally blind and studying full-time in a post-secondary institution in the United States.

One scholarship is available to a full-time employee also attending school part-time. 1 scholarship for $10,000 and 3 scholarships for $3000 have no additional restrictions. Twenty-two scholarships are awarded for $3000. Some have no additional restrictions, although some have female only restrictions and some have field of study restrictions. Contact National Federation Of The Blind, 805 Fifth Ave., Grinnel, IA 50122; 515-236-3366.

Fellowships And Grants For Advancement Of Women In Society

The AAUW provides funds through grants and fellowships to advance education, research, and self-development for women, and to foster equity and positive societal change. Applicants are not required to be members of AAUW.

Applicants must demonstrate scholarly or professional excellence and preference is given to women whose interests show a commitment to advancing the welfare of women and girls. Grants to individuals go up to $27,000, and include education, community action, and career development grants. A booklet is available that describes the various programs.

Contact American Association Of University Women Education Foundation (AAUW), 2201 N. Dodge Street, Dept. 148, Iowa City, IA 52243-4030; 319-337-1716; {www.aauw.org}.

SCHOLARSHIPS FOR LUTHERAN WOMEN

Women of the Evangelical Lutheran Church in America (Women of the ELCA) offers scholarships in three different categories. Scholarships for Lutheran Lay Women provides assistance to women of the ELCA in a variety of fields as they return to school after experiencing at least a two year interruption. The Arne Administrative Leadership Scholarship provides assistance to Lutheran women who are pursuing an education to prepare for an administrative position. The Herbert W. and Corrine Chilstrom Scholarship provides assistance to Lutheran women who are second-career students at ELCA seminaries and preparing for the ordained ministry in the ELCA.

Contact Women Of The Evangelical Lutheran Church In America, 8765 W. Higgins Road, Chicago, IL 60631-4189; 773-380-2730; 800-638-3522, ext. 2730; {e-mail: womnelca@elca.org}.

Musicians Eligible For Awards

The National Federation Of Music Clubs (NFMC) is dedicated to finding and fostering young musical talent. The Federation conducts annual Junior Festivals and offers more than a quarter of a million dollars in state and national competitions.

The awards NFMC offers are numerous. Age limits and categories vary greatly per award. Many awards include performance bookings. Almost all awards require NFMC membership. Contact the NFMC for a chart of competitions and awards. Contact National Federation Of Music Clubs (NFMC), 1336 North Delaware Street, Indianapolis, IN 46202-2481; 317-638-4003.

Scholarships For Female Jocks

Women's Sports Foundation offers scholarships to provide female high school student-athletes with a means to continue their athletic participation as well as their college education. The three scholarships offered for this purpose are The Linda Riddle/SGMA Scholarship, Mervyn's California/Women's Sports Foundation Scholarship and Gart Sports/Women's Sports Foundation College Scholarship. The Dorothy Harris Scholarship is offered to provide female graduate students in physical education, sports management, sports psychology or sports sociology with a means to attend graduate school. Contact Women's Sports Foundation, Eisenhower Park, East Meadow, NY 11554; 800-227-3988; {www.lifetimetv.com/WoSport}; {e-mail: WoSport@aol.com}.

Smart Science Majors Scholarships

The Clare Boothe Luce Program is intended "to encourage women to enter, study, graduate, and teach" in fields where there have been many obstacles to their advancement. These fields include physics, chemistry, biology, meteorology, engineering, computer science, and mathematics. Undergraduate scholarships are generally awarded for two years to a highly qualified female and solely based on merit. Graduate fellowships are awarded to highly qualified women who are doctoral candidates. Contact the Foundation for details.

The Clare Boothe Luce Program, The Henry Luce Foundation, Inc., 111 West 50th Street, New York, NY 10020; 212-489-7700; {www.hluce.org}.

$1500 For Engineering Students

Information Handling Services/SAE Women Engineers Committee Scholarship was established to encourage young women and minority students who are graduating from high school to enter the field of engineering. Applicants must have a minimum 3.0 GPA and be accepted into an ABET accredited engineering program. This $1500 award will be given for the freshman year only.

In addition, the Society offers over $27,000 worth of scholarships to engineering students at any accredited engineering programs. They also offer scholarships for use at over 50 specific universities. Contact the Society for more information and application deadlines. The Society Of Automotive Engineers, 400 Commonwealth Drive, Warrendale, PA 15096-0001; 724-772-8534.

Up to $5000 for Aspiring Journalists

The NAHJ Scholarship Fund was established to assist aspiring minority journalists pursuing a career in journalism. Applicants need not be a member of NAHJ, but must be a student enrolled full-time in a college for the entire academic year. Selection is based on academic excellence, a demonstrated interest to pursue a career in journalism and financial need.

High school seniors, college undergraduate or graduate students majoring in print or broadcast journalism are eligible for a $1000-$2000 NAHJ Scholarship. College juniors or seniors are eligible for the $5,000 Newhouse Scholarship Program. Contact National Association Of Hispanic Journalists, 1193 National Press Building, Washington, DC 20045-2100; 888-346-NAHJ; {www.nahj.org}.

$1000-$5000 For Broadcast Journalism Majors

The Foundation sponsors seven different scholarships for students seeking a career in electronic journalism. One of the seven awards is for graduate students only. Award amounts range from $1000-$5000. Applicants must be full-time students who have at least one year of college remaining and are officially enrolled in a college. Several of the awards are specific to minorities.

The Foundation also offers a variety of internship programs. Contact Radio And Television News Directors Foundation, RTNDF Scholarships, 1000 Connecticut Ave., NW, Suite 615, Washington, DC 20036; {www.rtndf.org}.

$1500 FOR MEDICAL AND DENTAL STUDENTS

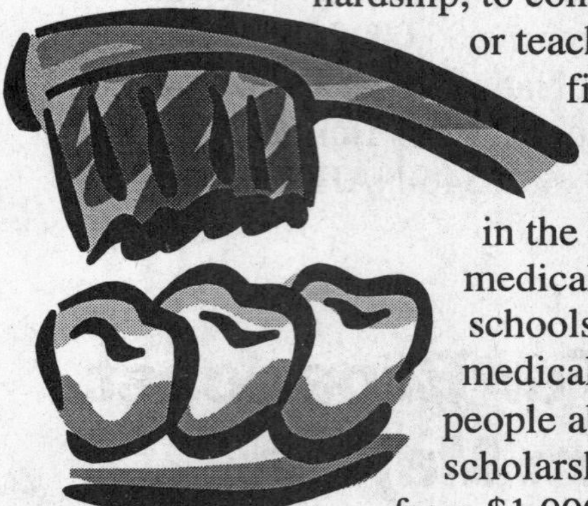

The CAMS awards scholarships to help qualified candidates, especially of Chinese descent, with financial hardship, to complete their study of research or teaching in the medical science field. This includes either undergraduate study in medical or dental schools in the U.S.A. or post-graduate medical study or research in schools participating in teaching in medical schools or helping Chinese people abroad. Four to six scholarships are awarded ranging from $1,000-$1,500. Contact Chinese-American Medical Society, Dr. H.H. Wang-Executive Director, 281 Edgewood Ave., Teaneck, NJ 07666; 201-833-1506; {www.camsociety.org}; {e-mail: hw5@columbia.edu}.

$6000 For Women Pursuing Sports Administration

The NCAA offers 12 scholarships to women and 12 scholarships to ethnic minorities who are college graduates and will be entering the first semester of their initial postgraduate studies. Applicants must be accepted into a sports administration or related program. Applicants must be pursuing a career in intercollegiate athletics such as coaching, sports medicine, athletics administration and other careers that provide a direct service to intercollegiate athletics. Each award is for $6000.

The Degree Completion program is for student athletes who have completed their eligibility for athletics-related aid at a Division I school and be within 30 hours of obtaining their degree. They can be funded five semesters part-time or two semesters full-time. They also offer eight $3,000 scholarships to college juniors majoring in sports journalism. Each year more than $1.7 million in scholarships is awarded. The NCAA also awards a variety of postgraduate scholarships.

Please contact Stanley D. Johnson, staff liaison. Contact The National Collegiate Athletic Association, 6201 College Boulevard, Overland Park, KS 66211-2422; 913-339-1906.

Women Pursuing CEO Or CFO Positions Eligible For Scholarships

The Foundation offers scholarships to women majoring only in finance or economics who are planning for a corporate business career in the private sector. They are targeting women who they believe are most likely to become tomorrow's CEO's or CFO's of major manufacturing companies. Applicants may range from high school seniors to Ph.Ds. The college of attendance must already be determined and that institution informed. The number of awards, as well as the amount, varies from year to year.

Contact The Karla Scherer Foundation, 737 North Michigan Avenue, Suite 2330, Chicago, IL 60611; 312-943-9191; {http://comnet.org/kschererf}.

$1000 For Females With A Love Of Flying

This wonderful fund is offered in remembrance of Nancy Horton who loved to fly! One award of $1000 is given to the recipient to further the student's flight training. Applicants must be at least 18 years old, have a minimum 3.0 GPA if in school, at least a private pilot, high recommendation from flight instructor, extra flight related activities and, an essay portraying one's love of flight.

Contact Nancy Horton "Touch The Face Of God" Scholarship, 4466 N.E. 91st Ave., Portland, OR 97220.

$1000-$2500 For Students Studying Real Estate

IREM offers the Brooker scholarship to increase participation of minorities in the real estate management industry. One graduate level award of $2500 and two undergraduate-level awards in the amount of $1000 are given. Applicants must be minority students who are U.S. citizens who have declared a major in real estate or in a related field and have a minimum GPA of 3.0. Students should have completed at least two courses in real estate at the time of application.

Contact George M. Brooker Collegiate Scholarship For Minorities, Institute of Real Estate Management, Attn: Brooker Scholarship, 430 N. Michigan Ave., Chicago, IL 60611-4090; 312-329-6008; {e-mail: gohlson@irem.org}.

$5000 For Students With Disabilities

EIF has established a scholarship which awards $5000 each to students with disabilities who are pursuing or about to pursue undergraduate or graduate studies directly related to the electronics industry. Selection is based on GPA, relevance of major, planned studies, career goals, outside activities, and essay questions on the scholarship. Contact Electronic Industries Foundation (EIF), Scholarship Award Committee, 2500 Wilson Boulevard, Suite 210, Arlington, VA 22201-3834; 703-907-7408.

$500-$1500 FOR PRESBYTERIAN CHURCH MEMBERS

The Presbyterian Church Higher Education Program provides $2 million dollars in grants, loans, and scholarships to students, both undergraduates and graduates, who belong to the Presbyterian Church. Grants range from $500-$2000 for studies.

One program is for students enrolled full-time and pursuing a medical profession. Other programs are for general studies. Applicants must be members of the Presbyterian Church (U.S.A.), U.S. citizens or permanent residents of the U.S., demonstrate financial need and be recommended by an academic advisor at the institution and by a church pastor. A booklet is available which lists the programs or you may check their website for more information.

Contact Presbyterian Church (U.S.A.), 100 Witherspoon Street, Louisville, KY 40202-1396; 502-569-5776; {www.theology.org/highed}.

Up To $4000 for Female Medical Students

AMWA Student Members are eligible for a variety of awards from the AMWA. The Wilhelm-Frankowski Scholarship of $4000 is offered to medical students attending an accredited U.S. medical or osteopathic medical school. The Janet M. Glasgow Essay Award of $1000 is presented for the best essay identifying a woman physician who has been a significant mentor and role model. The Carroll L. Birch Award of $500 is presented for the best original research paper written by a student member of the AWMA.

Loans are also available. Contact American Medical Women's Association Foundation (AMWA), 801 North Fairfax Street, Suite 400, Alexandria, VA 22314; 703-838-0500; {e-mail: mglanz@amwa-doc.org}.

$750 For Geoscience Thesis Work

The Association offers a scholarship program for women who require financial assistance to complete their thesis and to complete a masters or Ph.D. degree in a geoscience field. Applicant must be a woman whose education has been interrupted for at least one year, a candidate for an advanced degree in a geoscience field, and completing their thesis during the current academic year. The scholarship is to be used for typing, drafting, childcare or whatever it takes to finish the thesis. Two $750 scholarships will be awarded. Contact The Association For Women Geoscientists, Chrysalis Scholarships, G&H Production Company, LLC, #930, 518-17th Street, Denver, CO 80202; 303-534-0708; {e-mail: leete@macalstr.edu}.

$5000 For Training In Field Of Water Supply And Treatment

The American Water Works Association offers The Holly A. Cornell Scholarship to encourage and support outstanding female and/or minority students pursuing advanced training in the field of water supply and treatment. Current master's degree students or students who have been accepted into graduate school are eligible. The scholarship provides a one-time grant of $5000 to the most outstanding eligible candidate.

The Lars Scholarship is open to any student in a master's or doctorate program in science or engineering. There is a $5,000 scholarship for an M.S. student and a $7,000 scholarship for Ph.D. student. Contact American Water Works Association, 6666 W. Quincy Avenue, Denver, CO 80235; 303-347-6206.

Scholarships For Joining AFROTC

Air Force ROTC offers scholarships to high school seniors and high school graduates. Applicants must have a minimum GPA of 2.5 and minimum SAT scores of 1100, ACT scores of 24. The 2 or 3-year scholarships are offered to in-college students in all majors, but the highest concentration is in science and engineering fields. To qualify, applicants must have a minimum 2.65 GPA for science and engineering majors and a 3.0 GPA for all other majors and must hold an AFROTC Professional Officer Course allocation. If accepted for scholarship, students must pass a physical exam and a physical fitness test. Recipients must later serve on active duty to repay obligation. Contact AFROTC for more details. Contact Air Force ROTC, Headquarters AFROTC Scholarship Action Section, 551 E. Maxwell Blvd., Maxwell AFB, AL 36112-6106; 334-953-2091.

$1000 For Women Statisticians

The Gertrude Cox Scholarship is open to women who have been accepted into a graduate statistical program. Masters and doctorate students are encouraged to apply for the scholarship. Contact American Statistical Association, 1429 Duke St., Alexandria, VA 22314; 703-684-1221; {www.amstat.org}.

Scholarships For Spouse Or Children Of EOD Officer Or Technician

The EOD Memorial Scholarship Application can be viewed at the website below. Applicants must be an unmarried child under the age of 23 years, a widowed spouse who has never been remarried, or a spouse of an EOD officer or enlisted EOD technician of the Army, Marine Corps, Navy, or Air Force who have successfully completed NAVSCOLEOD. Applicants must also be a graduate of an accredited high school and be enrolled in or accepted for enrollment in a full-time undergraduate course of study at an accredited college/university or technical school beyond the high school level.

Money can be used for tuition, books, room, board, and other fees. The amount of the award varies each year. Contact EOD Memorial Scholarship Fund, Naval School, Explosive Ordnance Disposal, 309 Strauss Avenue, Indian Head, MD 20640-5040; 703-317-0635; {www.erols.com/ncerino/eodfund.html}.

Money For Grandmas

If you are fifty-four or older and have an idea for a project or program dealing with women, then this program is for you. The grants range from $500-$5,000. The projects cannot involve men or children. The projects need to be designed to enhance a skill or talent or produce a report or product that somehow involves women. Call for application guidelines. Contact The Thanks Be To Grandmother Winifred Foundation, P.O. Box 1449, Wainscott, NY 11975; 516-725-0323.

MONEY FOR MIDWIVES TO-BE

The American College of Nurse-Midwives provides scholarships to students in good standing who are enrolled in an accredited midwifery program. For application information contact the office listed below, or use their fax-on-demand system at 202-728-9898 and request document #9001. Contact American College of Nurse-Midwives, 818 Connecticut Ave., NW, Suite 900, Washington, DC 20006; 202-728-9860; {www.midwife.org}.

$500-$2500 For Ohio Engineering Majors

The Engineers Foundation of Ohio provides a variety of grants ranging from $500-$2500 for Ohio residents who meet a minimum grade point and SAT/ACT score. These grants are for students who have been accepted into engineering programs. For specific information about the grants and an application, please contact the office listed below. Contact Engineers Foundation of Ohio, 236 East Town St., Suite 210, Columbus, OH 43215; 614-228-8606; {www.geocities.com}.

UP TO $2,500 FOR RESPIRATORY CARE MAJORS

The American Respiratory Care Foundation awards grants ranging from $1,000 to $2,500 for students in respiratory therapy programs, both associate and baccalaureate degree programs. Awards generally include travel and registration to the annual conference. One award, the Morton B. Duggan, Jr. Memorial gives a preference to students from Georgia and South Carolina.

Contact American Respiratory Care Foundation, 1030 Ables Lane, Dallas, TX 75229; 972-243-2272; {www.aarc.org}.

Add Up Your Money Women Accountants

The Educational Foundation for Women in Accounting supports women in the accounting profession. They offer a variety of scholarships ranging from $1,250-$5000. The Laurels Fund Scholarships are one-year scholarships targeting women who are pursuing advanced accounting degrees.

Women in Transition Scholarship is for $4,000 and is given to women pursuing an accounting degree. This is for a woman who is in "transition" and was formerly called Displaced Homemaker Scholarship. Contact The Educational Foundation for Women in Accounting, Administrative Office, P.O. Box 1925, Southeastern, PA 19399; 610-407-9229; {www.efwa.org}.

A TOTAL OF $15,000 FOR WOMEN ACCOUNTING MAJORS

Each year the American Society of Women Accountants awards $15,000 in scholarships to women pursuing either a master's or bachelor's degree in accounting. The student can be attending full or part-time. Contact the office listed below for application information.

Contact American Society of Women Accountants, 60 Revere Dr., Suite 500, Northbrook, IL 60062; 800-326-2163; {www.aswa.org}.

Money For Human Resource Majors

The Society of Human Resource Management offers a variety of scholarships to undergraduate and graduate human resource majors. Awards range from $1,000-$5,000. Students must maintain a "C" average. Several of the awards are competitions in a research project or essay writing. Contact the office listed below for application information.

Contact Society for Human Resource Management, 1800 Duke St., Alexandria, VA 22314; 703-548-3440; {www.shrm.org}.

Money For Latinas

MANA, a national Latina organization, provides scholarships to Latinas who have good academic records and financial need. They offer a variety of scholarships. Contact the office listed below for application information. Contact MANA: A National Latina Organization, 1725 K St., NW, Suite 501, Washington, DC 20006; 202-833-0060; {www.hermana.org}.

$1000 For Real Estate Appraisers

The Appraisal Institute offers scholarships to minority students interested in the real estate appraisal field. The scholarship award of $1000 is for undergraduate or graduate degrees in the field. Contact Appraisal Institute, 875 North Michigan Ave., Suite 2400, Chicago, IL 60611; 312-335-4121; {www.appraisalinstitute.org}.

Confederates Unite

If you are a lineal descendant of worthy confederates, you may be eligible for scholarships through this organization. You must have certified proof of Confederate Military Record of one ancestor, and information on how to obtain this information is available. You also need recommendations, a 3.0 grade point average and more. There are several four-year scholarships without restrictions as to schools, major, or state of residency, and others that have some type of restriction. Send a self-addressed stamped envelope to the address listed below for information and application requirements. Contact United Daughters of the Confederacy, 3202 Superior Lane, Bowie, MD 20715.

Count On Accounting

The National Society of Public Accountants awards 30 scholarships per year, approximately $1,000 each. Students must have a 3.0 grade point average and major in accounting at a 2-year or 4-year college. Scholarships are awarded based upon academic excellence and financial need. Contact the Society for application information. National Society of Public Accountants, 1010 North Fairfax St., Alexandria, VA 22314; 703-549-6400; {www.nsacct.org}.

AT&T Labs Fellowship Program for Women & Minorities in Science & Tech

Outstanding minority and women students who plan to pursue Ph.D. studies in computers, engineering, and other communications-related fields are eligible to apply for the AT&T Fellowships. The students chosen as fellows will have a mentor assigned to them to help guide them through their studies. The fellowships cover most education expenses, an annual living stipend and more for up to five years of graduate studies.

For more information contact AT&T Labs Fellowship Administrator, Room C103, 180 Park Ave, Florham Park, NJ 07060; {www.att.com/attlabs/people/fellowships.html}.

$500-$1,500 for Smart Business Women

The American Business Women's Association offers a variety of scholarships to undergraduate and graduate business majors, and to students pursuing professional degrees. Awards range from $500-$1,500. Students must be female. Some awards are limited to residents of Anne Arundel County, Maryland. Contact American Business Women's Association, 1891 Poplar Ridge Rd., Pasadena, MD 21122; 301-255-1067; {www.abwahq.org}.

Up to $1000 for Legally Blind Women

The American Foundation for the Blind offers various support services and scholarships to undergraduate students who are legally blind. Some scholarships are restricted to specific majors; others require a short essay. They also offer several scholarships to students pursuing a Classical Music career. All are based on academic achievement. Contact American Foundation for the Blind, 15 W. 16th St., New York, NY 10011; {www.afb.org}.

Money for Smart Business Women

The Business and Professional Women's Association offers a variety of scholarships to women over the age of 25 who are returning to college after a break/delay in their education and plan on pursuing a business career. Some scholarships are intended for use during your junior and senior year only.

The Association considers financial need, academic achievement, recommendations and a personal statement in their decisions. The $1000 Kelly Services Second Career Scholarship is for women returning to or starting their education due to the death of a spouse or divorce, and is for use during any undergraduate year. The Association may also have loans available. Contact Business and Professional Women's Association, 2012 Massachusetts Ave., NW, Washington, DC 20036; 202-293-1200.

$500 for Meteorologists and Atmospheric Science Majors

Interested in a career in the Atmospheric Sciences? The American Geophysical Union offers undergraduate women a chance at $500! Contact American Geophysical Union, American Geophysical Union, 2000 Florida Ave., NW, Washington, DC 20009; 202-462-6903 {earth.agu.org or www.agu.org}.

Up to $3000 for Nuclear Scientists and Nuclear Engineers

The American Nuclear Society has a large variety of scholarships and research grants available to women who plan to pursue a career in the nuclear sciences. One scholarship awarded each year is reserved for women who are returning to school after a break/delay in their education. All scholarships can be applied for using one application form, which is available on their website. Contact American Nuclear Society, 555 N. Kensington Ave., La Grange Park, IL 60525; {www.ans.org}.

$500-$3,500 for Smart New York Women

The Foundation has various programs for Jewish female undergraduate students who live in New York, NY. Please write for further information, include a SASE. Contact Jewish Foundation for the Education of Women, 330 W. 58th St., New York, NY 10019.

$1,000 for Engineering, Math and Science Students

The Brookhaven Institute's Women in Science program targets women who have had their education interrupted due to financial, family, or other problems. Financial need is the primary consideration. Intended for use during your junior or senior year, the scholarship converts to a loan if you do not maintain good academic standing for two consecutive semesters. Contact Brookhaven Women in Science, P.O. Box 183, Upton, NY 11973; 516-344-7226.

$2000 for Smart Engineering Women

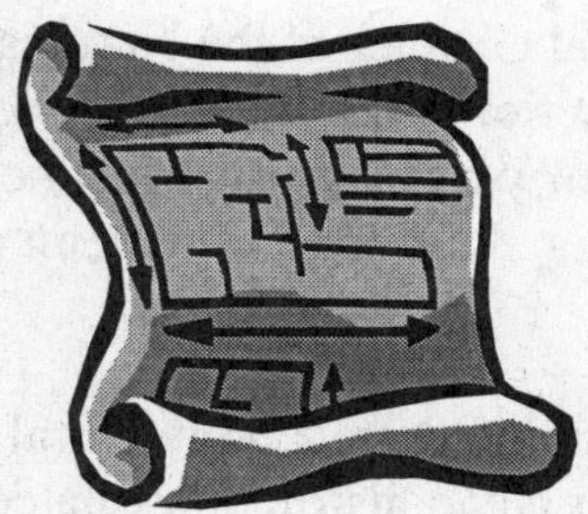

The National Society of Professional Engineers offers several scholarships to graduating high school seniors who are in the top 25% of their class and intend on pursuing a career in engineering. The scholarship is renewable, and requires a minimum GPA of 3.0. Contact National Society of Professional Engineers, 1420 King St., Alexandria, VA 22314; 703-684-2858; {www.nspe.org}.

Money for Smart Jewish Women in Massachusetts

Priority is given to those who are returning to school after a five year or longer absence. Financial need is the primary consideration, the awards may be used during any undergraduate field of study. A strong desire for financial independence is a plus. Contact National Council of Jewish Women, 75 Harvard Ave., Allston, MA 02134.

$1,000 FOR CALIFORNIA CONSTRUCTION WOMEN

The El Camino Real Chapter of the National Association of Women in Construction offers $1,000 to women entering their junior or senior year of study. Must be attending a college in California. Academic achievement is the primary consideration.

Women studying architecture, architectural engineering, civil engineering or any construction-related major are welcome to apply. Contact National Association of Women in Construction, El Camino Real Chapter 158, 333 W. Santa Clara St., Suite 110, San Jose, CA 95113; 408-998-4646.

$1,000 for Smart Journalism Women

The National Federation of Press Women offers several different scholarships, most paying around $1000, to high school seniors and college undergraduates pursuing a career in journalism. The Federation considers academic achievement, financial need, and potential for success in their decisions.

Contact National Federation of Press Women, 4510 W. 89th St., Prairie Village, KS 66207-2282; 913-341-0165.

Up to $500 for Activists at CUNY

For women attending any campus of the City University of New York. The Astraea Foundation offers two $500 awards annually to women who demonstrate political and social commitment to actively fighting for gay and lesbian civil rights. For use during any undergraduate year, lesbian sexual orientation is not a requirement - just commitment to lesbian civil rights. Financial need is considered but not required.

Contact Astraea National Lesbian Action Foundation, 116 E. 16th St., 7th Floor, New York, NY 10003; 212-529-8021; {www.imageinc.com/astraea}.

UP TO $2000 FOR WOMEN IN BROADCASTING

For undergraduate women planning on a career in radio or television broadcasting. Contact Opportunities for Women in Broadcasting, c/o The Citizen's Scholarship Foundation of America, 326 S. Minnesota Avenue, St. Peter, MN 56082; 507-931-1682; 507-931-8034.

$1000 for Daughters of Penelope

The Daughters of Penelope offers to members or children of members three different awards ranging from $1000 to $1500 for use during your undergraduate years. Academic achievement, financial need and an essay are required. Members of The Maids of Athena are also eligible to apply.

For application and information, check with your local chapter first, or the address below. Contact The Daughters of Penelope, 1909 Q St., NW, Suite 500, Washington, DC 20009; 202-234-9741.

Up to $1000 for Landscape Architects

The Foundation offers ten different programs assisting landscape architecture students. Some programs require written papers on the subject of landscape architecture, others require photos or slide of work you have done.

Please contact the Foundation for details. Landscape Architecture Foundation, 4401 Connecticut Ave., NW, Suite 500, Washington, DC 20008; 202-686-0068.

$500-$1000 for Kappa Kappa Gamma Women

If you are a member of Kappa Kappa Gamma and studying social work, special education, or rehabilitation, KKG has money for you!!

For application and information, please check with your college's chapter or send a SASE to the address below. Contact Kappa Kappa Gamma, 530 E. Town St., Columbus, OH 43216; 615-228-6515.

$500-$5,000 for Daughters of the Railroad

The Foundation offers 150 scholarships yearly to daughters of deceased employees of any railroad company. Preference is given to women who are about to graduate high school. Contact John Edgar Thomson Foundation, The Rittenhouse Claridge, Suite 318, Philadelphia, PA 19103; 215-545-6083.

$1,000 for Smart California Women

For undergraduate women studying in any college in California. Must have graduated from a high school in California. Based on financial need, academic achievement, community service, references. Contact Amaranth Fund Awards, California Mason Foundation, 1111 California St., San Francisco, CA 94109.

Up to $1,000 for Medical Women

For undergraduate women interested in pursuing a career in clinical healthcare or health administration. Contact American College of Medical Practice Executives, 104 Inverness Terrace East, Englewood, CO 80112; 303-799-1111; {www.ache.org}.

$1,000 for the Top Ten College Women

Each year, Glamour Magazine looks for the Top Ten College Women in America. Applications are taken during your junior year. Academic achievement, extracurricular activities, community service, personal statement, references and an essay are all considered — looking fantastic helps but isn't necessarily required. For full-time college juniors. Information for next year's contest will be available at the 800 number below in September, 1999. Contact Glamour Magazine, 350 Madison Ave., New York, NY 10017; 800-244-4526; {www.glamour.com}; {e-mail: ttcw@glamour.com}.

Lots of Money for All Kinds of Women in El Paso, TX

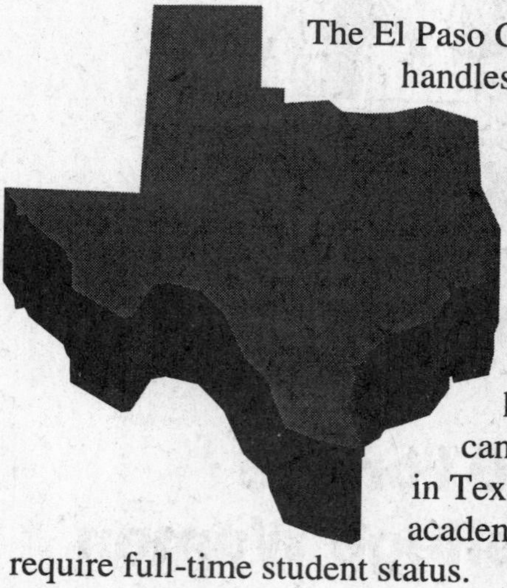

The El Paso Community Foundation handles scholarships for a large variety of foundations, with many different restrictions — some with none! But all are restricted to residents of El Paso, TX. Some are restricted to current high school seniors. Some can only be used at colleges in Texas. Most are based on academic achievement and require full-time student status.

For detailed information, contact The El Paso Community Foundation, 201 E. Main St., Suite 1616, El Paso, TX 79901.

Lots of Money for All Kinds of Women in Santa Barbara, CA

The Santa Barbara Foundation handles scholarships for a large variety of foundations, with many different restrictions — some with none! But all are restricted to residents of Santa Barbara, CA. Some are restricted to current high school seniors. Most are based on academic achievement and require full-time student status. For detailed information, contact Santa Barbara Foundation, 16 E. Carrillo St., Santa Barbara, CA 93101.

$6,000 for Graduate Women

The Amelia Earhart Fellowship, awarded annually by the Zonta International Foundation, is for women pursuing graduate level studies in aerospace, aeronautics, engineering and related studies. Academic achievement is the primary consideration. Contact Zonta International Foundation, 557 W. Randolph St., Chicago, IL 60661; 312-930-5848.

Up to $3000 for California Golfers

For women who are residents of southern California, this renewable award is based primarily upon academic achievement and financial need. Must have an interest in golfing, however actual skill in golfing is not a consideration. Must be attending or planning on attending a four-year college or university full-time. Contact Gloria Fecht Memorial Scholarship Foundation, 402 W. Arrow Highway, Suite 10, San Dimas, CA 91773; {www.womensgolf.org}.

A CALL TO ACTION — FOR MONEY!

The Call to Action Essay Contest is for undergraduate women who live in California and are studying business, education, health care, law enforcement or social service. Up to $5,000 is awarded to the winning essay, topic changes yearly.

Please write or contact your financial aid office for information. Contact Governor's Conference for Women, A Call To Action, Office of the Governor, 300 S. Spring St., 16th Floor, Los Angeles, CA 90013.

Up to $10,000 for Young Women

Girls Incorporated offers several scholarships and contests to its members, including a national academic scholarship contest worth $10,000. Must be a high school student in grades 10 through 12, under age 19, and a member of Girls Incorporated. Contact Girls Incorporated, 120 Wall St., New York, NY 10005.

Money for Women Ministers

For undergraduate women attending college full-time who are preparing for the ministry. Please include SASE with requests for information. Contact Disciples of Christ Church, P.O. Box 1986, Indianapolis, IN 46206.

Money for Women in Oregon

The Oregon State Scholarship Commission manages a large variety of scholarship offers for women who are residents of Oregon. Some of the opportunities for undergraduate women include:

The Agricultural Women-in-Network Scholarship for college sophomore and junior students attending college in Oregon, Washington, or Idaho. Primarily based on financial need and academic achievement, you must be planning on pursuing an agricultural-related career.

The Private 150 Scholarship Program, for current college juniors and seniors studying business. The Professional Land Surveyors Scholarship, for use during your junior or senior year. Must be attending any college in Oregon and plan on a career in surveying, cartography, or related careers.

Contact Oregon State Scholarship Commission, 1500 Valley River Dr., Suite 100, Eugene, OR 97401-7020.

Over $1 Million Available for Farmers

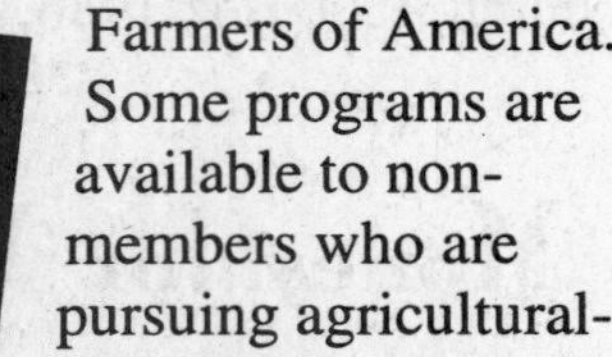

Over 300 different scholarship programs are available to members of the Future Farmers of America. Some programs are available to non-members who are pursuing agricultural-related degrees. Details and applications are available at the website. Contact Future Farmers of America, Inc., Scholarship Office, P.O. Box 68960, Indianapolis, IN 46268-0960; {www.ffa.agriculture.com/activities/activitiessectionpg.html}.

$250 for Teaching in Oregon

This renewable scholarship is for undergraduate students who plan on teaching in Oregon upon completion of their education degree. Preference is given to those who plan on teaching at the elementary or secondary school levels. Contact Oregon PTA, 531 SE 14th Ave., Room 205, Portland, OR 97214.

$3,500 for Broadcasting in Oregon or Washington

For current undergraduate students attending any college in Oregon or Washington who intend on pursuing a career in broadcasting. Academic achievement is the primary consideration. Contact Oregon Association of Broadcasters, P.O. Box 20037, Portland, OR 97220.

UP TO $1000 FOR SHEEP

For undergraduate students who are studying agriculture, animal science, veterinary medicine, or animal husbandry and intend on pursuing a career in the Sheep industry. Must be a resident of Oregon. Contact Oregon Sheep Growers Association, 1270 Chemeketa St., NE, Salem, OR 97301; 503-364-5462.

Tuition and up to $13,500 for Smart Graduate Students

The A.W. Mellon Fellowship in Humanistic Studies is designed to encourage and prepare students of exceptional academic promise for teaching and scholarship careers in humanistic studies. Students majoring in American studies, art history, the classics, comparative literature, cultural anthropology, english literature, foreign language, history, the philosophy of science, and related majors are welcome to apply. For use at the graduate level of study, this highly competitive and prestigious award grants tuition, fees, and a stipend of up to $13,500 to 80 people yearly. Contact The A.W. Mellon Fellowship in Humanities, Woodrow Wilson National Fellowship Foundation, CN 5329, Princeton, NY 08543-5329; 609-452-7007; {www.wwnff.org}.

Money for Dietetic Technicians

The American Dietetic Association offers various scholarships to students who are studying dietetics or nutrition, and plan on a career in dietetics. Must be entering your first year of study in an ADA-accredited dietetic technician program. Financial need and academic achievement are the primary considerations. Contact American Dietetic Association, 216 W. Jackson Blvd., Suite 800, Chicago, IL 60606-6995; 312-899-0040; {www.eatright.org}.

Up to $1,500 for Dental Hygienists

The Association offers a large variety of scholarships to students who plan on a career as a dental hygienist. Most awards are limited to current college juniors, however some are open to all undergraduate students. Some of their programs target students studying for a certificate in dental hygiene, others target minority students. Applications and information are available at their website. Financial need and academic achievement are the primary considerations. Contact American Dental Hygienists Association, 444 N. Michigan Ave., Suite 3400, Chicago, IL 60611; 312-440-8944; {www.adha.org}.

$2,500 FOR NURSES

The Eight and Forty Scholarship, offered by the American Legion, was established to assist current registered nurses (RN's) who wish to advance their career for positions in supervision, administration or teaching. Students are to have prospects of being employed in specific positions in hospitals, clinics, or health departments on completion of their education and the position must have a full-time and direct relationship to lung and respiratory control.

For more information, contact the address listed below. Contact The American Legion, Attn: Eight and Forty Scholarships, P.O. Box 1055, Indianapolis, IN 46206; {www.legion.org/educasst.htm}.

Up to $10,000 for Handicapped Musicians

This music competition is open to students who are blind, deaf, learning disabled, or physically disabled. An audition tape is required. Check with your local Very Special Arts Organization, or the address below for further information. Contact Very Special Arts and the Panasonic Electronics Company, 1300 Connecticut Ave., NW, Washington, DC 20036; 800-933-8721; {www.vsarts.org}.

Up to $5,000 for Food Service Experience

The National Restaurant Association has two different programs available. The Industry Assistance Grants offer up to $1000 to further the education of those who have at least three years experience in food service. The Undergraduate Scholarships Program offers up to $5,000 to current college sophomores and juniors who have at least a 3.0 GPA. You must also have at least 1000 hours of work experience in the food service industry. Contact National Restaurant Association Educational Foundation, 250 S. Wacker Drive, Suite 1400, Chicago, IL 60606-5834; 800-765-2122, ext. 760; {www.foodtrain.org}.

Up to $9,000 for Women from Developing Countries

Five awards are available, each up to $9,000 for female students from developing countries. Must show service to women and/or children. Must be 25 years of age or older. Must be planning on returning to your home country within two years.

Contact Margaret McNamara Memorial Fund, World Bank, Q-5-080, 1818 H Street, NW, Washington, D.C. 20433; 202-473-5804; {www.erols.com/prlinn/ mmmf.html}, {e-mail: wservices1@worldbank.org}.

Up to $2,500 for Respiratory Care

The American Respiratory Care Foundation has several different programs available to both undergraduate and graduate students studying health care and medical areas related to respiratory care.

For all programs, you must have at least a 3.0 GPA, be a U.S. Citizen, and be attending a school that is approved by the American Medical Association. Most awards require an original paper on a respiratory care related subject. Contact American Respiratory Care Foundation, 11030 Ables Lane, Dallas, TX 75229-4593; 972-243-2272; {www.aarc.org}.

Up to $2,000 for Essays!

Applicants must research and write an essay on a topic to be determined by The Foundation. Applicants must contact The Heritage of America Scholarship Foundation to receive an application form and essay question. Open to current high school seniors, current undergraduate and graduate students. Essays and application forms must be postmarked on or before April 30.

Please include SASE with requests for information! Requests without SASE will not be responded to! Contact Heritage of America Scholarship Foundation, 8222 Thetford Lane, Houston, TX 77070.

$1,000 for Oregon High School Students

Five awards of $1,000 are available through the annual Cascade Policy Essay Competition. Based on an essay, the topic changes yearly. Private, public and homeschooled students are all encouraged to enter. All high-school age students are eligible to apply, not just college-bound seniors.

Contact Cascade Policy Institute, 813 SW Alder, Suite 450, Portland, OR 97205; 503-242-0900; {www.CascadePolicy.org/essay/essay99.htm}, {e-mail: Essay@CascadePolicy.org}.

Over $200,000 Available for Students with Norwegian Interests!

The Sons of Norway has several programs available. King Olav V Norwegian American Heritage Fund Students from Norway are also eligible to apply.

For U.S. students, you must demonstrate a keen and sincere interest in the Norwegian heritage. For Norwegian students, you must demonstrate a strong interest in American heritage. Students at the high school senior, college undergraduate and college graduate level are eligible to apply. Most awards are in the range of $250-$3,000.

Nancy Lorraine Jensen Memorial Scholarship Fund for women under the age of 35, who are either members of the Sons of Norway, or employees of NASA/Goddard Space Flight Center. Daughters and granddaughters of members or employees area also eligible to apply. Must be studying chemistry, chemical engineering, mechanical engineering, electrical engineering, or physics. For undergraduate study only, must have completed at least one semester of studies at time of application.

Contact King Olav V Norwegian American Heritage Fund, Sons of Norway Foundation, 1455 W. Lake St., Minneapolis, MN 55408; {www.sofn.com}.

Up to $1,500 for Returning Students

The P.E.O. Program for Continuing Education provides grants to women whose education has been interrupted and who find it necessary to resume studies due to changing demands in their lives. There must be a need for financial assistance with their educational expenses to improve their marketable skills. Must have been out of school for at least a year, must be within the last two years of finishing your degree, must be a citizen of either the United States or Canada.

Apply directly with a local P.E.O. Sisterhood chapter. Contact P.E.O. Sisterhood, 3700 Grand Avenue, Des Moines, IA 50312-2899, Attn: Executive Office.

Up to $3.5 Million for Young Women

The American Young Woman of the Year, a talent and scholarship contest, is for current high school seniors. It's based on SAT or ACT scores, GPA, transcript, interview, physical fitness, talent, poise, and appearance. Contact American Young Woman of the Year Program, P.O. Box 2786, Mobile, AL 36652.

Money for Graduate Students

Delta Sigma Theta has various programs available to graduate students who have demonstrated a commitment to serving their community. Must have at least a 3.0 GPA. Contact Century City Alumnae Chapter, Delta Sigma Theta Sorority, P.O. Box 90956, Los Angeles, CA 90009; 213-243-0594.

$1,000 for Young Feminists

Spinster's Ink offers an essay contest on "What Feminism Means to Me," for current female high school seniors. Winning essays will also be published in a national magazine. Contact Spinster's Ink, ATTN: Claire Kirch, 32 East First St. #330, Duluth, MN 55802; 218-727-3222; 800-301-6860; {www.spinsters-ink.com}.

Money for Texas Women Returning to School

The Ajay Castro Scholarship for Re-Entering Women provides financial assistance to women from Bexar County, Texas, who have been out of school for at least three years. Must be pursuing your first undergraduate degree, and must be studying a communications-related major. Contact Association for Women in Communications, San Antonio

Professional Chapter, P.O. Box 780382, San Antonio, TX 78278; 210-231-5799; {e-mail: jones@texas.net}.

Up to $2,500 for Nevada Women

The Nevada Women's Fund offers a large variety of programs to assist women in Nevada who wish to pursue a college education. Women studying at any academic level are welcome to apply, all programs are based primarily on academic achievement, financial need, and community service. Preference is given to women who are returning to school after a few years break and to single mothers. Most programs are renewable. Must attend college in Nevada.

Contact Nevada Women's Fund, P.O. Box 50428, Reno, NV 89513; 702-786-2335; {nwf.reno.nv.us}, {e-mail: staff@nwf.reno.nv.us}.

Money for Arkansas Single Parents

The Arkansas Single Parent Scholarship Fund is open to single parents (of either gender) who wish to begin or continue their higher education. Applicants must reside in a county where a Single Parent Scholarship Fund has been established — you can get a list of counties with this program by contacting the address below or your school's financial aid office. Contact Arkansas Single Parent Scholarship Fund, 614 East Emma Avenue, Suite 119, Springdale, AR 72764; 501-927-1402.

Up to $750 for Nursing or Teaching Women from Maine

This program is open to young women in Knox County, Maine, who wish to pursue an education in nursing or education. Students with financial need are given preference. Contact Barbara Thorndike Wiggin Fund, c/o Trust Department, Fleet Bank of Maine, P.O. Box 1280, Portland, ME 04104; 207-874-5232.

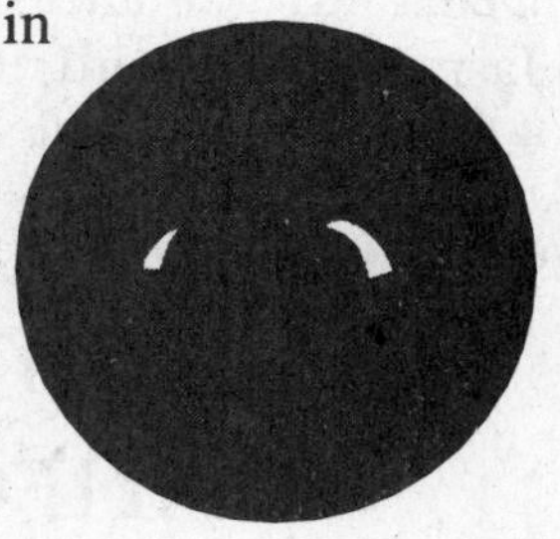

Up to $1,000 for Journalism Women in Washington

Women journalism majors entering their junior or senior year at any university in the state of Washington are eligible to apply. Contact Bobbi Mccallum Memorial Scholarship, Seattle Post-Intelligencer, 101 Elliott Avenue West, Seattle, WA 98119-4220; 206-448-8316.

$1,000 for Danish Sisterhood of America Women

Danish Sisterhood of America members, and their immediate families, are eligible to apply for a variety of programs offered by the Sisterhood. The awards can be used for either undergraduate or graduate work. You must have been a member for at least one year and have at least a 3.0 GPA. This award can also be used for studying in Denmark! Contact Danish Sisterhood of America, 8004 Jasmine Boulevard, Port Richey, FL 34668-3224; 813-862-4379.

Money for Palo Alto, California Women

Young women who are graduating from any high school in Palo Alto with a 3.0 or higher GPA are eligible to apply. Must be planning on attending a 4-year college or university, must be planning on studying science or a related major. Primary considerations for this award are athletic activities, community service, academic achievement and financial need. Please contact your high school's guidance counselor office or the address below for further information. Contact Peninsula Community Foundation, 1700 South El Camino Real, Suite 300, San Mateo, CA 94402-3049; 650-358-9369.

$1,000 for Texas Communication Women

Any woman attending any college or university in Texas who is studying journalism and has an interest in sports journalism is eligible to apply. Programs are available for both undergraduate and graduate level study.

Contact Texas Professional Communicators, P.O. Box 173, Denison, TX 75021-0173; 903-465-8567.

Money for Mathematical Woman

The American Mathematical Society has a variety of programs to reward outstanding undergraduate and graduate women in mathematics. Women in both the United States and Canada are eligible to apply. Contact American Mathematical Society, Attn: Executive Director, P.O. Box 6248, Providence, RI 02940-6248; 401-455-4000; 800-321-4AMS; {www.ams.org}, {e-mail: ams@ams.org}.

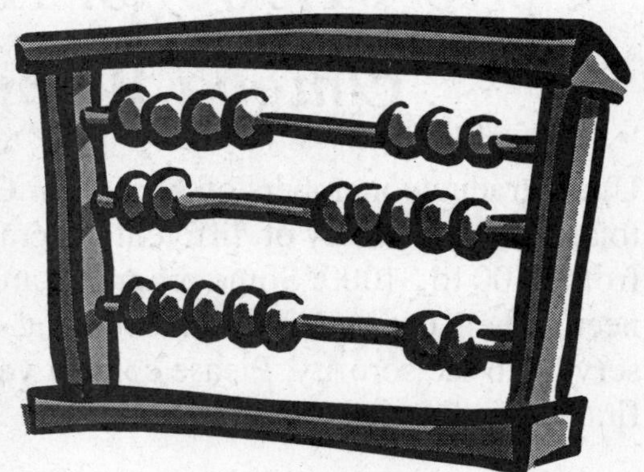

$100 FOR FOLK WOMEN

The Elli Kongas-Maranda Student Prize awards undergraduate and graduate students who submit papers or productions on women's traditional, vernacular, and local culture and/or work on feminist theory and folklore.

Contact American Folklore Society, Women's Folklore Section, c/o Clover Williams, Indiana University, Folklore Institute, 504 North Fess, Bloomington, IN 47405.

Up to $1,000 for Alpha Chi Omega Women

Undergraduate members of Alpha Chi Omega are eligible to apply for a variety of different programs offered, ranging from $400 to $1000. Some programs are based on financial need, others on academic achievement, most consider service to the sorority. Please contact your local chapter first for further information.

Contact Alpha Chi Omega Foundation, 5939 Castle Creek Parkway North Drive, Indianapolis, IN 46250-4343; 317-579-5050; {www.alphachiomega.org}.

$3,000 FOR SPORTS JOURNALISM

The Sports Journalism Scholarship Program is open to students entering their senior year who are interested in a career in sports journalism. Women and minorities are particularly encouraged to apply. Contact Freedom Forum, 1101 Wilson Boulevard, Arlington, VA 22209; 703-284-2814; {www.freedomforum.org/}, {e-mail: gpolicinski@freedomforum.org}.

Up to $3,000 for Western Art Women

The Grandma Moses Scholarship Program is for female high school seniors who plan on studying art at a college, university, or art school. Preference is given to women from the western states. Samples of your art work must be submitted, and the work must "manifest a congruence with the work of the famed folk artist, Grandma Moses." Contact Western Art Association, 13730 Loumont Street, Whittier, CA 90601.

Money for Rochester Women

High school students in and around the Rochester, New York area are eligible to apply. Over sixty different programs are available; requirements vary by program. Details on the various scholarships are available on the website Applications are only available through your high school guidance office, please do NOT write directly to the Foundation for information.

Contact Rochester Area Community Foundation, 500 East Avenue, Rochester, NY 14607-1912; 716-271-4100; {www.racf.org}.

Up to $2,500 for Hawaiian Women

The Hawaii Community Foundation has several programs available to women who are residents of Hawaii. Most programs require academic achievement, financial need, and full-time student status.

One program, the Jean Fitzgerald Scholarship, is for women who play tennis and have been active members of the Hawaii Pacific Tennis Association for at least four years. Contact Hawaii Community Foundation, 900 Fort Street Mall, Suite 1300, Honolulu, HI 96813; 808-566-5570.

Money for Jewish Women for Jesus

The Hazel Stone Memorial Scholarship is available to Jewish women who have committed their life to Jesus, plan on or are attending a Bible college or seminary, and are committed to an evangelistic career after graduation. Financial need is a primary consideration. Contact Jews for Jesus, 60 Haight Street, San Francisco, CA 94102; {www.jews-for-jesus.org}.

3M Engineering Awards

The National Action Council for Minorities in Engineering offers a variety of programs to minority women who have outstanding academic achievement, community service, and display a strong interest in math, sciences, and engineering areas. Programs are available at the high school, undergraduate and graduate level.

For most programs, students do not apply directly to NACME. Consult with your guidance counselor, program director, dean's office, financial aid officer or advisor to get information on the nomination process at your school or for applications. The application period for most programs is November through February. Contact National Action Council for Minorities in Engineering, 350 Fifth Avenue, Suite 2212, New York, NY 10118-2299; 212-279-2626; {www.nacme.org}.

Up to $2,500 for Music Women in Massachusetts

The Madelaine H. Soren Trust Scholarship is available to women music students who have graduated from a Massachusetts high school and wish to pursue their college education in the Boston area.

To apply, contact your high school's guidance counselor or administration office, they MUST nominate you for this program. Direct application is not available. Fifteen awards are made yearly. Contact Boston Safe Deposit and Trust Company, One Boston Place, Boston, MA 02108-4402; 617-722-7341.

Money for Navy Wives

The Mary Paolozzi Membership Scholarship is open to women who are wives of Navy personnel and have been members of the Navy Wives Club for at least two years. Financial need is considered.

Contact Navy Wives Club of America, P.O. Box 6971, Washington, DC 20032.

Money for Mennonite Women

The purpose of this program is to provide financial support to train emerging women church leaders around the world. Open to women from any country, this program helps with funding training at any level to prepare women for Mennonite church leadership. Training can include workshops for lay women who have very little education as well as course work for high school or college graduates.

Contact Mennonite Women International Women's Fund, 722 Main Street, P.O. Box 347, Newton, KS 67114; 316-283-5100.

Up to $1,000 for Women in Hunterdon County, New Jersey

The Mildred Preen Mortimer Woman-In-Transition Award is intended to provide financial aid to women in Hunterdon County, New Jersey, who are either returning to school after a break or who wish to pursue a second career. Financial need and desire for financial independence are the primary considerations. Contact Hunterdon Women's Fund, P.O. Box 183, Flemington, NJ 08822.

MONEY FOR WOMEN

Open to women from ages 3 to 20 (and men from ages 18-20), the purpose of this program is to "recognize and reward girls who could become tomorrow's leaders." Contestants must never have been married or have a child. In addition to appearance, academic achievement and community service are considered. Pageants are first held on the state level, winners then move on to the national competition. There is a $15 registration fee, and a $350 sponsor fee (which can be paid for by an individual's sponsors, family, friends, or through fund-raising.) Contact American Co-ed Pageants, 3695 Wimbledon Drive, Pensacola, FL 32504; 850-432-TEEN; {www.americanpageants.com/pageant.html}.

MONEY FOR BEAUTIFUL AFRICAN AMERICAN WOMEN

This annual competition is open to all African American women, including those who are married and/or have children, are eligible to enter this competition. The competition begins at the state level, winners move on to the national levels. Winners are chosen based on beauty, talent, and personality. There is a $40 application fee and a $550 sponsorship fee. The fees can be paid for by sponsors, fundraising, or by selling subscriptions to "Black America" magazine. Contact Miss Black America Pageant, P.O. Box 25668, Philadelphia, PA 19144; 215-844-8872.

Money for Talented Deaf Women

Miss Deaf America Pageant Awards. Must be deaf and between the ages of 18 and 28. The main objective of the Miss Deaf America Talent Pageant is "... to help us elevate the image and self-concept of deaf ladies throughout the United States. This is not an ordinary contest...beauty, poise, gracefulness are desirable qualities, but the biggest point is one's cultural talent performance. Talent is no longer the only thing; the women are judged across a broad spectrum of categories including community service, academics, current events, deaf culture, and more."

Contact National Association of the Deaf, 814 Thayer Avenue, Silver Spring, MD 20910-4500; 301-587-1788; TTY: 301-587-1789; {e-mail: nadinfo@nad.org}; {www.nad.org/mda.htm}.

$2000 for Deaf Graduate Women

The William C. Stokoe Scholarship is an annual award made to a deaf graduate student. The goal of the Stokoe Scholarship is to increase the number of deaf social scientists who are actively involved in research on sign language or the deaf community, whether in linguistics, psychology, anthropology, sociology, or other fields. Limited to deaf students who have graduated from a four-year college program and are pursuing part-time or full-time graduate studies in a field related to sign language or the deaf community, or a deaf graduate student who is developing a special project on one of these topics is eligible. Contact National Association of the Deaf, 814 Thayer Avenue, Silver Spring, MD 20910-4500; 301-587-1788; TTY: 301-587-1789; {www.nad.org/StokoeSch.html}, {e-mail: nadinfo@nad.org}.

More Money for Deaf Women

Scholarships are awarded to prelingually deaf or hard-of-hearing students who use speech and speechreading to communicate, and who are attending or have been admitted to a college or university program that primarily enrolls students with normal hearing. Applicants must have had a hearing loss since birth or before acquiring language with a 60dB or greater loss in the better ear in the speech frequencies of 500, 1000, and 2000 Hz.

Only the first 500 requests for applications will be accepted. Applications must be requested between November 1st and December 1st. Contact Alexander Graham Bell Association for the Deaf, 3417 Volta Place, N.W., Washington, DC 20007-2778; 202-337-5220 (Voice and TTY); {www.agbell.org/}.

$500 for Communications Women in Maine

This program is open to women of any age who are residents of Maine, will be enrolled in a communications or mass communications related college program. Financial need, academic achievement, career goals, and interest in communications are the primary consideration. Contact Maine Media Women, Attn: Katy Perry, Scholarship Committee, 9 Middle Street, Hallowell, ME 04347; 207-626-3242.

Money For Graphic Communication Majors

Over 300 awards of up to $1,000 are available annually to students who wish to pursue a career in graphic communications. High school seniors and current college students are eligible to apply. All students must be attending or planning on attending college full-time. Academic achievement and career goals are the primary considerations, although references and extracurricular activities are also considered. All awards are renewable provided a 3.0 GPA or above is maintained. Winners also receive a complimentary membership in the Graphic Arts Technical Foundation. Contact National Scholarship Trust Fund of the Graphic Arts, Attn: Scholarship Competition, 200 Deer Run Road, Sewickley PA 15143-2600; 412-741-6860; 800-910-GATF; {www.gatf.org}, {e-mail: info@gatf.org}.

Up to $5,000 for Desert Shield/Desert Storm Veterans and their Spouses and Children

This program provides financial assistance to Veterans of Desert Storm/Desert Shield. Highest preference is given to the children and spouses of men and women who lost their lives while on active duty in these campaigns. At the time of this writing, the schools participating in this program are: University of Arizona, Baylor University, Florida State University, George Mason University, University of

Houston, Loyola University of New Orleans, Norfolk State University, Northeastern University, University of Oklahoma, Rice University, Roosevelt University of Chicago, Saint John's University, San Diego State University, Seton Hall University, Southern Methodist University, Texas A&M University, Texas Christian University, Texas Tech University, University of Texas at Austin, and Villanova University. You MUST apply directly with your school; Mobil Corp. does not accept direct applications for this program. Contact The Mobil Corporation Desert Shield/Desert Storm Scholarship Program, Mobil Corporation, 3225 Gallows Road, Fairfax, VA 22037-0001.

$1,000 for Naval Academy Children and Women

Eligible to apply for these scholarships are children of active, retired, or deceased; Navy or Marine Corps officers or enlisted personnel who are or were permanently stationed at the United States Naval Academy complex, children of current full-year members of the Naval Academy Women's Club, children of civilian employees of the Naval Academy and any current member of the Naval Academy Women's Club.

Applicants must be in their senior year of high school, or have graduated from high school, and plan on attending full-time at any 2-year or 4-year college or university, any art school or any technical/trade school. Contact Naval Academy Women's Club, P.O. Box 826, Annapolis, MD 21404-0826.

Money for Future Homemakers

The Future Homemakers of America offers members a large variety of scholarship and grant programs. Most are based on a combination of academic achievement, potential for success, community service, volunteer work, service to FHA, and career goals. Most programs are applied for directly from your local FHA chapter, please check with your local chapter for further information. Contact Future Homemakers of America, Inc., 1910 Association Drive, Reston, VA 20191-1584; 703-476-4900; 800-234-4425; {www.fhahero.org}; {e-mail: natlhdqtrs@fhahero.org}.

Red River Valley Fighter Pilots Association Scholarships

This scholarship is available to the dependent sons, daughters and spouses of any member of the U.S. Armed Forces who is listed as killed in action, missing in action, or prisoner of war from any combat situation involving our military since August, 1965. Any dependent child or spouse of any military aircrew member who was killed as a result of performing aircrew duties during non-combat missions and the dependents of any current or deceased Red River Valley Association member are also eligible to apply.

The program has paid out over 735 scholarships worth over $1,200,000 total since its inception. Individual awards vary depending upon the financial need of the applicant and the cost of their chosen college or university. Academic achievement, financial need, community service, and extracurricular activities are the primary considerations.

Contact Red River Valley Fighter Pilots Association, Red River Valley Association Foundation, c/o Al Bache, P.O. Box 1551, North Fork CA 93643; 209-877-5000, {www.eos.net/rrva/}; {e-mail: afbridger@aol.com}.

Money for Smart Women

American Mensa offers a variety of essay-based competitions and academic-achievement scholarship programs available through local chapters. Most programs are available to non-members. Please contact your local Mensa chapter (a list of chapters is available at the website) for more information.

Contact American Mensa, 1229 Corporate Drive West, Arlington, TX 76006-6103; 817-607-0060; {www.us.mensa.org}.

Money for Delta Gamma Women

The Delta Gamma Foundation offers scholarships for undergraduate work, fellowships for graduate study, and loans for any form of higher education beyond the sophomore year. They also offer several programs that specifically target blind members of Delta Gamma and members who are pursuing a career in the sciences. Undergraduate members with 3.0 or above GPA's are eligible to apply for grants of up to $1,000. Graduate members are eligible to apply for up to $2,500.

Contact Delta Gamma Foundation, 3250 Riverside Dr., Columbus, OH 43221-0397; 614-481-8169; {www.deltagamma.org/found/scholar.htm}.

Up to $1,000 for Slovenian Women's Union Members

Slovenian Women's Union members, who have been members for at least three years, are eligible to apply for five different scholarships awarded annually. Must plan on attending college full-time. Financial need, academic achievement, community service, and participation in the local organization are the main considerations. Please contact your local chapter for application information. Contact Slovenian Women's Union of America, 52 Oakridge Drive, Marquette, MI 49855.

Up to $8000 for Nebraska Women in English

The Norma Ross Walter Scholarship is offered to current high school seniors and recent high school graduates who live in Nebraska and plan on majoring in English. This scholarship is renewable for four years, and is paid out at $2,000 a year, provided a minimum GPA of 3.0 in English is maintained. Must be graduating or have already graduated from any Nebraska high school. Information on this program should be available at your guidance counselor's office. Contact Willa Cather Foundation, 326 N. Webster, Red Cloud, NE 68970; 402-746-2653.

At least $9,000 for International Women in Education

The International Teacher Education Scholarship is open to single women under 30 years old who are from countries OTHER THAN the United States, and wish to receive teacher training in the United States. Alpha Delta Kappa members are not eligible for this program.

After receiving the scholarship, the winner is expected to return to their home country to work in education for at least one year, within three years of receiving the scholarship. Contact Alpha Delta Kappa, 1615 W. 92nd St., Kansas City, MO 64114; 816-363-5525.

$1,000 for Jewish Women in Los Angeles

The Women Helping Women program offers up to $1,000 a year to female residents of Los Angeles County who are entering or returning to school. Married or single women are eligible, women who are returning to school after a break and/or have children are given priority. Primary consideration is financial need. Contact National Council of Jewish Women, Los Angeles Chapter, 543 N. Fairfax Ave., Los Angeles, CA 90036-1715; 213-655-3807.

Up to $2,500 for Geological Women

The Geological Society of America offers a variety of scholarships and research grants to undergraduate students. Both members and nonmembers of the Society are eligible to apply. Preference for women studying at universities in the south-central and midwestern region of the United States. Must be studying geology or earth-science related majors. Contact Geological Society of America, 3300 Penrose Pl., Boulder, CO 80301-0140; 303-447-2020; {www.geosociety.org}.

Up to $300 for Phi Gamma Nu Women

Members of Phi Gamma Nu are eligible to apply for scholarships of up to $300. Open only to undergraduate students who are studying business or related majors. Also have small loans available (usually around $200 per year).

Contact Phi Gamma Nu, 6745 Cheryl Ann Dr., Seven Hills, OH 44131; 216-524-0934.

Money for Washington Accounting Women

The Mary M. Fraijo Scholarship is offered to women who live in the state of Washington and are part-time or full-time undergraduate or graduate students in accounting. Applicants must have completed at least 60 credit hours towards their degree, but do not need to be a member of the American Society of Women Accountants. Primary considerations are academic achievement, financial need and references.

Contact American Society of Women Accountants, Inland Northwest, Chapter No. 4, Attn: Leslie Miller, P.O. Box 2903, Spokane, WA 99220-2903.

Up to $2,000 for Hotel Women

The American Express Scholarship Program is offered to students who are currently working at least 20 hours a week

at any AH&MA member hotel or resort. Dependent children of current employees are also eligible to apply. Part-time and full-time students attending either a two-year or four-year college or university are eligible to apply. Must be majoring in hotel or hospitality related majors. Work experience, financial need, academic achievement, community service and career goals are the primary considerations. Contact American Hotel Foundation, 1201 New York Ave., NW, Suite 600, Washington, DC 20005-3931.

Up to $4,500 for African-American Colorado Women

Current African-American high school seniors who plan on attending any college in Colorado are eligible to apply. Must have been a Colorado resident for at least five years and have never enrolled in college. Financial need is the primary consideration, although academic achievement and references are also considered. Contact Sachs Foundation,

90 S. Cascade Ave., Suite 1410, Colorado Springs, CO 80903; {www.frii.com/~sachs}.

Money for Welding Women

Any student intending to pursue a career in welding technology is eligible to apply for the American Welding Society's District Scholarship program. These renewable scholarship awards may be used at any school in the United States with a welding or materials joining program, including technical/vocational schools. Financial need is the primary consideration. Applications are available at the website. Contact The American Welding Society, 550 NW LeJeune Rd., Miami, FL 33126; 800-443-9353; {www.aws.org}.

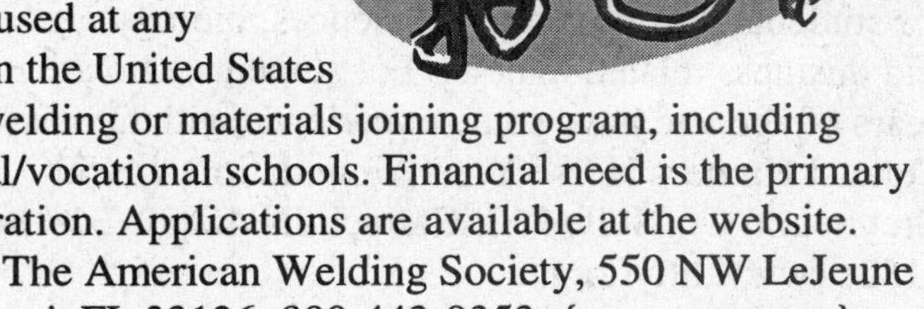

$500 for Homeschooled Californians

To be eligible to apply, you must be a resident of California who has been homeschooled for at least 4 years, your parents must be a member of the CHEA. Contact Christian Home Educators Association of California, Inc., Attn: Scholarship Committee, P.O. Box 2009, Norwalk, CA 90651-2009.

Money for Horse Racers

Have any experience with harness racing? Then the Harness Horse Youth Foundation may have some money you can apply for! They offer several scholarship programs for students pursuing animal sciences, biology, agricultural, and business related majors. For students who are under 24 years of age and have some experience with harness racing. Contact Harness Horse Youth Foundation, 14950 Greyhound Ct., Suite 210, Carmel, IN 46032; 317-848-5132; {www.hhyf.org}.

Up to $2,000 for California Real Estate Students

For current California students enrolled at any California two-year or four-year degree who plan on a career in real estate. Acceptable majors include but are not necessarily limited to: real estate brokerage, real estate finance, real estate management, real estate law and related areas. Also, current realtors in California who wish to pursue advanced education or degrees are eligible to apply. Contact California Association of Realtors, 525 S. Virgil Ave., Los Angeles, CA 90020; 213-739-8200.

Up to $2,500 for Architectural Women in California

The Association offers California women who are either residents of California or non-residents attending school in California and are studying architecture the opportunity to apply for several scholarships that they offer. Must be a current undergraduate student. Contact Association for Women in Architecture, 2550 Beverly Blvd., Los Angeles, CA 90057; 213-389-6490.

Up To $3,000 If You Live Near A Tyson Food Plant

If you live near a Tyson Foods plant and are a full-time undergraduate student with at least a 2.5 GPA, you may be eligible to apply for up to $3,000! Those majoring in agribusiness, agricultural related majors, computer science, and other majors are eligible for this renewable scholarship. Contact Tyson Foundation, Inc., 2210 W. Oaklawn Dr., Springdale, AR 72762; 501-290-4955.

Up to $2,000 for Connecticut Construction Women

For Connecticut residents pursuing a construction-related career. Primary considerations for this renewable award are academic achievement, personal statement, financial need and an interview. Contact Connecticut Building, Congress Scholarship Fund, 2600 Dixwell Ave., Hamden, CT 06514-1833; {www.constructioncorner.com/cbc/}.

Up to $1,500 for DECA Women

For current members of DECA who are planning on studying marketing, merchandising, or management. Members of the Future Business Leaders of America are also eligible to apply for some of the awards. Contact your local DECA chapter for further information, or the website. Contact DECA - Distributive Education Club of America, 1908 Association Drive, Reston, VA 20191-4013; 703-860-5000; {www.deca.org}.

MONEY FOR PETROLEUM WOMEN

The Desk and Derrick Educational Trust offers women in the United States and Canada who are studying business, engineering, natural resources or technology related majors and intend to pursue a career in the petroleum industry an opportunity to apply for $1,000. Financial need and academic achievement are the primary considerations. For use during your junior, senior, or graduate years. Contact Desk and Derrick Educational Trust, 4823 S. Sheridan, Suite 308A, Tulsa, OK 74145; 918-622-1675.

Up to $10,000 for Executive Women

Executive Women International offers over 100 scholarship awards ranging from $100-$10,000 every year to women who wish to pursue a four-year degree in business or related majors. Must apply while you are still a high school junior and plan on attending a four-year college. Awards are renewable. Contact Executive Women International, 515 S. 700 East, Suite 2E, Salt Lake City, UT 84102; 801-355-2800.

Money for Ham Radio Women

Do you have an interest in ham radios? Have you an amateur or general radio license? Then you might want to check in with the American Radio Relay League. They offer a large number of different scholarships for amateur radio operators, most of which have very few restrictions! Contact American Radio Relay League, 225 Main St., Newington, CT 06111; 203-666-1541; {www.arrl.org}.

$500 for Kansas Communications and Journalism Women

Kansas Press Women has several scholarships available to women who are residents of Kansas and are about to enter their senior year in college. Must be a journalism or communications major and studying at a college in Kansas. Preference is given to students with a strong interest in writing. Contact Kansas Press Women, Inc., 115 N. Pinecrest, Wichita, KS 67208; 316-268-6367.

$3,000 for Speaking Women

For current full-time junior, senior and graduate students with a strong interest in public speaking. Applications and information are available at the website. Contact National Speakers Association, 1500 S. Priest Dr., Tempe, AZ 85281; {www.nsaspeaker.org}.

Up to $1,000 for Dental Women

The American Association of Women Dentists has several academic achievement-based scholarships available to current junior and senior dental students who are members of the Association. Contact American Association of Women Dentists, 401 N. Michigan Ave., Chicago, IL 60611; 312-527-6757.

Up to $10,000 for Heating, Refrigerating and Air Conditioning

For students studying electrical engineering, electronics, heating, air conditioning, refrigeration technology, or other majors with intention on pursuing a career in the heating, refrigeration and/or air conditioning industry. Must have at least two years left before graduation, a 3.0 GPA or above, attending a ABET-accredited school, and financial need. Contact American Society of Heating, Refrigerating and Air Conditioning Engineers, Inc., 1791 Tullie Circle, NE, Atlanta, GA 30329-1683; 404-636-8400; {www.ashrae.org}.

Up to $3,000 for Logistics

For full-time undergraduate students pursuing a logistics or related major at any four-year college. Must have at least a 3.0 GPA. Contact SOLE-The International Logistics Society, 8100 Professional Pl., Suite 211, New Carrollton, MD 20785; {www.sole.org}.

$1,500 for Safety Engineers

Two awards annually for student members of the American Society of Safety Engineers. Must be attending college full-time with a minimum GPA of 3.0, studying a safety engineering related major, and plan on pursuing a career in safety engineering. Contact American Society of Safety Engineers Foundation, 1800 E. Oakton, Des Plaines, IL 60018; 847-699-2929.

$1,000 for Food Technology

Current junior and senior students in food science, food engineering, and food technology majors with outstanding academic achievement and a strong desire to pursue a career in food science or food engineering are eligible to apply for a variety of scholarships offered by the Institute.

Direct application is not available, you must have your department chairman or other school administrator recommend you for an award. Contact Institute of Food

Technologists, 221 N. LaSalle St., Suite 300, Chicago, IL 60601; 312-782-8424.

Money for Lutheran Women in Mental Retardation

Interested in a career in service to the mentally disabled? Bethesda Lutheran Homes offers a large variety of scholarships to students in social services, nursing, legal services, special education, health administration, education, therapy, and related majors. Must be an active, communicant member of a Lutheran church. Must be at least a college sophomore.

Please call or write for more information about available programs. Contact Bethesda Lutheran Homes and Services, Inc., National Christian Resource Center, 700 Hoffman Dr., Watertown, WI 53094-6294; 920-261-3050; {www.bethesdainfo.org}.

Money for Michigan Nurses

Up to $500 is available for sophomores, juniors, and seniors who are residents of Michigan and are attending a college in Michigan. Must be pursuing a nursing degree and have at least a 2.0 GPA. Preference is given to students who plan on working as a nurse in Michigan upon graduation. Contact Michigan League for Nursing, 33150 Schoolcraft Rd., Suite 201, Livonia, MI 48150-1646.

Up to $1,000 for Black Nurses

Members of the National Black Nurses Association are eligible to apply for several scholarships that average $1,000. Must have completed at least one year of school at time of application and be an African American. Primary considerations are academic achievement, potential for success, references, and involvement in the African American community.

When requesting information, please include a SASE with two stamps on it. Contact National Black Nurses Association, Inc., 1511 K St., NW, Suite 415, Washington, DC 20005.

Up to $2,500 for Oncology Nurses

A variety of scholarships are available to current registered nurses who wish to further their education and pursue careers as oncology nurses. Some awards are specifically for minority students, others are for current oncology nurses who have contributed to the field of oncology nursing. Some of the programs require a $5 application fee. Contact Oncology Nursing Foundation, 501 Holiday Dr., Pittsburgh, PA 15220; 412-921-7373; {www.ons.org}.

Up to $1,000 for Jewelry and Gems

The Gemological Institute of America offers students over the age of 17 a variety of different scholarship programs. All require that the applicant be pursuing a gemology-related major and plan on pursuing a career in the gemology field. Must be attending or planning on attending a school with a Gemological Institute accredited program of study.

Contact Gemological Institute of America, 5345 Armada Dr., Carlsbad, CA 92008-4698; 760-603-4005.

Up to $5000 for Composers

The Society offers a variety of contests and competitions for original compositions and musical scores. Some programs are available only to members of the Society. Most require a taped performance of your original music.

Contact American Society of Composers, Authors, and Publishers Foundation, ASCAP Building, One Lincoln Plaza, New York, NY 10023-2399; 212-621-6327; {www.ascap.com}.

Up to $3,000 for Parapsychology Students

For undergraduate and graduate students who can show a very strong and serious interest in parapsychology through coursework, research, essays, term papers and dissertations. Students who have only a minor interest are not eligible. Contact Parapsychology Foundation, 228 E. 71st St., New York, NY 10021; 212-628-1550; {www.parapsychology.org}.

Up to $3,000 for Christians

Several grants are available to undergraduate and graduate students who are pursuing a Master of Divinity degree at any accredited theological or seminary school. Students from midwestern states and those who plan on serving in a local church ministry are given preference. Ph.D. students are not eligible. Must be between the ages of 25 and 55 and have a strong Christian faith. Contact Opal Dancey Memorial Foundation, 45 South St., Croswell, MI 48422; 810-679-4729.

Up to $3,000 for Travel Agents

The American Society of Travel Agents has a large variety of scholarship programs available for undergraduate students pursuing a career in the travel and tourism industry. Some of the scholarships are restricted to women re-entering the work force after a few year's break, some are restricted to members only, others are open to current high school seniors and college undergraduates. Some of the programs are available to students attending an accredited travel school.

Please check the website or write for more information. Contact American Society of Travel Agents, Scholarship Foundation, 1101 King St., Suite 200, Alexandria, VA 22314-2187; 703-739-2782; {www.astanet.com}.

Up to $4,000 for Physical Therapy and Occupational Therapy Women

Allied Resources offers current college juniors, seniors and graduate students who have no more than two years left to complete their physical therapy or occupational therapy degree up to $4,000. All recipients must agree to work through Allied Resources after graduation. Please include a SASE with requests for information. Contact Allied Resources, 810 Regal Drive, Huntsville, AL 35801; 800-217-7870.

Money for Native American Single Parents

The Schuyler Meyer Jr. Scholarship is for single parents who have at least one child under the age of 18, are attending college full-time, and have at least a 2.0 GPA. Must be at least 25% Native American or Alaskan American (Inuit) and have tribal recognition. Open to students studying any major. Financial need is a primary consideration. Contact American Indian Science and Engineering Society, 5661 Airport Blvd., Boulder, CO 80301-2339; 303-939-0023.

Up to $2,500 for Marine Veterans

The Fifth Marine Division Scholarship is available to current high school seniors and college undergraduate students who are children of any Fifth Marine Division veteran. The veteran must be a member of the Fifth Marine Division Association. Financial need is the primary consideration — total family income must be below $45,000 in order to be considered, although academic achievement is also considered. Contact Marine Corps Scholarship Foundation, P.O. Box 3008, Princeton, NJ 08543-3008; 800-292-7777; {www.marine-scholars.org}.

Money for Civitan Members

Members of Civitan who are current college juniors, seniors or graduate students are eligible to apply for a variety of local and national scholarships offered through Civitan. Most programs are based primarily on academic achievement and community service.

Please check with your local chapter for information, or the website below. When writing for information, please include a SASE with three stamps on it. Contact Civitan International Foundation, P.O. Box 130744, Birmingham, AL 35213-0744; {www.civitan.org}.

Money for DeMolay Members

Current and former members of DeMolay are eligible to apply. There are no restrictions on what major you are studying. Scholarships are based primarily upon financial need, academic achievement, character and community service. Award amounts vary, but on average are $800. DeMolay members should also check with their local chapter for local scholarships. Contact DeMolay Foundation, 10200 N. Executive Hills Blvd., Kansas City, MO 64153; {www.demolay.org}.

Money for Non-Commissioned Officers Association Members

The Non-Commissioned Officers Association offers a variety of programs to its members and their children. Of particular interest is the Betsy Ross Educational Fund, which awards $250 to members who wish to take classes to improve their job skills. Other scholarships are available to spouses and children of members.

Please include a SASE with requests for information. Contact Non Commissioned Officers Association, P.O. Box 33610, San Antonio, TX 78265-3610; 610-653-6161.

Money for Girl's Club Members

Teenagers between the ages of 14 and 18 who are members of the Girl's Club for at least one year are eligible to apply for scholarships ranging between $2,000 and $8,000. Must apply for this scholarship through your local Girl's Club chapter — direct application is not available. Must have at least a 3.0 GPA in high school. Academic achievement, community service, and leadership potential are the primary consideration. Contact Reader's Digest Foundation, 1230 W. Peachtree St., NW, Atlanta, GA 30309.

Money for Royal Neighbors

Current high school students who have been members of the Royal Neighbors of America are eligible to apply for a variety of scholarships offered worth up to $2,000. Must be under 20 years of age. Primary considerations are academic achievement, service to Royal Neighbors, and community service. Contact Royal Neighbors of America, 230 16th St., Rock Island, IL 61201-8645; 309-788-4561.

Money for Maine Women

The Maine Community Foundation has a variety of programs available to current high school seniors and college undergraduates who are residents of Maine. Most require that you attend school in Maine. Applications are sent to local high schools and colleges every year, so check with your guidance counselor or financial aid office first for information. Contact Maine Community Foundation, P.O. Box 148, Ellsworth, ME 04605; 207-667-9735.

Up to $10,000 for Non-Traditional Michigan Women

Michigan women who have been out of school for at least four years and plan on attending any campus of the University of Michigan are eligible to apply. Each year, they offer up to 35 scholarships ranging from $1,000 to $10,000. Financial need is the primary consideration. Contact Center for the Education of Women, 330 E. Liberty St., Ann Arbor, MI 48104-2289; 734-998-7210.

More Money for Hawaiian Women

Female college juniors, seniors, and graduate students who are residents of Hawaii and have a strong interest in women's studies and commitment to serving women are eligible to apply. Must be attending a four-year college.

Contact Kilohana United Methodist Church, 1536 Kamole St., Honolulu, HI 96821.

$1,000 for Sculpture

For students who have created figurative or representational sculpture. Must include up to 10 photos of your work with application. Please include a SASE with requests for information. Contact National Sculpture Society, 1177 Avenue of the Americas, 15th Floor, New York, NY 10036; 212-764-5645.

Money for Vermont Women

The Vermont Student Assistance Corporation manages a large variety of scholarship offers for women (and men) who are residents of Vermont. Awards range from $500 to over $5,000. Requirements vary greatly for individual programs, please contact them and request their free scholarship booklet for Vermont residents. Contact Vermont Student Assistance Corporation, P.O. Box 2000, Winooski, VT 05404-2000; 802-655-9602; {www.vsac.org}.

Money for Louisiana Residents

A variety of scholarships and loans are available for Louisiana residents who are attending college or university in Louisiana. For undergraduate students only. Academic achievement is the primary consideration. Contact Willis and Mildred Pellerin Foundation, P.O. Box 400, Kenner, LA 70063-0400.

Money for Non-Traditional Native Americans

The Association offers several programs to assist Native American single parents or displaced homemakers. Awards are intended to assist with the costs of child care, transportation, and basic living expenses while finishing your education. Primary consideration is financial need. Must have either a certificate of degree of Indian blood or a Tribal enrollment card. Contact Association on American Indian Affairs, Inc., P.O. Box 268, Sisseton, SD 57262; 605-698-3998.

Up to $1000 for Lutheran Women

The Adult Degree Completion Scholarship Program is available to Lutheran women who are over age 25, full members of the Aid Association, and have an insurance policy or annuity in their name through the Association. Must be pursuing your first associate's or bachelor's degree.

Part time students are eligible to apply, however the award will be reduced. Contact Aid Association for Lutherans, 4321 N. Ballard Rd., Appleton, WI 54919-0001; 414-734-5721; {www.aal.org}.

MONEY FOR FLIGHT ATTENDANTS

Members and their dependent children are eligible to apply for this scholarship program. Must write an essay, topic changes yearly. Also considered is academic achievement and financial need. Contact Association of Flight Attendants, P.O. Box 212, Warrenton, VA 22186.

Money for New Hampshire Women

Residents of New Hampshire are eligible to apply for a large variety of programs offered through the Foundation. Only one application needs to be filled out for consideration of all programs that you may be eligible for. Some programs are restricted to handicapped students, others to those entering the Protestant ministry. For all programs, academic achievement and financial need is considered. Must sign an affidavit certifying that you do not smoke or drink alcohol. Undergraduate and graduate students at both 2 and 4 year vocational schools, colleges and universities are eligible to apply.

Contact New Hampshire Charitable Foundation, 37 Pleasant St., Concord, NH 03301-4005; 603-225-6641; {www.nhcf.org}.

Money for Asian Pacific Women in Los Angeles

The Asian Pacific Women's Network offers a variety of scholarship and support services to Asian Pacific women who live in the Los Angeles area and surrounding counties and wish to increase their job skills and educational background. Women returning to school after a break due to child rearing or financial difficulties, immigrant women, and refugees are especially encouraged to apply. Financial need is the primary consideration. Contact Asian Pacific Women's Network, P.O. Box 86995, Los Angeles, CA 90086; 213-891-6040; 909-596-5331.

Up to $1,500 for Chinese American Women

Current college juniors, seniors and graduate students of Chinese-American background who have at least a 3.0 GPA are eligible to apply for this scholarship. Please include a SASE with requests for information.

Contact Chinese-American Educational Foundation, P.O. Box 2217, Sunnyvale, CA 94087-0217.

MONEY FOR SOUTHERN CALIFORNIAN WOMEN

Current sophomore, junior or senior women with a 3.0 or above GPA and are attending any college in southern California are eligible to apply. Application is done through your financial aid office — you must have your financial aid officer nominate you. Direct application is not available.

Contact College Women's Club of Pasadena, Scholarship Foundation, P.O. Box 452, Pasadena, CA 91102.

Up to $2,000 for Short People

Students who are less than 4 feet 10 inches tall, along with their parents and children (regardless of height), are eligible to apply for several different scholarship programs offered by the Foundation. Current high school seniors and college undergraduates are eligible. Academic achievement, financial need, and leadership abilities or potential are the primary considerations. Contact Billy Barty Foundation, 929 W. Olive Avenue, Suite C, Burbank, CA 91506; 800-891-4022; 818-953-5410.

Money for African American Women

African American women who have completed at least one semester or two quarters of undergraduate studies with at least a 2.0 GPA are eligible to apply. Financial need is the primary consideration. Direct application is not available, you must be nominated by a member of the National Association of Colored Women's Clubs. Contact your local Club chapter for further information and to find a potential sponsor to nominate you.

NOTE: This award is offered only during even-numbered years. Contact National Association of Colored Women's Clubs, 5808 16th St., NW, Washington, DC 20011-2898; 202-726-2044.

Money for Baptist Acteens

Female high school seniors who are Southern Baptists and active in Acteens are eligible to apply. Primary considerations are character, church service, academic achievement, an essay and references. Amount awarded varies depending upon funding availability. Contact Woman's Missionary Union Foundation, P.O. Box 11346, Birmingham, AL 35202-1346; 205-408-5525.

$1,000 for African American Church of Christ Women

Undergraduate and graduate African American women who are members of the Church of Christ and are residents of southern California are eligible to apply. Priority is given to non-traditional women who are returning to college after a break, making a mid-life career change, or starting their college career after age 25. Contact United Church of Christ, Southern California Conference, 2401 N. Lake Ave., Altadena, CA 91001; 626-798-8082.

Up to $5,000 for Rhode Island Women

Rhode Island residents who are current college sophomores and juniors are eligible to apply for the Michael P. Metcalf Memorial Grants. These grants are to support or subsidize non-traditional educational opportunities, such as traveling for educational purposes, public service programs, etc., so long as the experience's primary purpose is to expand your horizons, perspective, and personal growth. Financial need must be established. Primary considerations are thoughtfulness of the proposal, creativity and motivation, and initiative. Contact Rhode Island Foundation, 70 Elm St., Providence, RI 02903; 401-274-4564.

$1000 for Lesbians in Louisiana

Louisiana residents who are affirmed and open Lesbians or Gays and over the age of 17 are eligible to apply. Must be attending any college or university at least three-quarter time. Community service, service to the Gay and Lesbian community, activism, leadership ability or potential and financial need are the primary considerations.

Contact Parents, Families and Friends of Lesbians and Gays, New Orleans Chapter, ATTN: Scholarship Committee, P.O. Box 15515, New Orleans, LA 70175; 504-895-3936; {www.gayneworleans.org/pflag/scholar.htm}.

$1000 for Asian Pacific American Women

Asian American women, including Chinese, Japanese, Filipino, Singaporean, Thai, Vietnamese, and Cambodian women who are entering their first year of college are eligible to apply. Current high school seniors or recent high school graduates must have at least a 3.0 GPA in high school. Older women will be considered based upon community service and financial need.

Contact Organization of Chinese Americans, Inc., 1001 Connecticut Ave., NW, Suite 707, Washington, DC 20036; 202-223-5000; {www.oca.org}.

Money for New Mexico Women

The Albuquerque Community Foundation offers a variety of scholarships. Current high school seniors and undergraduate students who are residents of New Mexico are eligible to apply. For all programs available, financial need is the primary consideration. Amount awarded is based upon need.

Contact Albuquerque Community Foundation, P.O. Box 36960, Albuquerque, NM 87176-6960; 505-883-6240.

$2,500 FOR HOME AND WORKSHOP WRITERS

Current high school seniors, college undergraduates, and graduate level students who have a strong interest in pursuing a career in the "do-it-yourself" market as a writer or journalist are eligible to apply, regardless of declared major.

Contact National Association of Home and Workshop Writers, c/o Frank Brugmeier Company, 7501 Woodstream Terrace, North Syracuse, NY 13212-1921; 315-458-0291.

Money for Massachusetts Baptist Women

Women who are residents of Massachusetts and members of an American Baptist Church in Massachusetts are eligible to apply. Must intend on rendering Christian Service in their chosen major or career, although there is no restriction on what major you may be studying. Primary considerations are academic achievement, financial need, dedication, character and values.

Contact American Baptist Women's Ministries of Massachusetts, 20 Milton St., Dedham, MA 02026-2967; 617-320-8100.

$1,500 for New York Women in Communications

Full-time undergraduate and graduate level women who are residents of New York and are studying communications, journalism, speech, broadcasting, and marketing are eligible to apply. Must have at least a 3.0 GPA and be attending a college or university in the New York City region and surrounding counties. Primary consideration is academic achievement and potential for success. Contact New York Women in Communications, Inc., 355 Lexington Ave., 17th Floor, New York, NY 10017-6603; 212-661-4737.

Up to $1,500 for Theater Women

Women who have outstanding dramatic talent and need financial assistance to continue their education are eligible to apply. Although preference is given to residents of Massachusetts, there is no restriction on residency. Applications must include recommendations from member(s) of the theatrical profession. Only applications from serious theater arts students of the highest talent will be considered — those with only a passing interest in dramatic arts and theater are not eligible. Contact Lotta M. Crabtree Trusts, 11 Beacon St., Suite 1110, Boston, MA 02108; 617-742-5920.

$1000 for Sigma Alpha Iota Women

Sigma Alpha Iota, a national organization for women musicians, offers a variety of scholarships and other support programs to its members. The Undergraduate Performance Scholarship is for outstanding performances in vocal and instrumental music, the String Performance

Scholarship is for outstanding string performances, and the Scholarship for the Visually Impaired is for members of the organization who are legally blind and are enrolled full-time in a music-related major. Contact Sigma Alpha Iota Philanthropies, Inc., 34 Wall St., Suite 515, Asheville, NC 28801-2710; 828-251-0606; {www.sai-national.org}.

Up to $2,000 for Jewelry Women

Women who are pursuing a jewelry-related career and are enrolled in a program that will enable them to achieve this goal are eligible to apply. Selection is based primarily upon skill in designing or creating unique pieces of jewelry, as determined by submitted photos or drawings of your work. Academic achievement, work experience, recommendations and financial need are also considered. Contact Women's Jewelry Association, 333B Route 46 W., Suite B201, Fairfield, NJ 07004; 201-575-7190.

$1,500 for Minnesota Nurses

College juniors and seniors who are either residents of Minnesota or attending college in Minnesota are eligible to apply for these scholarships which are funded by the American Cancer Society. Selection is based on an essay related to the nurse's role in caring for patients with cancer, research or public education on cancer, or a cancer-related subject of your choice. To apply, you do not need to be actually involved in oncology nursing or necessarily plan on a career as an oncology nurse. Contact Minnesota League for Nursing, P.O. Box 24713, Edina, MN 55424; 612-829-5891.

Money for Holistic Women

Nursing students and currently licensed nurses already in the workforce who have a strong interest in furthering their education in holistic health care or alternative health techniques are eligible to apply. Must have been a member of the Association for at least six months. Current nursing students must have at least a 3.0 GPA, financial need and career goals are also considered. Nurses who are already in the workforce are considered primarily on their work experience and interest in holistic health.

Contact American Holistic Nurses Association, 2733 E. Lakin Dr., P.O. Box 2130, Flagstaff, AZ 86003-2130; 520-526-2196.

$1,000 for California Nurses

Women who are already licensed Registered Nurses working in California and wish to return to school to pursue a B.S.N or graduate degree program are eligible to apply. Must attend school at least half-time and plan on finishing the degree within five years. If the winner doesn't finish their degree within five years, the scholarship reverts to a loan and must be repaid. References, commitment to nursing, work experience and financial need are the primary considerations. This award is renewable yearly depending upon academic achievement. Contact California Nurses Association, 1145 Market St., Suite 1100, San Francisco, CA 94103; 415-864-4141.

Money for Hispanic Nurses

Hispanic members of the Association who are pursuing diploma or certificate programs in nursing or associate or bachelor's degrees in nursing are eligible to apply. Academic achievement and financial need are the primary considerations. Contact National Association of Hispanic Nurses, 1501 16th St., NW, Washington, DC 20036; 202-387-2477.

Money for Wisconsin Nurses

Residents of Wisconsin who are currently enrolled in any college in Wisconsin and have completed at least half of the requirements needed for their degree are eligible to apply. Applications are available from the financial aid offices at all Wisconsin colleges, please do not write to the address below requesting an application as they do not send applications directly to students. Contact Wisconsin League for Nursing, 2121 E. Newport Ave., Milwaukee, WI 53211; 414-332-6271.

UP TO $2,000 FOR TRAVEL AND TOURISM WOMEN

The Foundation offers a variety of scholarships to travel and tourism students. For all programs, you must be enrolled full-time in a two or four-year school, have at least a 3.0 GPA, and be majoring in travel and tourism, hotel management, restaurant management, or a related major. You must be intending to pursue a career in the travel or tourism industry. Contact National Tourism Foundation, 5546 E. Main St, P.O. Box 3071, Lexington, KY 40596-3071; 606-226-4444.

$1,000 or More for Women Grocers

Members of the Women Grocer's of America, along with their children, spouses, employees, and grandchildren are eligible to apply. Must be a college sophomore or above with at least a 2.0 GPA enrolled in a food marketing, food service technology, business administration, business management, agribusiness or related major and plan on pursuing a career in the grocery industry. Hotel/restaurant management and public health majors are not eligible to apply.

Contact Women Grocers of America, 1825 Samuel Morse Dr., Reston, VA 20190-5317; 703-437-5300.

$2,500 for Diabetes Women

Women (and men!) who have Type 1 Diabetes and are planning on attending full-time any public or private undergraduate school in the United States are eligible to apply. The primary considerations for this award are outstanding service to the diabetes community, promotion of diabetes awareness in the community, or having overcome personal obstacles related to your diabetes, academic achievement, essays, and recommendations. Contact Lilly For Learning, Diabetes Scholarship Program, Eli Lilly and Company, Lilly Corporate Center, Drop Code 1625, Indianapolis, IN 46285; 800-88LILLY; {www.lilly.com/diabetes.scholarship/index.htm}.

Up to $10,000 for Government and Public Policy Women

This year-long fellowship program places women graduate students in Congressional offices to encourage more effective participation by women in policy formation at all levels. Preference is given to women who are studying government, public policy, women's issues or social sciences. Must be a U.S. citizen or legal resident. Send self-addressed, stamped business-sized envelope for information. Contact Women's Research And Education Institute, Congressional Fellowships for Women and Public Policy, 1750 New York Ave., NW; Suite 350, Washington DC 20006; 202-628-0444.

Up to $2,500 for Jewish Women in Washington, DC

The Irene Stambler Vocational Opportunities Grant Program is open to Jewish women who are residents of the Washington metropolitan area and need to improve their earning power because of divorce, separation or death of their spouses. Grants may be used to complete an educational or vocational program or start or expand a small business.

Contact Jewish Social Service Agency Of Metropolitan Washington, 6123 Montrose Road, Rockville, MD 20852; 301-881-3700.

Money for Grand Rapids, Michigan Women

Various scholarship programs are available to female residents of Grand Rapids, Michigan. Preference is given to students currently attending or planning on attending Grand Rapids Community College and intend on transferring to the University of Michigan upon graduation from GRCC.

Contact The Grand Rapids Foundation, 209-C Waters Bldg., 161 Ottawa Ave. NW, Grand Rapids MI 49503-2703; 616-454-1751.

$2000 for Graduate Historical Women

The Alice E. Smith Fellowship is open to any woman doing graduate level research in American history. Preference will be given to graduate research on history of the midwest or Wisconsin. Transcripts, work samples and references are not required nor sought. Four copies of a 2-page letter of application should describe in detail the applicant's current research. Send to State Historian at address below.

Contact State Historical Society Of Wisconsin, 816 State St., Madison, WI 53706; 608-264-6464.

$2,000 FOR WOMEN IN MASSACHUSETTS

Open to women who have lived in Massachusetts for at least five years. For graduate study in specific fields which change each year. Letter of endorsement from president of your local Women's Club is required. They also have a $600 scholarship program available for undergraduate women attending Mt. Ida College or Fisher College. Contact your local club or write to address below for complete information. Enclose self-addressed stamped envelope.

Contact General Federation Of Women's Clubs Of Massachusetts, Box 679, Sudbury, MA 01776-0679; 508-443-4569.

Up to $5,000 in No-Interest Loans for Jewish Women

Special no-interest-charged scholarship-loans available to active Jewish women women pursuing any undergraduate, graduate or professional degree. Must repay loan within ten years. Write for complete information.

Contact Samuel Lemberg Scholarship Loan Fund Inc., 60 East 42nd St., Suite 1814, New York, NY 10165.

Up to $400 for Jewish Women in Boston

The Amelia Greenbaum/Rabbi Marshall Lifson Scholarship Program is open to undergraduate Jewish women who are residents of Boston (or vicinity) and are attending any Massachusetts college or university. Primary consideration is financial need. Priority is given to those returning to school after a five-year or longer break in their education.

Contact National Council of Jewish Women, Greater Boston Section, 831 Beacon St., Newton Centre, MA 02159; 617-783-9660.

UP TO $1,000 FOR NEW YORK BUSINESS WOMEN

For women who are permanent residents of NY state. Fellowships for graduate study (master or doctorate) at an accredited NY state college or university. U.S. citizenship required. Applications available Oct. 1 through Jan. 31. Send a business-size, self-addressed stamped envelope for complete information.

Contact Business and Professional Women's Clubs, New York State Chapter, 7509 State Route 5, Clinton, NY 13323-3632; 315-735-3114.

$4000 for Bowling Women

Open to women under the age of 23 who are amateur bowlers and members in good standing with WIBC or YABA. Announcements regarding scholarships are sent to all member bowling alleys annually and also available from the address below. Please include self-addressed, stamped envelope with requests for information. Contact Young American Bowling Alliance, 5301 S. 76th St., Greendale, WI 53129.

$500 for San Mateo County, California Women

Awards for young women, age 16 to 26, who have attended a high school in San Mateo County, California. Must need financial support to re-enter a post-secondary school, community college, university, or vocational school. Award is to help young women who have dropped out of school for reasons beyond their control or have undergone unusual hardships to remain in school. Contact Peninsula Community Foundation, 1700 S. El Camino Real #300, San Mateo, CA 94402; 650-358-9369.

Up to $5,000 for Physically Disabled Women

Awards for physically disabled women in need of further education who are between 15 and 40 years old. Venture Club is an organization for young business and professional women sponsored by Soroptimist International of the Americas. Primary considerations are financial need and the capacity to profit from further education. Applicants should contact the nearest Venture Club or Soroptimist Club for application or send self-addressed, stamped envelope to the address below.

Contact Venture Clubs Of The Americas, Two Penn Center Plaza, Suite 1000, Philadelphia, PA 19102-1883; 215-557-9300; Fax: 215-568-5200; {e-mail: siahq@voicenet.com}.

Money for Louisiana Women

Student loans for college-bound young women who are residents of Louisiana. Contact Agnes T. Maguire Trust, c/o Premier Bank, Trust Department, P.O. Box 91210, Baton Rouge, LA 70821-9210; 504-332-4011.

Money for Delta Phi Epsilon Women

Scholarships for women students who are members of Delta Phi Epsilon Sorority. Daughters or granddaughters of members are also eligible to apply. Applications available in January. Write or e-mail Ellen Alper, Executive Director, at address below. Contact Delta Phi Epsilon Educational Foundation, 734 West Port Plaza, Suite 271, St. Louis, MO 63146; 314-275-2626; {e-mail: ealper@conentric.net}; {www.dphie.org }.

At least $500 for Women in National Security

Women studying engineering, computer science, physics, mathematics, business, law, international relations, political science, operations research, economics, and other fields relevant to a career in the areas of national security and defense are eligible to apply. Must be a U.S. citizen, have at least a 3.25 GPA, demonstrate financial need, and currently attending an accredited university/college. College juniors, seniors and graduate students attending either part-time or full-time are eligible to apply. Must have a strong interest in pursuing a career related to national security. Applications are online or send self-addressed, stamped envelope to the address below.

Contact HORIZONS Scholarship Foundation, Women in Defense, c/o ADPA, 2101 Wilson Blvd., Suite 400, Arlington, VA 22201-3061; 703-247-2552; {www.adpa.org/wid/horizon/Scholar.htm}, {e-mail: dnwlee@moon.jic.com}.

Money To Study Women Education Issues

One award for a graduate student, and one award for a postgraduate or non-student. Research project on any topic relevant to the education and personal and professional development of women and girls. Each submission is to have a single author. All entries must be original and not previously published or under review elsewhere. Contact National Association For Women In Education, 1325 18th St., NW, Suite 210, Washington, DC 20036-6511; 202-659-9330.

Money for Behavioral Science Women

Scholarships and grants open to women who are postgraduates, graduate students, and professionals in the behavioral sciences. Awards support study and/or research projects. Preference (but not limited) to organizational behavior and business ethics. Contact National Chamber Of Commerce For Women, 10 Waterside Plaza, Suite 6H, New York, NY 10010; 212-685-3454.

$250 for Writing about Christian Women

$250 to the author of the best essay published during the previous calendar year on any aspect of the role of women in the history of Christianity. Please include self addressed, stamped envelope with requests for information. Contact American Society Of Church History, P.O. Box 8517, Red Bank, NJ 07701.

$1,000 for African American Writing Women

Scholarships for African-American women pursuing careers in writing and/or journalism. Must major in English or journalism in a four-year university, have at least a 2.5 GPA, and demonstrate financial need. Contact Women On Books, 879 Rainier Ave. N., Suite A105, Renton, WA 98055; 206-626-2323.

Up to $1,500 for Public Service Women

COMPA offers two academic scholarships, five travel grants, and a $1,000 gift to the college that has the largest number of student registrants at its annual conference. Travel grants are for attending the conference. For minority women pursuing full-time education in the public administration, public service or public policy and are committed to excellence in public service and administration in city, county, state, and federal governments. Contact Conference Of Minority Public Administrators, P.O. Box 3010, Fort Worth, TX 76113; 817-871-8325; {www.compa.org}.

Up to $5,000 for Minority Women in Technology

The Association offers several scholarship awards to minority women studying science, mathematics, engineering and applied technology who intend to pursue a technology-related career. Local chapters may also have scholarships available. Contact National Technical Association, Inc., 6919 North 19th St., Philadelphia, PA 19126-1506; 215-549-5743; {www.huenet.com/nta}.

Money for Flying Women

Open to women whose goal is to fly the world's airlines. Award is intended to assist with achieving advanced pilot ratings, such as the U.S. FAA ATP certificate or equivalent; they also have other scholarship awards available to women studying any major but planning on an aviation career. Applicants must have a U.S. FAA Commercial Pilot Certificate with an Instrument Rating and a First Class medical or equivalent and a minimum of 750 flight hours. Contact International Society Of Women Airline Pilots, 2250 E. Tropicana Ave., Suite 19-395, Las Vegas, NV 89119-6594.

$2,000 for Opera Women in Connecticut

The Jenny Lind Competition for Sopranos is open to women between 18 and 25 years of age who have had formal training in operatic or concert singing but have not reached professional status. Only residents or students in Connecticut may apply. Contact Barnum Festival, 1070 Main St., Bridgeport, CT 06604.

$3,500 for Medical Women

Women who have already achieved their bachelor's degree from any American university and are attending or planning on attending any accredited medical school are welcome to apply. Must be studying medicine and be intending on pursuing a general practice career (but not in psychiatry.) Contact Cartland Shackford Medical Fellowships, c/o Wellesley College, Secretary, Graduate Fellowships, Career Center, Wellesley MA 02181; 617-283-3525.

Up to $4,000 for Medical Women in Illinois

Medicine-leading to an M.D.degree for U.S. citizens who are residents of Illinois and either accepted to or already attending any accredited medical college. Must be a legal resident of Illinois. Preference given to women who have lived in Dekalb County. Contact Nesbitt Medical Student Foundation, c/o National Bank & Trust Co., 230 West State St., Sycamore, IL 60178.

Money for Native American Women in the Humanities

Open to women of Native American heritage who are pursuing academic programs at the graduate level in the humanities or social sciences. Contact D'arcy McNickle Center for American Indian History, Attn: Cynthia Soto, 60 West Walton St., Chicago, IL 60610-3380; 312-255-3564.

Money for Mental Health Women

Open to holders of a Ph.Ds, M.D.s, or equivalent degrees who are interested in pursuing careers in mental health services research. Minorities and women are especially encouraged to apply. Fellows will improve their knowledge of public mental health systems and services and increase their theoretical, methodological, and analytic skills during the two-year program. Contact National Association of State Mental Health Program Directors Research Institute, Noel A. Mazade Ph.D, Exec Director, 66 Canal Center Plaza, Suite 302, Alexandria, VA 22314; 703-739-9333.

Money for Women in Sports Journalism

Must be studying journalism or communications and intend on pursuing a career in sports journalism. Open to current college juniors only. Scholarships include a six to ten week internship. Minorities are especially encouraged to apply. Contact Sports Journalism Institute, Sports Illustrated, 1271 Avenue of the Americas, New York, NY 10020-1393; 212-522-6407.

Money for Political Science Women in Maryland

Undergraduate women who are residents of Montgomery County, Maryland and studying political science, government, or public administration and attending any college in Maryland are eligible to apply. Send self-addressed stamped envelope for application and complete information. Contact Lavinia Engle Scholarship Foundation, c/o Judith Heimann, 6900 Marbury Rd., Bethesda, MD 20817; 301-229-4647.

Money for Unitarian Women

Limited funding available for active, involved Unitarian women at both the Undergraduate and Graduate level. Some funds are set aside specifically for children of Unitarian ministers. One program, the Ministerial Education Fund, is specificallly for students enrolled in a Masters of Divinity degree program intending on pursuing a career as a Unitarian minister.

Contact Unitarian Universalist Association, 25 Beacon St., Boston, MA 02108, 617-742-7025; {www.uua.org}.

Up to $5,000 for Environmental Public Policy Women

College sophomores and juniors pursuing a career in environmental public policy are welcome to apply for this highly competitive scholarship award. Direct application is not available. Application and nomination forms are sent to colleges annually, if your department chairman or financial aid office does not have information on this program, have your financial aid officer contact the Foundation for information. They also have a highly regarded internship opportunity available.

Contact The Morris K. Udall Foundation, 803/811 E. 1st St., Tucson, AX 85719; 520-670-5529; {www.udalfoundation.org}.

Money for Chiropractic Women

The Association offers several programs to student members who are college juniors or above. Awards are only available at colleges and universities where ICA student chapters are located. Please check with your local chapter for information. Contact International Chiropractors Association, 1110 N. Glebe Rd., Suite 1000, Arlington, VA 22201; 703-528-5000.

$1000 for Aviation Women in Los Angeles

Three scholarships available to women living in the greater Los Angeles area who wish to pursue a career in aviation. Must be at least 18 years old at time of application. Please include a self-addressed, stamped envelope with requests for information. Contact San Fernando Valley Ninety-Nine's, P.O. Box 8160, Van Nuys, CA 91409; 818-989-0081.

Up to $10,000 for Texas Women

Several hundred scholarships worth more than $1,000,000 are awarded annually to outstanding high school seniors in the Houston, Texas area. Some funds are also available to students in Texas but living outside of Houston. Most programs are available to students pursuing any major. Must plan on attending college full-time. Contact Houston Livestock Show and Rodeo, P.O. Box 20070, Houston, TX 77225-0070; 713-791-9000; {www.hlsr.com}.

Up to $2,000 for Nursing

The Aliene Ewell Scholarship Program offered by Chi Eta Phi is for undergraduate women planning on a career in nursing. Must be recommended by a current member of Chi Eta Phi. Primary considerations are financial need, academic achievement, and potential for success. Contact Chi Eta Phi Sorority, 3029 13th St., NW, Washington, DC 20009; 202-232-3858.

Up to $5000 for Ethics Women

Scholarship essay contest open to full time juniors and seniors in an accredited 4 year college or university. Essay must be on a ethics-based topic, such as "Why are we here and how are we to meet our ethical obligations" or reflecting on an ethical aspect of a public policy issue. The prizes are 2 at $500, 1 at $1500, 1 at $2500 and 1 at $5000.

Please write for more information. Include a self-addressed stamped envelope with requests. Contact Elie Wiesel Prize In Ethics Essay Contest, Elie Wiesel Foundation for Humanity, 380 Madison Avenue, 20th Floor, New York, NY 10017.

Up to $3000 for Women in Technology

The AFCEA offers several scholarship programs for students. For all scholarships, you must be a full-time student attending a 4-year college or university, a U.S. citizen, studying electrical engineering, aerospace engineering, electronics, computer science, computer engineering, physics, or mathematics, and must have a GPA of 3.4 on 4.0 scale or better.

The General John A. Wickham Scholarship accepts applications from current college juniors and seniors. The Ralph W. Shrader Scholarship is for postgraduate students working towards a master's degree in any of the above majors, or communications technology, communications engineering, or information management. At least one scholarship award is set aside specifically for a woman candidate, provided all eligibility criteria is met.

Please include a self-addressed and stamped envelope with information on field of study when writing to request information and application. Contact AFCEA Educational Foundation, 4400 Fair Lakes Ct., Fairfax, VA 22033-3899; 703-631-6149; 800-336-4583, ext. 6149; {www.afcea.org}; {e-mail: scholarship@afcea.org};.

At least $750 for Pennsylvania Journalism Women

The Pennsylvania Women's Press Association offers a competitive scholarship of at least $750. To be eligible, one must be a Pennsylvania resident, a print journalism major in a four-year or graduate-level program in a Pennsylvania college or university, and be classified as a junior, senior or graduate student for Fall term. The winner will be selected on the basis of proven journalistic ability, dedication to journalism and general merit. Contact PWPA Scholarship Committee, c/o Teresa Spatara, P.O. Box 152, Sharpsville, PA 16150; {www.regiononline.com/~pwpa/}.

$1,000 for Communications Women in New York

Women who are residents of New York, studying communications, and members or a child of a member of the American Legion Auxiliary, the American Legion Juniors, or the American Legion, any New York chapter.

Graduates of Girls State are also eligible to apply. Must be attending or planning on attending an accredited four-year college. Contact New York State Legion Press Association, P.O. Box 1239, Syracuse, NY 13201-1239.

Up to $10,000 for Education Women in Delaware

This is a renewable scholarship loan program. Current high school seniors or undergraduate college students who are Delaware residents, studying education, and attending any Delaware university are eligible to apply. Must have at least a 2.75 GPA. Must agree to teach in Delaware one year for each year the award was received or pay back the loan.

Contact Delaware Higher Education Commission, 820 North French Street, Fourth Floor, Wilmington, DE 19801.

$1000 for Vocational Women in Minnesota

Applicant must be a Minnesota high school senior planning to go to vocational school. Selection is based upon financial need, academic achievement, promise of leadership ability, and good character. Students planning on attending a two-year or four-year college are not eligible to apply. Contact Minnesota Federation of Teachers, Scholarship Committee, 168 Aurora Avenue, St. Paul, MN 55103.

Up to $4,000 for Journalism Women

High school seniors who show an interest in a career in the newspaper business, broadcasting, and journalism are eligible to apply. Primary considerations are financial need, academic achievement, character, and potential for success. Contact F. Ward Just Scholarship Foundation, c/o Kennedy, 805 Baldwin Ave, Apt. 308, Waukegan, IL 60085-2359.

$1000 for Lesbian Women

Each year, after a highly competitive application process, Legacy awards several $1000 scholarships to outstanding lesbian undergraduate and graduate full-time students. Must have at least a 3.0 grade point average, and demonstrate a commitment or contribution to the lesbian community. Other considerations are financial need, academic performance, honors, personal or financial hardship, and most especially, service to the lesbian community. Further information and applications are available at the website.

Contact An Uncommon Legacy Foundation, Inc., Scholarship Committee, 150 West 26th St., Suite 602, New York, NY 10001; 212-366-6507; {www.uncommonlegacy.org}; {e-mail: uncmlegacy@aol.com}.

$1000 for Clinical Laboratory Technology Women

The Society offers several scholarships to both undergraduate and graduate members. Check with your local chapter first for information. Contact International Society for Clinical Laboratory Technology, 917 Locust St., Suite 1100, St. Louis, MO 63101-1413.

Up to $13,000 for Scuba Diving Women

Open to undergraduate women who are certified SCUBA divers and between the ages of 21 and 25. Academic achievement is also considered. Contact Our World Underwater Scholarship Society, P.O. Box 4428, Chicago, IL 60608; 312-666-6525; {www.owu.ycg.org}.

Up to $10,000 for Smart Women

This highly competitive scholarship program is based primarily upon academic achievement. Open to both men and women, you must apply for this during your high school senior year. Other considerations include leadership potential, essay, and recommendations. Must have at least a 3.0 GPA, must take the PSAT/NMSQT during your

Junior year and score 167 or better. If you did not take the PSAT, SAT scores of 1160 or above will also be accepted.

Contact AdamsVision USA Scholar-Leadership Award, 440 Louisiana, Suite 1250, Houston, TX 77002; 888-294-4969; {www.adamsvision.com}; {e-mail: avision@ hic.net}.

Up to $10,000 for Women with Community Service

The Target All-Around Scholarship program is available to both men and women who are current high school seniors and legal U.S. residents. Must be planning on attending any vocational/technical, two-year, or four-year school full-time. Primary consideration is the amount and quality of time you have spent in service to your community as a volunteer. Applications are available every September at all Target stores.

Contact Target All-Around Scholarship, c/o Citizens' Scholarship Foundation of America, Inc., 1505 Riverview Rd., P.O. Box 297, St. Peter, MN 56082; 800-537-4180.

$2,500 for Peaceful Women

The Nuclear Age Peace Foundation awards two scholarships to undergraduate or graduate ethnic minority students. Primary consideration is a three-page essay on ways to achieve peace in the Nuclear Age, and how you hope to contribute to peace. Financial need and academic achievement are also considered.

Contact Nuclear Age Peace Foundation, Lena Chang Scholarship Awards, 1187 Coast Village Rd, Suite 123, Santa Barbara, CA 93108; 805-965-3443; {www.napf.org}; {e-mail: wagingpeace@napf.org}.

Money for Chess Players

High school juniors and seniors who excel in academics, chess play and sportmanship are eligible to apply. Primary considerations are an essay regarding how chess has had a positive influence on your life, academic achievement, and recommendations.

Contact U.S. Chess Federation, c/o Sharon Brunetti, 3054 NYS Route 9W, New Windsor, NY 12553; 914-562-8350; {www.uschess.org}.

Up to $1,500 for Wives of Overseas Active Duty Service Members

Open only to spouses residing with an active duty service member stationed overseas. A grant of up to 50% of tuition for on-base education programs, up to a maximum of $300 per undergraduate term, or $350 per graduate term, and $1,500 per academic year is available. Do not need to be a full-time student.

Contact Navy-Marine Corps Relief Society, Education Division, 801 N. Randolph St., Suite 1228, Arlington, VA 22203-1978; 703-696-4960.

Money for Connecticut Women

Current high school seniors who are residents of Waterbury, Connecticut are eligible to apply. Financial need is the primary consideration. Check with your high school counselor or administration office for application and information, or at the address below. Contact Elisha Leavenworth Foundation, 35 Park Pl., Waterbury, CT 06702.

Money for Operating Room Nurses

Scholarship awards covering tuition and fees are available to current Registered Nurses who are members of AORN and wish to return to college to continue or advance their education. Must have at least a 3.0 GPA and attend a four-year college. Graduate students are welcome to apply.

Contact Association of Operating Room Nurses Foundation, Credentialing Division, 10170 E. Mississippi Ave., Denver, CO 80231; 303-755-6300; 800-755-2676, ext. 8229; {www.aorn.org}; {e-mail: tbarlow@aorn.org}.

$1000 for Seattle Women in Service to the Homeless

Seven scholarships are available to high school seniors who are residents of Seattle and plan on attending college full-time. Must have a committed interest to the plight of the homeless and have demonstrated community service to the homeless. Financial need, recommendations and an essay are also considered.

Contact Windermere Foundation Scholarship, College Planning Network, Attn: Vicki Breithaupt, Campion Tower, 914 E. Jefferson, Seattle, WA 98112-5366; 206-323-0624; {www.collegeplan.org}.

$1,000 To Study Farming

Current college sophomores and juniors who are members of or children of members of the Society and plan on studying any agricultural-related major, agricultural engineering, or biological engineering are eligible to apply. Primary consideration is financial need, although academic achievement is also considered. Contact American Society of Agricultural Engineers, 2950 Niles Rd., St. Joseph, MI 49085; 616-428-6336; {www.asce.org}.

$500 for Graduate Women in Lesbian Studies or Jewish Women Studies

The Graduate Scholarship in Lesbian Studies awards $500 to a student who will be doing research for or writing a master's thesis or Ph.D. dissertation in lesbian studies. The Scholarship in Jewish Women's Studies awards $500 to a graduate student who is enrolled full-time for the fall semester and whose area of research is Jewish Women's Studies.

Contact National Women's Studies Association, University of Maryland, 7100 Baltimore Blvd., Suite 500, College Park, MD 20740; 301-403-0525; {www.nwsa.org/scholarship.htm}.

Money For Delaware Women Over Age 20

Young women who are at least 20 years old, have graduated high school or achieved a GED, have been accepted to any Delaware two year or four year college, and are residents of Delaware are eligible to apply. Financial need is the only consideration. Contact Wilmington Women in Business, Inc., P.O. Box 2310, Wilmington, DE 19899; Attn: Scholarship Committee; {www.wwb.org/fresh.htm}.

Money for Washington, DC Women in Communications

Current junior or senior female students studying communications, advertising, journalism, public relations, marketing, graphic arts, or a related field are eligible to apply. Must have at least a 3.0 GPA, work experience in communications or related field, active in extra-curricular activities including family obligations, volunteer work, club and organization involvement that show versatility and commitment.

Contact Association of Women in Communications, Washington DC Chapter, Attn: Maralee Csellar, Vice President of Student Affairs, 1754 Westwind Way, McLean, VA 22102-1606; {www.awic-dc.org}.

Money for Saginaw, Michigan Women

Each year, the Saginaw Community Foundation awards over 100 scholarships worth over $200,000 to area high school students and college students. Please check with your high school guidance counselor, college financial aid officer, or the address below for further information.

Contact Saginaw Community Foundation, 100 S. Jefferson, Suite 501, Saginaw, MI 48607; 517-755-0545.

$1000 for Culinary Women in Maine

The Maine Restaurant Association offers scholarships to current high school seniors who are residents of Maine and plan on pursuing a career in the restaurant business. Culinary arts majors are also eligible to apply. Primary considerations are financial need and academic achievement. Contact Maine Restaurant Association, P.O. Box 5060, Augusta, ME 04330.

Up to $1,500 for Georgia Women

Renewable scholarships available to undergraduate women who are residents of Georgia and studying anything except law, theology, or medicine (although nursing students may apply). Primary considerations are financial need and academic achievement. Preference given to women who live in Chatham County, Georgia.

Contact William F. Cooper Scholarship, c/o First Union National Bank-CMG, P.O. Box 9947, Savannah, GA 31412; 912-944-2154.

Up to $2,000 for Northern Virginia Women

Open to undergraduate women who are 23 years old or over and attending or planning on attending an accredited college or university in northern Virginia. If your planned course of study is not available at any northern Virginia schools, this award may be used at institutions outside of northern Virginia. Primary consideration is financial need.

Contact Junior League of Northern Virginia, 7921 Jones Branch Dr., Suite 320, McLean VA 22102; 703-893-0258.

Job Training Through Uncle Sam

Uncle Sam wants you — to be working that is. The Federal government has developed several different programs to help you find a new career, get the training you need to move up in your present job, or find a new skill if you lost your old job. Many of these programs will cover childcare, transportation, and relocation costs to get you on your way up the job ladder.

Become A Journeyman

Getting a good job does not always mean that you must attend college or trade school, but no one will readily admit that. There are apprenticeship programs all over the country that will provide free on-the-job training — and you will learn while you earn. Apprentices learn each skill of a job by carrying it out step by step under the close supervision of a skilled craft worker. An apprenticeship involves planned, day-by-day supervised training on the job, combined with technical instruction. Length of training varies depending on the job and is determined by standards adopted by a particular industry. The minimum term of apprenticeship is one year, but can be as long as four. Currently there are over 800 apprenticeable occupations, including cook, air craft mechanic, electrician, computer programmer, tool maker, and welder. For more information, look in the blue pages of your phone book for the Bureau of Apprenticeship located in your state, or you may contact Bureau of Apprenticeship and Training, U.S. Department of Labor, 200 Constitution Ave., NW, Room N4649, Washington, DC 20210; 202-219-5921; {www.doleta.gov/indiv/apprent.htm}.

State Contacts

Alabama
U.S. Department of Labor
Bureau of Apprenticeship and Training
950 22nd St., North
Birmingham, AL 35203
205-731-1308

Alaska
U.S. Department of Labor
Bureau of Apprenticeship and Training
3301 C St., Suite 201
Anchorage, AK 99503
907-271-5035

Arizona
Department of Economic Security
438 W. Adams St.
Phoenix, AZ 85003
602-252-7771 Ext. 114

U.S. Department of Labor
Bureau of Apprenticeship and Training
Suite 302
3221 North 16th St.
Phoenix, AZ 85016
602-640-2964

Arkansas
U.S. Department of Labor
Bureau of Apprenticeship and Training
700 West Capitol St.
Little Rock, AR 72201
501-324-5415

California
Division of Apprenticeship Standards
Department of Industrial Relations
45 Freemont St.
Suite 1040
San Francisco, CA 94105
415-975-4251

U.S. Department of Labor
Bureau of Apprenticeship and Training
Suite 1090-N
1301 Clay St.
Oakland, CA 94612
510-637-2951

Colorado
U.S. Department of Labor
Bureau of Apprenticeship and Training
721 19th St., Room 469
Denver, CO 80202
303-844-4826

Connecticut
Apprenticeship Program Manager
Connecticut Labor Department
200 Folly Brook Blvd.
Wethersfield, CT 06109
860-566-2450

U.S. Department of Labor
Bureau of Apprenticeship and Training
135 High St., Room 367
Hartford, CT 06103
203-240-4311

Delaware
Apprenticeship and Training Section
Division of Employment and Training
4425 N. Market St.
Station 313
P.O. Box 9828
Wilmington, DE 19809
302-761-8121

U.S. Department of Labor
Bureau of Apprenticeship and Training
844 King St.
Wilmington, DE 19801
302-573-6113

District of Columbia
D.C. Apprenticeship Council
500 C St., NW, Suite 241
Washington, DC 20001
202-724-7246

Florida
Apprentice Section
Bureau of Job Training
Department of Labor
1320 Executive Center Dr.
Atkins Building, Suite 200
Tallahassee, FL 32399
850-488-9250

U.S. Department of Labor
Bureau of Apprenticeship and Training
227 North Bronough St.
Tallahassee, FL 32301
850-942-8336

Georgia
U.S. Department of Labor
Bureau of Apprenticeship and Training
61 Forsyth St., SW
Atlanta, GA 30303
404-562-2323

Hawaii
Apprenticeship Division
Department of Labor and Industrial Relations
830 Punchbowl St.
Room 334
Honolulu, HI 96813
808-586-8877

U.S. Department of Labor
Bureau of Apprenticeship and Training
300 Ala Moana Blvd.
Honolulu, HI 96850
808-541-2519

Idaho
U.S. Department of Labor
Bureau of Apprenticeship and Training
3050 North Lakeharbor Lane
Boise, ID 83703
208-334-1013

Illinois
U.S. Department of Labor
Bureau of Apprenticeship and Training
230 South Dearborn St.
Room 708
Chicago, IL 60604
312-353-4690

Indiana
U.S. Department of Labor
Bureau of Apprenticeship and Training
46 East Ohio St., Room 414
Indianapolis, IN 46204
317-226-7592

Iowa
U.S. Department of Labor
Bureau of Apprenticeship and Training
210 Walnut St., Room 715
Des Moines, IA 50309
515-284-4690

Kansas
Apprenticeship Director
Department of Human Resources
401 S.W. Topeka Blvd.
Topeka, KS 66603
785-296-4161

U.S. Department of Labor
Bureau of Apprenticeship and Training
444 SE Quincy St., Room 247
Topeka, KS 66683
785-295-2624

Kentucky
Apprenticeship Director
Division of Employment Standards and Mediation
Kentucky Labor Cabinet
1047 U.S. 127 South
Suite 4
Frankfort, KY 40601
502-564-2784

U.S. Department of Labor
Bureau of Apprenticeship and Training
600 Martin Luther King Place
Louisville, KY 40202
502-582-5223

Louisiana
Director of Apprenticeship
Louisiana Department of Labor
1001 North 23rd St.
P.O. Box 94094
Baton Rouge, LA 70804
504-342-7820

U.S. Department of Labor
Bureau of Apprenticeship and Training
501 Magazine St.
New Orleans, LA 70130
504-589-6103

Maine
Apprenticeship Standards
Department of Labor
Bureau of Employment Services
55 State House Station

Augusta, ME 04333
207-624-6431

U.S. Department of Labor
Bureau of Apprenticeship and Training
68 Sewall St., Room 401
Augusta, ME 04330
207-622-8235

Maryland
Apprenticeship and Training Council
1100 North Eutaw St.
Sixth Floor
Baltimore, MD 21201
410-767-2968

U.S. Department of Labor
Bureau of Apprenticeship and Training
300 West Pratt St.
Room 200
Baltimore, MD 21201
410-962-2676

Massachusetts
Division of Apprentice Training
Department of Labor and Workforce
100 Cambridge St.
Room 1107
Boston, MA 02202
617-727-3488

U.S. Department of Labor
Bureau of Apprenticeship and Training
Room E-370
JFK Federal Building
Boston, MA 02203
617-565-2288

Michigan
U.S. Department of Labor
Bureau of Apprenticeship and Training
Room 304
801 South Waverly
Lansing, MI 48917
517-377-1746

Minnesota
Division of Apprenticeship
Department of Labor and Industry
443 Lafayette Rd.
4th Floor
St. Paul, MN 55155
651-296-2371

U.S. Department of Labor
Bureau of Apprenticeship and Training
316 Robert St.
Room 134
St. Paul, MN 55101
651-290-3951

Mississippi
U.S. Department of Labor
Bureau of Apprenticeship and Training
100 West Capitol St.
Jackson, MS 39269
601-965-4346

Missouri
U.S. Department of Labor
Bureau of Apprenticeship and Training
1222 Spruce St.,
St. Louis, MO 63103
314-539-2522

Montana -
Apprenticeship and Training Program
Montana Department of Labor
715 Front St.
Helena, MT 59620
406-447-3210

U.S. Department of Labor
Bureau of Apprenticeship and Training
301 South Park Ave.
Room 396- Drawer #10055
Helena, MT 59626
406-441-1076

Nebraska
U.S. Department of Labor
Bureau of Apprenticeship and Training
Room 801
106 South 15th St.
Omaha, NE 68102
402-221-3281

Nevada
Labor Commissioner
Nevada Apprenticeship Council
555 E. Washington Ave.
Suite 4100
Las Vegas, NV 89101
702-486-2660

U.S. Department of Labor
Bureau of Apprenticeship and Training
301 Stewart Ave., Room 311
Las Vegas, NV 89101
702-388-6396

New Hampshire
Director of Apprenticeship
State Office Park South
95 Pleasant St.
Concord, NH 03301
603-271-6297

U.S. Department of Labor
Bureau of Apprenticeship and Training
143 North Main St., Room 205
Concord, NH 03301
603-225-1444

New Jersey
U.S. Department of Labor
Bureau of Apprenticeship and Training
Parkway Towers
Building E- 3rd Floor
485 Route #1, South
Iselin, NJ 08830
908-750-9191

New Mexico
Apprenticeship Director
New Mexico Department of Labor

501 Mountain Rd., NE
Albuquerque, NM 87102
505-841-8989

U.S. Department of Labor
Bureau of Apprenticeship and Training
505 Marquette, Room 830
Albuquerque, NM 87102
505-766-2398

New York
Apprentice Coordinator
NYS Department of Labor
State Campus Building #12, Room 140
Albany, NY 12240
518-457-4391

U.S. Department of Labor
Bureau of Apprenticeship and Training
Leo O'Brien Federal Building
Room 809
North Pearl & Clinton Ave.
Albany, NY 12207
518-431-4008

North Carolina
Apprenticeship Division
Department of Labor
4 West Edenton St.
Raleigh, NC 27601
919-733-7540

U.S. Department of Labor
Bureau of Apprenticeship and Training
Somerset Park, Suite205
4407 Bland Rd.
Raleigh, NC 27609
919-790-2801

North Dakota
U.S. Department of Labor
Bureau of Apprenticeship and Training
New Federal Building
Room 332
304 East Broadway
Bismarck, ND 58501
701-250-4700

Ohio
Director of Apprenticeship
State Apprenticeship Council
Bureau of Apprenticeship Services
145 S. Front St.
Columbus, OH 43215
614-644-2242

U.S. Department of Labor
Bureau of Apprenticeship and Training
Room 605
200 North High St.
Columbus, OH 43215
614-469-7375

Oklahoma
U.S. Department of Labor
Bureau of Apprenticeship and Training
1500 South Midwest Blvd.
Suite 202
Midwest City, OK 73110
405-732-4338

Oregon
Apprenticeship and Training Division
Bureau of Labor and Industry
800 NE Oregon St.
Room 32
Portland, OR 97232
503-731-4891

U.S. Department of Labor
Bureau of Apprenticeship and Training
1220 SW 3rd Ave.
Portland, OR 97204
503-326-3157

Pennsylvania
Apprenticeship and Training Council
Labor and Industry Building
7th and Forster St.
Room 1301
Harrisburg, PA 17120
717-787-4763

U.S. Department of Labor
Bureau of Apprenticeship and Training
Federal Building
228 Walnut St.
Room 773
Harrisburg, PA 17108
717-221-3496

Rhode Island
Apprenticeship Training Programs
Department of Labor
610 Manton Ave.
Providence, RI 02909
401-457-1859

U.S. Department of Labor
Bureau of Apprenticeship and Training
Federal Building
100 Hartford Ave.
Providence, RI 02909
401-528-5198

South Carolina
U.S. Department of Labor
Bureau of Apprenticeship and Training
Strom Thurmond Federal Building
1835 Assembly St.
Room 838
Columbia, SC 29201
803-765-5547

South Dakota
U.S. Department of Labor
Bureau of Apprenticeship and Training
Oxbow I Building, Room 204
2400 West 48th St.
Sioux Falls, SD 57105
605-330-4326

Tennessee
U.S. Department of Labor
Bureau of Apprenticeship and Training
1321 Murfreesboro Rd.
Suite 541
Nashville, TN 37210
615-781-5318

Texas
U.S. Department of Labor
Bureau of Apprenticeship and Training
2320 LaBranch St.
Houston, TX 77004
713-750-1696

Utah
U.S. Department of Labor
Bureau of Apprenticeship and Training
1600 West 2200 South
Suite 101
Salt Lake City, UT 84119
801-975-3650

Vermont
Apprenticeship and Training
Department of Labor and Training
5 Green Mountain Dr.
P.O. Box 488
Montpelier, VT 05620
802-828-5082

U.S. Department of Labor
Bureau of Apprenticeship and Training
11 Elmwood Ave., Room 612
Burlington, VT 05401
802-951-6278

Virginia
Apprenticeship Director
Department of Labor and Industry
13 South 13th St.
Richmond, VA 23219
804-786-2381

U.S. Department of Labor
Bureau of Apprenticeship and Training
700 Centre, Suite 546
704 East Franklin St.
Richmond, VA 23219
804-771-2488

Washington
Apprenticeship Program Manager
Department of Labor and Industries
P.O. Box 44530
46 Legion Way S.E.
Olympia, WA 98504
360-902-5320

U.S. Department of Labor
Bureau of Apprenticeship and Training
1400 Talbot Rd. South
Renton, WA 98055
206-277-5214

West Virginia
U.S. Department of Labor
Bureau of Apprenticeship and Training
1108 Third Ave., Suite 203
Huntington, WV 25301
304-528-7540

Wisconsin
Dept of Workforce Develp
Division of Workforce Excellence
Bureau of Apprenticeship Standards

7201 E. Washington Ave.,
Room 211
P.O. Box 7972
Madison, WI 53707
608-266-3133

U.S. Department of Labor
Bureau of Apprenticeship and Training
212 East Washington Ave.,
Room 303
Madison, WI 53703
608-264-5377

Wyoming
U.S. Dept. of Labor Bureau of Apprenticeship and Training
1912 Capitol Ave.#508
Cheyenne, WY 82001
307-772-2448

Free Training If You Are Laid Off

If you have found yourself on the losing end of a plant closing or mass layoff, apply for money and re-training under the Economic Dislocation and Worker Adjustment Assistance Act. The program is administered by each state, and because of that, the program differs from state to state. Under certain circumstances, states may also authorize service for displaced homemakers.

Workers can receive classroom, occupational skills, and/or on-the-job training to qualify for jobs in demand. Basic and remedial education, entrepreneurial training, and instruction in literacy or English-as-a-second-language may be provided. For more information contact your state Department of Labor in the blue pages of your phone book, or you may contact Office of Worker Retraining and Readjustment Programs, U.S. Department of Labor, Room N-5426, 200 Constitution Ave., NW, Washington, DC 20210; 202-219-5577; {www.doleta.gov/programs/factsht/edwaa.htm}.

State Dislocated Worker Contacts

Alabama
Workforce Development Division
Alabama Department of Economic and Community Affairs
401 Adams Ave.
P.O. Box 5690
Montgomery, AL 36103
334-242-5300
800-562-4916

Alaska
Division of Community and Rural Development
Department of Community and Regional Affairs
333 West 4th Ave., Suite 220
Anchorage, AK 99501
907-269-4658

Arizona
Dislocated Worker Coordinator
Job Training Partnership Act
1789 West Jefferson, Site Code 920Z
Phoenix, AZ 85005
602-542-2484

Arkansas
Arkansas Employment Security Department
P.O. Box 2981
Little Rock, AR 72203
501-682-3137

California
Displaced Worker Services Section
Job Training Partnership Division
Employment Development Department
P.O. Box 826880
Sacramento, CA 94280
916-654-8275

Colorado
Dislocated Worker Unit
Governor's Job Training Office
720 South Colorado Blvd.

Suite 550
Denver, CO 80222
303-620-4200
800-388-5515

Connecticut
CT Department of Labor
Dislocated Worker Unit
200 Folly Brook Blvd.
Wethersfield, CT 06109
203-566-4290

Delaware
Division of Employment and Training
Delaware Department of Labor
4425 North Market St.
Wilmington, DE 19809
302-761-8117

District of Columbia
Dislocated Worker Unit
Department of Employment Services
500 C St., NW
Washington, DC 20001
202-724-7130

Florida
Bureau of Workforce Program Support
Division of Labor, Employment and Training
1320 Executive Center Dr.
Atkins Building
Room 200
Tallahassee, FL 32399
850-488-9250
800-633-3572

Georgia
Georgia Department of Labor
Sussex Place
Suite 440
148 International Blvd., NE
Atlanta, GA 30303
404-656-6336

Hawaii
Workforce Development Division
Department of Labor and Industrial Relations
830 Punchbowl St.
Room 329
Honolulu, HI 96813
808-586-8812

Idaho
Dept. of Employment
317 Main St.
Boise, ID 83735
208-334-6298

Illinois
Job Training Division
Department of Commerce and Community Affairs
620 East Adams St.
Springfield, IL 62701
217-785-6006

Indiana
Indiana Department of Employment and Training Services
Program Operations Division
10 North Senate Ave.
Indianapolis, IN 46204

317-232-7461
800-437-9136

Iowa
Division of Workforce Development
Iowa Department of Economic Development
1000 East Grand Ave.
Des Moines, IA 50319
515-281-5365
800-562-4692

Kansas
Job Training Director
Department of Human Resources
Division of Employment and Training
401 SW Topeka Blvd.
Topeka, KS 66603
785-296-7876

Kentucky
Office of Training and Reemployment
Workforce Development Cabinet
275 East Main
3 Floor West
Frankfort, KY 40601
502-564-5360

Louisiana
Special Programs Section
Office of Labor Federal Training Program
P.O. Box 94094
Baton Rouge, LA 70804
504-342-7637

Maine
Dislocated Worker Unit
Hallow/Annex Central Building
55 State House Station
2nd Floor
Augusta, ME 04330
207-624-6390

Maryland
Department of Labor, Licensing and Regulations
Office of Employment and Training
1100 North Eutaw St.
Room 310
Baltimore, MD 21201
410-767-2803

Massachusetts
Corporation for
Business, Work and Learning
The Schrafft Center
529 Main St., Suite 400
Boston, MA 02129
617-727-8158 ext. 319

Michigan
Dislocated Worker Unit
Michigan Jobs Commission
201 N. Washington Square
Lansing, MI 48913
517-373-6234

Minnesota
State Dislocated Worker Unit
Minnesota Department of Jobs and Training
390 North Robert St.

First Floor
St. Paul, MN 55101
612-296-7918
800-438-5627

Mississippi
Employment and Training Division
Mississippi Department of Economic and Community Development
301 West Pearl St.
Jackson, MS 39203
601-949-2234
800-762-2781

Missouri
Division of Job Development and Training
Department of Economic Development
P.O. Box 1087
Jefferson City, MO 65102
314-751-7796
800-877-8698

Montana
Dislocated Worker Unit
State Job Training Bureau
Montana Department of Labor and Industry
P.O. Box 1728
Helena, MT 59624
406-444-4500

Nebraska
Job Training Program Division
Nebraska Department of Labor
550 South 16th St.
Lincoln, NE 68509
402-471-9903

Nevada
State Job Training Office
Capitol Complex
400 West King St.
Suite 108
Carson City, NV 89710
702-687-4310
800-900-4614

New Hampshire
New Hampshire Job Training Coordinating Council
64-B Suncock Rd.
Concord, NH 03301
603-228-9500

New Jersey
Rapid Response Team
Labor Management Committee
New Jersey Department of Labor, CN 058
Trenton, NJ 08625
800-343-3919

New Mexico
EDWAA Coordinator
P.O. Box 4218
Santa Fe, NM 87502
505-827-6866

New York
Dislocated Worker Unit
NY State Department of Labor
State Office Campus, Bldg. 12
Albany, NY 12240
518-457-3101

North Carolina
Division of Employment and Training
NC Department of Commerce
441 N. Harrington St.
Raleigh, NC 27603
919-733-6383 Ext. 212
800-562-6333

North Dakota
Job Training Division
Job Service North Dakota
1000 E. Divide Ave.
P.O. Box 5507
Bismarck, ND 58502
701-328-2843
800-247-0981

Ohio
Dislocated Worker Unit
Ohio Bureau of Employment Services
145 South Front St.
P.O. Box 1618
Columbus, OH 43215
614-466-3817

Oklahoma
Oklahoma Employment Security Commission
Will Rogers Bldg., Room 408
2401 North Lincoln Blvd.
Oklahoma City, OK 73104
405-557-7294

Oregon
Dislocated Worker Unit
Economic Development Department
255 Capitol St., NE
3rd Floor
Salem, OR 97310
503-373-1995

Pennsylvania
Dislocated Worker Unit
Labor and Industry Building
12th Floor
7th and Forester Sts.
Harrisburg, PA 17120
717-772-0781

Rhode Island
EDWAA Coordinator
Department of Employment and Training
109 Main St.
Pawtucket, RI 02860
401-828-8283

South Carolina
Manpower Training Unit
P.O. Box 1406
Columbia, SC 29202
803-737-2601
800-922-6332

South Dakota
Job Training Partnership Act Administrator
South Dakota Department of Labor
Kneip Building
700 Governors Dr.
Pierre, SD 57501
605-773-5017
800-952-2316

Tennessee
Tennessee Dept. of Labor
Gateway Plaza
710 James Robertson Parkway, 4th Floor
Nashville, TN 37243
615-741-1031
800-255-5872

Texas
Work Force Development Division
Texas Workforce Commission
211 East 7th St., Suite 1000
Austin, TX 78701
512-936-0474
888-562-7489

Utah
Utah Department of Workforce Services
140 East 300 South
Suite 500
Salt Lake City, UT 84114
801-526-4312
888-848-0688

Vermont
Dislocated Worker Unit
Department of Employment and Training
P.O. Box 488
Montpelier, VT 05602
802-828-4177

Virginia
Virginia Employment Commission
P.O. Box 1358
Richmond, VA 23218
804-786-3037

Washington
Dislocated Worker Unit
Employment Security Department
Employment Security Bldg.
P.O. Box 9046
Olympia, WA 98507
360-438-4629

West Virginia
Governor's Administered Programs
Bureau of Employment Programs
Job Training Programs Div.
112 California Ave.
Charleston, WV 25305
304-558-1847

Wisconsin
Department of Labor, Industry and Human Relations
201 E. Washington Ave.
P.O. Box 7972
Madison, WI 53707
608-266-0745
888-822-5246

Wyoming
Job Training Program
Department of Employment
100 West Midwest
P.O. Box 2760
Casper, WY 82601
307-235-3601
800-730-9725

Free Training If You Lose Your Job From Increased Imports

Ever notice how so many products have gotten less expensive over the last ten years? Shirts that once cost $30 are now sold for $15. Televisions and VCRs — not to mention computers — have never been cheaper. Almost everything we now buy in the U.S. is being made overseas. If you lost your job because of imports, you can get help looking for a new job or get paid to get more training. The Trade Adjustment Assistance program will help you learn more marketable job skills, so you can move to greener employment pastures. You can receive up to 104 weeks of on-the-job and classroom training; you can receive 52 weeks of benefits after your unemployment expires if you are part of a job training program; you can receive $800 to travel for job hunting purposes; $800 to relocate for a job; and transportation expenses to job training programs. For more information contact your local employment services office in the blue pages of your phone book, or Office of Trade Adjustment Assistance, Employment and Training Assistance, U.S. Department of Labor, Room C4318, 200 Constitution Ave., NW, Washington, DC 20210; 202-219-5555; {www.doleta.gov}. For a listing of state contacts, see the list located after the next item.

Free Training For Those Who Lose Their Jobs Because Of Increased Trade With Mexico or Canada

NAFTA is not a dirty word, but a lot of U.S. workers swear it is a plan to put them out of work and ship their jobs where labor costs are cheaper — Canada, but more significantly to Mexico and other Latin American countries. In a dog-eat-dog global economy, there are no real borders. If you were laid off or lost your job because of the North American Free Trade Agreement (NAFTA), the government wants to help you find a new one, and probably one that pays you more than your last job. The NAFTA Transitional Adjustment Assistance Program is like a job skills and retraining SWAT team geared to provide rapid and early response to the threat of unemployment. The program includes on-site services to let workers know they are eligible; assessment of skills; financial and personal counseling; career counseling; job placement assistance; child care; transportation; income support for up to 52 weeks after worker has exhausted unemployment compensation while the worker is enrolled in training; relocation allowance; and more. For more information, contact your local employment services office in the blue pages of your phone book, or Office of Trade Adjustment Assistance, Employment and Training Assistance, U.S. Department of

Labor, Room C4318, 200 Constitution Ave., NW, Washington, DC 20210; 202-219-5555; {www.doleta.gov}.

State TAA-NAFTA Contacts

Alabama
Department of Industrial Relations
649 Monroe St., Room 330A
Montgomery, AL 36131
334-242-8635

Alaska
Employment Security Division
P.O. Box 25509
Juneau, AK 99802
907-465-5954

Arizona
Department of Employment Security
P.O. Box 6666
Phoenix, AZ 85005
602-495-1861

Arkansas
Arkansas Employment Security Department
P.O. Box 2981
Little Rock, AR 722-3
501-682-3747

California
Employment Development Department
P.O. Box 826880
Attn: MIC40
Sacramento, CA 94280
916-654-9305

Colorado
Department of Labor and Employment
Two Park Central, Suite 400
1515 Arapahoe St.
Denver, CO 80202
303-620-4201

Connecticut
Connecticut Department of Labor
Employment Security Division
200 Folly Brook Blvd.
Wethersfield, CT 06109
860-566-2424

Delaware
Division of Employment and Training
P.O. Box 9828
4425 North Market St.
Wilmington, DE 19809
302-761-8117

District of Columbia
Office of Unemployment Compensation
D.C. Department of Employment Services

500 C St., NW, Room 515
Washington, DC 20001
202-724-7274

Florida
Department of Labor and
Employment Security
1320 Executive Center Dr.
Room 200, Atkins Building
Tallahassee, FL 32399
850-488-9250

Georgia
Georgia Department of Labor
148 International Blvd.
Room 440
Atlanta, GA 30303
404-656-6336

Hawaii
Department of Labor and
Industry
830 Punchbowl St., Room 329
Honolulu, HI 96813
808-586-8820

Idaho
Idaho Department of Labor
317 Main St.
Boise, ID 83735
208-334-6314

Illinois
Department of Employment
Security
401 South State St., 7th Floor
Chicago, IL 60605
312-793-6805

Indiana
Department of Workforce
Development
10 North Senate Ave.
Indianapolis, IN 46204
317-232-7186

Iowa
Department of Workforce
Development
1000 E. Grand Ave.
P.O. Box 10332
Des Moines, IA 50306
515-281-4981

Kansas
Department of Human
Resources
512 S.W. 6th Ave.
Topeka, KS 66603
785-291-3470

Kentucky
Department of Employment
Services
2nd Floor West
CHR Building
275 E. Main St.
Frankfort, KY 40621
502-564-5334

Louisiana
Louisiana Department of
Labor
1001 N. 22nd St.
P.O. Box 94094
Baton Rouge, LA 70804
504-342-8753

Maine
Maine Department of Labor
Bureau of Employment Services
55 State House Station
Augusta, ME 04330
207-624-6390

Maryland
Department of Labor, Licensing and Regulations
Division of Employment and Training
1100 N. Eutaw St.
Baltimore, MD 21201
410-767-2832

Massachusetts
Corporation for Business, Work and Learning
Schrafft Center
529 Main St.
Boston, MA 02129
617-727-8158

Michigan
Employment Security Agency
7310 Woodward Ave.
Detroit, MI 48202
313-876-5374

Mississippi
Employment Security Commission
P.O. Box 1699
Jackson, MS 39215
601-961-7544

Missouri
Department of Labor and Industrial Relations
Division of Employment Security
P.O. Box 59
Jefferson City, MO 65104
573-751-3784

Montana
Department of Labor and Industry
Job Service Division
P.O. Box 1728
Helena, MT 59624
406-444-3351

Nebraska
Department of Labor
P.O. Box 94600
Lincoln, NE 68509
402-471-3406

New Hampshire
New Hampshire Employment Security
P.O. Box 9505
Manchester, NH 03108
603-656-6608

New Jersey
Department of Labor
Central Regional Office
506 Jersey Ave.
New Brunswick, NJ 08901
732-937-6249

New Mexico
Department of Labor
P.O. Box 1928
Albuquerque, NM 87103
505-841-8452

New York
Department of Labor
State Office Building
Campus #12, Room 156
Albany, NY 12240
518-457-3101

North Carolina
Employment Security
Commission
Workforce Development
Division
P.O. Box 26988
Raleigh, NC 27611
919-733-6745

North Dakota
Job Service of North Dakota
1000 East Divide Ave.
P.O. Box 5507
Bismarck, ND 58506
701-328-2817

Ohio
Bureau of Employment
Services
145 South Front St.
P.O. Box 1618
Columbus, OH 43216
614-644-2706

Oklahoma
Employment Security
Commission
Will Rogers Memorial Office
Building
2401 North Lincoln
P.O. Box 52003
Oklahoma City, OK 73152
405-557-7274

Oregon
Job Training Administration
Attn: DWU
255 Capitol St.
Salem, OR 97310
503-947-1665

Pennsylvania
Dept. of Labor and Industry
7th and Forster Sts.
Room 1100
Harrisburg, PA 17120
717-783-8050

Rhode Island
Department of Labor and
Training
175 Main St.
Pawtucket, RI 02860
401-277-3450

South Carolina
Employment Security
Commission
P.O. Box 1406
Columbia, SC 29202
803-737-3096

South Dakota
Department of Labor
Kniep Building
700 Governors Dr.

Pierre, SD 57501
605-773-5017

Tennessee
Dept. of Employment Security
Davy Crockett Building
11th Floor
500 James Robertson Parkway
Nashville, TN 37245
615-741-1948

Texas
Texas Workforce Commission
101 E. 15th St.
Austin, TX 78778
512-305-9638

Utah
Department of Workforce Services
140 East 300 South
P.O. Box 45249
Salt Lake City, UT 84145
801-526-4309

Vermont
Department of Employment Security
P.O. Box 488
5 Green Mountain Dr.
Montpelier, VT 05602
802-828-4177

Virginia
Virginia Employment Security
703 East Main St.
Room 308
Richmond, VA 23219
804-786-8825

Washington
Employment Security Department
P.O. Box 9046
Mail Stop 6000
Olympia, WA 98507
360-438-4645

West Virginia
Division of Employment Service
Bureau of Employment Programs
112 California Ave.
Charleston, WV 25305
304-558-2850

Wisconsin
Department of Workforce Development
201 E. Washington
P.O. Box 7946
Madison, WI 53707
608-266-0745

Wyoming
Department of Employment
200 West Midwest
P.O. Box 2760
Casper, WY 82602
307-235-3284

Free Training For Teens And Unemployed Adults

The Job Training Partnership Act (JTPA) provides job training services for disadvantaged adults and youth, dislocated workers, the elderly, and others who face significant employment barriers. Free services include an assessment of an unemployed individual's needs and abilities and a strategy of services, such as classroom training, on-the-job training, job search assistance, work experience, counseling, basic skills training, and support services, such as transportation and child care.

There are hundreds of JTPA sites across the U.S. To locate your nearest one, look in the blue pages of your phone book or contact Office of Employment and Training Programs, U.S. Department of Labor, 200 Constitution Ave., NW, Room N4469, Washington, DC 20210; 202-219-6236; {www.doleta.gov}.

State JTPA Contacts

Alabama
Job Training Division
Alabama Department of
Economic and Community
Affairs
401 Adams Ave.
P.O. Box 5690
Montgomery, AL 36103
334-242-530

Alaska
Division of Community and
Rural Development
Department of Community and
Regional Affairs
333 W. 4th Ave.
Suite 220
Anchorage, AK 99501
907-269-4520

Arizona
Division of Employment and
Rehabilitation Services
1789 W. Jefferson
P.O. Box 6123
Suite 901A
Phoenix, AZ 85005
602-542-4910

Arkansas
Arkansas Employment
Security Department
Two Capitol Mall, Room 506
Little Rock, AR 72203
501-683-2121

California
Employment Development
Department
800 Capitol Mall, MIC 83
P.O. Box 826880
Sacramento, CA 95814
916-654-8210

Colorado
Governor's Job Training Office
720 S. Colorado Blvd.
Suite 550
Denver, CO 80222
303-758-5020

Connecticut
Connecticut Department of
Labor
200 Folly Brook Blvd.
Wethersfield, CT 06109
203-566-4280

Delaware
Employment and Training
Delaware Department of Labor
P.O. Box 9828
Newark, DE 19809
302-761-8110

District of Columbia
District of Columbia
Department of Employment
Services
500 C St., NW, Suite 600
Washington, DC 20001
202-724-7130

Florida
Department of Labor and Employment Security
2012 Capital Circle, Southeast
Suite 303
Tallahassee, FL 32399
850-922-7021

Georgia
Georgia Department of Labor
148 International Blvd., NE
Atlanta, GA 30303
404-656-3011

Hawaii
Department of Labor and Industrial Relations
830 Punchbowl St., Room 329
Honolulu, HI 96813
808-586-8844

Idaho
Idaho Department of Employment
317 Main St.
Boise, ID 83735
208-334-6110

Illinois
Department of Commerce and Community Affairs
620 E. Adams St.
Springfield, IL 62701
217-785-6454

Indiana
Indiana Department of Workforce Development
10 N. Senate Ave.
Room SE 302
Indianapolis, IN 46204
317-233-5661

Iowa
Iowa Department of Economic Development
Division of Workforce Development
100 E. Grand
Des Moines, IA 50319
515-281-5365

Kansas
Kansas Department of Human Resources
401 SW Topeka Blvd.
Topeka, KS 66603
913-296-7474

Kentucky
Office of Training and Reemployment
Workforce Development Cabinet
275 E. Main St., 2 West
Frankfort, KY 40621
502-564-5360

Louisiana
Office of Labor
P.O. Box 94094
Baton Rouge, LA 70804
504-342-7693

Maine
Department of Labor
20 Union St.
P.O. Box 309

Augusta, ME 04332
207-287-3788

Maryland
Labor, Licensing and Regulations
1100 N. Eutaw St., Room 600
Baltimore, MD 21201
410-767-2400

Massachusetts
Corporation for Business, Work, and Learning
The Schrafft Center
529 Main St., Suite 400
Boston, MA 02129
617-727-8158

Michigan
Michigan Jobs Commission
201 N. Washington Square
Lansing, MI 48909
517-373-6227

Minnesota
Minnesota Department of Economic Security
390 N. Robert St., 1st Floor
St. Paul, MN 55101
651-296-3700

Mississippi
Department of Economic and Community Development
Employment Training Division
301 W. Pearl St.
Jackson, MS 39203
601-949-2234

Missouri
Department of Economic Development
2023 St. Mary's Blvd.
Jefferson City, MO 65102
573-526-8229

Montana
Department of Labor and Industry
State Job Training Bureau
P.O. Box 1728
Helena, MT 59624
406-444-2416

Nebraska
Department of Labor
P.O. Box 94600
550 S. 16th St.
Lincoln, NE 68509
402-471-9792

New Hampshire
New Hampshire Job Training Coordinating Council
64-B Old Suncook Rd.
Concord, NH 03301
603-228-9500

New Jersey
State of New Jersey
Department of Labor
CN 055
Trenton, NJ 08629
609-292-2323

New Mexico
New Mexico Department of Labor

P.O. Box 1928
Albuquerque, NM 87103
505-841-8409

New York
New York State Department of Labor
State Office Campus
Building 12
Albany, NY 12240
518-457-2741

North Carolina
Division of Employment and Training
Department of Commerce
111 Seaboard Ave.
Raleigh, NC 27604
919-733-7979

North Dakota
Governor's Employment and Training Forum
P.O. Box 5507
Bismarck, ND 58502
701-328-2836

Ohio
Ohio Bureau of Employment Services
145 S. Front St., 4th Floor
Columbus, OH 43215
614-466-3817

Oklahoma
Security Commission
2401 N. Lincoln
Will Rogers Bldg.
Room 408
Oklahoma City, OK 73152
405-557-5329

Oregon
Oregon Economic Development Department
255 Capitol St., NE, Suite 399
Salem, OR 97310
503-373-1995

Pennsylvania
Employment Security and Job Training
Pennsylvania Department of Labor and Industry
7th and Forster Sts.
Room 1700
Harrisburg, PA 17120
717-787-3907

Rhode Island
Department of Employment and Training
101 Friendship St.
Providence, RI 02903
401-277-3600

South Carolina
South Carolina Employment Security Commission
1550 Gadsden St.
P.O. Box 995
Columbia, SC 29202
803-737-2617

South Dakota
Department of Labor
Kneip Bldg.
700 Governor's Dr.

Pierre, SD 57501
605-773-3101

Tennessee
Department of Labor
710 James Robertson Pkwy.
4th Floor
Nashville, TN 37243
615-741-3031

Texas
Workforce Development
Division
Texas Workforce Commission
101 E. 15th St.
Austin, TX 78778
512-436-2654

Utah
Department of Worforce
Services
140 East 300 South
Salt Lake City, UT 84111
802-531-3780

Vermont
Vermont Department of
Employment and Training
P.O. Box 488
Five Green Mountain Dr.
Montpelier, VT 05601
802-828-4325

Virginia
Governor's Employment and
Training Division
701 E. Broad St.
Richmond, VA 23219
804-786-2315

Washington
Employment and Training
Division
605 Woodland Square Loop
P.O. Box 9046
M/S 6000
Olympia, WA 98507
360-438-4611

West Virginia
Bureau of Employment
Programs
Job Training Programs
Division
112 California Ave., Room
610
Charleston, WV 25305
304-558-2630

Wisconsin
Division of Jobs, Employment
and Training Services
P.O. Box 7972
Madison, WI 53707
608-266-2439

Wyoming
Employment Resources
Division
P.O. Box 2760
Casper, WY 82602
307-235-3254

Free Training for Workers Laid Off Because Their Factories Complied With Air Pollution Laws

Federal air pollution laws on the books are certainly better than none at all. Look at Mexico City's respiratory fatalities due to industrial smoke.

Even though the government has shut down your factory because of pollution or environmental questions, Uncle Sam will help you get back on your feet with free training programs and unemployment services. Those eligible for this program include dislocated workers who are unlikely to return to their previous industries or occupations, and who have been terminated or laid off due to a decision to reduce employment as a result of a company's compliance with the requirements of the Clean Air Act.

For more information, contact your state job training office, check the State Dislocated Worker Contacts on page 330, or Office of Worker Retraining and Adjustment Programs, Employment and Training Administration, U.S. Department Labor, Room N5426, 200 Constitution Ave., NW, Washington, DC 20210; 202-219-5577; {www.doleta.gov}.

Free Training If You Are Laid Off Due To Defense Cutbacks

Thousands of communities around the country have felt the fallout of the end of the Cold War. And the fallout has been economic, not nuclear. Base closings mean no jobs — pure and simple. Fortunately, the Defense Conversion Adjustment (DCA) Program provides retraining and other assistance for workers hurt by defense cutbacks.

The DCA Program offers retraining and readjustment services tailored to meet each individual participant. Long-term training, including educational and occupational, is encouraged. Those eligible include workers who lose their jobs because of plant closings or mass layoffs due to reduced U.S. defense expenditures or closed military facilities.

For more information contact your state job training office, check the State Dislocated Worker Contacts on page 330, or Office of Worker Retraining and Adjustment Programs, Employment and Training Administration, U.S. Department Labor, Room N5426, 200 Constitution Ave., NW, Washington, DC 20210; 202-219-5577; {www.doleta.gov}.

Free Training If You Are Laid Off By A Defense Contractor

If you have been laid off or fired because the company you worked for was on the wrong end of cutbacks at the U.S. Department of Defense, you may qualify to be retrained for another job.

The Defense Diversification Program (DDP) provides retraining and readjustment assistance to workers and military personnel dislocated by defense cutbacks and base closings, as well as career planning support and assistance. Those eligible for the program include civilian employees of the Department of Defense, Department of Energy, and defense contractors who have been terminated or laid off, or have a notice of termination or layoff.

For more information contact your state job training office, check the State Dislocated Worker Contacts on page 330, or Office of Worker Retraining and Adjustment Programs, Employment and Training Administration, U.S. Department Labor, Room N5426, 200 Constitution Ave., NW, Washington, DC 20210; 202-219-5577; {www.doleta.gov}.

How To Make A High School Diploma Worth More

The School-to-Work program provides money to States and local partnerships of business, labor, government, education, and community organizations to develop school-to-work systems. School-to-Work is based on the concept that education works best and is most useful for future careers when students apply what they learn to real life, real work situations. School-to-Work has three core elements: School-based learning, Work-based learning, and Connecting Activities. School-to-Work looks different in each state and locality.

Contact your state office to learn more. State offices can be contacted from the list below; or National School-To-Work Learning and Information Center, 400 Virginia Ave., SW, Room 210, Washington, DC 20024; 800-251-7236; {www.stw.ed.gov}.

School-to-Work Grantees

Alabama
Center for Commerce
Room 424
401 Adams Ave.
Suite 380
Montgomery, AL 36103
334-242-5300
www.noicc.gov

Alaska
Alaska Department of Education
801 W. 10th St., Suite 200
Juneau, AK 99801
907-465-8726
E-mail: {Sally_Saddler@educ.state.ak.us}.

Arizona
Arizona Department of Commerce
STW Division
3800 North Central Ave.
Building D
Phoenix, AZ 85012
602-280-8130
www.state.az.us/commerce

Arkansas
Arkansas Career Opportunities Initiative
Department of Workforce
3 Capitol Mall
Room 506D
Little Rock, AR 72201
501-682-1579

California
Department of Education High School Division
Assistant Superintendent and Director
721 Capitol Mall, 4th Floor
Sacramento, CA 94244
916-657-2532

Colorado
Colorado School-to-Career Partnership
1580 Logan St., Suite 410
Denver, CO 80203
303-894-2060
www.state.co.us/gov_dir/ltgov/schooltowork/index.html

Connecticut
Connecticut State Department of Education
Acting Associate Commissioner of Education
25 Industrial Park Rd.
Middletown, CT 06457
860-807-2005

Delaware
Delaware Department of Public Instruction
Vocational-Technical Education & STW Transition
Townsend Building
Federal & Lockerman Streets
Dover, DE 19901
302-739-4638

District of Columbia
DC Public Schools
Corporation and Community Relations
825 N. Capitol, NE
8th Floor, Room 8144
Washington, DC 20002
202-442-5155

Florida
Florida Department of Education
325 West Gaines St.
Unit 754
Tallahassee, FL 32399
850-488-7394

Georgia
Workforce Development Initiatives
Georgia Department of Technical & Adult Education
1800 Century Place, Suite 400
Atlanta, GA 30345
404-679-1658

Hawaii
Hawaii School-to-Work Opportunities
State Executive Director
874 Dillingham Blvd.
Honolulu, HI 96817
808-845-9432
www.hdo.k12.hi.us/stwo

Idaho
Idaho School-to-Work
Executive Director
650 W. State St., Suite 300
P.O. Box 83720
Boise, ID 83720
208-332-6928
http://netnow.micron.net/~stw/index.html

Illinois
Office of the Governor
107 Stratton Building
Springfield, IL 62706
217-782-1145

Indiana
Department of Workforce Development
State STW Director
10 N. Senate Ave., SE
Room 302 Indiana Government Center
Indianapolis, IN 46204
317-232-1832
www.dwd.state.in.us

Iowa
Workforce Development Administrative Center
Grimes State Office Building
3rd Floor
Des Moines, IA 50319
515-242-5611

Kansas
Kansas State Department of Education
Coordinator, School-to-Careers
120 SE 10th Ave.
Topeka, KS 66612
785-296-3915

Kentucky
Executive Director
Berry Hill Annex
700 Louisville Rd.
Frankfort, KY 40601
502-564-5901
www.state.ky.us/agencies/wforce/

Louisiana
Office of Lifelong Learning
School-to-Work Liaison
P.O. Box 94004
Baton Rouge, LA 70804
504-342-2094
www.leeric.lsu.edu/stw

Maine
Department of Education
Workforce Education and School-to-Work Opportunities
23 State House Station
Augusta, ME 04333
207-287-5854

Maryland
Department of Education
Assistant State Superintendent
200 West Baltimore St.
Baltimore, MD 21201
410-767-0157

Massachusetts
Massachusetts Office for School-to-Work Transition
350 Main St.
Malden, MA 02148
781-388-3300 ext. 311
www.stw.bssc.org

Michigan
Michigan Jobs Commission
Office of Workforce Development
201 North Washington Square
Victor Office Center
Fifth Floor
Lansing, MI 48913
517-335-5858
www.mjc.state.mi.us

Minnesota
Minnesota Department of Children, Families and Learning
Office of Lifework Development
1500 Highway 36 West
Roseville, MN 55113
651-582-8427
http://children.state.mn.us

Mississippi
Mississippi Department of Education
Central High School Building
359 North West St.
Jackson, MS 39205
601-359-1737

Missouri
Missouri Department of Elementary and Secondary Education
Assistant Director
School-to-Work
P.O. Box 480
Jefferson City, MO 65102
573-751-4192

Montana
Office of the Commissioner of Higher Education
Director for Workforce Development
2500 Broadway
Helena, MT 59620
406-444-0316
www.montan.edu/wochesw/docs/webpage.html

Nebraska
Nebraska Alliance for Learning
STW Director
301 Centennial Mall South
Lincoln, NE 68509
402-471-3741
www.ded.state.ne.us/stw/stw.html

Nevada
Nevada Dept. of Education
State School-to-Careers Coordinator
700 E. Fifth St.
Carson City, NV 89701
775-687-9243

New Hampshire
Department of Education
Educational Consultant
101 Pleasant St.
Concord, NH 03301
603-271-3729

New Jersey
New Jersey Department of Education
Office of School-to-Work Initiatives
100 Riverview Plaza
Trenton, NJ 08625
609-633-0665
www.state.nj.us.gov.educ

New Mexico
Office of the Governor
Governor's Education Policy Advisor/STW Coordinator
State Capitol Bldg., Suite 400
Santa Fe, NM 87503
505-827-3078
www.edd.state.nm.us/ST

New York
New York State Education Department
Assistant Commissioner, Workforce Preparation and Continuing Education
89 Washington Ave.
Room 319 EB
Albany, NY 12234
518-474-8892
www.nysed.gov/workforce/work.html

North Carolina
Commission on Workforce Preparedness
School-to-Work Transition
116 West Jones St.
Raleigh, NC 27603
919-715-3300

North Dakota
North Dakota/STW Opportunities System

State Capitol, 15th Floor
Bismarck, ND 58505
701-328-3074

Ohio
Ohio School-to-Work
131 North High St.
Suite 500
Columbus, OH 43215
614-728-4630
www.ohio-stw.com

Oklahoma
Department of Vocational and Technical Education
State Coordinator
1500 West Seventh Ave.
Stillwater, OK 74074
405-743-5158
www.okvotech.org

Oregon
Oregon Department of Education
Coordinator, School-to-Work Teams
255 Capitol St., NE
Salem, OR 97310
503-378-3584 Ext. 350

Pennsylvania
Pennsylvania Department of Education
School-to-Work Opportunities Liaison
333 Market St., 5th Floor
Harrisburg, PA 17126
717-772-4177

Rhode Island
Rhode Island School-to-Work Director
610 Manton Ave., 3rd Floor
Providence, RI 02909
401-222-4922

South Carolina
Office of the Governor
STW Coordinator
1429 Senate St., Room 912A
Columbia, SC 29201
803-734-8410

South Dakota
Department of Labor
STW Coordinator
700 Governors Dr.
Pierre, SD 57501
605-773-5017
www.state.sd.us/dol/jtpa/stw.htm

Tennessee
Department of Education
Executive Director
710 James Robertson Parkway, 6th Floor
Nashville, TN 37243
615-532-5942
www.state.tn.us/education/stchpage.html

Texas
Texas Workforce Commission
Research Specialist III
STW Coordinator
1117 Trinity St., Room 326T

Austin, TX 787778
512-936-3267

Utah
Utah State Office of Education
Coordinator, School to Careers
250 East 500 South
Salt Lake City, UT 84111
801-538-7850

Vermont
Vermont Department of
Employment and Training
5 Green Mountain Dr.
P.O. Box 488
Montpelier, VT 05601
802-828-4301
www.det.state.vt.us

Virginia
Virginia Business-Education
Partnership
100-101 North 9th St.
Fifth Floor
Richmond, VA 23219
804-692-0244
www.state.va.us/vbep

Washington
Office of Superintendent of
Public Instruction
Secondary Education and
Career Preparation
Old Capitol Building
600 Washington St., SE
Olympia, WA 98504
360-753-2062
www.wa.gov/wtb

West Virginia
Director
1900 Kanawha Blvd., East
Building 6, Room 235
Charleston, WV 25305
304-558-2389

Wisconsin
Department of Workforce
Development, Connecting
Education & Work
Division Administrator
201 East Washington Ave.
Room 231X
Madison, WI 53702
608-266-0223

Wyoming
Office of Workforce
Development
Herschler Building
122 W. 25th St.
Cheyenne, WY 82002
307-777-7639

Free Training For Dead Beat Dads

No one likes a deadbeat dad, but Uncle Sam understands that many fathers fall behind in child support not because they're evil, wicked, mean, and nasty. Some just don't have a job and not much training to make them qualified for many jobs.

The Parents Fair Share Program was a demonstration program of the Administration for Children and Families (part of the U.S. Department of Health and Human Services), and was designed to help parents get the training they need to get a paycheck to help with child support. The demonstration program has since ended, but many of the sites continue to provide job readiness and job skills training.

For more information, contact one of the sites below:

California
Los Angeles County Fair Share, Bureau of Family Support Operations, 5770 South Eastern Ave., Commerce, CA 90024; 323-889-2954.

Florida
Duvall County Parents' Fair Share, Employment and Training Security, Department of Labor, 421 W. Church St., Jacksonville, FL 32202; 904-798-4720.

Massachusetts
Massachusetts JOBS Parents' Fair Share Project, Springfield Employment Resource Ctr., Inc., 140 Wilbraham Ave., Springfield, MA 01109; 413-737-9544.

Michigan
Non-Custodial Parent Program, 385 Leonard NE, Grand Rapids, MI 49503; 616-458-6350.

New Jersey
Operation Fatherhood, Union Industrial Home For Children, 4 N. Broad St., Trenton, NJ 08608; 609-695-3663.

Ohio
Options for Parental Training and Support, Montgomery County Department of Human Services, 14 W. Fourth St., Dayton, OH 45402; 937-225-4077.

Triple Your Salary With Job Training For Migrant And Farm Workers

Migrant workers and seasonal laborers are some of the hardest working people in America. Yet when the crops are all picked or the economy sags, they are some of the first to be out of a job. And most of these people live just at the poverty level to begin with.

Fortunately, the government has a special job training program to help them find less backbreaking work. Participants can receive a weekly allowance at the current minimum wage and learn new work skills in classroom and on-the-job training programs, work experience in new employment areas, job development and placement services, relocation and education assistance, and more.

For more information contact your local job training office, or U.S. Department of Labor, Office of Special Targeted Programs, Division of Migrant and Seasonal Farmworker Programs, Room N-4641, 200 Constitution Ave., NW, Washington, DC 20210; 202-219-5500; {www.wdsc.org/msfw}.

Migrant and Seasonal Farmworker Programs

Alabama
Alabama Department of Economic and Community Affairs
401 Adams Ave.
Montgomery, AL 36103
334-242-5100

Alabama Opportunity Program
224 Church St., Suite D
Huntsville, AL 35801
205-536-8218

Arizona
Portable Practical Educational Preparation, Inc.
806 East 46th St.
Tucson, AZ 85713
520-622-3553

Arkansas
Arkansas Human Development Corporation
Suite 800, 300 S. Spring St.
300 Spring Building
Little Rock, AR 72201
501-374-1103

California
Employers Training Resource
County of Kern
2001 28th St.
Bakersfield, CA 93301
805-861-2495

Center for Employment Training
701 Vine St.
San Jose, CA 95110
408-287-7924

Proteus, Inc.
4612 West Mineral King Ave.
P.O. Box 727
Visalia, CA 93279
559-733-5423
www.proteusinc.org

Central Valley Opportunity Center, Inc.
1748 Miles Court
P.O. Box 2307
Merced, CA 95348
209-383-2415
www.elite.net/~cvocplan/

Colorado
Rocky Mountain Ser/Jobs for Progress, Inc.
3555 Pecos St.
P.O. Box 11148
Denver, CO 80211
303-480-9394

Connecticut
New England Farm Workers' Council, Inc.
191 Franklin Ave.
Hartford, CT 06114
860-296-3518

Delaware
Telamon Corp.
504 North Dupont Highway
Dover, DE 19901
302-734-1903

Florida
Adult Migrant and Seasonal Farm Workers Program
Suite 200
3801 Corporex Park Dr.
Corporex Plaza Two
Tampa, FL 33619
813-744-6303

Georgia
Telamon Corporation
Suite 140, Building D
2720 Sheraton Dr.
Macon, GA 31204
912-750-7134
www.telamon.org

Hawaii
Maui Economic Opportunity, Inc.
189 Kaahumanu
P.O. Box 2122
Kaului, HI 96732
808-871-9591

Idaho
Idaho Migrant Council
104 North Kimball
P.O. Box 490
Caldwell, ID 83606
208-454-1652

Illinois
Illinois Migrant Council
16th floor
28 East Jackson Blvd.
Chicago, IL 60604
312-663-1522

Indiana
Transition Resource Corporation
Suite 0-2
2511 East 46th St.
Indianapolis, IN 46205
317-547-1924
www.telamon.org

Iowa
Proteus, Inc.
175 NW 57th Place
Des Moines, IA 50313
515-244-5694
www.netins.net/showcase/proteus

Kansas
SER Corporation of
Kansas/SER Rural Initiatives
709 East 21st
Wichita, KS 67214
316-264-5372

Kentucky
Kentucky Farmworker
Programs, Inc.
1844 Lyda St., Suite 210
P.O. Box 51146
Bowling Green, KY 42102
502-782-2330

Louisiana
Motivation, Education and
Training, Inc.
1055 Laurel St.
Baton Rouge, LA 70802
504-343-0301

Maine
Training and Development
Corporation
14 High St.
Ellsworth, ME 04605
207-667-7543

Maryland
Telamon Corp.
237 Florida Ave.
Salisbury, MD 21801
410-546-4604

Massachusetts
New England Farm Workers'
Council, Inc.
1628-1640 Main St.
Springfield, MA 01103
413-781-2145

Michigan
Telamon Corp.
Suite C
6250 West Michigan Ave.
Lansing, MI 48917
517-323-7002

Minnesota
Motivation Education and
Training Inc.
1900 Highway 294, NE
Suite 2040
Wilmar, MN 56201
320-231-5174

Mississippi
Mississippi Delta Council for
Farm Workers Opportunities,
Inc.
1005 State St.
Clarksdale, MS 38614
601-627-1121

Missouri
Rural Missouri, Inc.
1014 Northeast Dr.
Jefferson City, MO 65109
573-635-0136

Montana
Rural Employment
Opportunities, Inc.
25 South Ewing St., 5th Floor
P.O. Box 831
Helena, MT 59624
406-442-7850

Nebraska
NAF Multicultural Human Development Corp.
416 East 4th St.
P.O. Box 1459
North Platte, NE 69103
308-534-2630

Nevada
Center for Employment Training
520 Evans Ave.
Reno, NV 89512
702-348-8668

New Hampshire
Farm Workers' Council, Inc.
370 Union St.
Manchester, NH 03103
603-622-8199

New Jersey
New Jersey Rural Opportunities
510-12 E. Landis Ave.
Vineland, NJ 08360
609-696-1000

New Mexico
Home Education Livelihood Program, Inc.
5101 Copper NE
Albuquerque, NM 87017
505-265-3717

New York
Rural Opportunities, Inc.
400 East Ave.
Suite 401
Rochester, NY 14604
716-546-7180

North Carolina
Telamon Corp.
3937 Western Blvd.
P.O. Box 33315
Raleigh, NC 27636
919-851-7611
www.telamon.org

Telamon Corp.
Suite 200
4917 Waters Edge Dr.
Raleigh, NC 27606
919-851-6141
www.telamon.org

North Dakota
Midwest Farmworker Employment and Training Inc.
Suite D
1323 South 25th St.
Fargo, ND 58106
701-241-8442

Ohio
Rural Opportunities Inc.
320 West Gypsy Lane Rd.
P.O. Box 186
Bowling Green, OH 43402
419-354-3552

Oklahoma
ORO Development Corp.
Suite 204
5929 North May Ave.
Oklahoma City, OK 73112
405-840-7077

Oregon
Oregon Human Development Corp.
Suite 110
9620 SW Barbur Blvd.
Portland, OR 97219
503-245-2600
www.1stop.org/washco/ohdc/

Pennsylvania
Rural Opportunities, Inc.
2nd Floor
1300 Market St.
Lemoyne, PA 17043
717-731-8120

Puerto Rico
Commonwealth of Puerto Rico
Department of Labor and Human Resources
21st Floor
505 Munoz Rivera Ave.
Hato Rey, PR 00918
809-472-6620

South Carolina
Telamon Corp.
1413 Calhoun St.
P.O. Box 12217
Columbia, SC 29211
803-256-8528
www.telamon.org

South Dakota
Midwest Farmworker
Employment and Training, Inc.
121 W. Dakota St.
Pierre, SD 57501
605-224-0454

Tennessee
Tennessee Opportunity Program For Seasonal Farm Workers, Inc.
1370 Hazelwood Dr.
Suite 207
P.O. Box 925
Smyrna, TN 37167
615-459-3600

Texas
Motivation, Education and Training, Inc.
307 North College
P.O. Box 1749
Cleveland, TX 77328
281-592-6483

Utah
Private Industry Council, Inc.
Futures Through Training, Inc.
533 26th St., Suite 204
Ogden, UT 84401
801-394-9774

Vermont
Central Vermont Community Action Council, Inc.
195 US Rt. 302-Berlin
Barre, VT 05641
802-479-1053

Virginia
Telamon Corp.
4915 Radford Ave.
Suite 202A
Richmond, VA 23220
804-355-4676
www.telamon.org

Washington
Director of Employment Training
Washington State Migrant Council
105-B South 6th St.
Sunnyside, WA 98944
509-837-5443

West Virginia
Telemon Corp.
100 Williamsport Ave.
Martinsburg, WV 25401
304-263-0916

Wisconsin
DILHR- Employment and Training
Room 231-X
201 East Washington Ave.
P.O. Box 7972
Madison, WI 53707
608-267-7273
www.dwd.state.wi.us

United Migrant Opportunity Services
929 West Mitchell St.
P.O. Box 04129
Milwaukee, WI 53204
414-671-5700

Wyoming
Northwestern Community Action Programs of Wyoming, Inc.
1922 1/2 Robertson Ave.
P.O. Box 158
Worland, WY 82401
307-347-6185

Free Jobs and Training for Dropouts Interested in Construction Careers

Bottom line: most construction jobs pay really well. If you like the work, training in the construction industry can fatten the paycheck even further. If you get the itch, you might even want to become an engineer, or — better yet — become someone who gets to use the wrecking ball.

Young men and women can get experience in the construction trades, while helping to build housing for the homeless under the Youthbuild program. Participants get hands-on training in the rehabilitation and construction of housing, as well as valuable off-site education. Low income kids between the ages of 16 and 24 are eligible to participate.

For more information about sites across the country check out the list below, or contact Office of Economic Development, Community Planning and Development, U.S. Department of Housing and Urban Development, Washington, DC 20410; 202-708-2035.

Youthbuild Sites

Alabama
Birmingham Enterprise Community, Inc.
1200 Tuscaloosa Ave., West
Birmingham, AL 35211
205-322-3117

Arizona
City of Phoenix
200 West Washington
Phoenix, AZ 85003
602-262-4032

Town of Guadalupe
9050 S. Avenida Del Yaqui
Guadalupe, AZ 85283
602-730-8030

California
Century Center for Economic Opportunity
17216 S. Figueroa St.
Gardena, CA 90248
310-255-3070

Community Services And Employment Training
2150 S. Mooney Blvd.
Visalia, CA 93277
209-732-4194

Excelsior Education Center
14564 7th St.
Victorville, CA 92392
760-245-4264, ext. 22

Neighborhood Housing Services of the Inland Empire, Inc.
390 North D St.
San Bernardino, CA 92405
909-884-6891

Pacific Asian Consortium In Employment
1541 Wilshire Blvd.
Los Angeles, CA 90017
213-353-3982

Sonoma County People for Economic Opportunity
555 Sebastopol Ave.
Santa Rosa, CA 95401
707-544-6911

Venice Community Housing Corp.
318 Lincoln Blvd., Suite 225
Venice, CA 90291
310-399-4100

Connecticut
Co-Opportunity Inc.
117 Murphy Rd.
Hartford, CT 06114
860-236-3617

District of Columbia
Arch Training Center, Inc.
2427 Martin Luther King, Jr. Ave., SE
Washington, DC 20012
202-889-6344

Latin American Youth Center
3045 15th St., NW
Washington, DC 20009
202-483-1140

Sasha Bruce Youthwork, Inc.
741 8th St., SE
Washington, DC 20003
202-675-9340

Florida
City of Jacksonville
117 W. Duval St.
Jacksonville, FL 32202
904-630-6440
Gainesville Housing Authority
1900 SE 4th St.
Gainesville, FL 32602
352-371-3180

Illinois
Youthbuild McLean County
1312 W. Monroe
Bloomington, IL 61701
309-827-7505

Louisiana
Louisiana Technical College-Tallulah
Old Highway 65 South
Tallulah, LA 71282
318-574-4820

Maine
Portland West Neighborhood Planning Council
155 Brackett St.
Portland, ME 04102
207-775-0105

Maryland
Southern Area Youth Services, Inc.
4710 Auth Place
Suite 620
Suitland, MD 20746
301-702-9730

Massachusetts
Massachusetts Job Training, Inc.
332 Main St., Suite 601
Worcester, MA 01608
508-753-2991

Nueva Esperanza inc.
401 Main St.
Holyoke, MA 01040
413-533-9442

Old Colony Y Services Corp.
320 Main St.
Brockton, MA 02301
508-584-1100 ext. 21

People Acting in Community Endeavors, Inc.
P.O. Box 5626
New Bedford, MA 02742
508-999-9920

Youthbuild Boston, Inc.
504 Dudley St.
Roxbury, MA 02119
617-445-8887

Michigan
Neighborhood Information and Sharing Exchange
200 Paw Paw
Benton Harbor, MI 49022
616-925-3948

Oakland Livingston Human Service
196 Oakland Ave.
Pontiac, MI 48343
248-209-2622

Washtenaw County
220 North Main St.
Ann Arbor, MI 48105
734-994-2435

Missouri
Youth Education and Health in Soulard
1921 South 9th St.
St. Louis, MO 63014
314-436-1400

Montana
Human Resource Development Council of District IX, Inc.
321 East Main
Suite 300
Bozeman, MT 59715
406-587-4486

Nebraska
Chadron Community Development Corp.
P.O. Box 978
Chadron, NE 69337
308-432-4346

New Hampshire
Odyssey House, Inc.
P.O. Box 780
Hampton, NH 03843
603-929-3038 Ext. 341

New Jersey
Atlantic City Youthbuild
1 South Carolina Ave.
Atlantic City, NJ 08401
609-345-4575

Isles, Inc.
10 Wood St.
Trenton, NJ 08618
609-393-5656 ext. 14

New Jersey Community Development Corp.
13 1/2 Van Houten St.
Paterson, NJ 07505
973-225-0555

Paterson Coalition for Housing, Inc.
262 Main St.
Paterson, NJ 07505
973-684-5998

New Mexico
Youthbuild New Mexico Coalition, Inc.
115 Second St., SW
Albuquerque, NM 87102
505-244-9505

New York
New York Housing Authority
250 Broadway
New York, NY 10007
212-306-8424

The Urban League of Rochester, NY, Inc.
265 N. Clinton Ave.

Rochester, NY 14605
716-325-6530

Youth Action Programs and Homes, Inc.
218 East 106th St.
New York, NY 10029
212-860-8190

North Carolina
Housing Authority of the City of High Point
500 East Russell Ave.
High Point, NC 27260
336-887-2661

River City Community Development Corp.
501 E. Maine St.
Elizabeth, NC 27909
252-331-2925

UDI Community Development Corp.
P.O. Box 1349
631 United Dr.
Durham, NC 27702
919-544-4597

Ohio
Community Action Commission of Fayette County
324 E. Court St.
Fayette County, OH 43160
740-335-7282

Cuyahoga County Youthbuild
112 Hamilton Court
Cleveland, OH 44114
216-443-8160

Improved Solutions for Urban Systems, Inc.
100 N. Jefferson St.
Suite 602
Dayton, OH 45402
937-223-2323

Private Industry Council of Trumbull County, Inc.
815 Youngstown Warren Rd.
Niles, OH 44446
330-652-2095

Oklahoma
Housing Authority of the City of Tulsa
415 E. Independence
Tulsa, OK 74148
918-581-5777

Oregon
City of Portland
808 SW Third Ave.
Portland, OR 97204
513-286-9350

Pennsylvania
Crispus Attucks Community Development Corp.
605 S. Duke
York, PA 17403
610-921-6997

Housing Authority City of Pittsburgh
200 Ross St.

Pittsburgh, PA 15219
412-456-5085

Philadelphia Youth for Change
Charter School
619 Catherine St.
Philadelphia, PA 19147
215-627-8671

Youthbuild Pittsburgh, Inc.
7129 Hamilton Ave.
Pittsburgh, PA 15208
412-242-7709

South Carolina
Telamon Corp.
P.O. Box 12217
Columbia, SC 29211
803-256-7411

Tennessee
Tennessee Technology Center
at Memphis
550 Alabama Ave.
Memphis, TN 38105
901-527-9617

Texas
American Institute for
Learning
422 Congress Ave.
Austin, TX 73701
512-472-3395

Community Development
Corporation of Brownsville
1150 East Adams St.
Brownsville, TX 78520
956-541-4955

Gulf Coast Trades Center
P.O. Box 515
New Waverly, TX 77358
409-344-6677

Harlingen Community
Development Corp.
518 East Harrison
Harlingen, TX 78550
956-421-2351

Harris County Youthbuild
1310 Prairie
Houston, TX 77002
713-755-4766

Vermont
King Street Youth Center
14 South Williams St.
Burlington, VT 05401
802-862-6736

Randolph County Housing
Authority
1200 Harrison Ave.
Elkins, WV 26241
304-636-6495

Southern Appalachian Labor
School
P.O. Box 127
Kincaid, WV 25119
304-442-3157

Wisconsin
809 N. Broadway, 3rd Floor
Milwaukee, WI 53202
414-286-2034

Milwaukee Community
Service Corps.
Milwaukee Christian Center
1150 E. Beady St.
Milwaukee, WI 53202
404-276-6272

Operation Fresh Start Inc.
1925 Winnebago St.
Madison, WI 53704
608-244-4721

Free Job Training and More For Foster Care Teens

All kinds of free help is out there for teenagers in foster care — and young adults who have been raised in foster homes — to get the job skills they need to make a good life on their own. The Independent Living program helps foster care youth between the ages of 16 and 21, in getting a GED or a driving permit and provides assistance in filling out college applications. Those who live out in the country can even get free transportation to job training programs that can assure them of a good paying career track.

For more information, contact your foster care worker, or to learn your state contact for the Independent Living program contact Division of Child Welfare, Children's Bureau, Administration for Children and Families, P.O. Box 1182, Washington, DC 20013; 202-205-8740; {www.acf.dhhs.gov/programs/cb/programs/index.htm}.

Independent Living State Coordinators

Alaska
Alaska Division of Family and Youth Services
P.O. Box 110630
Juneau, AK 99811
907-465-2145

Alabama
Alabama Department of Human Resources
1050 Government St.
Suite 201
Mobile, AL 36604
334-433-4456

Arizona
Arizona Department of Economic Security
1717 W. Jefferson, 3rd Floor
Phoenix, AZ 85007
602-542-5120

Arkansas
Arkansas Division of Children and Family Services
P.O. Box 1437, Slot 819
Little Rock, AR 72203
501-682-8453

California
California Department of Social Services
744 P St.
MS 19-78
Sacramento, CA 95814
916-324-9084

Colorado
Colorado Department of Human Services
1575 Sherman St., 2nd Floor
Denver, CO 80203
303-866-3228

Connecticut
DCYS
505 Hudson St.
Hartford, CT 06106
860-550-6471

District of Columbia
Department of Human Services
Independent Living Programs
65 I St., SW, Room 219
Washington, DC 20024
202-727-1534

Delaware
Division of Child Protective Services
1825 Faulkland Rd.
Wilmington, DE 19805
302-633-2659

Florida
Florida Department of Health and Rehabilitative Services
1317 Winewood Blvd.
Tallahassee, FL 32399
850-921-1883

Georgia
Division of Family and Children Services
2 Peachtree St., NW
Atlanta, GA 30303
404-657-3459

Hawaii
Hawaii Department of Human Services
Family and Adult Services
810 Richards St., Suite 400
Honolulu, HI 96809
808-586-5668

Idaho
Idaho Department of Health and Welfare
P.O. Box 83720
Boise, ID 83720
208-334-38000

Illinois
Illinois Department of Children and Family Services
406 E. Monroe Station, #75
Springfield, IL 62701
217-785-2467

Illinois Department of Children and Family Services
Research and Demonstration Unit
1921 S. Indiana
Chicago, IL 60616
312-808-5240

Indiana
Indiana Department of Public Welfare
Children and Family Services
402 W. Washington St.
Room W364
Indianapolis, IN 46204
317-232-4631

Iowa
Division of Adults, Children, and Family Services
Hoover State Office Building
Des Moines, IA 50319
515-281-6786

Kansas
Youth and Adult Services
Docking State Office Building
9155 SW Harrison, 5th Floor
Topeka, KS 66606
913-368-8165

Kentucky
Kentucky Department of Social Services
Children and Youth Services, 6W

275 E. Main St.
Frankfort, KY 40621
502-564-2147

Louisiana
Louisiana Department of Social Services
Office of Community Services
P.O. Box 3318
Baton Rouge, LA 70821
504-342-2279

Office of Community Services
P.O. Box 61210
New Orleans, LA 70161
504-342-2268

Maine
Maine Department of Human Services
11 State House Station
Augusta, ME 04333
207-287-5060

Maryland
Maryland Department of Human Resources
Independent Living Coordinator
311 W. Saratoga St.
Suite 572
Baltimore, MD 21201
410-767-7634

Massachusetts
Massachusetts Department of Social Services
24 Farnsworth St.
Boston, MA 02110
617-727-0900

Michigan
Michigan Department of Social Services
235 S. Grand, Suite 511
Lansing, MI 48909
517-373-2083

Minnesota
Minnesota Department of Human Services
444 Lafayette Rd.
St. Paul, MN 55155
612-296-7635

Mississippi
Department of Human Services
Office of Social Services
P.O. Box 352
Jackson, MS 39205
601-359-4982

Missouri
Missouri Division of Family Services
P.O. Box 88
Jefferson City, MO 65103
314-751-4319

Montana
Department of Family Services
P.O. Box 8005
Cogswell Bldg. 1
1400 Broadway
Helena, MT 59620
406-444-5900

Nebraska
Nebraska Department of Social Services
301 Centennial Mall South
State Office Building
Lincoln, NE 68509
402-471-9434

Nevada
Nevada State Welfare/ Department of Human Resources
Division of Child and Family Services
6171 W. Charleston Blvd., Bldg. 15
Las Vegas, NV 89158
702-486-6014

New Hampshire
New Hampshire Division for Children, Youth, and Family
Bureau of Children
6 Hazen Dr.
Concord, NH 03301
603-271-4706

New Jersey
Division of Youth and Family Services
1 S. Montgomery St.
CN 717- Fifth Floor
Trenton, NJ 08625
609-292-0887

New Mexico
Department of Children, Youth and Family
707 Broadway NE, #500
Albuquerque, NM 87102
505-841-9500

New York
NYS Department of Social Services
40 N. Pearl St., Floor 11-A
Albany, NY 12243
518-474-9586

North Carolina
Care Program
North Carolina Division of Social Services
325 N. Salisbury St.
Raleigh, NC 27603
919-733-4622

North Dakota
North Dakota Department of Human Services
600 E. Boulevard Ave.
Bismarck, ND 58505
701-328-4934

Ohio
Ohio Department of Human Services
Family Enhancement Services
65 East Sate St., 5th floor
Columbus, OH 43215
614-728-4733

Oklahoma
Oklahoma Department of Human Services
P.O. Box 25352
Oklahoma City, OK 73125
405-521-4364

Oregon
Oregon Children's Service Division
Program Development Grant Support
500 Summer St., NE
Salem, OR 97310
503-945-6619

Pennsylvania
Pennsylvania Department of Public Welfare
DPW-OCYF
P.O. Box 2675
Harrisburg, PA 17105
717-783-3984

Rhode Island
Rhode Island Department of Children and Families
610 Mt. Pleasant Ave., Bldg. 10
Providence, RI 02908
401-457-4503

South Carolina
South Carolina Department of Social Services
P.O. Box 1520
Columbia, SC 29202
803-734-3515

South Dakota
Department of Social Services
Office of Child Protection Services
700 Governor's Dr.
Pierre, SD 57501
605-773-3227

Tennessee
Tennessee Department of Human Services
Social Services Policy Development
400 Deaderick St., 14th Floor
Nashville, TN 37248
615-532-5644

Texas
Texas Department of Protective and Regulatory Services
P.O. Box 149030, MC E-558
Austin, TX 78714
512-438-5442

Utah
Utah Dept. of Social Services
120 N. 200 W.
P.O. Box 45500
Salt Lake City, UT 84103
801-538-4070

Vermont
Vermont Department of Social Services
103 S. Main St.
Waterbury, VT 05676
801-241-2131

Virginia
Independent Living Program Coordinator
Virginia Department of Social Services
730 E. Broad St.
Richmond, VA 23219
804-692-1293

Washington
Division of Children and Family Services
4045 Delridge Way Southwest, Suite 400
Seattle, WA 98106
206-933-3538

Wisconsin
Wisconsin Department of Health and Social Services
One W. Wilson St.
P.O. Box 8916, Room 465
Madison, WI 53708
608-266-5330

West Virginia
West Virginia University
Independent Living Program Manager
955 Harman Run Rd.
Morgantown, WV 26505
304-558-7980

Wyoming
Department of Family Service
324 Hathaway Bldg.
Cheyenne, WY 82001
307-777-5878

Free Job Training, GED Courses, And Guaranteed Jobs For High School Kids And Poverty Zone Drop Outs

Growing up in poverty today isn't what it was earlier this century. In years past, a life of poverty was much harder. There was no government assistance, no food stamps, no volunteer organizations willing to spend time helping anyone out.

Youth Fair Chance is a new community based program that gives money directly to areas where problems for kids are greatest — high poverty zones. The purpose of Youth Fair Chance is to serve kids who just aren't getting what they need from traditional job training and placement programs. Some of the special kinds of help kids can receive include: employment and training, help staying in school, assistance in dealing with drug and gang involvement, participation in sports and recreation, family support, and more. Kids and young adults between 14-30 years of age who reside in rural and urban communities are eligible.

For more information on the program or to locate the site nearest you, contact Office of Policy and Research, Employment and Training Administration, U.S. Department of Labor, 200 Constitution Ave., NW, Washington, DC 20210; 202-219-8668; {www.doleta.gov}.

Need Money But Out Of Work

If you have been laid off or your company has downsized you out of your job through no fault of your own, then help is out there for you. Unemployment compensation is the government's first line of defense against the ripple effects of unemployment.

By cash payments made directly to laid off workers, the program ensures that at least a significant proportion of the necessities of life, such as food, shelter, and clothing, can be met while a search for work takes place. There are no federal standards for benefits, in terms of qualifying requirements, benefit amounts, or duration of the regular benefits. All states do require that a person work a certain amount of time or earn a specified amount of wages to qualify for the program.

Unemployment benefits can often be extended in certain circumstances.

To learn more contact your local Unemployment Office that can be found by looking in the blue pages of your phone book. If you need more information, you may also contact the main office at Unemployment Insurance Service, Employment and Training Administration, U.S. Department of Labor, 200 Constitution Ave., NW, Washington, DC 20210; 202-219-5200; {www.doleta.gov}.

Want Your High School Diploma?

People drop out of or fail to complete high school for many different reasons. But one thing is clear; getting your high school diploma or GED is the key to advancement. GED stands for General Educational Development. When you take a GED test, it tests your knowledge and ability in five different areas: writing skills, social studies, science, interpreting literature and the arts, and mathematics. GED tests are given at sites all across the United States. There are several ways to learn where the nearest GED test site is located. You can contact your local Board of Education, which may also know about free or cheap preparation classes. You can also contact your State Department of Adult Education, which you can locate by looking in the blue pages of your phone book. The GED Information Hotline is operated by the American council on Education, One Dupont Circle, NW, Suite 250, Washington, DC 20036; 800-62-MY-GED; {www.acenet.edu/calec/ged/home.html}.

Free Help For Migrant Workers Who Want To Get Their GEDs

Migrant farmworkers who missed out completing high school because of the demands of seasonal work schedules now qualify for a little known program called the Migrant Education High School Equivalency Program.

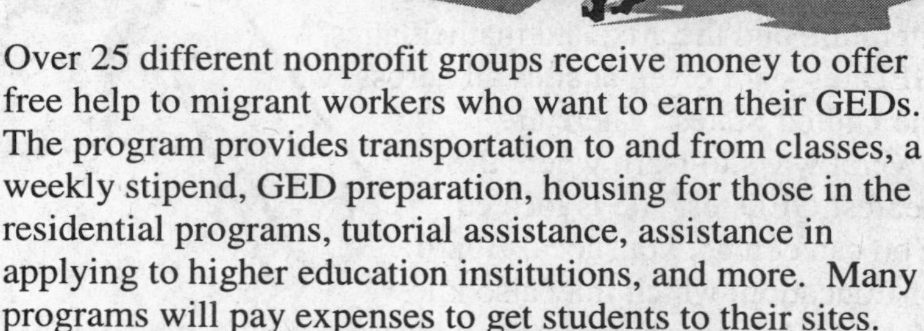

Over 25 different nonprofit groups receive money to offer free help to migrant workers who want to earn their GEDs. The program provides transportation to and from classes, a weekly stipend, GED preparation, housing for those in the residential programs, tutorial assistance, assistance in applying to higher education institutions, and more. Many programs will pay expenses to get students to their sites.

Many are residential programs, where you can live while you are studying to complete your GED. You even get your meals there!

For more information or to locate a site near you contact Office of Migrant Education, U.S. Department of Education, 600 Independence Ave., SW, Room 4100, Washington, DC 20202; 202-260-1124; 800-234-8848; {www.ed.gov/offices/OESE/MEP}.

Free Tutoring And Financial Counseling For Migrant Workers Who Want To Go To College

Migrant workers who are attending college for the first time experience a number of difficulties that are unique to them. To help these workers make a smooth transition into the academic environment of college, the government created the College Assistance Migrant Program (CAMP). CAMP provides intensive services during students' first year in college including campus tours, application assistance, housing orientation, academic advising, tutoring, financial aid, health services, and more. For more information or to locate a site near you, contact Office of Migrant Education, U.S. Department of Education, 600 Independence Ave., SW, Room 4100, Washington, DC 20202; 202-260-1124; 800-234-8848; {www.ed.gov/offices/OESE/MEP}.

Free Tutors and Other Services To Help Low-Income School Dropouts Reach College

Talent Search is a special program that provides funding to help youth from disadvantaged backgrounds re-enter the educational system, complete high school, and go on to the college of their choice.

Program services include academic, financial and personal counseling, career exploration and aptitude testing, financial aid application assistance, preparation for college entrance exams, and more. Talent Search programs are sponsored by colleges, public or private agencies or organizations, with candidates between the ages of 11 and 27 years.

To find a site near you contact Division of Student Services, Education Outreach Branch, Division of Postsecondary Education, U.S. Department of Education, 600 Independence Ave., SW, Washington, DC 20202; 202-708-4804; {www.ed.gov/offices/OPE/HEP}.

Free Help In Getting A College Degree

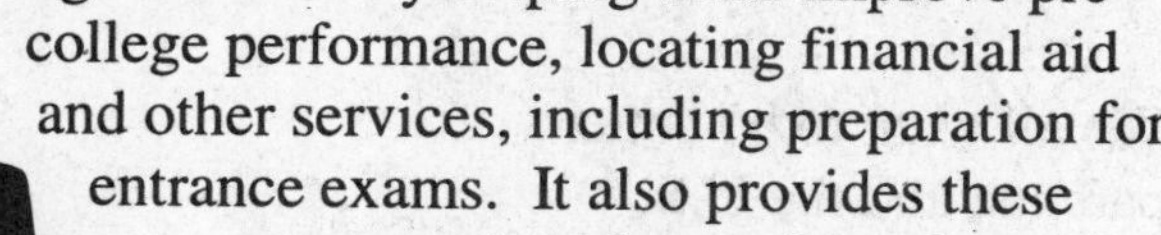

Upward Bound helps disadvantaged high school students prepare for college entrance by helping them improve pre-college performance, locating financial aid and other services, including preparation for entrance exams. It also provides these services for students from families where neither parent holds a college degree and for first-generation military veterans.

Program services include instruction in reading, writing and study skills, academic, financial and personal counseling, tutoring, assistance in completing college entrance and financial aid applications, and more. Those eligible must have completed the 8th grade and be between the ages of 13 and 19 and demonstrate a need for support.

To learn more or to locate an Upward Bound program near you contact Division of Student Services, Division of Postsecondary Education, U.S. Department of Education, 600 Independence Ave., SW, Room 5065, Washington, DC 20202; 202-708-4804; {www.trioprograms.org}.

Free Training For Parents To Make Them Better At Doing Homework

We all want to be better parents, and the U.S. Department of Education wants that too. It gives money to hundreds of programs across the country that shows parents how to become more involved in their children's education. The program is called Even Start, and it focuses on parents of children up to seven years old.

Even Start is a family literacy program that integrates early childhood education and adult literacy training. It provides adult basic education, including helping parents learn to read or teach English as a second language. It also integrates parenting education with early childhood education. For more information or to find a site near you contact Even Start, U.S. Department of Education, 600 Independence Ave., SW, Room 4400, Washington, DC 20202; 202-260-0958; {www.ed.gov/offices/OESE/CEP}.

Free Job Training And Education For Kids And High School Dropouts

Are you or someone you love a high school drop out? Need some help sticking with a program? Job Corps may be for you. This is the nation's largest residential education and training program for disadvantaged youth. There are 111 centers in 46 states, the District of Columbia and

Puerto Rico. It is a full-time year-round residential program that offers a comprehensive array of training, education and supportive services, including supervised dormitory housing, meals, medical care, and counseling. The job training covers a variety of occupational trades and more.

To learn about Job Corps contact Office of Job Corps, U.S. Department of Labor, 200 Constitution Ave., NW, Room N4510, Washington, DC 20210; 202-219-8550, 800-733-JOBS; {www.jobcorps.org}.

State Job Corps Listings

Alabama

Montgomery Job Corps
1145 AirBase Blvd.
Montgomery, AL 36109
334-262-8883
Fax: 334-265-2339

Gadsden Job Corps
Region: IV
P.O. Box 286
Gadsden, AL 35902
205-547-6222
Fax: 205-547-9040
Special Features: Vocational offerings are being taught by Gadsden State Community College
Job Training: Advanced Word Processing, Secretary, Home Health Aide, Carpentry, Auto Repair Technician, Electrician

Alaska

Alaska Job Corps Center
Region X
750 Cope Industrial Way
Palmer, AK 99645
907-746-8800
Fax: 907-746-8810
Job Training: Carpentry, Building and Apartment Maintenance, Heavy Equipment Operator, Food Service, Painter, Health Occupations, Clerical

Arizona

Fred G. Acosta Job Corps
Region: IX
902 South Campbell Ave.
Tucson, AZ 85719
520-792-3015
Fax: 520-628-1552

Special Feature: ESL for Hispanic and Asian students
Job Training: Clerical, Sales Cl Ret Tr, Auto Repair Technician, Electronics Assembler, Auto Body Repair, Electrician, Plumber, Building and Apartment Maintenance

Phoenix Job Corps
Region: IX
518 South Third St.
Phoenix, AZ 85004
602-254-5921
Fax: 602-340-1965
Special Features: ESL for Hispanic, Asian and Eastern European students
Job Training: Off-center Programs, Clerical, Sales Person, Nurses Aide, Electronics Assembler, Painter, Plasterer, Cement Mason, Carpenter, Bricklayer, Building and Apartment Maintenance

Arkansas

Cass Civilian Conservation
Region: VI
USDA, Forest Service
HCR 63, Box 219
Ozark, AR 72949
501-667-3686
Fax: 501-667-3689
Job Training: Food Service, Welder, Building and Apartment Maintenance, Cement Mason, Operating Engineer, Carpenter, Bricklayer, Painter

Little Rock Job Corps
Region: VI
2020 Vance St.
Little Rock, AR 72206
501-376-4600
Fax: 501-376-6152
Special Feature: Handicapped accessible
Job Training: Clerical, Food Service, Nurses Aide, Building and Apartment Maintenance, Plumber

Ouachita Civilian Conservation
Region: VI
USDA
Forest Service
570 Job Corps Rd.
Royal, AR 71068
501-767-2707
Fax: 501-767-2768
Job Training: Welder, Building and Apartment Maintenance, Painter, Plasterer, Cement Mason, Carpenter, Bricklayer

California

Inland Empire Job Corps
Region: IX
3173 Kerry St.
San Bernardino, CA 92405
909-887-6305
Fax: 909-887-8635
Special Feature: ESL for Asian students

Job Training: Clerical, Bookkeeper, Building and Apartment Maintenance, Carpenter, Tilesetter, Sales Cl Ret Tr, Food Service, Machinist, Surveyor Assist I, Landscaping, Welder, Off-center Programs

Long Beach Job Corps
1903 Santa Fe Ave.
Long Beach, CA 90810
562-983-6304
Fax: 562-983-6393

Los Angeles Job Corps
Region: IX
1106 South Broadway
Los Angeles, CA 90015
213-748-0135
Fax: 213-746-4549
Special Feature: ESL for Hispanic, Asian and Ethiopian students
Job Training: Nurse Licensed Practical, Clerical, Food Service, Offset Duplicating Machine Operator, Electronics Tech, Computer Programmer, Radiology Cl Technician, Accounting Clerk, Ward Clerk, Teacher Aide, Machinist, Welder, Auto Repair Tech, Data Entry, Building and Apartment Maintenance

Sacramento Job Corps
Region: IX
3100 Meadowview Rd.
Sacramento, CA 95832
916-393-2880
Fax: 916-424-2872
Special Features: Handicapped accessible, ESL for Hispanic and Asian students
Job Training: Clerical, Building and Apartment Maintenance, Sales Cl Ret Tr, Food Service, Security Guard, Painter, Plasterer, Cement Mason, Surveyor Assist I, Landscaping, Operating Engineer, Carpenter

San Diego Job Corps
Region: IX
1325 Iris Ave.
Imperial Beach, CA 92154
619-429-8500
Fax: 619-429-3909
Special Features: ESL for Hispanic, Asian and Ethiopian students, child care for non-residential students
Job Training: Clerical, Bookkeeper, Sales Cl Ret Tr, Food Service, Nurses Aide, Grounds Keeper, Auto Repair Technician, Electronics Assembler, Welder, Painter, Plasterer, Cement Mason, Carpenter, Bricklayer, Tilesetter, Solar Installer, Nursery School Attendant

San Jose Job Corps
Region: IX
3485 E. Hills Dr.

San Jose, CA 95127
408-937-3200
Fax: 408-254-5663
Special Features: ESL for Hispanic, Asian and Ethiopian students, child care for non-residential students
Job Training: Building and Apartment Maintenance, Food Service, Electronics Technician, Drafter Assist, Computer Programmer, Off-center Programs, Clerical, Teller, Computer Operator, Accounting Clerk Landscape Gardener, Machinist, Auto Repair Technician, Offset Duplicating Machine Operator, Electronics Tester, Welder, Electrician, Carpenter, Dental Assist, Nursing Assist, Clerical

Treasure Island Job Corps
Region: IX
National Maritime Union
Job Corps Training
Bldg. 363 Treasure Island
San Francisco, CA 94130
415-362-4436
415-362-4458
Fax: 415-395-4219
Job Training: Deckhand, Advanced Food Service

Colorado

Collbran Civilian Conservation
Region: VIII
USDI, Bureau of Reclamation
Route 1, 5760
Highway 33
Collbran, CO 81624
303-487-3576
Fax: 303-487-3823
Job Training: Clerical, Food Service, Welder, Painter, Dental Asst, Carpentry, Cement Mason

Connecticut

Connecticut Job Corps Center
455 Wintergreen Ave.
New Haven, CT 06515
203-397-3775
Fax: 203-392-0299

District of Columbia

Potomac Job Corps
Region: III
No. 1 DC Village Lane, SW
Washington, DC 20032
202-574-5000
Fax: 202-563-7069
Special Feature: Childcare for non-residential students
Job Training: Clerical, Data Entry, Bookkeeper, Nurses Aide, Security Guard, Landscape Gardener, Electrician, Painter, Plasterer, Cement Mason, Carpenter, Bricklayer, Plumber, Train Clerk

Florida

Gainesville Job Corps
Region: IV
5301 NE 40th Terrace

Gainesville, FL 32609
352-377-2555
Fax: 352-374-8257
Special Features: Handicapped accessible, ESL for Hispanic students, alternative learning program, National Honor Society.
Job Training: Clerical, Cashier Checker, Food Service, Nurses Aide, Auto Repair Technician, Electronics Assembler, Building and Apartment Maintenance, Auto Body Repair, Painter, Carpenter, Tilesetter, Plasterer

Jacksonville Job Corps
Region: IV
205 West Third St.
Jacksonville, FL 32206
904-353-5904
Fax: 904-359-4747
Job Training: Clerical, Secretary, Terminal Operator, Cosmetologist, Nursery School Attendant, Food Service, Auto Body Repair, Auto Repair Technician, Small Engine Mechanic, AC Refrigerator Mechanic, Machinist, Offset Duplicating Machine Operator, Welder, Electronics Assembler Diesel Mechanic, Medical Assist, Nurse Licensed Practical, Surgical Technician, Home Health Aide, Cement Mason, Carpenter, Bricklayer, Electrician, Plumber, Pipefitter Marine

Miami Job Corps
Region: IV
3050 NW 183rd St.
Miami, FL 33055
305-626-7800
Fax: 305-626-7857
Special Features: ESL for Hispanic and Creole students, National Honor Society
Job Training: Clerical, Data Entry, Food Service, Accounting Clerk, Hotel Clerk, Sales Cl Ret Tr, Building and Apartment Maintenance, Welder

Georgia

Atlanta Job Corps Center
Region: IV
239 West Lake Ave., NW
Atlanta, GA 30314
404-794-9512
Fax: 404-794-8426
Special Features: ESL for Amerasians, off-center college programs
Job Training:, Clerical, Center Food Service, Nurses Aide, Building and Apartment Maintenance, Data Entry, Off-center programs

Brunswick Job Corps
Region: IV
4401 Blynco Parkway

Brunswick, GA 31520
912-264-8843
Fax: 912-267-7192
Job Training: Clerical, Food Service, Welder, Auto Body Repair, Nurses Aide, Horticulture Wkr I, Electrician, Painter, Carpenter, Plumber, Building and Apartment Maintenance

Turner Job Corps
Region: IV
2000 Schilling Ave.
Albany, GA 31708-7501
912-883-8500
Fax: 912-434-0383
Special Feature: BSA Explorer Post
Job Training: Clerical, Sales Cl Ret Tr, Food Service, Nurses Aide, Horticulture Wkr I, Auto Repair Technician, Offset Duplicating Machine Operator, Welder, Electrician, Painter, Carpenter, Bricklayer, Building and Apartment Maintenance, Cement Mason, Plasterer, Brick Masonry, Carpentry, Painting, Cement Masonry, Computer Specialist, Construction Estimator

Hawaii

Hawaii Job Corps
41-467 Hihimanu St.
Waimanalo, HI 96795
808-259-6001
Fax: 808-259-7907

Idaho

Centennial Job Corps
3201 Ridgecrest Dr.
Nampa, ID 83687
208-442-4500
Fax: 208-442-4506

Illinois

Joliet Job Corps
Region: V
1101 Mills Rd.
Joliet, IL 60433
815-727-7677
Fax: 815-723-7052
Job Training: Clerical, Food Service, Health Occupations, Auto Repair Technician, Dispensing Optician, Painter, Building and Apartment Maintenance, Tilesetter

Golconda Civilian Conservation
Region: V
USDA, Forest Service
Route 1
Box 104A
Golconda, IL 62938
618-285-6601
Fax: 618-285-3121
Job Training: Building and Apartment Maintenance, Food Service, Welder, Painter, Carpenter, Bricklayer, Clerical, Electrician

Chicago Job Corps
3348 S. Kedzi
Chicago, IL 60623

773-847-9820
Fax: 773-847-9823

Indiana

Atterbury Job Corps Center
Region: V
P.O. Box 187
Edinburg, IN 46124
812-526-5581
Fax: 812-525-9551
Special Feature: ESL for Hispanic and Asian students
Job Training:, Clerical, Food Service, Health Occupations, Auto Repair Technician, Building and Apartment Maintenance, Welder, Plasterer, Cement Mason, Carpenter, Bricklayer, Painter, Glazier, Retail Sales, Heavy Equipment Operator, Sign Painter, Heavy Equipment Mechanic

Independence JCC
Region: V
17 West Washington St.
Indianapolis, IN 46204
317-684-2555
Fax: 317-231-2375
Job Training: Computer Service Technician, Medical Records Transcriptionist, Aviation, Clerical

Iowa

Denison Job Corps
Region: VII
Highway 30 East
P.O. Box 608
Denison, IA 51442
712-263-4192
Fax: 712-263-6910
Job Training: Clerical, Security Guard, Food Service, Nurses Aide, Building and Apartment Maintenance, Welder, Painter, Carpenter, Bricklayer, Nurse Licensed Practical, Plumber, Rental Equipment, Electrician

Kansas

Flint Hills Job Corps
Region: VII
P.O. Box 747
Manhattan, KS 66502-0007
785-537-7222
Fax: 785-537-9517
Job Training: Clerical, Food Service, Health Occupations, Plumber, Building and Apartment Maintenance, Carpenter, Cement Mason

Kentucky

Carl D. Perkins Job Corps
Region: IV
Box G-1
Goble Roberts Rd.
Prestonsburg, KY 41653
606-886-1037
Fax: 606-886-6048
Job Training: Food Service, Electrician, Carpenter, Bricklayer, Building and Apartment Maintenance,

Health Occupations, Retail Sales

Earl C. Clements Job Corps
Region: IV
2302 US Highway 60 East
Morganfield, KY 42437
502-389-2419
Fax: 502-389-1134
Special Feature: ESL for Hispanic and Asian students
Job Training: Auto Body Repair, Bricklayer, Building and Apartment Maintenance, Carpenter, Secretary, Electrician, Food Service, Home Health Aide, Landscape Technician, Offset Duplicating Machine Operator, Computer Service Technician, Telephone Station Installer, Painter, Plumber, Welder, Auto Repair Technician, Heavy Equipment Operator, Diesel Mechanic, Auto Parts Clerk

Great Onyx Civilian Conservation
Region: IV
USDA, National Park Service
Mammoth Cave National Park
3115 Ollie Ridge Rd.
Mammoth Cave, KY 42259
502-286-4514
Fax: 502-286-8824
Job Training: Clerical, Cement Mason, Food Service, Auto Repair Technician, Welder, Painter, Carpenter, Bricklayer, Building and Apartment Maintenance

Frenchburg Civilian Conservation
Region: IV
USDA
Forest Service
Box 935
Mariba, KY 40345
606-768-2111
Fax: 606-768-3080
Job Training: Clerical, Food Service, Auto Repair Technician, Painter, Cement Mason, Carpenter, Bricklayer

Pine Knot Civilian Conservation
Region: IV
USDA, Forest Service
Pine Knot, KY 42635
606-354-2176
Fax: 606-354-2170
Job Training: Food Service, Auto Repair Technician, Welder, Painter, Cement Mason, Carpenter, Bricklayer

Whitney Young Job Corps
Region: IV
P.O. Box 307
Simpsonville, KY 40067
502-722-8862
Fax: 502-722-8719
Special Feature: National Honor Society
Job Training: Secretary, Food Service, Home Health Aide,

Welder, Building and Apartment Maintenance, Carpenter, Bricklayer

Louisiana

New Orleans Job Corps
Region: VI
3801 Hollygrove St.
New Orleans, LA 70118
504-486-0641
Fax: 504-486-0823
Special Feature: National Honor Society
Job Training: Secretary, Hotel Clerk, Sales Cl Ret Tr, Food Service, Home Health Aide, Building and Apartment Maintenance, Auto Repair Technician, Welder, Carpenter, Cosmetology

Shreveport Job Corps
Region: VI
2815 Lillian St.
Shreveport, LA 71109
318-227-9331
Fax: 318-222-0768
Job Training: Clerical, Food Service, Nurses Aide, Security Guard, Building and Apartment Maintenance, Welder, Painter, Cement Mason, Carpenter, Off-center Programs

Maine

Penobscot Job Corps
Region: I
1375 Union St.
P.O. Box 8148
Bangor, ME 04401
207-990-3000
Fax: 207-942-9829
Special Feature: Handicapped accessible
Job Training: Secretary, Clerical, Bookkeeper, Food Service, Nurses Aide, Welder, Building and Apartment Maintenance, Wastewater Treatment

Loring Job Corps
RR #1, Box 1727
Limestone, ME 04750
207-328-4212
Fax: 207-328-4219

Maryland

Woodstock Job Crops
Region: III
10900 Old Court Rd.
Randallstown, MD 21133
410-461-1100
Fax: 410-461-5794
Job Training: Clerical, Bookkeeper, Food Service, Nurses Aide, Welder, Plasterer, Cement Mason, Carpenter, Landscape Gardener, Electrician, Painter, Bricklayer, Cosmetology, Retail Sales, Building and Apartment Maintenance

Woodland Job Corps
Region: III
3300 Fort Meade Rd.

Laurel, MD 20724
301-725-7900
Fax: 301-497-8978
Special Features: Moderate hearing and sight impaired accessible. ESL classes
Job Training: Clerical, Data Entry, Bookkeeper, Food Service, Nurses Aide, Plasterer, Painter, Carpenter, Building and Apartment Maintenance, Cement Mason

Massachusetts

Grafton Job Corps
Region: I
P.O. Box 575
Route 30
North Grafton, MA 01536
508-839-6904
Fax: 508-839-9781
Special Feature: Solo Parent Program in conjunction with Rhode Island Dept. of Health and Human Services
Job Training: Clerical, Food Service, Nurses Aide, Painter, Data Entry, Teacher Aide, Janitor I (Building Service), Cement Mason, Landscape Gardener, Plumber, Electrician, Building and Apartment Maintenance

Westover Job Corps
Region: I
16 Johnson Dr.
Westover Air Force Base
Chicopee, MA 01022
413-593-5731
Fax: 413-593-5170
Special Features: ESL for Hispanic and Asian students, evening program with child care for non-residential students
Job Training: Clerical, Computer Operator, Food Service, Nurses Aide, Auto Repair Technician, Welder, Painter, Carpenter, Bricklayer, Hotel Clerk, Sign Painter, Plumber, Glazier, Electrician, Landscape Technician

Fort Devens Job Corps
192 MacArthur Ave.
Devens, MA 01432
978-784-2600
Fax: 978-784-2721

Michigan

Detroit Job Corps
Region: V
10401 East Jefferson Ave.
Detroit, MI 48214
313-821-7000
Fax: 313-821-7126
Job Training: Clerical, Health Occupations, Welder, Building and Apartment Maintenance, Computer Operator, Visual Arts

Grand Rapids Job Corps
Region: V
110 Hall St. SE
Grand Rapids, MI 49507

616-243-6877
Special Feature: BSA Explorer Post
Job Training: Clerical, Food Service, Health Occupations, Auto Repair Technician, Welder, Carpenter, Building and Apartment Maintenance, Data Entry

Flint-Genessee Job Corps
2400 N. Saginaw St.
Flint, MI 48505
810-232-1131
Fax: 810-232-6835

Minnesota

Hubert H. Humphrey Job Corps
Region: V
1480 North Snelling Ave.
St. Paul, MN 55108
612-642-1133
Fax: 612-642-0123
Job Training: Clerical, Food Service, Health Occupations, Data Entry, Welder, Building and Apartment Maintenance, Auto Repair Technician, Carpenter

Mississippi

Batesville Job Corps Center
Region: IV
Route 3, Box 2J
Batesville, MS 38606
601-563-4656
Fax: 601-563-1644
Job Training: Clerical, Retail Sales, Food Service, Auto Repair Technician, Welder, Building and Apartment Maintenance, Lithograph Painter, Health Occupations

Gulfport Job Corps
Region: IV
3300 20th St.
Gulfport, MS 39501
601-864-9691
Fax: 601-865-0154
Job Training: Medical Assistant, Secretary, Home Health Aide, Welder, Electrician, Carpenter, Bricklayer, Plumber, Building and Apartment Maintenance, Data Entry, Advanced Career Training

Mississippi Job Corps
Region: IV
P.O. Box 817
Crystal Springs, MS 39059
601-892-3348
Fax: 601-892-3719
Special Feature: National Honor Society
Job Training: Bricklayer, Plumber, Building and Apartment Maintenance, Clerical, Health Occupations, Landscape Technician, Retail Sales, Food Service, Welder, Electrician, Carpenter, Advanced Career Training

Missouri

Excelsior Springs Job Corp
Region: VII
701 St. Louis Ave.
Excelsior Springs, MO 64024
816-637-5501
Fax: 816-637-1806
Job Training: Food Service, Clerical, Nurses Aide, Welder, Building and Apartment Maintenance, Painter, Cement Mason, Carpenter, Data Entry, Word Processing, Geriatric Nurse Assistant, Advanced Career Training

Mingo Civilian Conservation
Region: VII
USDI
Fish and Wildlife Service
Route 2, Box 133
Puxico, MO 63960
573-222-3537
Fax: 573-222-3801
Special Feature: BSA Explorer Post
Job Training: Clerical, Food Service, Nurses Aide, Auto Repair Technician, Welder, Painter, Operating Engineer, Carpenter, Bricklayer, Building and Apartment Maintenance

St. Louis Job Corps
Region: VII
4333 Goodfellow Blvd.
St. Louis, MO 63120
314-679-6200
Fax: 314-679-6244
Special Feature: Child care for non-residential students
Job Training: Clerical, Data Entry, Food Service, Nurses Aide, Security Guard, Welder, Painter, Train Clerk, Plasterer, Cement Mason, Carpenter, Building and Apartment Maintenance, Advanced Career Training

Montana

Kicking Horse Job Corps
Region: VIII
2000 Mollman Pass Trail
Ronan, MT 59864
406-644-2217
Fax: 406-644-2343
Job Training: Clerical, Food Service, Forester Aide, Diesel Mechanic, Operating Engineer, Carpenter, Building and Apartment Maintenance, Dental Assist, Medical Assist

Trapper Creek Civilian Conservation
Region: VIII
USDA
Forest Service
5139 West Fork Rd.
Darby, MT 59829
406-821-3286
Fax: 406-821-4730 Ext.179
Job Training: Clerical, Food Service, Welder, Electrician,

Painter, Cement Mason, Carpenter, Stock Clerk, Building and Apartment Maintenance

Anaconda Civilian Conservation Center
Region: VIII
USDA, Forest Service
1407 Foster Creek Rd.
Anaconda, MT 59711
406-563-3476
Fax: 406-563-8243
Job Training: Welder, Clerical, Painter, Carpenter, Operating Engineer, Construction Equipment Mechanic, Bricklayer, Food Service

Nebraska

Pine Ridge Civilian Conservation
Region: VII
USDA, Forest Service
Star Route #1, Box 39F
Chadron, NE 69337
308-432-3316
Fax: 308-432-4145
Job Training: Clerical, Food Service, Welder, Painter, Plasterer, Cement Mason, Carpenter, Bricklayer

Nevada

Sierra Nevada Job Corps
Region: IX
5005 Echo Ave.
Reno, NV 89506
702-972-5627
Fax: 702-972-6480
Special Features: ESL for Hispanic and Asian students
Job Training: Medical Assistant, Clerical, Food Service, Security Guard, Janitor I, Landscape Gardener, Auto Repair Technician, Welder, Painter, Plasterer, Cement Mason, Carpenter, Bricklayer, Electrician, Plumber, Building and Apartment Maintenance, Advanced Career Training

New Jersey

Edison Job Corps
Region: II
500 Plainfield Ave.
Edison, NJ 08817-2587
732-985-4800
Fax: 732-985-8551
Special Features: ESL for Hispanic, Asian and East Indian students, 22-24 year of age pilot program, accessible for hearing and sight impaired students
Job Training: Carpenter, Bricklayer, Tilesetter, Building and Apartment Maintenance, Plumber, State of NJ Auto Repair Technician, Security, Electrician, Horticulture, Clerical, Health Occupations, Painter, Food Service, Bookkeeper

New Mexico
Roswell Job Corps
Region: VI
P.O. Box 5970
Roswell, NM 88201
505-347-5414
Fax: 505-347-2243
Special Feature: ESL for Hispanic students
Job Training: Secretary, Food Service, Home Health Aide, Building and Apartment Maintenance, Electrician, Painter, Carpenter, Plumber, Clerical, Health Occupations, Advanced Career Training

Albuquerque Job Corps Center
Region: VI
1500 Indian School Rd., NW
Albuquerque, NM 87104
505-842-6500
Fax: 505-247-3262
Special Feature: English as a Second Language for Hispanic students
Job Training: Clerical, Data Entry, Sales Clerk, Food Service, Nurses Aide, Security Guard, Welder, Appliance Repair, Electrician, Carpenter, Plumber, Building and Apartment Maintenance, Security Guard, Welder, Cosmetology

New York
South Bronx Job Corps
Region: II
1771 Andrews Ave.
Bronx, NY 10453-6803
718-731-7700
Fax: 718-731-3543
Special Features: ESL for Hispanic students, day care for non-residential students
Job Training: Clerical, Bookkeeper, Ward Clerk, Food Service, Carpenter, Plumber, Building and Apartment Maintenance, Nurses Aide

Cassadaga Job Corps
Region: II
Glascow Rd.
Cassadaga, NY 14718
716-595-8760
Fax: 716-595-3963
Job Training: Interior Design, Clerical, Food Service, Painter, Carpenter, Plumber, Building and Apartment Maintenance, Off-center Programs, Nurses Aide

Delaware Valley Job Corps
Region: II
P.O. Box 325
Callicoon, NY 12723-4762
914-887-5400
Fax: 914-887-4762
Special Feature: ESL for Hispanic students
Job Training: Clerical, Food Service, Auto Repair Technician, Electronics Assembler, Auto Body Repair, Electrician, Painter, Hotel

Clerk, Health Occupations, Building and Apartment Maintenance, Retail Sales, Security Guard

Glenmont Job Corps
Region: II
P.O. Box 993
Route 144
Glenmont, NY 12077-0993
518-767-9371
Fax: 518-767-2106
Job Training: EKG Technician, Medical Assistant, Clerical, Food Service, Building and Apartment Maintenance, Nurses Aide, Auto Repair Technician, Auto Body Repair, Data Entry, Cosmetologist

Iroquois Civilian Conservation
Region: II
USDI, National Park Service
11780 Tibbits Rd.
Medina, NY 14102
716-798-7000
Fax: 716-798-7046
Special Feature: National Honor Society
Job Training: Clerical, Welder, Electrician, Painter, Plasterer, Carpenter, Bricklayer

Oneonta Job Corps
Region: II
Box 51A, Rd. No. 4
Oneonta, NY 13820-9325
607-433-2111
Fax: 607-433-1629
Special Feature: Solo Parent dorm and Day Care center for mothers and 30 children
Job Training: Clerical, Food Service, Nurses Aide, Auto Repair Technician, Auto Body Repair, Welder, Electrician, Plumber, Tile Setter, Nursery School Attendant, Hotel Clerk

North Carolina

Oconaluftee Civilian Conservation
Region: IV
USDI, National Park Service
200 Park Circle
Cherokee, NC 28719
828-497-5411
Fax: 828-497-4417
Job Training: Plasterer, Cement Mason, Carpenter, Bricklayer, Food Service, Auto Repair Technician, Welder, Painter, Building and Apartment Maintenance

Kittrell Job Corps
Region: IV
Kittrell College
P.O. Box 278
Kittrell, NC 27544
252-438-6161
Fax: 252-492-9630
Job Training: Clerical, Sales Cl Ret Tr, Food Service, Nurses Aide, Painter, Carpenter,

Bricklayer, Building and Apartment Maintenance

Schenck Civilian Conservation
Region: IV
USDA, Forest Service
98 Schenck Dr.
Pisgah Forest, NC 28768
828-877-3291
Fax: 828-877-3028
Job Training: Food Service, Auto Repair Technician, Welder, Painter, Carpenter, Bricklayer, Building and Apartment Maintenance, Forester Aide, Landscape Technician

Lyndon Johnson Civilian Conservation
Region: IV
466 Job Corps Dr.
Franklin, NC 28734
828-524-4446
Fax: 828-369-7338
Job Training: Food Service, Welder, Building and Apartment Maintenance, Cement Mason, Carpenter, Bricklayer, Clerical, Painter

North Dakota

Burdick Job Corps Center
Region: VIII
1500 University Ave., W
Minot, ND 58701
701-838-9976
Fax: 701-838-9979
Job Training: Auto and Farm Machinery Parts, Auto and Farm Equipment Mechanic, Food Service, Clerical, Building and Apartment Maintenance, Health Occupations, Carpenter

Ohio

Cincinnati Job Corps
Region: V
1409 Western Ave.
Cincinnati, OH 45214
513-651-2000
Fax: 513-651-2004
Job Training: Clerical, Food Service, Building and Apartment Maintenance, Auto Repair Technician, Welder, Carpenter

Cleveland Job Corps
Region: V
10660 Carnegie Ave.
Cleveland, OH 44106
216-795-8700
Fax: 216-795-1109
Job Training: Clerical, Retail Sales, Data Entry, Operator, Health Occupations, Data Entry, Building and Apartment Maintenance

Dayton Job Corps
Region: V
3849 Germantown Pike
Dayton, OH 45418
937-268-6571

Fax: 937-268-5339
Special Feature: National Honor Society
Job Training: Clerical, Hotel Clerk, Food Service, Health Occupations, Painter, Electronics Assembler, Carpenter, Building and Apartment Maintenance

Oklahoma

Guthrie Job Corps
Region: VI
P.O. Box 978
600 Academy Rd.
Guthrie, OK 73044-0978
405-282-9930
Fax: 405-282-4977
Job Training: Drafter Clerical, Food Service, Nurses Aide, Security Guard, Offset Duplicating Machine Operator, Welder, Electrician, Floor Layer, Painter, Carpenter, Plumber, Building and Apartment Maintenance, Word Processing, Physical Therapy, EKG Technician, Medical Lab Assistant, Respiratory Therapy, Phlebotomist, Nurse Licensed Practical

Talking Leaves Job Corps
Region: VI
P.O. Box 948
Tahlequah, OK 74465
918-456-9959
Fax: 918-456-3508
Special Feature: Child care for non-residential students
Job Training: Clerical, Food Service, Auto Body Repair, Building and Apartment Maintenance, Health Occupations, Cosmetology, Front End Mechanic, Auto Repair Technician, Welder, Electrician, Carpenter, Diesel Mechanic

Treasure Lake Civilian Conservation
Region: VI
USDI
Fish and Wildlife Service
Route 1, Box 30
Indiahoma, OK 73552
405-246-3203
Fax: 405-246-8222
Special Feature: Child care for non-residential students
Job Training: Food Service, Health Occupations, AC Refrigeration Mechanic, Electrician, Painter, Plasterer, Cement Mason, Carpenter, Bricklayer

Tulsa Job Corps
Region: VI
1133 N. Lewis Ave.
Tulsa, OK 74110
918-585-9111
Fax: 918-592-2430
Special Features: Vision and hearing impaired accessible,

BSA Explorer Post, child care for non-residential students
Job Training: Clerical, Nurses Aide, Security Guard, Food Service, Cosmetologist, Electronics Assembler, Carpenter, Building and Apartment Maintenance, Painter, Barber

Oregon

Springdale Site
Region: X
31224 E. Crown Point Hwy.
Troutdale, OR 97060
503-695-2245
Fax: 503-695-2254
Special Feature: Child care
Job Training: Clerical, Food Service, Nurses Aide, Auto Body Repair, Building and Apartment Maintenance, Sign Painting

Timber Lake Civilian Conservation
Region: X
USDA, Forest Service
59868 E. Highway 224
Estacada, OR 97023
503-834-2291
Fax: 503-834-2333
Job Training: Food Service, Forester Aide, Welder, Painter, Plasterer, Carpenter, Building and Apartment Maintenance

Tongue Point Job Corps
Region: X
Astoria, OR 97103
503-325-2131
Fax: 503-325-5375
Job Training: Building and Apartment Maintenance, Landscape Gardener, Food Service, Electronics Assembler, Welder, Painter, Plasterer, Cement Mason, Carpenter, Glazier, Seamanship, Electrician, Lithographic Printer, Nursing Assist, Dental Assist, Accounting Clerk, Clerical

Angell Civilian Conservation Center
Region: X
USDA
Forest Service
335 NE Blogett Rd.
Yachats, Oregon 97498
503-547-3137
Fax: 503-547-4236
Special Features: English as a Second Language for Asian, Micronesian, and Hispanic
Job Training: Clerical, Food Service Center, Forester Aide, Auto Repair Technician, Welder, Painter, Carpenter, Bricklayer

Wolf Creek Civilian Conservation
Region: X
USDA
Forest Service
2010 Opportunity Lane

Glide, OR 97443-9733
541-496-3507
Fax: 541-496-0015
Job Training: Food Service, Forester Aide, Welder, Painter, Plasterer, Cement Mason, Carpenter, Building and Apartment Maintenance, Clerical

Pivot Job Corps
2508 NE Everett
Portland, OR 97232
503-916-6170
Fax: 503-916-6168

Pennsylvania

Keystone Job Corps
Region: III
#1 Foothills Dr.
P.O. Box 37
Drums, PA 18222
570-788-1164
Fax: 570-788-1119
Special Features: ESL for Asian, Ethiopian and Hispanic students, off-center training at Tobyhanna Army Depot
Job Training: Clerical, Food Service, Nurses Aide, Floor Layer, Carpentry, Electrician, Building and Apartment Maintenance, Plumbing, Painting, Bricklayer, Cement Masonry, Plasterer

Philadelphia Job Corps
Region: III
4601 West Market St.
Philadelphia, PA 19139
215-471-9689
Fax: 215-747-8552
Job Training: Clerical, Food Service, Nurses Aide, Building and Apartment Maintenance

Pittsburgh Job Corps
Region: III
Highland Dr.
Pittsburgh, PA 15206
412-441-8700
Fax: 412-441-1586
Special Feature: Child care for non-residential students
Job Training: Electronics, Drafter Assist, Surveyor Assist I, Nurse General Duty, Radiological Technician, Med-Lab Assist, Respiratory Therapy, Medical Assistant, Program Aide, Legal Secretary, Secretary, Stenographer, Computer Operator, Medical Records Clerk, Teacher Aide, Food Service, Nursery School Attendant, Hotel Clerk, Auto Body Repair, Diesel Mechanic, Building and Apartment Maintenance, Independent Truck Operator, Clerical, Nurses Aide

Red Rock Job Corps
Region: III
P.O. Box 218
Lopez, PA 18628
570-477-2221

Fax: 570-477-3046
Job Training: Clerical, Bookkeeper, Nurses Aide, Landscape Gardener, Auto Repair Technician, Carpenter, Bricklayer, Plumber, Electrician, Painter, Building and Apartment Maintenance, Cosmetologist

Puerto Rico

Ramey Job Corps
Region: II
P.O. Box 643
Ramey, PR 00604-0463
787-890-2030/2505
Fax: 787-890-4749
Job Training: Nurse Licensed Practical, Clerical, Food Service, Front End Mechanic, Electrician, Cement Mason, Carpenter, Plumber, Home Health Aide

Arecibo Job Corps Center
Region: II
P.O. Box 544
Garrochales, PR 00652-0540
787-881-2300
Fax: 787-881-7243
Job Training: Nurse Licensed Practical, Clerical, Home Health Aide, Auto Body Repair, Electrician, Building and Apartment Maintenance

Barranquitas Job Corps Center
Region: II
P.O. Box 68
Barranquitas, PR 00794
787-857-5200
Fax: 787-857-2262
Job Training: Nurse Licensed Practical, Clerical, Furniture Upholsterer, Electrician, Cement Mason, Building and Apartment Maintenance

South Carolina

Bamberg Job Corps Center
Region: IV
P.O. Box 967
200 South Carlisle St.
Bamberg, SC 29003
803-245-5101
Fax: 803-245-5915
Job Training: Clerical, Food Service, Nurses Aide, Auto Body Repair, Welder, Cement Mason, Carpenter, Plumber, Building and Apartment Maintenance, Retail Sales

South Dakota

Boxelder Civilian Conservation
Region: VIII
USDA
Forest Service
P.O. Box 110
Nemo, SD 57759
605-348-3636
Fax: 605-348-3636
Job Training: Clerical, Food Service, Auto Repair Technician, Welder, Carpenter, Bricklayer, Building and

Apartment Maintenance, Painter

Tennessee

Memphis Job Corps
1555 McAlister Dr.
Memphis, TN 38116
901-396-2800
Fax: 901-396-2892

Jacobs Creek Civilian Conservation
Region: IV
USDA, Forest Service
Drawer W-Route No. 1
Bristol, TN 37620
423-878-4021
Fax: 423-878-7034
Job Training: Food Service, Construction Equipment Mechanic, Welder, Painter, Cement Mason, Operating Engineer, Carpenter, Bricklayer

Texas

David L. Carrasco Job Corps
Region: VI
11155 Gateway West
El Paso, TX 79935
915-594-0022
Fax: 915-591-0166
Special Feature: ESL for Hispanic students
Job Training: Clerical, Cosmetology, Food Service, Health Occupations, Auto Repair Technician, Electronics Tester, Welder, Building and Apartment Maintenance

Gary Job Corps
Region: VI
P.O. Box 967
San Marcos, TX 78667-0987
512-396-6652
Fax: 512-396-6666
Special Feature: ESL for Asian, Ethiopian and Hispanic students
Job Training: Clerical, Accounting Clerk, Construction Equipment Mechanic, Retail Sales, Building and Apartment Maintenance, Food Service, Meat Cutting, Auto Repair Technician, Auto Body Repair, Auto Parts Clerk, Carpentry, Electrician, Bricklayer, Cement Mason, Tile Setter, Painter, Heavy Equipment Operator, Machinist, Welder, Lithographic Printer, Material Handler, Health Occupations, Dental, Advanced Training, Automotive Diagnostic, Peripheral Equipment Operator, Environmental Control

Laredo Job Corps
Region: VI
P.O. Box 1819
101 Island St.
Laredo, TX 78044-1819

956-727-5147
Fax: 956-727-1937
Special Features: ESL for Hispanic students, Advance Vocational Training (AVT), horses on center
Job Training: Clerical, Bookkeeper, Food Service, Welder, Electrician, Carpenter

McKinney Job Corps
Region: VI
P.O. Box 750
McKinney, TX 75069-8003
972-542-7941
Fax: 972-542-8870
Job Training: Clerical, Food Service, Health Occupations, Lithographic Printing, Material Handler, Electrician, Painter, Plasterer, Cement Mason, Carpenter, Bricklayer, Plumber, Building and Apartment Maintenance, Security/Correctional Officer, Desktop Publishing, Bookkeeper, Data Entry, Word Processing

Utah

Clearfield Job Corps
Region: VIII
P.O. Box 160070
Clearfield, UT 84016
801-774-4000
Fax: 801-773-8906
Special Feature: ESL for Hispanic and Asian students
Job Training: Clerical, Welder, Building and Apartment Maintenance, Offset Duplicating Machine Operator, Auto Body Repair, Auto Repair Technician, Food Service, Nurses Aide, Machinist, Bookkeeper, Auto Parts Clerk, Auto Repair Technician, Diesel Mechanic, Auto Body Repair, Off-center Programs

Weber Basin Civilian Conservation
Region: VIII
USDI
Bureau of Reclamation
Rural Free Delivery (RFD) No. 6
Ogden, UT 84405
801-479-9806
Fax: 801-476-5985
Job Training: Clerical, Food Service, Welder, Painter, Carpenter, Bricklayer, Health Occupations, Building and Apartment Maintenance

Vermont

Northlands Job Corps
Region: I
100-A MacDonough Dr.
Vergennes, VT 05491
802-877-2925
Fax: 802-877-2699
Job Training: Clerical, Bookkeeper, Food Service,

Nurses Aide, Auto Repair Technician, Auto Body Repair, Welder, Building and Apartment Maintenance

Virginia

Blue Ridge Job Corps Center
Region: III
245 West Main St.
P.O. Box 425
Marion, VA 24354
540-783-7221
Fax: 540-783-1751
Job Training: Medical Assist, Medical Secretary, Clerical, Bookkeeper, Ward Clerk, Accounting Clerk, Nurses Aide, Sales Cl Ret Tr, Food Service, Teacher Aide, Diesel Mechanic, Building and Apartment Maintenance, Welder, Machinist

Flatwoods Civilian Conservation
Region: III
USDA, Forest Service
Rt. 1 Box 2111
Coeburn, VA 24230
703-395-3384
Fax: 703-395-2043
Job Training: Welder, Painter, Plasterer, Cement Mason, Carpenter, Bricklayer, Plumber, Electrician

Old Dominion Job Corps
Region: III
P.O. Box 278
Monroe, VA 24574
804-929-4081
Fax: 804-929-3511
Job Training: Clerical, Bookkeeper, Sales Cl Ret Tr, Food Service, Nurses Aide, Auto Repair Technician, Electrician, Painter, Carpenter, Bricklayer, Plumber, Building and Apartment Maintenance, Landscape Gardener

Washington

Cascades Job Corps
Region: X
2267 Northern State Rd.
P.O. Box 819
Sedro Woolley, WA 98284
360-856-3400
Fax: 360-856-3419
Special Feature: Handicapped designated for hearing and sight impaired
Job Training: Dental Assist, Clerical, Food Service, Building and Apartment Maintenance, Landscape Technician, Cable TV Installer, Painter, Plasterer, Cement Mason, Carpenter, Nurses Aide

Columbia Basin Civilian Conservation
Region: X
USDI
Bureau of Reclamation
Building 2402
6739 24th St.

Moses Lake, WA 98837
509-762-5581
Fax: 509-762-9540
Job Training: Dental Assist, Building and Apartment Maintenance, Food Service, Painter, Plasterer, Cement Mason, Carpenter, Tilesetter, Welder, Nurses Aide

Curlew Civilian Conservation
Region: X
USDA
Forest Service
Star Route, Box 100
Wauconda, WA 98859
509-779-4611
Fax: 509-779-4328
Special Feature: High School Diploma Program
Job Training: Clerical, Food Service, Forester Aide, Auto Repair Technician, Construction Worker, Welder, Painter, Carpenter, Bricklayer, Building and Apartment Maintenance

Fort Simcoe Civilian Conservation
Region: X
USDI
Bureau of Reclamation
40 Abella Lane
White Swan, WA 98952
509-874-2244
Fax: 509-874-2342
Job Training: Food Service, Auto Repair Technician, Truck Driver, Auto Body Repair, Painter, Plasterer, Carpenter, Bricklayer, Heavy Equipment Operator, Heavy Equipment Mechanic, Clerical, Dental

West Virginia

Charleston Job Corps
Region: III
1000 Kennawa Dr.
Charleston, WV 25311
304-925-3200
Fax: 304-925-7127
Job Training: Clerical, Computer Operator, Food Service, Nurses Aide, Offset Duplicating Machine Operator, Drafter, Cosmetologist, Cashier Checker, Nurse Licensed Practical, Stenographer, Diesel Mechanic, Welder, Electrician, Auto Body Repair, Auto Repair Technician, Nursery School Attendant, Commercial Artist, Carpenter, Building and Apartment Maintenance

Harpers Ferry Civilian Conservation
Region: III
USDI
National Park Service
P.O. Box 237
Harpers Ferry, WV 25425
304-725-2011
Job Training: Painter, Plasterer, Cement Mason, Carpenter, Bricklayer,

Building and Apartment Maintenance, Clerical

Wisconsin

Blackwell Civilian Conservation Center
Region: V
USDA
Forest Service
Route 1 Box 233A
Laona, WI 54541
715-674-2311
Fax: 715-674-4305
Special Feature: Handicapped accessible
Job Training: Food Service, Building and Apartment Maintenance, Electrician, Welder, Painter, Carpenter, Bricklayer, Clerical

State And National Job Training Programs

Not only does the Federal Government offer job training programs, but state, national, and local organizations do so as well. Here is a listing to get you started.

To give you an idea of what is available, The Single Parent/Homemaker Project Services in Greensburg, IN and the Center for Displaced Homemakers in Shreveport, LA provide vocational education, job training, career counseling, job placement and life management training, as well as support groups for single parents. The Institute of Social and Economic Development in Iowa City, IA and the Grand Rapids Opportunities for Women in Grand

Rapids, MI want to encourage self-sufficiency through the growth of a small business and will provide services to help you begin your endeavor. Hard Hatted Women in Cleveland, OH and Tradeswomen of Purpose in Philadelphia, PA allow women to learn the construction trades through various apprenticeship and training programs.

Don't forget to also contact your local One-Stop Career Center and your state Department of Labor office listed at the beginning of each state to learn more about job training programs near you.

State Job Training

National

The following is a list of national associations and agencies available to guide you in finding resources in your local area.

America's Learning eXchange

The American Association of Community Colleges has partnered with the U.S. Department of Labor to support learners, employers, and training suppliers. The vehicle is the web-based America's Learning eXchange. ALX can connect you with the training and education you need. It is intended to be a breakthrough resource for workers entering the job force, people interested in lifelong learning, and employers looking for enhanced performance. Their website is like a one-stop electronic marketplace for lifelong learning resources. The links there will lead you to tens of thousands of training offerings and providers—everything from continuing education courses to Internet-based training, from traditional classroom-based courses to CD-ROM and video instruction. Check out {www.alx.org/}.

Help For The Homeless

The International Union of Gospel Missions is made up of over 250 member organizations. They are located primarily in North America, with other member missions in South Africa, India, South America, and Australia. Many member organizations offer job training as a part of their mission though programs vary by location. Most of those holding Organizational Membership follow the traditional "rescue mission model," providing meals, housing, and spiritual help for the homeless. Many offer other innovative services aimed at the addicted, urban youth, the mentally ill, and other needy people in their communities.

To find a service provider near you, refer to the website below or contact International Union Of Gospel Missions, 1045 Swift Ave., Kansas City, MO 64116-4127; 816-471-8020; {www.iugm.org/missions.html}.

Training With Goodwill

Along with offering many services, Goodwill Industries is also one of the world's largest non-profit providers of employment and training services for people with disabilities and other disadvantaging conditions. Their goal is to equip people with the skills they need to find and sustain competitive employment by overcoming any obstacles that may be preventing them from working.

Goodwill's job training and placement programs are designed to meet the needs of local communities so programs tend to vary by location. Typical services offered include vocational evaluation, work adjustment, career counseling, job placement and transitional employment opportunities. Workshops covering stress management, personal finance, responsible parenting and other "life skills " are also common. Examples of career-specific job training that may be offered in your area include careers in banking, customer service, health care, and adaptive technology among others.

There are 187 Goodwill organizations in the United States and Canada. To locate one near you, call 800-664-6577 or contact their headquarters at Goodwill Industries International, Inc., 9200 Rockville Pike, Bethesda, MD 20814; 301-530-6500; TTD: 301-530-9759; {www.goodwill.org/home.html}.

Learn Skills Online

Does your lifestyle or location prevent you from entering a conventional learning center? This one is a cyber university for women! Women's International Electronic University promotes the empowerment of women online by facilitating access to training in skills such as information technology, health promotion and living skills. They have no physical address, so visit their website to learn more at {www.wvu.edu/~womensu/}.

Economic Independence For Women

Women In Community Service (WICS) is dedicated to reducing the number of young women living in poverty by promoting self-reliance and economic independence. The organization actively addresses critical national issues surrounding employment, job training, welfare reform, poverty, and cultural diversity. Each year, WICS volunteers and staff help more than 150,000 low-income women and young adults by providing support services, mentoring and workforce preparation programs nationwide.

With service centers located throughout the country, contact the national office to locate one near you. Women In Community Service, 1900 N. Beauregard St., Suite 103, Alexandria, VA 22311; 703-671-0500; 800-442-9427; Fax: 703-671-4489; {www.wics.org/}; {e-mail: WICSNatl@aol.com}.

Considering a Non-traditional Career?

The Institute for Women in Trades, Technology & Science (IWITTS) is dedicated to integrating women into the full range of trades, technology and science careers in which they are underrepresented: from engineer to police officer, pilot, automotive technician, electrician and web master, to name just a very few. To accomplish this mission, IWITTS serves as a resource nationally to the education and job-training systems and employers.

Contact them at Institute for Women in Trades, Technology & Science (IWITTS), 3010 Wisconsin Ave. NW, Suite E-10, Washington, D.C. 20016; 202-686-7275, {www.serve.com/iwitts}; {e-mail: iwitts@aol.com}.

Christian Programs

Ursuline Companions in Mission is a Christian association of lay women and men who seek to make a difference in the lives of the poor through a variety of programs including job training. They have service delivery sites in Delaware, Illinois, Kentucky, Minnesota, Missouri, New Mexico, and Ohio. Programs vary from location to location.

For more information, contact Ursuline Companions In Mission, Sr. Jane Quinlan, College of New Rochelle, College Center, Room 155, New Rochelle, NY 10805; 914-654-5270; Fax: 915-654-5290; {www.theursulines.org}; {e-mail: ursulinecomp@hotmail.com}.

The Old Reliable

The YWCA has long been committed to providing women and girls with the education, training, and support they need to provide for themselves and their families. The YWCA's spectrum of offerings in this area include basic lifeskills training, English courses, GED courses, adult education, welfare to work programs, structured training curricula, training for non-traditional employment, career counseling, entrepreneurial workshops, job clubs and more.

Local YWCAs tailor their programs and services to meet the needs of the women, families and employers in their local communities. To find the YWCA in your area contact: YWCA of the USA, Empire State Building, Suite 301, 350 Fifth Avenue, New York, NY 10118; 212-273-7800; Fax: 212-465-2281; {www.ywca.org/index.html}.

Networking For Hi-Tech Women

Webgrrls International provides a web-based forum for women in or interested in new media and technology to network, exchange job and business leads, form strategic alliances, mentor and teach, intern and learn skills needed to succeed in an increasingly technical workplace and world. They offer ongoing workshops focusing on enhancing business and communication such as refining negotiating skills. The original chapter was founded in New York City and many new branches continue to be added around the country. For more information, contact

212-642-8012; {www.webgrrls.com/ny}; {e-mail: nyc@webgrrls.com}.

Training On An International Level

The Centre for Development and Population Activities (CEDPA) is a women-focused non-profit international organization founded in 1975. CEDPA's mission is to empower women at all levels of society to be full partners in development. All CEDPA activities are designed to advance gender equity. Working with partner non-governmental organizations and networks in more than 37 countries, CEDPA designs, implements, monitors, and evaluates projects in family planning and reproductive health, family life education, women's participation in empowerment, youth services, and international advocacy for women and girls.

The Women in Management (WIM) leadership training workshop is CEDPA's flagship capacity-building initiative. During this five-week tuition-based workshop, WIM participants from around the world hone leadership and management skills with peers for a dynamic dialogue. This training program is designed for women working in government, non-governmental, and community-based organizations who design, manage, and evaluate gender-equitable development programs and women working in a wide range of professions who have demonstrated leadership potential in areas related to gender-equitable development. The goal of the Women in Management program is to enhance women's leadership capacity for managing strategic responses to health, economic, education, and other development challenges.

For more information, contact Workshops Coordinator, CEDPA, 1717 Massachusetts Avenue, NW, Suite 200, Washington, DC 20036; 202-667-1142; Fax: 202-332-4496; {www.cedpa.org/}; {e-mail: ketty@cedpa.org}.

Displaced Homemakers

Are you forced to go into the work world suddenly? Do you need help getting your job skills upgraded? Women Work! can help you. They have over 1400 sites across the country to help women from diverse backgrounds achieve economic self-sufficiency through job readiness, education, training and employment. Women Work! provides these services through a network of programs in every state. Women Work! also takes on the toughest women's employment issues and fights for them in Congress and in state legislatures.

For more information on Women Work! or to find a location near you contact Women Work!, 1625 K Street NW, Suite 300, Washington, DC 20006; 800-235-2732; 202-467-6346; Fax: 202-467-5366; {www.womenwork.org/}; {e-mail: womenwork@womenwork.org}.

Help for Southwestern Low-Income Young Women

Job Corps is a school to work program that gives low-income young women, ages 16-24, a chance at a fresh start and a promising future. At Job Corps, young women receive the educational, vocational and social skills training they need to compete in today's challenging job market. Since 1964, over 1.5 million youth have participated in the program and have found the independence they've been looking for. The training is free for the trainee and there is an exciting variety of training programs. Job Corps Centers are located in Arizona, California, Nevada, and Utah. Contact René E. Nutter, 582 Market St. Suite #719, San Francisco, CA 94104; 415-981-821; Fax: 415-981-8433; {http://proudofit.org/}; {e-mail: r9desi00@jcdc.jobcorps.org}.

Resources for Women Business Owners

The National Foundation for Women Business Owners (NFWBO) is a central source of information and statistics on women business owners and their businesses providing non-profit research, leadership development and entrepreneurial training. Their website has a large collection of related links. Contact National Foundation for Women Business Owners, 1100 Wayne Avenue, Suite 830, Silver Spring, MD 20910-5603; 301-495-4975; Fax: 301-495-4979; {www.nfwbo.org/index.htm}; {e-mail: NFWBO@worldnet.att.net}.

Grow Your Business With Expert Advice

The Women's Network for Entrepreneurial Training (WNET) links seasoned entrepreneurs with women whose businesses are ready to grow. In a year-long program, experienced women business owners provide technical business advice and training to women with lesser skills and experience. For more information please contact the local SBA District Office in your area. Go to the Small Business Administration's Home Page and click on the SBA Resources icon to find the office nearest you.{www.sbaonline.sba.gov/}.

Network With Other Businesswomen

The mission of the American BusinessWomen's Association is to bring together businesswomen of diverse occupations and to provide opportunities for them to help themselves and others grow personally and professionally through leadership, education, networking support and national recognition. ABWA believes education and training are key to helping women grow personally and professionally. The Association supports education by providing continuing education programs and products, which enhance members business skills.

Members receive discounts on a variety of products and services, including career-focused books and audiotapes, seminars by national seminar providers and computer application classes. For more information, contact

American Business Women's Association, 9100 Ward Parkway, PO Box 8728, Kansas City, MO 64114-0728; 816-361-6621; Fax: 816-361-4991; {www.abwahq.org/}; {e-mail: abwa@abwahq.org}.

Train For Well Paid Work

Wider Opportunities for Women (WOW) has worked for more than 30 years both nationally and in its home community of Washington, DC to achieve economic independence and equality of opportunity for women and girls. WOW can help you learn to earn, with programs emphasizing literacy, technical and non-traditional skills, welfare-to-work transition, and career development. Since 1964, WOW has trained more than 10,000 women for well paid work. The location of their national office is WOW, 815 15th Street, NW, Suite 916, Washington, DC 20005; 202-638-3143; Fax: 202-638-4885; {www.w-o-w.org/default.htm}; {e-mail: info@w-o-w.org}.

Network with Professional Women of Color

Professional Women of Color (PWC) is a non-profit organization that provides workshops, seminars, group discussions as well as networking sessions to help women of color more effectively manage their personal and professional lives. There is a $50 annual Membership Fee to join PWC. Contact Professional Women of Color, PO Box 5196, New York, NY 10185; 212-714-7190; {e-mail: www.pwconline.org/}.

Entrepreneurial Training For Women of Color

If you would like to become more self-sufficient, check out the economic entrepreneurial centers run by the National Council of Negro Women (NCNW). For more information, contact National Council of Negro Women, Christine Toney, Executive Director, Lucenia Dunn,

Director of Programs, 633 Pennsylvania Avenue, NW, Washington, DC 20004; 202-737-0120; Fax: 202-737-0476; {www.ncnw.com}; {e-mail: ncnwbpdc@erols.com}.

Online Training For Women Business Owners

You can receive information, training, and opportunities for online networking to women business owners wherever you are at any time of the day. The Online Women's Business Center (OWBC) provides these services through an Internet site.

This "virtual" women's business center works in unison with, and as an extension of, more than 54 Women's Business Centers (WBC) throughout the United States that have contributed actively to its creation. The combined efforts of the WBCs and OWBO create unlimited possibilities for reaching women who want instant access to information, personal guidance and insight into business management skills, particularly if they do not have a WBC nearby or if their current employment prevents them from visiting a WBC during operating hours. OWBC was developed on behalf of the U. S. Small Business Administration's (SBA) Office of Women's Business Ownership (OWBO) and several corporate sponsors who joined forces in a unique public/private partnership.

For more information, contact Online Women's Business Center, Paula Aryanpur, Project Director, Bill J. Priest

Institute for Economic Development, 1402 Corinth Street, Suite 209, Dallas, TX 75215-2111; 214-565-0447; Fax: 214-565-7883; {www.onlinewbc.org}; {e-mail: virtual@onramp.net}.

Free Job Training and Part-Time Jobs For Those Age 55 And Over

The Senior Community Service Employment Program

offers part-time training and employment opportunities for eligible low-income persons 55 years of age and older in a variety of public or private non-profit community service settings, such as senior centers, nutrition programs, social service agencies, libraries, environmental projects, and many others. The program provides seniors with income and the opportunity to learn new skills or improve the ones they already have. There are sites in every state that offer training and employment.

To learn about the site nearest you contact Division of Older Worker Program, Employment and Training Administration, U.S. Department of Labor, 200 Constitution Ave., NW, Room 4641, Washington, DC 20210; 202-219-5904; {www.wdsc.org/owprog/index.html}.

States

The following is a state-by-state listing of resources and contacts providing services and programs to meet your needs.

Alabama

One-Stop Career Centers

A network of One-Stop Career Centers throughout the state offers a wide range of employment related services including job training. Services vary by location. To find a location near you, please refer to the website {http://wtw.doleta.gov/ohrw2w/recruit/where.htm}. To learn more about the services they offer, contact your state coordinator. Mr. Mickey Hutto, One-Stop Coordinator Workforce Development Division, Alabama Department of Economic and Community Affairs, P.O. Box 5690, 401 Adams Avenue, Montgomery, AL 36103-5690; 334-242-5300; Fax: 334-242-5855.

Job Service Offices

A system of Employment Service/Job Service offices is located within every state with the goal of assisting millions of job seekers and employers. While services may vary from location to location, many provide job training, skills assessment and related services. With approximately 1,800 Employment Service/Job Service offices nationwide there is bound to be one near you. To learn more about the services offered in your area, contact your state administrator. Dottie Blair Cieszynski, Director, Department of Industrial Relations, 649 Monroe Street, Room 204, Montgomery, AL 36130; 334-242-8990; Fax: 334-242-3960.

Career Center

The Shoals Career Center, part of Alabama Career Center System is now open. The vision of the career center is to utilize all equipment and training resources to develop a well-trained, qualified, and diverse workforce for Alabama. The center strives to serve as the primary connection between employers and qualified workers. For more information, contact Shoals Career Center, Town Plaza Shopping Center, 500 South Montgomery Ave., Suite 102, Sheffield, AL 35660; 256-381-0611; Fax: 256-381-9972; {www.dir.state.al.us/es/JTPA/shoalscc.html}.

Job Loss Program

The TAP program uses a case management approach to assist customers in coping with the traumatic effects of losing their jobs. Highly trained, experienced case managers offer free job development, resume preparation assistance, direct referral to jobs, Internet job search, and other job and career related assistance to dislocated workers eligible for services under Title III of the Job Training Partnership Act. For more information, contact Alabama State Employment Service, 115 North 7th Street, Gadsden, AL 35901; 205-546-4667; Fax: 205-546-6603 or Alabama State Employment Service, 500 S. Montgomery Ave, Suite 102, Sheffield, AL 35660; 256-383-5610; Fax: 256-383-4983; {www.dir.state.al.us/es/jtpa/index.html}.

Assistance For Your New or Existing Business

The Women's Business Assistance Center (WBAC) provides training seminars and one-on-one counseling for the south Alabama and northwest Florida area. It is located in the Center for Entrepreneurial Excellence, a former school campus that was purchased and renovated by the City of Mobile and Mobile County. It is now a business incubator and training center. Their physical address is Women's Business Assistance Center, Kathryn Cariglino, Director, 1301 Azalea Road, Suite 201A, Mobile, AL 36693 (Mailing Address: P. O. Box 6021, Mobile, AL 36660); 334-660-2725; 800-378-7461; Fax: 334-660-8854; {http://ceebic.org/~wbac}; {e-mail: wbac@ ceebic.org}.

Women Work!
Find yourself suddenly in need of employment? Get the training and support you need to make the transition into the workforce. Women Work! is a national membership organization dedicated to helping women from diverse backgrounds achieve economic self-sufficiency through job readiness, education, training and employment. Alabama Women Work!, Linda Waide, President, Northwest Shoals Community College, PO Box 2545, Muscle Shoals, AL 35662; 256-331-5321.

Help For Single Parents, Displaced Homemakers and Single Pregnant Women
The Alabama Department of Revenue offers programs designed to assist single parents, displaced homemakers and single pregnant women in gaining marketable skills and attaining self-sufficiency through high wage career/technical training. They can provide you with additional support services such as assessment, personal and career counseling, employability skills training, self-esteem building and child care. Emphasis is placed on serving individuals with the greatest financial need. Contact Alabama Department of Revenue, P.O. Box 327001, Montgomery, AL 36132-7001; 334-242-1170; {www.alsde.edu/careertech/alabama1/GenderEq.htm#SingleParent}.

Alaska

One-Stop Career Centers
A network of One-Stop Career Centers throughout the state offers a wide range of employment related services including job training. Services vary by location. To find a location near you, please refer to the website {www.jobs.state.ak.us/} or {http://wtw.doleta.gov/ohrw2w/recruit/where.htm}. To learn more about the services they offer, contact your state coordinator.

Mr. Remond Henderson, DCRA, Division of Administration and Finance, P.O. Box 112100, Juneau, AK 99811-2100; 907-465-4709; Fax: 907-465-8760.

Ms. Ann Spohnholz, Alaska Job Center Network Project Manager, Alaska Job Center Network Division of Community and Rural

Development, 3890 University Lake, Bldg # 110, Anchorage, AK 99508; 907-786-1399; Fax: 907-786-1396; {e-mail: aspohnholz@ comregaf.state.ak.us}.

Job Service Offices

A system of Employment Service/Job Service offices is located within every state with the goal of assisting millions of job seekers and employers. While services may vary from location to location, many provide job training, skills assessment and related services. With approximately 1,800 Employment Service/Job Service offices nationwide there is bound to be one near you. To learn more about the services offered in your area, contact your state administrator. Rebecca Nance, Director, Alaska Department of Labor, Employment Security Division, P.O. Box 25509, Juneau, AK 99802-5509; 907-465-2712; Fax: 907-465-4537.

Unemployment Program

The state of Alaska wants to help you get back to work. That's why they created the State Training and Employment Program (STEP). They offer you training or retraining for new or emerging industries and technologies. Persons are eligible who are unemployed and receiving unemployment insurance benefits, or who have exhausted their UI benefits; are employed but likely to lose their job within six months due to the job's elimination, or due to obsolescence of their job skills; or have worked in a job covered by unemployment insurance during the last three years but are ineligible for benefits because the job was seasonal, temporary, part-time, or wage contributions were insufficient, or due to underemployment. For more information, contact Katherine A. Brown, Grants Administrator, Division of

Community and Rural Development, Department of Community and Regional Affairs, P.O. Box 112100 (150 Third Street, Room 111), Juneau, AK 99811-2100; 907-465-4863; Fax: 907-465-3212; {e-mail: kbrown@ComRegAf.state.ak.us}.

Prepare for Work

The Department of Health and Human Services offers a program called JOBS - Job Opportunities and Basic Skills. If you are an AFDC recipient, they can help you prepare for and find employment. Through aptitude and interest testing, they help identify your strength areas to match you with appropriate employers. Contact Jobs Program, Val Horner, Program Manager, 350 Main Street, Room 310, P.O. Box 110640, Juneau, AK 99811-0640; 907-465-3349; 907-465-5154; {http://health.hss.state.ak.us/htmlstuf/pubassis/jobs/job.htm}.

Help for Women-owned Microenterprises

WOMEN$ Fund is a microenterprise training and microlending program for women entrepreneurs in Anchorage, AK. They provide training classes in entrepreneurship, technical assistance, individual mentoring and seed money for your women-owned small businesses, helping you to gain economic self-sufficiency. For more information, WOMEN$ Fund, A Program of the YWCA of Anchorage, Kathryn J. Maieli, Program Director, Sharon Richards, YWCA Executive Director, 245 West Fifth Avenue, P. O. Box 102059, Anchorage, AK 99510-2059; 907-274-1524; Fax: 907-272-3146; {e-mail: ywcaak@alaska.net}.

Network With Alaskan Women Online

The Alaska Women's Network's purpose is to further the empowerment of Alaskan women through sharing of information, education and support and through encouraging the development of skills which will enable women to assume leadership roles in building a better world. To achieve this purpose, they maintain a statewide communications network between Alaskan women and women's organizations, through electronic means that can be a valuable resource in helping you identify job-training opportunities. Point your browser to {www.juneau.com/akwomen/network.html}.

Assistance for Women in Construction

Alaskan Tradeswomen Network reaches out to all women involved in construction and related trades. They provide a support network, mentoring, aid/assistance, and continuing education. Contact: Alaskan Tradeswomen Network, P.O .Box 240712, Anchorage, AK 99524-0712; 907-566-2200; {e-mail: cacurtis@ Alaska.net}.

Networking and Training for Women Environmental Professionals

Alaska Women's Environmental Network creates networking opportunities and leadership training programs for Alaskan women working in the environmental field. AWEN members include women from state and national conservation groups, state and federal land management agencies, Alaskan businesses, educators and artists. They can improve your leadership and communications skills, help you pursue leadership positions in environmental fields, link you to like-minded women through a diverse, statewide network and support system, and find a mentor for you to improve professional and personal skills and lessen isolation. They also publish a directory of Alaskan women in environmental fields. Contact: Martha Levensaler, 750 W. 2nd Ave. #200, Anchorage, AK 99501; 907-258-4810; Fax: 907-258-4811; {e-mail: levensaler@nwf.org}.

Employment Education And Training Programs

The Alaska Human Resource Investment Council is the lead state planning and coordinating entity for federal, state, and local employment and training and human resource programs. They can provide you with employment education, training programs, and services to insure you have the skills and opportunities necessary to earn a living wage. JoAnn Henderson is the Chair and can be contacted at AHRIC, 3610 C Street, Suite 380, Anchorage, AK 99503; 907-269-7489; Fax: 907-269-7489; {e-mail: AHRIC@gov.state.ak.us}.

Arizona

One-Stop Career Centers

A network of One-Stop Career Centers throughout the state offers a wide range of employment related services including job training. Services vary by location. To find a location near you, please refer to the website {http://wtw.doleta.gov/ohrw2w/recruit/where.htm}. To learn more about the services they offer, contact your state coordinator.

Ms. Terry Palmer, Quality Initiatives Manager, One-Stop Lead, Arizona Department of Economic Security Division of Employment and Rehabilitation Services, Site Code 901A, 1789 W. Jefferson, P.O. Box 6123, Phoenix, AZ 85007; 602-542-1250; Fax: 602-542-2273

Ms. Linda J. Blessing, Arizona Department of Economic Security, Site Code 010A, 1717 W. Jefferson, PO Box 6123, Phoenix, AZ 85005-6123; 602-564-5331; Fax: 602-564-7452.

Job Service Offices

A system of Employment Service/Job Service offices is located within every state with the goal of assisting millions of job seekers and employers. While services may vary from location to location, many provide job training, skills assessment and related services. With approximately 1,800 Employment Service/Job Service offices nationwide there is bound to be one near you. To learn more about the services offered in your area, contact your state administrator. Linda J. Blessing, Director, Department of Economic Security, P.O. Box 6123-010A, Phoenix, AZ 85005; 602-542-5678; Fax: 602-542-5339.

Food Stamp Recipients

If you are using food stamps, the state of Arizona would like to train you for work. Their Food Stamp Employment & Training Policy provides you with skills and training assistance towards gaining the skills and experience which lead to employment and decreased long-term FS dependence. They can assist you with job searching, job readiness, unsubsidized employment, on-the-job training, unpaid work experiences, community service programs, vocational education training, high school/secondary education, remedial education, General Education Diploma (GED), and English for Speakers of Other Languages (ESOL). They provide guidance and support and activities that help build your confidence, recent work history, and enhance skills you already possess. Contact Janice M. Wood, Food Stamp Employment & Training Policy Specialist, JOBS Administration, 1789 West Jefferson, SC-720A, Phoenix, AZ 85007-3202; 602-542-6542; Fax: 602-542-6310.

Referral Agencies

A great place to begin your search for job training is Arizona's Workforce Development Unit. Through a process called Individual Referral Certification (IRC), the Department of Education has linked together partners in employment and training to meet the customized training needs and employment goals of eligible participants. Acting as a catalyst, the ADE's Workforce Development Unit functions as a liaison among eligible participants, referral agencies, and training facilities. Training and technical assistance is provided to referral agencies. By contacting the Workforce Development Unit, you can join the nearly eight hundred participants each year who are placed into individualized training programs to assist them in becoming gainfully employed. Contact Connie Stewart, Manager, Denise Pawlak, Coordinator, Arizona Department of Education, 1535 West Jefferson, Bin #39, Phoenix, AZ 85007; 602-542-5142; Fax: 602-542-3818; {e-mail: Stewar@mail1.ade.state.az.us}; {e-mail: dpawlak@mail1.ade.state.az.us}.

Single Parent And Displaced Homemakers Gain New Skills

If you are a single parent or displaced homemaker, Arizona Department of Education's Vocational Equity in Arizona offers you employment preparatory services such as instruction in basic academic and occupational skills. They can assist you in attaining vocational competencies and marketable skills. Contact Arizona Department of Education, 1535 West Jefferson Street, Phoenix, AZ 85007; 602-542-

4361; 800-352-4558; {http://internet.ade.state.az.us/aboutade/}; {e-mail: ADE@mail1.ade.state.az.us}.

The following is a list of regional service providers from their website at {internet.ade.state.az.us/programs/foundations/stw/equity/sph-dh.htm}.

- STEP Program AZ Western CC, PO Box 929,Yuma, AZ 85366-0929; 520-344-7699, ext. 23; Fax: 520-344-7730; Angelica Diaz de Leon & Yolanda Rios.

- Working in New Directions (WIND), Central AZ CC, Superstition Mt. Campus, 273 Old West Hwy., Apache Junction, AZ 85219; 602-288-4033; Fax: 602-288-4038; Sharon Stinard.

- Working in New Directions (WIND), Central AZ CC, Main Campus, 8470 N. Overfield Rd. Coolidge, AZ 85228; 520-426-4422; Fax: 520-426-4234; Barbara Meyer.

- Single Parent Program, Cochise CC, 901 N. Colombo, Sierra Vista, AZ 85635; 520-364-0223; Fax: 520-364-0236; Joanne Darbee.

- Self PRIDE Program, Coconino CC, 3000 N 4th St., #17, Flagstaff, AZ 86004; 520-527-1222, ext. 323; Fax: 520-526-1821; Diana Bedore.

- Single Parents/Homemakers Eastern, AZ CC, 600 Church St., Thatcher, AZ 85552; 520-428-8317; Fax: 520-757-0850; Hopi Fitz-William.

- Re-Entry And Change (REACH), Mohave CC, 1971 Jagerson Ave., Kingman, AZ 86401; 520-757-0850; Fax: 520-757-0896 Jane Barkhurst

- REACH, Mohave CC North Campus, PO Box 980, Colorado City, AZ 86021-0980; 520-875-2799; Fax: 520-875-2831; Peggy Oakleaf.

- REACH, Mohave CC Valley Campus, 3400 Hwy 95, Bullhead City, AZ 86442; 520-758-3926; Fax: 520-758-4436; Patricia Post.

- REACH, Mohave CC Lake Havasu Campus, 1977 W. Acoma Blvd, Lake Havasu, AZ 86403; 520-855-7812; Fax: 520-453-1836; Jackie Binenfeld & Geri DeBellis.

- Women in Progress, WIP Pima CC Downtown Campus, 1255 N. Stone, Tucson, AZ 85709-3000; 520-206-6293, 520-206-6135; Fax: 520-206-6201; Mini Montez.

- WIP Pima CC Community Campus, 1901 N. Stone, Tucson, AZ 85705; 520-206-6408, 520-206-3968; Fax: 520-206-6542; Beth Hunter.

- WIP Pima CC West Campus, 2202 W. Anklam Rd., Tucson, AZ 85709-0001; 520-206-6645; Fax: 520-206-6847; Nadia Villalobos.

- WIP Pima CC Desert Vista Campus, 5901 S. Calle Santa Cruz, Tucson, AZ 85709-6010; 520-295-5099; Fax: 520-295-5055; Karen Engelsen.

- WIP Pima CC East Campus, 8181 E. Irvington Rd., Tucson, AZ 85709-4000; 520-722-7606; Fax: 520-722-7690; Deborah Lloyd.

- New Directions, Yavapai CC, 601 Blackhills, Clarkdale, AZ 86324; 520-634-6528, Fax: 520-634-6549; Barbara Duncan.

- AZ Women's Education & Employment (AWEE), 640 N. 1st Ave., Phoenix, AZ 85003; 602-223-4333; Fax: 602-223-433; Marie Sullivan, Director, Mary Lou Yetman, Pat Gregan.

- AWEE-North, 914 E. Hatcher, #135, Phoenix, AZ 85021; 602-371-1216; Fax: 602-534-2773; Mary Kelly & Pattie Fessler.

- AWEE-Prescott, 161 S. Granite, Suite C, Prescott, AZ 86303; 520-778-3010; Fax: 520-778-0737; Ginger Johnson, Carol Basinger, Ann Balowski.

- Center for New Directions, 1430 N. 2nd St., Phoenix, AZ 85004; 602-252-0918; Fax: 602-253-2628; Yolanda Rohrer, Director, Susan Schmidt, Laura Valadez.

- Center for New Directions East Valley, 943 S. Gilbert, Suite 204, Mesa, AZ 85204; 602-507-8619; Fax: 602-507-8618; Joyce Vidal-Thornburg.

- Center for New Directions West Valley, 6010 W. Northern, #304, Glendale, AZ 85301; 602-435-8530; 602-435-2392; Barbara Estrada.

- Adult Vocational Training Project (AVTP), Pima County AVTP, 1630 S. Alvernon, Suite 104, Tucson, AZ 85711; 520-327-8733; Fax: 520-327-8904; Peg Nash.

- Project for Homemakers in AZ Seeking Employment (PHASE), U of A PHASE, 1230 N. Park Ave., #209, Tucson, AZ 85721; 520-621-3902; Fax: 520-621-5008; Diane Wilson.

- Transition Works, NAU, P.O. Box 6025, Flagstaff, AZ 86011-6025; 520-523-4564; Fax: 520-523-6395; Carol Eastman.

- Career Success Program, Yavapai CC, Prescott Valley Business Center, 6955 Panther Path, Prescott Valley, AZ 86314; 520-772-8368; Fax: 520-772-8861; Kim Ewing.

Learn Construction Skills

The Family Self-Sufficiency Housing Program is a construction/training company created by the Housing Authority of the City of Nogales. If you are interested in learning construction related work skills, they would like to hire you for projects and on-the-job training. Their concept is to eliminate the "mobilization costs" of hiring outside contractors while providing employment and training for the community. For more information, contact Rebecca T. Swanson, Nogales

Housing Authority, P.O. Box 777, Nogales, AZ 85628; 520-287-4183; {www. nhc.org/infoproj/jobinfo.htm}; {e-mail: nha@dakotacom.net}.

Help For Single Parents and Displaced Homemakers Reentering College

The COMPASS program is a college re-entry program for single parents and displaced homemakers located at Cochise Community College in Sierra Vista and Douglas, AZ. The program focuses on the special needs of single parents and displaced homemakers who are looking to upgrade their employment and job readiness skills. They can provide support services while you are enrolled in college and ease your transition into the workforce.

Services can be customized to your individual needs and may include: financial assistance; academic planning; career counseling; summer school sponsorships; personal counseling and support; job-readiness training; academic skills workshops; personal/professional development credit classes; information on non-traditional careers; support groups; new student orientation; life skills workshops; lending library; newsletters mailings; referrals; mentor guidance and support. For more information about this program you can contact Compass, Cochise College, 4190 W. Hwy. 80, Douglas, AZ 85607; 520-364-7943; {www.cochise.org/spp/}.

Economic Independence

If you are unemployed or underemployed, Arizona Women's Education and Employment can help you move to economic independence and well being through the dignity of work. They can provide job readiness training, job search support, job placement, guidance to keep a job, and support for transportation and child care. The program is a series of classes, workshops, and one on one sessions. Please contact AWEE-AZ Women's Education and Employment, 640 N. 1st Ave., Phoenix, AZ 85003; 602-223-4338.

Self-Employment Training For Women and Minorities

Are you a low-income individual who would like to start or expand a small business? The Self-Employment Loan Fund, Inc. (SELF) is a private non-profit organization that can provide you with training, technical assistance, and loan access. The training sessions are ten to fourteen weeks in length with the outcome of a completed business plan. Upon the completion of the business plan, participants are eligible for SELF's peer lending process, called Borrower's Circles. These circles of three to eight individuals provide an avenue for support, debt repayment, and continuing business education. SELF serves all of Maricopa County and will soon be providing services in Graham and Gila counties. For more information, contact Self-Employment Loan Fund, Inc. (SELF), Jean Rosenberg, Director, Andrea Madonna, Project Manager, 201 North Central Avenue, Suite CC10, Phoenix, AZ 85073-1000; 602-340-8834; Fax: 602-340-8953; {e-mail: self@uswest.net}.

Arkansas

One-Stop Career Centers

A network of One-Stop Career Centers throughout the state offers a wide range of employment related services including job training. Services vary by location. To find a location near you, please refer to the website {http://wtw.doleta.gov/ohrw2w/recruit/where.htm}. To learn more about the services they offer, contact your state coordinator.

Travis Beebe, One-Stop Lead Arkansas Employment Security Department, #2 Capitol Mall (Zip 72201), P.O. Box 2981, Little Rock, AR 72203; 501-682-5630.

Job Service Offices

A system of Employment Service/Job Service offices is located within every state with the goal of assisting millions of job seekers and employers. While services may vary from location to location, many provide job training, skills assessment and related services. With approximately 1,800 Employment Service/Job Service offices nationwide there is bound to be one near you. To learn more about the services offered in your area, contact your state administrator. Phil Price, Director, Employment Security Department, P.O. Box 2981, Little Rock, AR 72203-2981; 501-682-2121; Fax: 501-682-2273.

Other State Programs

The Arkansas Department of Labor periodically schedules training seminars on a variety of work related topics. For a schedule, refer to the website {www.state.ar.us/labor/pr02.htm}. For information on the program content, or how to register for a conference, call Cynthia Kaelin at 501-682-1767. For all other information, contact Department of Labor, 10421 West Markham, Little Rock, AR 72205; 501-682-4500; Fax: 501-682-4535; {e-mail: becky.bryant@mail.state.ar.us}.

Career Help for Single Parent and Displaced Homemaker Students

If you are a single parent or displaced homemaker intent upon gaining job skills, your local community college has a special program for you. Specifically, they can provide career counseling and personality assessments, goal setting, time management, and communication skills. Their services are presented as modules which are five hours long each and focus on the above mentioned items. To find a service provider near you, refer to the list below or contact Garland County Community College, Dana Murphy, Coordinator, 101 College Drive, Hot Springs, AR 71913-9174; 501-760-4243; 501-760-4244; {e-mail: dmurphy@ admin.gcc.ar.us}.

Satellite Offices

- Crowley's Ridge Technical Institute, P.O. Box 925, Forrest City, AR 72335; Contact: Brenda McBride; 870-633-5411.

- Northwest Technical Institute, P.O. Box Drawer A, Springdale, AR 72765-1301; Contact: Debbie Hobbs; 501-751-8824.

- Pulaski Technical College, 2020 W. Third, Suite 520, Little Rock, AR 72205; Contact: Sylvia Crockett; 501-372-7261.

- Phillips Community College of U of A, P.O. Box 427, Dewitt, AR 72042; Contact: Kay Eldridge; 870-946-3506.

- Southern Arkansas University Tech, 133 Jackson St., Camden, AR 71701; 870-777-0117.

- Southern Arkansas Development Council, Inc., P.O. Box 574, Hope, AR 71801; Contact: Gloria Hudson; 870-777-8892.

- Westwark Community College, P.O. Box 3649, Fort Smith, AR 72913; Contact: Jo Hines; 501-452-8994.

Training For Trainers

If you work professionally with those returning to the workforce, the Arkansas Public Administration Consortium can help you further develop your skills. In order to improve the quality of public services in Arkansas, they offer public administration education and management training opportunities for public and non-profit organizations. All APAC courses, while not traditional college courses, are eligible for Continuing Education Units (CEUs). APAC administers the following training programs: Certified Employment Manager (CEMP); Certified Public Manager (CPM); Certified Volunteer Manager (CVM); MPA Internship Placements; Neighborhood Leadership Program (NLP); Volunteer Management 101; TEAM UP! (Training for Employment And Management); Fund Raising Certificate (FRC). Fees are usually $100-$175 for a two-day class. For further information contact Arkansas Public Administration Consortium, Library Room 523, University of Arkansas at Little Rock, 2801 South University Avenue, Little Rock, AR 72204; 501-569-3090; Fax: 501-569-3021; {www.ualr.edu/~iog/APAC.html}; {e-mail: apacprog@ualr.edu}.

Training for Non-High School or College Graduates

Looking for work without a degree can be a challenge. Conway Adult Education Center's Basic Skills Program can provide you with skills training in technical reading, technical math using work-based materials, or state-of-the-art computer training to meet the challenges of changing technology in the workplace. They also offer a high school equivalency program for adults who do not have a high school diploma, the GED (General Educational Development Testing Program). If language is a barrier, CAEC offers specialized ESL (English as a second language) courses to help non-native speakers communicate more effectively in the English language. Another program, WAGE, is a community-based work force development program that addresses the need to improve the basic skills of the unemployed. For more information, please contact: Karen Mellon, Work Place Coordinator, Conway Adult Education Center, 615 E. Robins Street, Conway, AR 72032; 501-450-4810; Fax: 501-450-4818; {www.caec.org/}; {e-mail: k.mellon@conwaycorp.net}.

California

One-Stop Career Centers

A network of One-Stop Career Centers throughout the state offers a wide range of employment related services including job training. Services vary by location. To find a location near you, please refer to the website {http://wtw.doleta.gov/ohrw2w/recruit/where.htm}. To learn more about the services they offer, contact your state coordinator. Mr. Jose Luis Marquez, One Stop Team Leader, Office of Workforce Policy Employment Development Department, P.O. Box 826880 MIC 77, Sacramento, CA 94280-0001; 916-654-9995; Fax: 916-654-9863; {e-mail: jmarquez@edd.ca.gov}.

Job Service Offices

A system of Employment Service/Job Service offices is located within every state with the goal of assisting millions of job seekers and employers. While services may vary from location to location, many provide job training, skills assessment and related services. With approximately 1,800 Employment Service/Job Service offices nationwide there is bound to be one near you. To learn more about the services offered in your area, contact your state administrator.

Victoria L. Bradshaw, Director, Employment Development Dept., P.O. Box 826880, MIC 83, Sacramento, CA 94280-0001; 916-654-8210; Fax: 916-657-5294

Mark Sanders, Dep. Dir. Operations, Employment Development Dept., P.O. Box 942880, MIC 86, Sacramento, CA 94280-0001; 916-654-9047; Fax: 916-653-3440.

Help Is Just A Phone Call Away

Forced to go into the work world suddenly or do you need help getting your job skills upgraded? Women Work! is for you. They have over 1400 sites across the country to help women from diverse backgrounds achieve economic self-sufficiency through job readiness, education, training and employment. Women Work! provides these services through a network of programs in every state. Women Work! also takes on the toughest women's employment issues and fights for them in Congress and in state legislatures. For more information on Women Work! or to find a location near you contact Women Work! Regional Representative, Region IX, Joanne Durkee, Displaced Homemaker Program, Mt. Diablo Adult Education, 1266 San Carlos Avenue, Concord, CA 94518; 510-685-7340, ext. 2786; Fax: 510-687-8217.

Opportunities in San Jose

MetroED is a collaborative education district in San Jose that prepares youth and adults to be sought-after employees and contributing community members who learn and earn for a lifetime. Their network of service providers include the following programs.

Central County Occupational Center Program-CCOC provides a wide variety of technical training options at the CCOC campus, and on high school and other campus locations throughout the county. Courses offered include training in over 32 occupational choices including electronics, manufacturing, business, automotive, construction, and health occupations. CCOC/P training serves high school juniors, seniors and adults. Contact CCOC, 760 Hillsdale Avenue, San Jose,

CA 95136; Office: 408-723-6400; Student Services: 408-723-6407; {www.metroed.net/ccoc.htm}.

Metropolitan Adult Education Program-MAEP provides learning opportunities in over 50 locations throughout San Jose and Campbell which serve a combined total of 43,000 adults around the clock in subjects including: English as a Second Language, citizenship preparation (offered in English and 5 other languages), adult basic education-literacy skills in reading, writing, and math, GED preparation, high school diploma program for adult students, short-term vocational certificate programs helping people gain skills to enter, or re-enter, the workforce, educational programs for older adults, childbirth and parenting education, and community interest programs for personal growth and job skills enhancement. For more information, contact Campbell Center (Western Region): 1224 Del Mar Avenue, San Jose, CA 95128; 408-947-2300; or Metropolitan Center (Southern Region): 760 Hillsdale Avenue, San Jose, CA 95136; 408-723-6450; or San Jose Center (Central Region): 1149 E. Julian Street, San Jose, CA 95116; 408-947-2311; {www.metroed.net/maep.htm}.

Metropolitan Technical Institute-MTI provides contract training to meet the academic and job skills needs of the commercial/industrial/health care community throughout the Bay Area. MTI specializes in designing customized training programs to meet specific customer needs. Contact Metropolitan Technical Institute, 105 North Bascom Avenue, Suite 104, San Jose, CA 95128; 408-918-6400; Fax: 408-918-6401; {www.metroed.net/mti.htm}.

Training For Low-Income People

The Center for Employment Training (CET) is a private, non-profit, community based organization that provides quality employment training for those who need it most. They offer extensive life skills and workplace know-how instruction through a program that includes job preparedness training, job development and placement. CET keeps students in training until they are placed and conducts follow-up on all placements to ensure stable employment and job growth. CET's primary activity is classroom skill training, which is provided year-round. CET does not screen applicants through testing, but accepts anyone who is willing to do the necessary work. Courses are offered on an open-entry, open-exit basis and students complete training at their own pace.

CET training is intensive, with students attending 5 days and 35 to 40 hours per week for an average of seven months. CET training is competency based, highly individualized, and hands-on. The average training course at CET maintains a 20-1 student/ teacher ratio. CET uses basic skills instruction and human development conducted in a simulated work setting. At least twenty-five job training options are offered at CET nationwide. These include automated office skills, building maintenance, electronic assembly, medical assistant, truck driving, and shipping/receiving. Skill offerings vary from one center to another. A typical CET center offers 4-5 skills and may serve up to 250 persons annually. To locate a service center near you, refer to the list below or contact CET Corporate Offices, 701 Vine St., San Jose, CA 95110; 408-287-7924; 800-533-2519 (for your local center); {www.best.com/~cfet/main.htm}; {e-mail: cfet@ best.com}.

CET Service Centers in California

- South Third St., El Centro, CA 92243; 760-337-6565; Fax: 760-353-5589.

- East Washington Ave., Suite A, Escondido, CA 92025; 619-347-4808; Fax: 619-747-8238.

- Arroyo Circle, Gilroy, CA 95020; 408-842-6484; Fax: 408-842-7158.

- Jackson Street, Building A, Indio, CA 92201; 619-347-4808 Fax: 619-342-4563.

- South Spring St., Los Angeles, CA 90013; 213-687-9350; Fax: 213-687-9353.

- Capwell Drive, Oakland, CA 94621; 510-568-6166; Fax: 510-568-6723.

- South C Street, Oxnard, CA 93030; 805-487-9821; Fax: 805-486-8762.
- La Cadena Dr., Riverside, CA 92501; 909-680-0238; Fax: 909-680-0125.
- 65th Street, Sacramento, CA 95828; 916-393-7401; Fax: 916-393-7347.
- Monterey St., Salinas, CA 93901; 408-424-0665; Fax: 408-424-4743.
- Market Street, San Diego, CA 92102; 619-233-6829; Fax: 619-233-6350.
- Mission Street, San Francisco, CA 94103; 415-255-8880 Fax: 415-252-0990.
- Vine Street, San Jose, CA 95110; 408-287-7924; Fax: 408-294-7849.
- West Fifth Street, Suite 120, Santa Ana, CA 92701; 714-568-1755; Fax: 714-568-1331.
- West Morrison, Santa Maria, CA 93454; 805-928-1737; Fax: 805-928-1203.
- Avenida Alvarado, Unit A, Temecula, CA 92590; 909-676-7514; Fax: 909-694-0913.
- Blanca Lane, Watsonville, CA 95076; 408-728-4551; Fax: 408-728-1659.

Training Programs in Oakland

The Oakland Private Industry Council offers services to people who need to earn a high school diploma or GED, update skills, or prepare for a new career. They also work with many community based agencies which provide job training and placement services to local residents. PIC administers the following employment and training programs in partnership with the City of Oakland. All training programs include assistance with job search and placement. PIC is an equal opportunity service provider; auxiliary aid is available upon request for persons with disabilities. For more information, refer to the list below and call the program(s) which interest you.

Note: This is not a comprehensive directory of vocational programs, but a list of programs funded by the Oakland PIC. Main address: Oakland Private Industry Council ("The PIC"), 1212 Broadway, Suite 300, Oakland, CA 94612; 510-891-9393; {www.oaklandpic.org/programs.asp}.

- *American Viet League* - Training in basic skills, English as a second language, and computerized accounting skills. Vickie Nguyen, 255 International Blvd., Oakland, CA 94606; 510-834-7971; Fax: 510-834-7974.

- *Asian Neighborhood Design* - Training in manufacturing technologies (including Auto CAD and CNC), construction-related trades and basic education. Daniel Duvernay or David Meiland, 1890 Campbell Street, Oakland, CA 94607; 510-433-1370; Fax: 510-433-1375.

- *ASSETS Senior Employment Opportunities Program* - Training in life skills, early childhood development, general office procedures, typing, bookkeeping, computer programs and customer service skills. Also, work experience. Brendalynn Goodall, City of Oakland, 250 Frank Ogawa Plaza, Suite 4353, Oakland, CA 94612; 510-238-3535; Fax: 510-238-7207.

- *Berkeley Adult School* - Training in general clerical, medical clerical, nursing assistant/home health aide, warehouse/forklift, accounting clerk and restaurant occupations. ESL, GED/HS diploma preparation. Contact Berkeley Adult School, 1222 University Avenue, Berkeley, CA 94702; 510-644-8970; Fax: 510-644-8789.

- *Building Opportunities for Self-Sufficiency (BOSS)* - Pre-employment skills preparation and training in office skills, culinary preparation and janitorial skills. Contact Building Opportunities for Self-Sufficiency, 356 15th Street, Oakland, CA 94612; 510-834-2231; Fax: 510-465-0837.

- *Career Resources Development Center* - Training in computer applications, business math and English, 10-key and typing, customer service and cash register use. Career Resources Development Center, 320 13th Street, Oakland, CA 94612; 510-268-8886; Fax: 510- 268-0688.

- *Catholic Charities* - Pre-employment and basic skills training. Vocational ESL, bilingual job counseling and assessment and on-the-job training. Aldric Chau, 707 Jefferson Street, Oakland, CA 94607; 510-465-0642; Fax: 510-465-4044

- *Center for Employment Training* - Training in office skills, shipping/receiving, machine tool operator and building maintenance. Gil Rodriguez, 8390 Capwell Drive, Oakland, CA 94621; 510-568-6166; Fax: 510-568-6723.

- *Cypress Mandela/Women in Skilled Trades Training Center* - Pre-apprentice construction training, lead abatement, hazardous materials and asbestos removal skills. Jeri Robinson, 2229 Poplar Street, Oakland, CA 94607; 510-208-7350; Fax: 510-835-3726.

- *Dislocated Workers Program* - PIC contracts with agencies and institutions to provide training in a variety of growing fields. Revelina Valmores, 1212 Broadway, Suite 200, Oakland, CA 94612; 510-768-4440; Fax: 510-451-4049.

- *East Bay Asian Youth Center* - Basic skills training, GED preparation and training in desktop publishing. Contact East Bay

Asian Youth Center, 2025 East 12th Street, Oakland, CA 94606 ; 510-533-1092; Fax: 510-533-6825.

- *English Center for International Women* - Four levels of intensive ESL instruction. Occupational training includes word processing and spreadsheet skills. Deborah Taylor, Mills College, 5000 MacArthur Blvd., Oakland, CA 94613; 510-430-2064; Fax: 430-2259.

- *Jobs for Homeless Consortium* - Training in carpentry, janitorial, and clerical occupations. David Lyons or Nina Grotch, 1722 Broadway, Oakland, CA 94612; 510-251-6241; Fax: 251-6093.

- *Local 250 Health Care Workers Union* - Pre-employment skills and on-the-job training as certified nursing assistants. Joan Braconi, 560 20th Street, Oakland, CA 94612; 510-251-1250; Fax: 510-763-2680.

- *Oakland Chinese Community Council* - Entrepreneurial training for home-based child care centers. Nhang Luong, 168 11th Street, Oakland, CA 94607; 510-839-2022; Fax: 510-839-2435.

- *Oakland Unified School District, Adult Education* - Basic education training, GED preparation and training in nursing assistant, home health aide, clerical, computer operation, security and janitorial skills. Offered at many sites across Oakland. Contact Oakland Unified School District, 1025 2nd Avenue, Portable 15, Oakland, CA 94606; 510-879-8131; Fax: 510-879-1840.

- *Oakland Unified School District, Exceptional Children's Program* - Basic education instruction, workplace education and labor market orientation. On-site job training and job mentoring. Contact Exceptional Children's Program, 4655 Steele Street, Oakland, CA 94619; 510-879-1763; Fax: 510-879-1769.

- *Scotland Youth and Family Center* - Basic and pre-employment skills training, California HS Proficiency Exam preparation/testing,

GED preparation and work experience. Hanna McQuinn, 1651 Adeline Street, 2nd Floor, Oakland, CA 94607; 510-832-4544; Fax: 510-832-3521.

- *Spanish Speaking Citizens' Foundation and Lao Family Community Development, Inc.* - Training in dietary aide and dietary clerk fields. Work experience at hospital or public health facility. Rosario Flores, 1470 Fruitvale Avenue, Oakland, CA 94601; 510-261-7839; Fax: 510-261-2968.

- *Stepping Stones Growth Center* - Training in janitorial, grounds maintenance, boat cleaning and detailing, recycling, and utility and stock clerk occupations. Jerry Joseph, 311 MacArthur Boulevard , San Leandro, CA 94577; 510-568-3331; Fax: 510-568-416.

- *Summer Youth Employment and Training Program* - Program starts in June. Offers labor market orientation, job readiness and work experience. Kelly Robinson, Oakland Private Industry Council, 1212 Broadway, Suite 300, Oakland, CA 94612; 510-891-9393; Fax: 510-839-3766.

- *Youth Employment Partnership* - Computer training, including: word processing, data entry, database management, spreadsheets and the Internet. Business communications and math. GED preparation. Opportunity for work experience and internships. Construction and lead abatement skills training. Dennis Smith or Mark Henderson, 1411 Fruitvale Avenue, Oakland, CA 94601; 510-533-3447; Fax: 510-533-3469.

Get The Help You Need To Start Your Own Business

Founded in 1976, the American Woman's Economic Development Corporation is the premier national not-for-profit organization committed to helping entrepreneurial women start and grow their own businesses. Based in New York City, AWED also has offices in southern California, Connecticut and Washington, D. C. Join over 100,000 women who have benefitted from formal course instructions, one-to-one business counseling, seminars, special events and peer group support. AWED's goal is to increase the start-up, survival and expansion rates of small businesses. Contact American Woman's Economic Development Corporation (AWED), Suzanne Tufts, President and CEO, 71 Vanderbilt Avenue, Suite 320, New York, NY 10169; 212-692-9100; Fax: 212-692-9296.

California Branch Offices

- You can benefit from two long-term training modules depending on your stage in owning your own business. The Women's Enterprise Development Corporation was previously known as California AWED which began in 1989 with SBA funding to assist the growing number of women business owners in Los Angeles. Their Neighborhood Entrepreneurial Program is a 12-18 session start up program, often stressing home-based businesses and/or preliminary skill building, for low-income residents of particular neighborhoods and targeted communities in Los Angeles, Long Beach, and elsewhere. Typically, it is offered at no cost. Starting Your Own Business ($240) is for beginning business owners. Managing Your Own Business ($525) is for women who have been in business at least one year with gross receipts over $50,000. Courses are in six languages: Chinese, English, Japanese, Khmer, Korean and Spanish. For more information contact Women's Enterprise Development Corporation, Phil Borden, Executive Director, 100 West Broadway, Suite 500, Long Beach, CA 90802; 562-983-3747; Fax: 562-983-3750; {www.wedc.org/}; {e-mail: wedc1@aol.com}.

- Orange County has the third largest concentration of women-owned businesses in the nation (ranking just behind New York and Los Angeles). AWED Orange County follows the same AWED curriculum described above which includes the core program, plus a two-hour pre-business seminar and a monthly group counseling program. For more information, contact Women's Enterprise

Development Corporation, Linda Harasin, Acting Executive Director, 2301 Campus Drive, Suite 20, Irvine, CA 92715; 310-983-3747; Fax: 310-9830-3750.

Enhance Your Business Skills Close To Home

If you live in lower-income communities around San Francisco, particularly Fruitvale, San Antonio and Central East Oakland, the Women's Initiative for Self Employment can provide you with training and technical assistance in establishing your own business. The English language program consists of a two-week business assessment workshop, a fourteen-week business skills workshop and a four-week workshop on writing a business plan. The Spanish language program parallels the English but is in modular format. WI also offers business support services including one-on-one consultations, peer networking and support groups, and special seminars. They provide training in locations close to their client base, in shopping centers, etc.

Contact Women's Initiative for Self Employment (WI), Barbara Johnson, Executive Director, 450 Mission Street, Suite 402, San Francisco, CA 94105; 415-247-9473; Fax: 415-247-9471; {e-mail: womensinitsf@igc.apc.org}; {Oakland Site e-mail: wioakland@ igc.apc.org}; {Spanish Site e-mail: wialas@igc.apc.org}.

Looking For A Job Or Planning A Career In Sacramento, S.F., L.A. or San Diego?

JobStar is the right place to start your career, plan your job campaign or negotiate a good salary. They have comprehensive listings for programs related to employment in Sacramento, S.F., L.A. or San Diego including job training opportunities.

The listings are too numerous to include here. However, to give you an idea of what is available, the list below includes programs concerned with job training just in the Los Angeles area. Note that the list below does not include programs concerned with job placement and other non-training related services. If you are interested in these services or would like more information, refer to their website below. If the Internet is not readily available to you, don't forget that your local library will probably have access. {http://jobstar.org/index.htm}.

- *Brady JobNet* serves primarily lower-income individuals and families in East Los Angeles and surrounding areas, but anyone is welcome. Free services include employment readiness seminar in English and Spanish, help with resumes and interviews, job placement, job club, and computer center. For more information, contact Brady JobNet, 717 S. Brady Avenue, Los Angeles, CA 90022; 213-722-4495.

- *Career Encores* is a non-profit program that assists adults age 50 and over with employment opportunities. Job preparation training offered in two Career Transition Centers (Burbank and mid-Wilshire.) Special attention is given to the needs of older persons and their services are free. For more information, contact Career Encores, 3700 Wilshire Blvd., Suite 200, Los Angeles, CA 90010; 800-833-6267.

- *Chicano Service Action Center* - Los Angeles offers free job training and placement for low-income people of any nationality. Training in office work, warehousing, and other trades. Must be 22 or older with proper ID, residency and income to qualify. Call for additional Van Nuys location. For more information, contact Chicano Service Action Center - Los Angeles, 134 East First Street, Los Angeles, CA 90012; 213-253-5959.

- *Chinatown Service Center* is a non-profit organization whose free programs include employment training, basic skills remediation, job placement, career planning & referrals to vocational training centers. They serve Asians and other immigrants, refugees and other Americans in the greater L.A. area. Multicultural, multi-lingual staff speak Chinese dialects, Vietnamese, Cambodian, Spanish and English. For more information, contact Chinatown Service Center, 767 N. Hill Street, Suite 400, Los Angeles, CA 90012; 800-733-2882.

- *Forty Plus of Southern California* is a non-profit, cooperative membership organization open to executives, managers & professionals seeking new employment or a career change. They offer job search preparation, interviewing assistance, computer training, unadvertised job market and have free orientations. For more information, contact Forty Plus of Southern California, 3450 Wilshire Boulevard, Suite 510, Los Angeles, CA 90010; 213-388-2301.

- *Jewish Vocational Services* is a non-profit, nonsectarian service organization providing a full range of skills assessment, training, job search & consulting services to job seekers & employers on a sliding fee basis. They have special services for immigrants, disabled, students, downsized workers, outplacement professionals, career changers. Entertainment Networking Group is for persons either in or seeking to enter the entertainment industry. Must be L.A. resident, 18 or older. For more information, contact Jewish Vocational Services, 5700 Wilshire Boulevard #2303, Los Angeles, CA 90036; 323-761-8888.

- *Central Job Service* offers free career counseling, vocational testing, job search skills workshops, computerized job matching and placement, job club. EDD Home Page has information on job services, unemployment insurance and locations of 22 offices throughout L.A. County. For more information, contact L.A. Central Job Service, Employment Development Department, 158 W. 14th Street, Los Angeles, CA 90015; 213-744-2244.

- *L.A. Works* provides a free comprehensive system of training, placement and career planning for job seekers throughout southern California. For more information, contact L.A. Works, 5200 Irwindale, Ave., Suite130, Irwindale, CA 91706; 626-960-3964.

- *Los Angeles County Regional Occupational Programs* is one of 12 Regional Occupational Education Programs throughout L.A. County. Programs are offered at high schools, adult schools, community colleges, private postsecondary schools and community or business facilities. Students learn entry-level skills in a wide variety of occupational fields including animal care, banking, nursing, food service, retail sales and electronics. Applicants must be at least 16 years of age. Call for additional locations. Free to high school students, fees for adults. For more information, contact Los Angeles County Regional Occupational Programs, 20122 Cabrillo Lane, Cerritos, CA 90703; 562-403-7382.

- *Los Angeles Urban League* offers free employment services focused on African Americans and other minorities, but open to anyone age 15 years or older. The League assists job-ready applicants and employers through counseling, workshops and a job bank. Services include pre-employment preparation, job development, on-the-job training and placement in computers, automotive, electronics and other trades. Call for additional Pasadena and Pomona locations. For more information, contact Los Angeles Urban League, 3450 Mount Vernon Drive, Los Angeles, CA 90008; 213-299-9660.

- *The Maxine Waters Employment Preparation Center* is one of 6 Los Angeles Unified School District Skills Centers offering short-term vocational training designed to get people working. Each site offers training specialties suited to the surrounding community. Services include extensive vocational counseling in addition to job training and placement. Adult Basic Education and GED high school diploma testing are also offered. Programs are adaptable with open entry, open exit and flexible scheduling to meet individual needs. They serve a culturally diversified population throughout L.A. County aged 14 and older and students may enroll concurrently with regular school. There is a small registration fee. For information on additional locations & special community-based programs for particular groups, contact Maxine Waters Employment Preparation Center, Los Angeles Unified School District Skills Centers, 10925 S. Central Avenue, Los Angeles, CA 90059; 213-564-1431.

- *Mexican American Opportunity Foundation* is a non-profit agency offering free services that include job listings, computer training, on-the-job training with partial reimbursement to employers; work experience for preschool teacher's aides, basic skills training in reading and math, limited paid internships for youths 18-21. For more information, contact Mexican American Opportunity Foundation, 401 N. Garfield Avenue, Montebello, CA 90640; 213-890-9600.

- *Pacific Asian Consortium in Employment* is a community-based agency offering youth & adult free job training and transitional workshops, job preparation, referral and placement to low-income individuals age 22 and older. Training & technical assistance is available for low-income entrepreneurs, educational/leadership development for high school dropouts and at-risk youth. Call for additional information on Gardena location. For more information, contact Pacific Asian Consortium in Employment (PACE), 1541 Wilshire Blvd., Suite 407, Los Angeles, CA 90017; 213-389-2373.

- *Southeast L.A. County Private Industry Council* offers one-stop employment and training programs & services for laid-off workers, the unemployed and low-income. They have special services for youth seeking G.E.D. and older workers (over 55). Career Center offers resources, workshops. If eligible, you may qualify for individual or in-depth training programs. Their services are free but some services are only for eligible clients. For more information, contact Southeast L.A. County Private Industry Council, 10900 E. 183rd St., #350, Cerritos, CA 90703; 562-402-9336.

- *Southern California Indian Center* is a non-profit organization serving the American Indian community. Provides free employment assistance and vocational training to American Indians, Native Alaskans and Native Hawaiians who are unemployed, underemployed or economically disadvantaged. Services include annual job fair, training, resume & job application preparation, job search techniques, job listings and referrals and educational workshops for parents. For more information and additional locations, contact Southern California Indian Center, 3440 Wilshire Blvd., Los Angeles, CA 90010; 213-387-5772.

- *Verdugo Private Industry Council* is one of 6 federally funded Private Industry Councils (PICs) in the greater L.A. area. Applicants may qualify for one or more reasons including layoff, long-term unemployment or income below poverty levels. Their free services include educational, vocational & on-the-job training; job-search skills and placement; dislocated workers program; older workers programs and youth training programs. For more information and additional locations, contact Verdugo Private Industry Council, 706 W. Broadway, Suite 202, Glendale, CA 91204; 818-409-0476.

- *Women at Work* is a non-profit, drop-in career and job resource center serving unemployed and underemployed women (and men) in the greater L. A. area seeking jobs or changing careers. Services include job listings, job market information, career library, career workshops, career counseling, occupational testing, special employment programs, job search support groups, computer classes, self-serve computer lab. Fees are involved and may vary. For more information, contact Women at Work, 50 North Hill Avenue, Suite 300, Pasadena, CA 91106; 626-796-6870.

Help With Procurement for Advanced Business Owners

The Women Business Owners Corporation (WBOC) forecasts and develops business opportunities in the government and major corporate markets for women business owners. WBOC also assists women suppliers in marketing their goods and services and acquiring the skills necessary to succeed in these markets. The SBA's Office of Women's Business Ownership has provided the initial funding for development of the WBOC Procurement Institute and procurement training to women suppliers through WBOC's world wide website. Contact Women Business Owners Corporation, Kathleen Schwallie, President, 18 Encanto Drive, Palos Verdes, CA 90274-4215; 310-530-7500; Fax: 310-530-1483.

Help For Northern CA Small Business Owners

WEST Company serves micro enterprise owners in rural northern California. Through their Build a Better Business training and consulting program, they assist clients in developing a business plan for both start-up and expansion purposes. They make individual and peer loans; assist with the formation of business networks; and have started a cross-generational technology-mentoring program. For more information, contact:

West Company, Sheilah Rogers, Executive Director, 367 North State Street, Suite 201, Ukiah, CA 95482; 707-468-3553; Fax: 707-462-8945.

West Company, Carol Steele, Loan Fund Manager, 340 North Main Street, Fort Bragg, CA 95437; 707-964-7571; Fax: 707-961-1340.

Learn To Work At A Job Usually Filled By Men

The Job Training Network in Alliance with the Private Industry Council is a successful partnership between public and private sectors, which provides valuable employment and training programs throughout Santa Barbara County. One of their many client services is Non-traditional Options for Women (N.O.W.) that offers women an array of training programs in jobs usually filled by men. Contact Job Training Network, 228 W Carrillo St. # C, Santa Barbara, CA 93101-6159; 805-882-3675; {www.jtnwinjobs.org/}.

Network And Learn From Other Women In Management

Women In Management (WIM) is a non-profit educational corporation for the advancement of women into management positions. Open to everyone, regardless of your place on the career path, WIM's annual membership costs only $65 per person. They host monthly meetings in the southern California area for managers, entrepreneurs, administrative assistants, the self-employed and anyone who would like to make contacts, develop leadership skills, establish rewarding relationships and advance their career. They also offer scholarships for education to their members. WIM does not have a permanent address, since all of their board positions are on a volunteer basis and the people who fill the positions change annually. You can reach them at 800-531-1359, {www.wimworks.com}; {e-mail: mail@WIMworks.com}.

Nearly Free Job Training Classes
The Norwalk-LaMirada Adult School provides classes and career counseling at practically no cost. While their information is limited on their offerings, according to locals, their program is extremely popular. Contact Norwalk-LaMirada Adult School, Attention: Donatella, 12820 Pioneer Boulevard, Norwalk, CA 90650; 562-868-0431.

I Could Do That Guy's Job
Women In Non-traditional Employment Roles' (WINTER) mission is to encourage and support women's training, employment, and retention in high wage, high skill jobs. The common bond is that all share the goal of opening more doors for women. As a member, you can take advantage of training workshops, job counseling, job search assistance and referrals. Other organizational activities include: educating members on job rights, skill building, safety, and other issues; holding monthly support group meetings; publishing monthly newsletter; publicizing job and apprenticeship openings; advocating for equal employment opportunity; networking with other organizations on labor issues; promoting active involvement of women in unions; providing technical assistance to employers, unions, community based organizations, and schools; producing videos on women in non-traditional jobs; engaging in research investigating job segregation; organizing speaker's bureau. Contact Ebony Shakoor-Akbar, Women In Non-traditional Employment Roles, P.O. Box 90511, Long Beach, CA 90809-0511; 310-590-2266; {www.ttrc.doleta.gov/wanto/}.

Training For Virtually Any Job!
Private Industry Council, Inc. offers job training in health/human services; clerical; administration/management; cosmetology; construct/manufacturing; mechanical/repair; agriculture/forestry; transportation; education/child development; legal/law enforcement; technical/computer; and communication/marketing. They also offer a huge variety of job-related services at the following three locations.

Jobtree located in the EDD Office, 2523 S. Mooney Blvd., Visalia, CA 93277; 209-737-4226; Fax: 209-737-4320

Tulare County Workforce Development Center, 1249 N. Cherry, Tulare, CA 93274; 209-685-2680; Fax: 209-685-2567

Tulare County Workforce Development Center (located in the EDD Office), 61 N. Second St., Porterville, CA 93257; 209-782-4718; Fax: 209-782-4786; {www.climbthejobtree.org/}.

Training & Employment Center

The Napa County Training and Employment Center (TEC) is a nationally recognized, service-integrated, one-stop career center offering comprehensive career and employer services which are designed to enhance options for job seekers and employers alike. Focusing on solutions and positive outcomes, as well as customer satisfaction, TEC offers responsive services designed to enhance employability and employment options. Their services include: competency-based job readiness skills training; job search workshops; networking opportunities; vocational and career assessment; computerized labor market information; resume preparation; vocational skills training; academic programs including high school diploma and GED preparation; English as a second language and basic literacy courses; immediate employment referral for job seekers with marketable skills; career resource center; retraining for new skills; job development and placement assistance; and personalized support services. For more information, contact Training & Employment Center, 2447 Old Sonoma Road, Napa CA 94558; 800-289-1872.

A Handful of Other Training Opportunities

- *North Valley Private Industry Council* offers vocational and on-the-job training, counseling, support services, job referrals and placement for youth, seniors, and unemployed, laid-off workers. Contact North Valley Private Industry Council, 505 W. Olive Avenue, #550, Sunnyvale, CA 94086; 408-730-7232; (TDD) 408-730-7501.

- *Opportunities Industrialization Center West* offers job training for economically disadvantaged, unemployed, or underemployed adults and youth. Contact Opportunities Industrialization Center West (OICW), 1200 O'Brien Drive, Menlo Park, CA 94025; 650-322-8431.

- *San Jose Job Corps Center* offers remedial education, recreation, GED preparation, vocational training, and a residential program for youth age 16-24. Contact San Jose Job Corps Center, East Hills Drive, San Jose, CA 95127; 408-254-5627.

- *Santa Clara County Office of Education* - Regional Occupational Programs offers career and vocational training for adults, out-of-school youth, and high school students age 16 or over. Contact Santa Clara County Office of Education, 575 W. Fremont Avenue, Sunnyvale, CA 94087; 408-733-0881.

Colorado

One-Stop Career Centers

A network of One-Stop Career Centers throughout the state offers a wide range of employment related services including job training. Services vary by location. To find a location near you, please refer to the website {http://wtw.doleta.gov/ohrw2w/recruit/where.htm}. To learn more about the services they offer, contact your state coordinator.

Ms. Ledy Garcia-Eckstein, Executive Director, Workforce Coordinating Council, 1580 Logan Street, Suite 410, Denver, CO 80203; 303-894-2077; Fax: 303-894-2064; {e-mail: gareckl@ capitol.state.co.us}

Mrs. Judy Richendifer, Director, Office of Employment and Training Programs Colorado Department of Labor and Employment, 1515 Arapahoe Street, Tower 2, Suite 400, Denver, CO 80202-2117; 303-620-4204; Fax: 303-620-4257; {e-mail: judi.Richendifer@state.co.us}.

Job Service Offices

A system of Employment Service/Job Service offices is located within every state with the goal of assisting millions of job seekers and employers. While services may vary from location to location, many provide job training, skills assessment and related services. With approximately 1,800 Employment Service/Job Service offices nationwide there is bound to be one near you. To learn more about the services offered in your area, contact your state administrator. John J. Donlon, Executive Director, Department of Labor & Employment, Tower 2, Suite 400, 1515 Arapahoe Street, Denver, CO 80202-2117; 303-620-4701; Fax: 303-620-4714.

Help For Low-income Latina Women

The Mi Casa Resource Center for Women, Inc. provides quality employment and education services that promote economic independence for low-income, predominantly Latina women and youth. You can receive educational counseling, job readiness and job search training, life skills development, job placement, non-traditional and computer skills training. If you lean towards owning your own business, you can receive training on how to start a business and develop business plans with micro-loans available to program graduates. Other services include: youth development, drop-out prevention, leadership training and responsible decision making, provided through two youth programs - Mi Carrera (My Career) and Fenix (teen-pregnancy, AIDS and STD prevention program). Contact Mi Casa Resource Center for Women, Inc., Agnes Talamantez Carrol, Director of Business, 571 Galapago Street, Denver, CO 80204; 303-573-0333; Fax: 303-607-0872; {www.micasadenver.org}; {e-mail: acarrol@micasadenver.org}.

Job Training Has Advantages

Hone your job skills at The Training Advantage. They can help prepare you for participation in the labor force by increasing your occupational and educational skills. Their free services include: assessment of job skill level and training needs; job and career counseling; information and training for women in non-traditional jobs; classroom training in occupational skills; academic skills training, including GED preparation, math, English, reading; work experience programs and internships; on-the-job training in an occupational skill; in-house computer training; and supportive services. For more information, contact:

The Training Advantage, 11 South Park, P.O. Box 2146, Montrose, CO 81402; 970-249-2234; {www.montrose.org/hospital/resource/pages/training_advantage.htm}.

The Training Advantage, Director: Mary Layton; P.O. Box 800, 285 Lakin Street, Ignacio, CO 81137; 970-563-4517; Fax: 970-563-4504; {www.ignacio.co.us/sucap/index.html}.

Connecticut

One-Stop Career Centers

A network of One-Stop Career Centers throughout the state offers a wide range of employment related services including job training. Services vary by location. To find a location near you, please refer to the website {http://wtw.doleta.gov/ohrw2w/recruit/where.htm}. To learn more about the services they offer, contact your state coordinator.

Deborah M. Nanfito, Programs and Services Coordinator, Connecticut Department of Labor, 200 Folly Brook Blvd, Wethersfield, CT 06109; 860-566-2533; Fax: 860-566-1520

Jean E. Zurbrigen, Deputy Commissioner, Connecticut Department of Labor, 200 Folly Brook Blvd., Wethersfield, CT 06109; 860-566-4388; Fax: 860-566-1520.

Job Service Offices

A system of Employment Service/Job Service offices is located within every state with the goal of assisting millions of job seekers and employers. While services may vary from location to location, many

provide job training, skills assessment and related services. With approximately 1,800 Employment Service/Job Service offices nationwide there is bound to be one near you. To learn more about the services offered in your area, contact your state administrator. James P. Butler, Commissioner, State Labor Department, 200 Folly Brook Boulevard, Wethersfield, CT 06109-1114; 860-566-4384; Fax: 860-566-1520.

Information Hotline

The Education and Employment Information Center has a hotline to provide you with the information you need to get on your career track. This service is offered by the Department of Higher Education and the Board of Governors for Higher Education. Call 800-842-0229 or, in the Hartford area call 860-947-1810; {www.ctdhe.commnet.edu}.

Help For Displaced Homemakers

The State of Connecticut offers a Displaced Homemakers Program that is designed to help you become economically self-sufficient. They offer you information, referral, counseling, assessment of skills, job training for various occupations, job placement, and support services, such as child care and transportation assistance. Use the list below to locate a service center near you or refer to the website for updated information. {www.ctdol.state.ct.us/progsupt/jobsrvce/discjt.htm}

- Region I: Ansonia/Waterbury, Danbury/Torrington, Bridgeport/Stamford, Norwalk, Greenwich YWCA of Eastern Fairfield County - "Job Readiness Program", Connie Condon, Executive Director, 753 Fairfield Avenue, Bridgeport, CT 06604; 203-334-6154 Fax: 203-579-8882.

- YWCA of Greenwich - "New Horizons", Jacqueline Majors-Miles, Executive Director, 259 East Putnam Avenue, Greenwich, CT 06830; 203-869-6501, ext. 218.

- YWCA of Darien/Norwalk - "Beginning Again", Rita Shaughnessey, Executive Director, 49 Old Kings Highway North, Darien, CT 06820; 203-655-2535.

- YWCA of Waterbury - "Step by Step", Margaret Sumpter, Executive Director, 80 Prospect Street, Waterbury, CT 06702; 203-754-5136, ext. 3311.

- Region II: New Haven, Meriden, Middletown YWCA of Meriden - "Open Door", Shane Rood, Executive Director, 169 Colony Street, Meriden, CT 06450; 203-235-9297; Fax: 203-237-7571.

- "New Transitions" Program, c/o Red Cross Building, 703 Whitney Avenue, New Haven, CT 06511; 203-776-8453.

- Region III: Hartford, New Britain, Bristol Hartford College for Women of the University of Hartford - "Look Forward", Gail Champlin, Director - Counseling Center, 50 Elizabeth Street, Hartford, CT 06105; 860-768-5619; Fax: 860-768-5680.

- YWCA of New Britain - "Look Forward", Nancy Heiser, Executive Director, 22 Glen Street, New Britain, CT 06051; 860-225-4681, ext. 288; Fax: 860-826-7026

- Region IV: Northeast: Willimantic/Danielson Southeast: Norwich/New London ACCESS Agency, Incorporated, Kerrie Jones Clark, Executive Director, 1315 Main Street, Willimantic, CT 06226; 860-450-7400, ext. 749; Fax: 860-450-7477.

- ACCESS-Multiservices, Lorraine Griffith, Director, 16H Maple Street, Danielson, CT 06239; 860-774-0418; Fax: 860-450-7477.

- ACCESS-Multiservices, Pamela St. John, Program Supervisor, 106 Truman Street, New London, CT 06320; 860-442-4630; Fax: 860-447-1826.

Learn Construction Skills

The Ansonia Housing Authority formed Curtisey Corporation, a non-profit entity, to provide training and employment activities for its tenants and other low-income individuals enabling them to transition from welfare roles to self-sufficiency. If you are interested in learning construction oriented work skills, they would like to hire you for projects and on-the-job training. The program offers on-the-job employment training and a Family Self-Sufficiency/Innovations Network. For more information, contact Kathy Lester, Curtisey Corporation, 88 Main Street, Ansonia, CT 06401; 203-732-0411; Fax: 203-734-3283; {www.nhc.org/infoproj/jobinfo.htm}.

Educational Center for Women

Caroline House is located in one of the most devastated areas in Bridgeport, CT. For the past four years the School Sisters of Notre Dame, Wilton Province, have ministered and taught in this learning center that is available to needy women who want to learn English as a second language (ESL), basic computer, and life resource learning skills. Each day about 45 women attend classes together with their preschool children. Within the same facility, children are attending preschool. For further information, contact Maureen Fleming, SSND, Caroline House, 574 Stillman Street, Bridgeport, CT 06608; 203-334-0640; Fax: 203-334-0640.

Help For Women Entrepreneurs

Connecticut women are lucky to have an American Woman's Economic Development Corporation office in their state. Connecticut's programs follow the New York AWED model, offering Start Your Own Business and Managing Your Own Business training seminars and provides individual seminars and workshops. They also may be able to provide you with loan packaging assistance. (See listing under "New York" for more information or contact American Woman's Economic Development Corporation, Fran Pastore, Connecticut Manager, 2001 W. Main Street, Suite 140, Stamford, CT 06902; 203-326-7914; Fax: 203-326-7916.

Delaware

One-Stop Career Centers

A network of One-Stop Career Centers throughout the state offers a wide range of employment related services including job training. Services vary by location. To find a location near you, please refer to the website {http://wtw.doleta.gov/ohrw2w/recruit/where.htm}. To learn more about the services they offer, contact your state coordinator.

Mr. Michael M. Benefield Jr., Director, DOL/Division of Employment and Training, 4425 N. Market Street, Wilmington, DE 19809-0828; 302-761-8000; Fax: 302-761-6621; {e-mail: M.Benefield@DET-ADMIN@DOL}

Mr. Robert Clarkin, Employment and Training Administrator, State of Delaware, 4425 N. Market Street, Wilmington, DE 19809-0828; 302-761-8102; Fax: 302-761-6617; {e-mail: Clarken@DET-MIS@DOL}.

Job Service Offices
A system of Employment Service/Job Service offices is located within every state with the goal of assisting millions of job seekers and employers. While services may vary from location to location, many provide job training, skills assessment and related services. With approximately 1,800 Employment Service/Job Service offices nationwide there is bound to be one near you. To learn more about the services offered in your area, contact your state administrator. Darrell J. Minott, Secretary of Labor, State Department of Labor, 4425 North Market Street, Wilmington, DE 19802; 302-761-8000; Fax: 302-761-6621.

Other State Programs
The state of Delaware has designed a program to get you back to work. Their ABC program combines all programs that the state offers to welfare clients including job training. Services are provided to clients through the joint efforts of DSS, Department of Labor, the Economic Development Office and Contractors. For more information, contact Beverly Ennis, Workforce Development, Delaware Economic Development Office, 99 Kings Highway, Dover, DE 19901; 302-739-4271; {e-mail: bennis@state.de.us}

For more information about the Delaware Department of Health and Social Services Division of State Service Centers, contact Anne M. Farley, Director, Lorraine Mekulski, Deputy Director, 1901 N. Du Pont

Highway, Chas Debnam Bldg., New Castle, DE 19720; 302-577-4961; Fax: 302-577-4975; {e-mail: dhssinfo@state.de.us}.

Christian Programs

Ursuline Companions in Mission is a Christian association of lay women and men who seek to make a difference in the lives of the poor through a variety of programs including job training. They have service delivery sites in Delaware, Illinois, Kentucky, Minnesota, Missouri, New Mexico, and Ohio. Programs vary from location to location. For more information, contact Ursuline Companions In Mission, Sr. Jane Quinlan, College of New Rochelle, College Center, Room 155, New Rochelle, NY 10805; 914-654-5270; Fax: 915-654-5290; {www.theursulines.org}; {e-mail: ursulinecomp@hotmail.com}.

Search For A Job Online

The Virtual Career Network is a sophisticated online search engine concerned with all things related to employment in Delaware. While no specific programs are offered for women, the Job Seeker Services area allows you to create your resume and place it in a talent bank accessible by employers. You can also search through an electronic job bank for the job of your choice, to research occupations that may be of interest, and to review training opportunities. For example, by entering your chosen field i.e. secretary, the system makes suggestions as to where to obtain training for that occupation. Check out the website at {www.vcnet.net/}.

District of Columbia

Job Service Offices

A system of Employment Service/Job Service offices is located within every state with the goal of assisting millions of job seekers and employers. While services may vary from location to location, many provide job training, skills assessment and related services. With approximately 1,800 Employment Service/Job Service offices nationwide there is bound to be one near you. To learn more about the services offered in your area, contact your state administrator Mr. Gregory P. Irish, Director, DC Department of Employment Services, 500 C Street, NW, Room 600, Washington, DC 20001; 202-724-7100.

Opportunities for Women

All Kinds Of Opportunities For Women in DC

You are fortunate to live near the National Women's Business Center. They have many programs for women at all stages of business development including Introduction to Business Ownership; Making it Happen; Up and Running; Marketing: Getting Results; Managing a Business with Accountability; Federal Procurement Series; The Advanced Training Institute; The Business Council; The Roundtable; The Business Laboratory; and The Bottom Line.

The National Women's Business Center, located in downtown Washington, DC also has an office at the SBA District Office, co-located with a Small Business Development Center sub-center to maximize the exposure to and utilization of business training and counseling with several SBA resource partners. Contact National Women's Business Center, Beth Cole, Executive Director, Arlinda Halliburton, Director, Patti Berens, Director, 1250 24th Street, NW, Suite 350, Washington, DC 20037; 202-466-0544; 202-466-0581; SBA office 202-606-4000, ext. 278; {www.womenconnect.com/womensbusinesscenter}; {e-mail: wbc@patriot.net}.

School of Tomorrow

If you or someone you know is unemployed, underemployed or part of the working poor, the School of Tomorrow can help you get on track. The School provides a full array of educational and vocational training programs, including commercial drivers' training, computer skills and GED preparation. Over 150 adult students are currently attending classes. For more information, contact Gospel Rescue Ministries of Washington DC, 810 5th Street, NW, Washington, DC 20001; 202-842-1731; Fax: 202-898-0285.

Culinary Training For The Unemployed

You can learn all the necessary skills to gain employment as a kitchen worker. The DC Central Kitchen operates out of a fully equipped 10,000 square foot, health code-approved industrial kitchen. The twelve-week training course follows a curriculum prepared in cooperation with Cornell University's School of Hotel Management, and includes all facets of entry-level work in a professional kitchen. Class size varies from 10 to 20 students each cycle. Participants attend classes Monday through Friday, from 8:30 AM to 3:30 PM. Instruction is provided by full-time staff chefs in all areas of kitchen skills. The training program emphasizes not only the technical aspects of kitchen work, but also the importance of punctuality, following directions, and positive work attitudes. Participants' self-sufficiency and esteem increases as a result of enhanced job skills, which is key to the transition out of homelessness. Upon successful completion of the program, graduates work actively with DC Central Kitchen staff to connecting with a network of area food service employers. For more information, contact DC Central Kitchen, 425 Second Street, NW, Washington, DC 20001; 202-234-0707; Fax: 202-986-1051; {e-mail: dccentralkitchen.org}; {www.dccentralkitchen.org/Job_Training.html}.

Homeless Women Eat While Learning Kitchen Skills

At the Dinner Program for Homeless Women, any woman (and her children) may receive an appetizing and nutritious dinner in a stable and safe environment, and be provided the support and opportunity needed to achieve her full potential. In addition to basic services, the Dinner Program provides a food services training program to five trainees per cycle. Each cycle lasts three-to-four months, depending upon the individual. Trainees learn to prepare and serve meals in a sanitary environment. They also receive weekly case management services to assist with goals related to employment, housing, and special needs such as substance abuse and mental health issues. In addition, women seeking training in other fields are referred to Jobs Have Priority (JHP) and Jubilee Jobs, who provide job training and placement assistance. For more information, contact Dinner Program for Homeless Women, 945 G Street, NW, Washington, DC 20001; 202-737-9311; Fax: 202-347-7217; {www.idsonline.com/userweb/cwilson/dinner.htm}.

Get The Help You Need To Start Your Own Business

Founded in 1976, the American Woman's Economic Development Corporation is the premier national not-for-profit organization committed to helping entrepreneurial women start and grow their own businesses. Based in New York City, AWED also has offices in southern California, Connecticut and Washington, DC. Join over 100,000 women who have benefitted from formal course instructions, one-to-one business counseling, seminars, special events and peer group support. AWED's goals is to increase the start-up, survival and expansion rates of small businesses. Contact American Woman's Economic Development Corporation (AWED), Suzanne Tufts, President and CEO, 71 Vanderbilt Avenue, Suite 320, New York, NY 10169; 212-692-9100; Fax: 212-692-9296.

Training, Training, Training

Another national program that locals can benefit from is Wider Opportunities for Women (WOW) which works nationally and in its home community of Washington, DC to achieve economic independence and equality of opportunity for women and girls. What began as a local Washington effort to help women help themselves has become a multi-faceted women's employment organization, recognized nationally for its skills training models, technical assistance, and advocacy for women workers. WOW can help you learn to earn, with programs emphasizing literacy, technical and non-traditional skills, welfare-to-work transition, and career development as they have for 30 years. Join the more than 10,000 women WOW has trained for well paid work since 1964. Contact the National Office: WOW, 815 15th Street, NW, Suite 916, Washington, DC 20005; 202-638-3143; Fax: 202-638-4885.

Local Training Office: WOW, 204 Riggs Road, NE, Washington, DC 20011; 202-526-7066; Fax: 202-526-4030; {www.w-o-w.org/default.htm}; {e-mail: info@w-o-w.org}.

Florida

One-Stop Career Centers

A network of One-Stop Career Centers throughout the state offers a wide range of employment related services including job training. Services vary by location. To find a location near you, please refer to the website {http://wtw.doleta.gov/ohrw2w/recruit/where.htm}. To learn more about the services they offer, contact your state coordinator.

Ms. Kim Doyle, Brevard Local Learning Lab, 1519 Clearlake Road, Suite A-116, Cocoa, FL 32922; 407-504-2060; Fax: 407-504-2065; {www.brevard.cc.fl.us/joblink}; {e-mail: kdoyle@job-link.net}.

Ms. Kathleen McLeskey, Director Division of Jobs and Benefits, Florida Department of Labor and Employment Security, 1320 Executive Center Drive, Atkins Building, Suite 300, Tallahassee, FL 32399-0667; 904-488-7228; Fax: 904-487-1753.

Job Service Offices

A system of Employment Service/Job Service offices is located within every state with the goal of assisting millions of job seekers and employers. While services may vary from location to location, many provide job training, skills assessment and related services. With approximately 1,800 Employment Service/Job Service offices nationwide there is bound to be one near you. To learn more about the services offered in your area, contact your state administrator. Doug Jamerson, Secretary, Department of Labor & Employment Security, 2012 Capital Circle, SE, Suite 303 Hartman Building, Tallahassee, FL 32399-2152; 904-922-7021; Fax: 904-488-8930.

Unemployment Compensation /Benefit Eligibility

The Florida Training Investment Program was established as a statewide three year pilot program designed to extend unemployment compensation benefit eligibility to dislocated workers throughout Florida who have lost their jobs, have limited marketable skills, and enroll in vocational training intended to lead to employment in an occupation for which there is a labor market demand. Applications for the training investment program may be obtained at any Florida unemployment compensation claims office, job service office or by writing to: Division Of Unemployment Compensation, Tip Unit, Bureau Of Claims And Benefits, 234 Caldwell Building, Tallahassee, FL 32399-0225; 850-921-3893.

You Can Get A "Man's" Job and Wages

Central Florida Jobs & Education Partnership, Inc. strives to train and find employment for women in non-traditional jobs that allows them to earn typically higher wages. Just last year, 40 women were trained and placed in non-traditional jobs and are now earning up to $40.00 per hour and average $10.05 per hour. You can receive training in: truck driving, computer electronics, drafting, police/corrections officer, auto mechanic, electrician, assemblers/packagers, air conditioning tech, and auto sales. For more information, contact CFJEP, 1801 Lee Road, Suite 307, Winter Park, FL 32789; 407-741-4365; Fax: 407-741-4394; {www.cfjep.com/}; {e-mail: kacornett@ hotmail.com}.

Grow Your Own Business

The Women's Business Development Center can provide you with quality business education, technical assistance and access to capital. Their focus is on women, minorities and low- and moderate-income individuals who are starting or growing their own businesses. Business education programs incorporate both traditional and non-traditional methods of learning. In classroom settings, business owners and professionals teach participants about entrepreneurship, market research, financial analysis and business planning. Non-traditional programs include one-on-one business counseling, a mentor/protege program, business specialty workshops and networking forums. The Center also assists clients with preparation of loan packages and will present loans to financial institutions. The Center has been designated an intermediary for the SBA Women's Prequalification Loan Program and has a satellite office in downtown Miami at the SBA's Business Resource Center. Social skills training for women on welfare has been initiated and will be offered with dual goals of enhancing employability as well as providing the first step to self-employment. For more information: Women's Business Development Center (WBDC), Christine Kurtz-White, Director, 10555 West Flagler Street, Room 2612, Miami, FL 33174; 305-348-3951, 305-348-3903; Fax: 305-348-2931; {e-mail: obermann@fiu.edu} (Program Coordinator); {e-mail: rojasm@fiu.edu} (Financial Consultant).

Training For Low-Income People

The Center for Employment Training (CET) is a private, non-profit, community based organization that provides quality employment training for those who need it most. They offer extensive life skills and workplace know-how instruction through a program that includes job preparedness training, job development and placement. CET keeps students in training until they are placed and conducts follow-up on all placement to ensure stable employment and job growth. CET's primary activity is classroom skill training, which is provided year-round. CET does not screen applicants through testing, but accepts anyone who is willing to do the necessary work. Courses are offered on an open-entry, open-exit basis and students complete training at their own pace. CET training is intensive, with students attending 5 days and 35 to 40 hours per week for an average of seven months. CET training is competency based, highly individualized, and hands-on from day one. The average training course at CET maintains a 20-1 student/teacher ratio. CET's unique mode of training involves an integration of skill training, basic skills instruction and human development conducted in a simulated work setting. At least twenty-five job training options are offered at CET nationwide. These include automated office skills, building maintenance, electronic assembly, medical assistant, truck driving, and shipping/receiving. Skill offerings vary from one center to another. A typical CET center offers 4-5 skills and may serve up to 250 persons annually. For more information, contact their national headquarters: CET Corporate Offices, 701 Vine St., San Jose, CA 95110; 408-287-7924; 800-533-2519; {www.best.com/~cfet/main.htm}; {e-mail: cfet@best.com}.

In Florida, contact Center for Employment Training, 301 Southwest 14th Ave., Delray Beach, FL 33444; 561-265-1405; Fax: 561-243-2596; {e-mail: mailto:d_gainer@cetmail.cfet.org}.

Find A Mentor For Your Women Owned Business Endeavor

The mission of the Women Business Owners Of North Florida is to create and recognize opportunities to lift up the successes of women in the business world, both individually and collectively. What this means for you is that WBO will support your vision with practical educational opportunities and with mentors who offer encouragement, advice and networking assistance. Contact Women Business Owners Of North Florida, P.O Box 551434, Jacksonville, FL 32255-1434; 904-278-9270; {www.jaxwbo.org/}.

The Old Reliable

The YWCA of Jacksonville has a transitional housing program in which they offer free employment training such as resume development and interview skills. A computer lab is onsite to develop computing skills. Program is only open to women living in the transitional housing program for which they pay 30% of their current income. Contact YWCA, 325 E Duval St., Jacksonville, FL 32202-2794; 904-354-6681.

Community Colleges

Florida is blessed with a large number of community colleges with special programs of interest to women. Several are described below.

- *Okaloosa-Walton Community College* offers their Single Parent/Displaced Homemaker Program. If you are returning to school because of a divorce, separation, or the death of a spouse, they can help you. The program assists students with education and training so they can enter the work force with marketable skills and abilities, a support system, referrals, tuition assistance, information leading to high wage vocational employment and textbook loans for qualified students. For more information, Okaloosa-Walton Community College, 100 College Boulevard, Niceville, FL 32578; 850-729-5291 or 850-678-5111; {www.owcc.cc.fl.us/departs/cont_ed/programs/single_displaced_home.html}.

- If you are in the job market due to a divorce, separation, death or disability of a spouse, supporting parent or family member or friend whose financial resources are now no longer available, *Valenica Community College* has 2 programs for you.

  1. The *Displaced Homemaker Program* at Valencia Community College offers multiple services including: classes; follow-up assistance with job searches; individualized personal, educational and vocational counseling; monthly seminars for personal and professional growth; and individual intake appointments to establish specific needs. The Program serves Orange, Osceola, and Seminole Counties. Available at no charge to county residents, the Program also offers confidence building; career direction and assessment; employability skills; job search assistance; referral to social services, training and education; information and advisement; and life management skills. Displaced homemakers who qualify financially receive a weekly stipend from the Valencia Community College Foundation to help them pay for their transportation and child care costs while they attend the all day two-week "Building for Success" classroom sessions.

  2. To assist program graduates who require additional education to sharpen existing skills or to acquire new skills that will enable them to successfully enter the workplace with a meaningful and rewarding career to support themselves and their family, the *Displaced Homemaker Scholarship* is available to qualified applicants to the extent of available funding. Applicants for the Displaced Homemaker Scholarship must be graduates of the Displaced Homemaker Program, have evidence of financial need, exemplify scholastic ability, and must complete Valencia's financial aid application. Selection of the recipient of the Displaced Homemaker Scholarship is made by a Displaced Homemaker Staff Committee. Inquiries about this scholarship and requests for an application should be made to the Women's Center office, and should be filed as early as possible before the defined dates. Applicants selected as Displaced Homemaker Scholars are expected to write to the Displaced Homemaker

Program, in care of the Valencia Foundation, about their experiences at Valencia and the value of the scholarship. Valencia Community College Foundation, P.O. Box 3028, Orlando, FL 32802-3028; 407-317-7950; Fax: 407-317-7956; {www.valencia.org/442.html}; {e-mail: Valencia3@aol.com}.

- *Edison Community College* offers a Single Parent/Displaced Homemaker/Single Pregnant Woman Program. It is a grant-funded program with a mission to assist single pregnant women, single parents and displaced homemakers enrolled in Associate of Science Degree core courses to gain marketable skills and attain self-sufficiency through vocational training. Services you can take advantage of include scholarship funding; personal counseling; academic advising; vocational advising; financial aid advising; community referrals; career assessment; child care scholarship. Contact: Annette Massen Spates, Coordinator, Howard Hall 125, Fort Myers, FL 33919-5598; 941-489-9005; {www.edison.edu/departments/supportserv/singleparent.htm}.

- *Santa Fe Community College* Displaced Homemaker Program/Focus on the Future offers confidential assistance to homemakers who are 35 years of age or older who lack skills or experience in today's job market and have lost the financial support of a spouse or family member due to death, divorce, separation or disability. The program provides instruction in goal setting, personal growth and development (including financial planning, stress and time management) and job search techniques (including applications, resumes and interviewing). Individual and career counseling is also available to help people make the transition to independence through personal development, further education or employment. Free month-long classes and special workshops are scheduled throughout the year. Call the Displaced Homemaker Program: Focus on the Future at 352-395-5047 for further information. This program is made possible by a grant from the State of Florida, Department of Education. Northwest Campus, 3000 NW 83rd Street, Gainesville FL 32606; 352-395-SFCC (395-7322); {http://admin.santafe.cc.fl.us/~information/catalog/displaced.htm}.

The main campus contact is Santa Fe Community College, 401 NW 6th St., Gainesville, FL 32601; 352-395-5645.

- *Gateway to Health Education Center* has a program that is designed to assist single parents, single pregnant women, and displaced homemakers to enroll in college in A.S. degree programs that will prepare them for high-wage careers. They offer career assessment and advising, financial assistance for tuition and books to qualified participants, support groups and workshops. While the program is headquartered at the Health Education Center, the program coordinator keeps office hours on the St. Petersburg/ Gibbs and Clearwater Campuses and serves students collegewide. For more information, contact the Gateway to Health Education Center, 7200 66th Street North, Pinellas Park, Fl 33781; 813-341-3687; {http://hec.spjc.cc.fl.us/}.

- The *Roseanne Hartwell Women's Center* is part of the Florida Community College in Jacksonville. They have two programs of special interest to women. The Challenge program is designed to meet the specific needs of displaced homemakers. Specially trained staff conduct classes and provide advising with personal skills, as well as job placement. Five week classes are held continuously throughout the year. One and two day workshops are held at various times during the year. There is no fee for Challenge. For more information or to arrange for an interview call 604-633-8316

- *FCCJ's Gender Equity Program* can assist you with orientation to non-traditional careers such as automotive technology, carpentry, computer programming, electrical wiring, plumbing and welding to name a few. They also offer tuition assistance, book scholarships, child care, transportation assistance, employability skills training, and support groups. To see if you qualify or for more information on either program, contact FCCJ Downtown Campus, 101 W. State St., Jacksonville, FL 32202; 904-633-8390; Fax: 904-633-8496.

Help For Coconut Creek Displaced Homemakers:
The Displaced Homemaker Program provides career counseling and community agency referrals. Contact Displaced Homemaker Program, 1000 Coconut Creek Blvd., Bldg. 41, Coconut Creek, FL 33066; Carol Faber Director; 305-973-2398.

Georgia

One-Stop Career Centers
A network of One-Stop Career Centers throughout the state offers a wide range of employment related services including job training. Services vary by location. To find a location near you, please refer to the website [http://wtw.doleta.gov/ohrw2w/recruit/where.htm]. To learn more about the services they offer, contact your state coordinator.

Ralph Towler, One-Stop Lead, Assistant Commissioner, Employment Service, Sussex Place, Suite 600, I-48 International Blvd., NE, Atlanta, GA 30303-1751; 404-656-6380; Fax: 404-657-8285; {e-mail: parkerh@doleta.gov}

Ms. Marti Fullerton, Commissioner, Georgia Department of Labor, Sussex Place, Suite 600, 1-48 International Blvd., NE, Atlanta, GA 30303-1751; 404-656-3011; Fax: 404-656-2683; {e-mail: MartiFullerton@dol.state.ga.us}.

Job Service Offices
A system of Employment Service/Job Service offices is located within every state with the goal of assisting millions of job seekers and employers. While services may vary from location to location, many provide job training, skills assessment and related services. With approximately 1,800 Employment Service/Job Service offices nationwide there is bound to be one near you. To learn more about the services offered in your area, contact your state administrator. David Poythress, Commissioner, GA Department of Labor, 148 International Boulevard, NE, Atlanta, GA 30303; 404-656-3011; Fax: 404-656-2683.

Education and Training Services in Northwest Georgia

If you live in northwest Georgia and are looking for job training, you ought to know about the Northwest Georgia Career Depot. They offer a comprehensive system of education and job training programs designed for life-long learning in both formal training and self-directed learning formats. Among their many programs is the Family and Children Services that provides free pre-employment training for individuals who need temporary assistance while they are seeking employment. New Connections is a program for single parents and displaced homemakers with services that include assessment, counseling, job readiness and job search training, and life management skills. New Connections works with other programs to help students find appropriate training to become employed and the program is free. An Adult Literacy Program offers free training for the beginning reader through the General Equivalency Diploma (GED) or High School Diploma. Many counties now offer training in English as a second language.

For information on the Career Depot project, contact Gwen Dellinger, CVRDC, P.O. Box 1793, Rome GA 30162-1793; 706-295-6485; {e-mail: gdelling@cvrdc.org}; or Karen E. Howell, Coordinator, Northwest Georgia Workforce Development Project at the same address; {www.careerdepot.org/business.htm}; {e-mail: Vandy88@aol.com}.

Training For Female Prisoners and Low-income Women

Prison Ministries with Women offers a range of services that include fee based computer training for low-income women, non-traditional job training (renovation), housing for single women, one-on-one sponsoring, mentoring for women, counseling for ex-offenders, furniture, and household goods. Female prisoners and ex-prisoners are eligible for all services except computer training, low-income women for computer training. For more information, contact Prison Ministries with Women, 465 Boulevard, SE #205, Atlanta, GA 30312; 404-622-4314; Fax: 404-624-0313.

Help Is Just A Phone Call Away

Forced to go into the work world suddenly or do you need help getting your job skills upgraded? Women Work! is for you. They have over 1400 sites across the country to help women from diverse backgrounds achieve economic self-sufficiency through job readiness, education, training and employment. Women Work! provides these services through a network of programs in every state. Women Work! also takes on the toughest women's employment issues and fights for them in Congress and in state legislatures. For more information on Women Work! or to find a location near you contact Women Work! Regional Representative, Region IV, Department Of Technology and Adult Education, Lydia Webber, Director of Special Services, 1800 Century Place NE, Suite 400, Atlanta, GA 30345; 404-679-1654; Fax: 404-679-1675.

Training For Domestic Violence Victims

Gresham's Arms of Love serves battered women and their children by offering a resource center for job training and placement for clients, transitional housing, 24 hour child care for residents, legal advocacy, teen support groups, and women's support groups in metro Atlanta. For more information, contact Gresham's Arms of Love, Inc., P.O. Box 42188, Atlanta, GA 30311; 404-622-9944; Domestic Violence Resource Center, 215 Lakewood Way, Suite 1070, Atlanta, GA 30315; 404-622-9944.

Start Your Own Business

If you are planning, expanding or strengthening a business, the WEDA program is for you. It is a 21-seminar series for women business owners, lasting two-and-one-half hours each week. This program was condensed in 1995 to a five-hour program. WEDA also provides mentoring and one-on-one counseling. The majority of clients are African-American women; however, it is open to all individuals. Topics covered in the training program include marketing, business planning, accounting and finance, contract negotiation, and domestic and international procurement. Women's Economic Development

Agency (WEDA), Joyce Edwards, Chairperson for Board, 675 Ponce de Leon Avenue, Atlanta, GA 30308; 404-853-7680; Fax: 404-853-7677; {e-mail: dorothy.fletcher@internetmci.com}.

Hawaii

One-Stop Career Centers

A network of One-Stop Career Centers throughout the state offers a wide range of employment related services including job training.

Services vary by location. To find a location near you, please refer to the website {http://wtw.doleta.gov/ohrw2w/recruit/where.htm}. To learn more about the services they offer, contact your state coordinator.

Ms. Lorraine H. Akiba, Director, Department of Labor and Industrial Relations, 830 Punchbowl Street, Rm. 321, Honolulu, HI 96813; 808-586-8844; Fax: 808-586-9099

Ms. Elaine Young, Workforce Development Division Administrator, Department of Labor and Industrial Relations, 830 Punchbowl Street, Room 329, Honolulu, HI 96819; 808-586-8820; Fax: 808-586-8822.

Job Service Offices

A system of Employment Service/Job Service offices is located within every state with the goal of assisting millions of job seekers and employers. While services may vary from location to location, many provide job training, skills assessment and related services. With approximately 1,800 Employment Service/Job Service offices nationwide there is bound to be one near you. To learn more about the services offered in your area, contact your state administrator. Lorraine H. Akiba, Director, Department of Labor & Industrial Relations, 830 Punchbowl Street, Room 320, Honolulu, HI 96813; 808-586-8844; Fax: 808-586-9099.

Women Work!

Women Work! is a state affiliate of the national membership organization dedicated to helping women from diverse backgrounds achieve economic self-sufficiency through job readiness, education, training and employment. For more information, contact Hawaii Women Work!, Janet Morse, President, Hawaii Literacy, Inc., 200 N. Vineyard Blvd., Suite 403, Honolulu, HI 96817; 808-537-670; {e-mail: hliteracy@aol.com}.

Idaho

One-Stop Career Centers

A network of One-Stop Career Centers throughout the state offers a wide range of employment related services including job training. Services vary by location. To find a location near you, please refer to the website {http://wtw.doleta.gov/ohrw2w/recruit/where.htm}. To learn more about the services they offer, contact your state coordinator.

Ms. Cheryl Brush, Idaho Department of Labor, 317 Main Street, Boise, ID 83735, 208-334-6303; Fax: 208-334-6430; {e-mail: cbrush@labor.state.id.us}.

Ms. Pat Debban, Idaho Department of Labor, 317 Main Street, Boise, ID 83735; 208-334-6399; Fax: 208-334-6430; {e-mail: pdebban@labor.state.id.us}.

Job Service Offices

A system of Employment Service/Job Service offices is located within every state with the goal of assisting millions of job seekers and employers. While services may vary from location to location, many provide job training, skills assessment and related services. With approximately 1,800 Employment Service/Job Service offices nationwide there is bound to be one near you. To learn more about the services offered in your area, contact your state administrator. Roger B. Madsen, Director, Department of Labor, 317 Main Street, Boise, ID 83735; 208-334-6110; Fax: 208-334-6430.

Illinois

One-Stop Career Centers

A network of One-Stop Career Centers throughout the state offers a wide range of employment related services including job training. Services vary by location. To find a location near you, please refer to the website {http://wtw.doleta.gov/ohrw2w/recruit/where.htm}. To learn more about the services they offer, contact your state coordinator.

Mr. Herbert D. Dennis, Manager, One-Stop Lead, JTPA Programs Division Department of Commerce and Community Affairs, 620 East Adams, 6th Floor, Springfield, IL 62701; 217-785-6006; Fax: 217-785-6454; {e-mail: herb.dennis@accessil.com}.

Ms. Lynn Doherty, Director, Illinois Department of Employment Security, 401 South State Street, Suite 615 South, Chicago, IL 60650; 312-793-5700; Fax: 312-793-9306.

Job Service Offices

A system of Employment Service/Job Service offices is located within every state with the goal of assisting millions of job seekers and employers. While services may vary from location to location, many provide job training, skills assessment and related services. With approximately 1,800 Employment Service/Job Service offices nationwide there is bound to be one near you. To learn more about the services offered in your area, contact your state administrator. Lynn Doherty, Director, Department of Employment Security, 401 South State Street, Suite 624, Chicago, IL 60605; 312-793-9279; Fax: 312-793-9834.

Christian Programs

Ursuline Companions in Mission is a Christian association of lay women and men who seek to make a difference in the lives of the poor through a variety of programs including job training. They have service delivery sites in Delaware, Illinois, Kentucky, Minnesota, Missouri, New Mexico, and Ohio. Programs vary from location to location. For more information, contact Ursuline Companions In

Mission, Sr. Jane Quinlan, College of New Rochelle, College Center, Room 155, New Rochelle, NY 10805; 914-654-5270; Fax: 915-654-5290; {www.theursulines.org}; {e-mail: ursulinecomp@hotmail.com}.

Gain Computer Literacy and More

Erie Technology Center is a comprehensive computer laboratory dedicated to the computer and information literacy of community residents. It is a program of Erie Neighborhood House, a settlement house located in Chicago. The Technology Center provides free computer and information literacy training to adult students taking in English, General Equivalency Diploma (GED), basic literacy, math, and career preparation classes at Erie Neighborhood House. As part of their regular classes, students use technology tools to complete their class assignments, write autobiographies, compile statistics, and create graphs. In addition, specific training is also provided in common application software, interfacing with Windows 95, using network resources, e-mail, and the Internet.

Currently, the Technology Center offers both daytime and evening classes to meet working students' needs. Their Pathways to Success (PTS) program is a job training program preparing adults to find jobs in the banking industry, which typically offers benefits in addition to living wages. Students, most of whom receive public assistance, learn English, math, personal budgeting, finance, workplace and stress management in the four-month program. The Technology Center serves as a "smart classroom" for PTS students to experience technology tools that they will be using in the workplace. Specific training is provided in touch-keyboarding, 10-key, Microsoft Office Professional, e-mail, and the Internet. A program titled First Step: Women, Technology, and Literacy provides training to women struggling to enter and remaining in the workforce to comply with federal welfare-to-work legislation. Working with low-literacy students (less than 6th grade reading level), staff teaches a combination of basic literacy and computer skills in a modern workplace environment simulated in the Technology Center. Every seat has a computer and access to software tools. Learning exercises in the areas of reading, writing, and pre-employment workshops are used to teach computer literacy. For more information, contact Erie Neighborhood House, 1347 W Erie St., Chicago, IL 60622-5722; 312-666-3430; {www.luc.edu/depts/curl/prag/pragusr/erie/tech/tech2.htm}.

Find Out Where You Can Receive Job Training

The Workforce Center provides easy access to information about employment opportunities and job training to any Rock Island resident on a call or walk-in basis. Contact Walter Trice or Kristia Tinsley, Workforce Center, Martin Luther King Community Center, 630 Martin Luther King Drive, Rock Island, IL 61201; 309-732-2999; Fax: 309-732-2991.

Help In Evanston Township

Evanston Township General Assistance offers education and job training programs, including clerical training and GED preparation, and assists applicants in procuring employment. Provides substance abuse services and temporary financial assistance to eligible applicants. For more information, contact Evanston Township General Assistance, 2100 Ridge Ave., Room G-900, Evanston, IL 60201; 847-475-4481.

Technical Opportunities

The Joliet Junior College Institute of Economic Technology offers a program called Technical Opportunities Program for Women in Non-Traditional Careers. It consists of a 16-week course offered at no charge to interested women. The 120-hour hands-on program introduces women to specific career paths requiring acquisition of technical skills. The women are provided the foundation necessary to gain access to education, training and entry-level technical jobs. Program participants receive hands-on training in areas such as building and industrial maintenance, computer aided design/ architectural drafting, automotive service technology, electrical automated systems technology, electronics technology and chemical process operations technology. Three field trips to area manufacturers are included in the program, as well as stress management, workplace survival skills and job search on the Internet. For more information contact Sandy Cyrkiel at Joliet Junior College, 1215 Houbolt Road, Joliet, IL 60432-4077; 815-280-1526; 815-280-1506; {http://iet.jjc.cc.il.us/top.htm}.

Help Is Just A Phone Call Away

Forced to go into the work world suddenly or do you need help getting your job skills upgraded? Women Work! is for you. They have over 1400 sites across the country to help women from diverse backgrounds achieve economic self-sufficiency through job readiness, education, training and employment. Women Work! provides these services through a network of programs in every state. Women Work! also takes on the toughest women's employment issues and fights for them in Congress and in state legislatures. For more information on Women Work! or to find a location near you contact Women Work! Regional Representative, Region V, Displaced Homemaker Program, Lincoln Land Community College, Contact: Sherry Montgomery, Shepard Road, Springfield, IL 62794-9256; 217-786-2275; Fax: 217-786-2223.

Help For Women In Transition

Home of the Sparrow is a non-profit transitional shelter for homeless women, women with children and expectant mothers and their infants. They provide transitional shelter, referral services, support, and encouragement daily to those in need. Residents are provided with: in-house counseling; job training; job placement; financial counseling; educational assistance; parenting classes; and assistance securing permanent housing. They are always open. For more information please call or write: Executive Director Rev. Phyllis Mueller, Home of the Sparrow, P.O Box 343, McHenry, IL 60051; 815-344-5171; Fax: 815-363-6001; {http://user.mc.net/~sparrow/}.

Learn Job Skills In a Supportive Environment

The Enterprising Kitchen is an innovative non-profit organization that provides meaningful employment along with job training to impoverished women living in Chicago. Participants are paid to assemble, package and help market products such as handmade soaps and grain-based goods. They offer women without strong work histories the chance to work in a supportive environment as they acquire valuable work habits and job skills. The women they employ participate in a holistic curriculum specially geared to meet their particular needs so that the workday is divided between curriculum time and production. Participants are paid to learn and work in an environment designed to encourage independence and personal development. 100% of all proceeds directly benefits job training and employment for women. For more information, contact The Enterprising Kitchen, 4545 N. Broadway, Chicago, IL 60640; 800-818-6158; {www.concentric.net/~Flieb/}.

Gain Basic Job Skills

PASS Adult Education offers you the following services aimed at giving you basic skills for employment: adult basic education, secondary education, GED preparation, high school credit courses, introduction to computers, job seeking skills, literacy, family literacy programs, and English as a second language. They serve Warren, Henderson, and Mercer counties in Illinois. There is a $3 fee for the computer class. For more information, contact PASS Adult Education, 620 South Main #103, 620 South Main #15, Monmouth, IL 61462; 309-734-3818; Fax: 309-734-2041; {e-mail: pearson@misslink.net}.

Employment and Training Program For Women

The Southwest Women Working Together WETP provides education assistance and employment placement to displaced homemakers and single mothers. Job counselors often address the employment needs of women who are public aid recipients or homeless. In addition to financial aid and employment services, the program provides job readiness workshops, resume preparation classes, skills assessments, employment training seminars, and job support groups for women. Furthermore, the program sponsors an annual non-traditional job fair that introduces women to careers in fields that provide higher earning potential than traditional fields. For more information, contact Southwest Women Working Together, 4051 West 63rd Street, Chicago,

IL 60629; 773-582-0550; Fax: 773-582-9669; {www.swwt.org/}; {e-mail: swwt@megsinet.net}.

Training For Low-Income People

The Center for Employment Training (CET) is a private, non-profit, community based organization that provides quality employment training for those who need it most. They offer extensive life skills and workplace know-how instruction through a program that includes job preparedness training, job development and placement. CET keeps students in training until they are placed and conducts follow-up on all placements to ensure stable employment and job growth. CET's primary activity is classroom skill training, which is provided year-round. CET does not screen applicants through testing, but accepts anyone who is willing to do the necessary work. Courses are offered on an open-entry, open-exit basis and students complete training at their own pace. CET training is intensive, with students attending 5 days and 35 to 40 hours per week for an average of seven months. CET training is competency based, highly individualized, and hands-on from day one. The average training course at CET maintains a 20-1 student/teacher ratio. CET's unique mode of training involves an integration of skill training, basic skill instruction and human development conducted in a simulated work setting. At least twenty-five job training options are offered at CET nationwide. These include automated office skills, building maintenance, electronic assembly, medical assistant, truck driving, and shipping/receiving. Skill offerings vary from one center to another. A typical CET center offers 4-5 skills and may serve up to 250 persons annually. For more information, contact their national headquarters: CET Corporate Offices, 701 Vine St., San Jose, CA 95110; 408-287-7924; 800-533-2519; {www.best.com/~cfet/main.htm}; {e-mail: cfet@best.com}. In Illinois, contact Center for Employment Training, 1307 South Wabash Ave., 3rd Floor, Chicago, IL 60605; 312-913-0055; Fax: 312-913-0937; {e-mail: VFW9091@aol.com}.

Work At A Trade

The Illinois Department of Employment Security (IDES) in cooperation with educators, business and trade unions, will help you get the training you need for high-paying, skilled jobs through a program called Women Step Up To Opportunity. Contact any of these organizations for more information:

- Illinois Employment Security Department, 401 S State St., Chicago, IL 60605-1225; 312-793-5700.

- Illinois Department of Commerce and Community Affairs (DCCA), 620 E Adams St., Springfield, IL 62701-1615; 217-782-7500.

- Women Employed, 22 W Monroe St. # 1400, Chicago, IL 60603-2505; 312-782-3902.

Non-traditional Work

Women in Trades, in partnership with five organizations in different states, will provide technical assistance to employers, contractors, and labor organizations on mega construction projects in the Midwest. They will work with contractors and apprenticeship programs meeting their goals for hiring women in job sites. These groups refer qualified tradeswomen to jobs, and most provide pre-apprenticeship programs to give women the skills needed in apprenticeship programs. They can give information on career awareness on the range of job options for women too. For further information on programs in your state call: Lauren Sugerman, Executive Director, Chicago Women in Trades, 220 S. Ashland, Chicago, IL 60607; 312-942-1444 (For information specifically on pre-apprenticeship programs, at Chicago Women in Trades, contact Elise Wilson, Employment and Counseling Associate at the above phone number.)

Look At All These Programs For Women

Richland Community College has several programs designed around the career needs of women. All programs focus on employment and provide career guidance and job search assistance and you may be enrolled in more than one at a time.

- The *Options/Opportunities Programs* serve homemakers who are widowed, divorced, or separated and need help finding a job. They help low-income single parents, displaced homemakers, and men and women on public aid with tuition, child care, mileage, and books. Call 217-875-7200, ext. 232, for more information.

- The *Opportunities Program at RCC* assists with education, training and employment for TANF recipients. Post secondary, vocational skills, career assessment and non-traditional programs are available. Supportive services include child care and transportation. For referrals, call Barb Mosier at 217-875-7211, ext. 574.

- The *Displaced Homemaker Program* offers career training workshops, career counseling, educational assistance and job placement assistance to homemakers who are divorced, widowed or separated and need to work to survive. Call Kathy Chambers at 217-875-7211, ext. 576 or Bobbie Henson at ext. 572.

- The *Single Parent Program* offers career training workshops, career counseling, educational assistance, job placement assistance, tuition, and child care costs for low-income single parents or single pregnant women who enroll in vocational courses. Call Bobbie Henson at 217-875-7211, ext. 572 or Kathy Chambers at ext. 576.

- *Options In Technology* offers career training workshops, career counseling, educational assistance, job placement assistance, tuition, and child care costs for students who enroll in non-traditional courses or who seek non-traditional employment. Call Bobbie Henson at 217-875-7211, ext. 572, or Kathy Chambers at ext. 576.

- The *RCC Opportunities Center* offers 25-hour GED classes to TANF recipients. The focus is on entering the job market while obtaining a high school equivalency. Call Sandra Montgomery at 217-421-6568. For Job Readiness and Job Search referrals call Barb Mosier at 217-875-7211, ext. 574.

The RCC Opportunities Center is located at 1500 East Condit St., 2nd Floor. Call or write Richland Community College, One College Park, Decatur, IL 62521; 217-875-7200; {www.richland.cc.il.us/}.

Management Training

Founded in 1976, Women in Management was developed by a group of women in business to meet the need for training and support seminars for woman managers and women seeking management positions. The Near West Cook County Chapter was founded in 1991. Theirs is a membership organization. For more information, contact Patricia Davis, President, PRO Office Services, Oak Park, IL 60302; 708-386-3717; Fax: 708-848-4099; {www.oprf.com/WIM/index.html}; {e-mail: riz@megsinet.net}.

Other chapters in Illinois include:

- Women In Management Incorporated, 30 N Michigan Ave. # 508, Chicago, IL 60602-3404; 312-263-3636.

- Women-In-Management Incorporated, 2203 Lakeside Dr. # B, Deerfield, IL 60015-1265; 847-295-0370.

Women Entrepreneurs in Chicago

The Women's Business Development Corporation can provide you with a variety of entrepreneurial training courses and seminars: one-on-one counseling; financial assistance and loan packaging for micro-loans, the SBA Prequalification Loan Program and other SBA and government loan programs including the mentor/protege program. They also offer WBE certification and private and public sector procurement; annual conference and Women's Buyers Mart; and extensive advocacy and policy development for women's economic and business development issues. Founded in 1986, the WBDC serves women business owners in the greater Chicago area, and advocates for women business owners nationwide. Contact Women's Business Development Center (WBDC), Hedy Ratner and Carol Dougal, Co-Directors, Linda Darragh, Project Director Extension 22, 8 South Michigan Avenue, Suite 400, Chicago, IL 60603; 312-853-3477; Fax: 312-853-0145; {e-mail: wbdc@aol.com}.

Help For Illinois Displaced Homemakers

Illinois maintains a Network for Displaced Homemakers. There are 12 Displaced Homemaker Centers located throughout Illinois. Each provides services that assist displaced homemakers to achieve economic independence and become financially contributing members of society. A displaced homemaker is an individual who has worked in the home for a substantial number of years providing unpaid household services for family members, is not gainfully employed, had difficulty in securing employment, and was dependent on the income of another family member but is no longer supported by such income or was dependent on federal assistance but is no longer eligible for such assistance. Example of services offered are workshops, career life planning, counseling, and support groups, referrals to local community resources, identification of educational and training programs, job placement and job search assistance. The network itself functions as an information clearinghouse. Call for information and referrals to employment and training programs as well as to displaced homemaker centers in your geographical area or refer to the list below. Contact Kathy Malcolm - Coordinator, Black Hawk College, 301 42nd Ave., E. Moline, IL 61244; 309-755-2200, ext. 230; Fax: 309-755-9847; {e-mail: malcolmk@outr01.bhc.edu}.

- Alternatives, Elgin Community College, 51 South Spring Street, Elgin, IL 60123; 847-697-1000; Fax: 847-931-3919.

- Community Service Council of Northern Will County, 201 Normantown Road, Romeoville, IL 60446; 815-886-3324; Fax: 815-886-6340.

- Women's Resource Program, Black Hawk College Outreach Center, 301 42nd Avenue, East Moline, IL 61244; 309-755-2200, ext. 230; Fax: 309-755-9847.

- Fresh Beginnings, Rock Valley College, 3134 11th Street, Rockford, IL 61109; 815-395-6600; Fax: 815-395-1899.

- Lincoln Land Community College, 5250 Shepherd Road, P.O. Box 19256, Springfield, IL 62794-9256; 217-786-2335; 217-786-2227; Fax: 217-786-2223.

- Tri-County Urban League, 317 South MacArthur Highway, Peoria, IL 61405; 309-673-7474; Fax: 309-672-4366.

- Richland Community College Options Program, One College Park, Decatur, IL 62521; 217-875-7200; Fax: 217-875-6965.

- Olney Central College, 305 North West Street, Olney, IL 62450; 618-395-7777; Fax: 618-392-3293; {e-mail: Teelr@iecc.cc.il.us}.

- Evaluation and Development Center, Southern Illinois University/ Genesis, 500 C Lewis Lane, Carbondale, IL 62901; 618-453-2331; Fax: 618-453-6386: {e-mail: minton@midwest. net}.

- Women's Program, William Rainey Harper College, 1200 West Algonquin Road, Palatine, IL 60067-7398; 847-925-6558; Fax: 847-925-6890; {e-mail: Jkline@harper.cc.il.us}.

- Project Impact, Southwest Women Working Together, 4051 West 63 Street, Chicago, IL 60629; 773-582-0550; Fax: 773-582-9669.

- Women Employed Institute, 22 West Monroe, Suite 1400, Chicago, IL 60603; 312-782-3902; Fax: 312-782-5249.

- Illinois Department of Labor Displaced Homemaker Program, State of Illinois Building, 160 North LaSalle, Suite C-1300, Chicago, IL 60601-3150; 312-793-7111 direct; 312-793-2800 general; Fax: 312-793-5257.

Training For Hispanics

The Hispanic Connections program enrolls a minimum of forty people per year in a six-week job training program which addresses basic employability skills and provides an opportunity for on-the-job training with the assistance of local businesses and not-for-profit agencies. For more information, contact Hispanic Connections, 2610 West North Avenue, 2nd Fl., Chicago, IL 60647; 773-292-5180.

Indiana

One-Stop Career Centers

A network of One-Stop Career Centers throughout the state offers a wide range of employment related services including job training. Services vary by location. To find a location near you, please refer to the website {http://wtw.doleta.gov/ohrw2w/recruit/where.htm}. To learn more about the services they offer, contact your state coordinator.

Carol Baker, Director, Program Development, Indiana Department of Workforce Development Indiana Government Center, 10 N. Senate Avenue, Indianapolis, IN 46204-2277; 317-233-3919; Fax: 317-233-4793.

Job Service Offices

A system of Employment Service/Job Service offices is located within every state with the goal of assisting millions of job seekers and employers. While services may vary from location to location, many provide job training, skills assessment and related services. With approximately 1,800 Employment Service/Job Service offices nationwide there is bound to be one near you. To learn more about the services offered in your area, contact your state administrator.

Timothy Joyce, Commissioner, Department of Workforce Development, Indiana Government Center South, 10 North Senate Avenue, Room E204, Indianapolis, IN 46204-2277; 317-233-5661; Fax: 317-233-1670

Bruce Kimery, Assistant Commissioner/Comptroller, Department of Workforce Development Indiana Government Center South, 10 North Senate Avenue, Room E204, Indianapolis, IN 46204-2277; 317-232-7675; Fax: 317-233-1670.

Help For Women and Minorities

Are you an Indiana woman or minority who owns a business? The Women and Minorities in Business Group (WMBG) offers counseling for emerging and mature businesses. Client needs are determined, evaluated and advised at no cost. Services include: workshops and seminars, direct counseling, information clearinghouse and referral source, and general information including statistics regarding women- and minority-owned businesses. They also administer the Minority Outreach Resource Executive (MORE) Program in six regions. Apply Through: Indiana Small Business Development Corporation (ISBD Corp.), 1 N. Capitol Ave. # 1275, Indianapolis, IN 46204-2025; 317-264-2820.

Women Work!

Women Work! is a state affiliate of the national membership organization dedicated to helping women from diverse backgrounds achieve economic self-sufficiency through job readiness, education, training and employment. Contact Indiana Women Work!, Jill Littell, President, New Directions, P.O. Box 887, Vincennes, IN 47591; 812-885-5882.

Single Parent/Displaced Homemaker Programs

Get assistance with vocational education, job training, career counseling, job placement, and life management training. Also, support groups to single parent, homemaker, displaced homemaker or single pregnant women in Decatur County and most surrounding areas. Contact Single Parent/Homemaker Project Services, 1025 Freeland Rd, Greensburg, IN 47240; 812-663-8597; {www.treecity.com/library/resource/single.htm}.

Business Training

You can get assistance with tuition, books, uniforms, child care (licensed centers), and gas vouchers (transportation) for business training at the McDowell Adult Education Center. They will help in job seeking, including interviewing, resume preparation, and interest surveys. Contact McDowell Adult Education Center - BCSC Person in Charge: Nancy Rympa, Single Parent/Displaced Homemaker Program, 2700 McKinley Avenue, Columbus, IN 47201; 812-376-4451; {columbus.in.us/iris/irisonline/Content/Single_Parent_Displaced_Homemaker_Program_McDowell.html}.

Help For Farm and Migrant Workers

Transition Resources Corporation is a non-profit organization that serves the needs of farm workers, including migrant workers, and their families. They can help with free services that include financial and tutorial assistance for GED, Ivy Tech or other education, assessment and testing, career counseling, training, job placement. They also offer emergency help with food, financial, etc. To be eligible, you must have done farm work for at least 25 days or for $400. For more information, contact Transition Resources Corporation, 220 Clifty Drive, Unit J, Madison, IN 47250; 800-664-6066; 812-273-5451; Fax: 812-273-1881.

Learn To Be a Certified Nursing Assistant

The Certified Nursing Assistant Program at McDowell has a course where you can develop skills which could lead to entry level employment in the health care field. Special emphasis is placed on increasing skills for the job market; learning medical terminology, and understanding the everyday health needs of the patient, as well as one's self, one's family, and the elderly. Students who successfully complete one semester of Nurse Assistant training, may also qualify for long-term health care certification, after practicum training (2 week period) in a health care facility. Fees: $10 + books for high school; higher for non-credit students. Contact the Certified Nursing Assistant Program - McDowell, 2700 McKinley Ave., Columbus, IN 47201; 812-376-4451.

Help in Bartholomew County

The following are career service providers in Bartholomew County compiled from a list at {http://columbus.in.us/iris/search/query.asp}.

- You can take courses in marketing education, basic office services and entrepreneurship with opportunity for on-the-job training and community-based work with pay. There are no fees. Contact the Co-operative Office Education/Basic Office Services, 1400 25th Street, Columbus, IN 47201; 812-376-4240.

- Computer Training (Interim) is a company that can offer you free 90-minute classes throughout the week if you are actively seeking employment through Interim Personnel. Contact Computer Training (Interim), 1504 N. Lincoln, Greensburg, IN 47240; 812-379-1070; Fax: 812-663-9096.

- Computer Training (Kelly) provides free computer training courses for people registered with Kelly with all levels of prior computer skills. Schedules vary; call for details. Computer Training (Kelly), 810 Brown Street, Suite B, Columbus, IN 47201; 812-378-3757.

- Computer Training (Manpower) offers free computer training courses to clients who intend to seek employment through their services. Computer courses utilize a computer tutorial with help from a training assistant. Contact Computer Training (Manpower), 1309 North National Road, Columbus, IN 47201; 812-376-4111.

- The Columbus Housing Authority offers a program for individuals who are highly motivated for increased independence and currently on Housing Authority list. If you are residing in public housing, they offer you: child care, transportation, education, job development, job training, and counseling. Services are free. Contact Family Self-Sufficiency - Columbus Housing Authority, McClure Road, Columbus, IN 47201; 812-376-2523.

- The Columbus Area Career Connection offers you classes in: Agriscience & Technology, Child Educare, Construction/Building, Trades Cooperative, Office Education, Cosmetology, Culinary Arts, Electronics Engineering, Drawing/CAD, Family & Consumer Science, Health Occupations, Industrial Cooperative Education, Industrial Technology, Machine Trades, Printing, Power Systems/Auto Technology, and Welding. You can receive credit toward your high school diploma while experiencing both classroom and work-based training. You also get workplace skills while laying the foundation for life-long learning. There are no fees. For more information, contact Columbus Area Career Connection, 2650 Home Avenue, Columbus, IN 47201; 812-376-4240; Fax: 812-376-4699.

- Health Careers Training offers choices in dental, veterinarian, physical therapy, radiology or nurse assistant. Students are placed at work sites for on-the-job training. This is a fee-based program. For more information, contact Health Careers Training, 2650 Home Ave., Columbus, IN 47201; 812-376-4240.

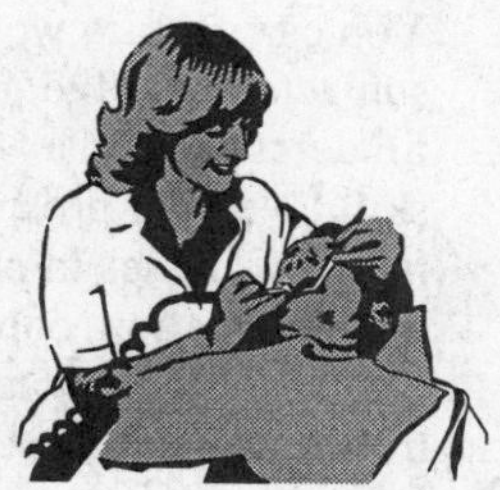

- Horizon House - Human Services, Inc. has a transitional shelter for homeless families who are highly motivated to make a permanent change in their lives. They can help you with job training/ coaching, short-term shelter; long-term case management; parenting classes; budget counseling; daily living skills; and nutrition classes. This office is also the intake site for after hours emergency lodging through the Salvation Army. There are no fees. Contact the Horizon House - Human Services, Inc., 724 Chestnut Street, P O Box 588, Columbus, IN 47202; 888-485-6137.

- IMPACT offers you job training and a work readiness program to help you become self-sufficient. Their services include: job training; education assistance; job placement; child care; transportation; medical coverage for up to 12 months; and limited financial assistance with uniforms, tools, etc. To be eligible, you must be a single parent, disabled parent, unemployed/ underemployed parent or teenage parent head of household; income and resource guidelines. There are no fees. Contact IMPACT (Indiana Manpower Placement & Comprehensive Training), 2330 Midway Street, Suite 3, Columbus, IN 47202; 812-376-9361.

- The Restaurant Dining-McDowell Education Center offers training in commercial food service. As a student, you will help operate a restaurant that serves lunch to the public three days a week. Call for information about fees. Contact Restaurant Dining-McDowell Education Center, 2700 McKinley Avenue, Columbus, IN 47201; 812-376-4451.

- You can acquire workplace skills while completing academic subjects needed to graduate and prepare for future education/work. Students receive a "Passport" that details their competency and skill levels for prospective employers and colleges. Services include: classes in physics, chemistry, biology, algebra, communication, composition, business, manufacturing and electronics; team teaching; peer tutoring; guest speakers; field trips; extensive hands-on instruction in tech lab. There are no fees. For more information, contact Technology Preparation Classes, 2650 Home Ave., Columbus, IN 47201; 812-376-4240.

- You can take free courses including topics such as building trades, welding, auto and diesel mechanics, electronics, printing, machine trades and drafting. Projects include: elaborate houses built; structures for Holiday Festival of Lights are hand forged and wired; microprocessor repair; computerized technology. For more information, contact Trade and Industry, 2650 Home Ave., Columbus, IN 47201; 812-376-4240.

- The Bartholomew County Division of Family & Children is a state agency that provides social services to adults, children, and families including job training. Contact Bartholomew County Division of Family & Children, 2330 Midway Street, Suite 3, PO Box 587, Columbus, IN 47202; 812-376-9361.

Iowa

One-Stop Career Centers

A network of One-Stop Career Centers throughout the state offers a wide range of employment related services including job training. Services vary by location. To find a location near you, please refer to the website {http://wtw.doleta.gov/ohrw2w/recruit/where.htm}. To learn more about the services they offer, contact your state coordinator.

Cynthia P. Eisenhauer, Director, One-Stop Lead, Iowa Department of Workforce Development, 1000 East Grand Avenue, Des Moines, IA

50319; 515-281-5365; Fax: 515-281-4698; {e-mail: Cynthia. Eisenhauer@iwd.state.ia.us}.

Job Service Offices

A system of Employment Service/Job Service offices is located within every state with the goal of assisting millions of job seekers and employers. While services may vary from location to location, many provide job training, skills assessment and related services. With approximately 1,800 Employment Service/Job Service offices nationwide there is bound to be one near you. To learn more about the services offered in your area, contact your state administrator. Cynthia Eisenhauer, Director, Department of Workforce Development, 1000 E. Grand Avenue, Des Moines, IA 50319; 515-281-5365; Fax: 515-281-4698; {www.state.ia.us/iwd/centers/files/offices.htm}.

Would You Like To Be Self-Employed?

The Institute of Social and Economic Development focuses on minorities, women, people with disabilities and low-income individuals. They encourage self-sufficiency through the growth of a small business and other self -employment opportunities. They can provide services for any person who wants to start or expand a business employing up to five employees, including the owner. For more information, contact Institute of Social and Economic Development, 1901 Broadway, Suite 313, Iowa City, IA 52240; 319-338-2331; Fax: 319-338-5824.

Training For Older Workers

The Older Worker Employment & Training program provides free training through part-time employment (20 hours/week). As an enrollee, you will be assigned to government agencies, non-profit corporations and schools that provide a "community service". You will be paid minimum wage with federal Older Americans Act funds. While in the program, you will also attend classroom training and gain experience that will lead to unsubsidized employment. This means a job not paid for by the program or other federal funds. Interested persons ages 55 years and over are encouraged to contact the Older Worker Employment & Training, Catherine Pratscher-Woods Coordinator, Great River Bend AAA, 736 Federal Street, Davenport, IA 52803; 319-324-9085; 800-892-9085; Fax: 319-324-9384.

Kansas

One-Stop Career Centers

A network of One-Stop Career Centers throughout the state offers a wide range of employment related services including job training. Services vary by location. To find a location near you, please refer to the website {http://wtw.doleta.gov/ohrw2w/recruit/where.htm}. To learn more about the services they offer, contact your state coordinator.

Mr. Roger Aeschliman, Acting Secretary, Kansas Department of Human Resource, 401 S. W. Topeka Blvd., Topeka, KS 66603-3182; 785-296-7474; Fax: 785-368-6294.

Heather Whitley, Director of Employment and Training, Kansas Department of Human Resources, Division of Employment and Training, 401 SW Topeka Blvd., Topeka, KS 66603-3182; 785-296-7874; Fax: 785-296-5112.

Job Service Offices

A system of Employment Service/Job Service offices is located within every state with the goal of assisting millions of job seekers and employers. While services may vary from location to location, many provide job training, skills assessment and related services. With approximately 1,800 Employment Service/Job Service offices nationwide there is bound to be one near you. To learn more about the services offered in your area, contact your state administrator. Wayne L. Franklin, Secretary, Kansas Department of Human Resources, 401 Topeka Boulevard, Topeka, KS 66603; 913-296-7474; Fax: 913-368-6294.

Kansas Job Training

Heartland Works, Inc. is a private company that administers job training in Kansas with Job Training Partnership Act. The focus of Heartland Works and JTPA is to assist individuals in becoming productive members of the workforce. Their services include basic skills training designed to help participants overcome deficiencies in reading, writing and math and prepare for the GED test, and career reemployment opportunities through an network of Career Reemployment Centers, where clients can interact with training representatives to conduct career research, attend career development workshops, create customized resumes/cover letters, practice their job search skills and attend computer classes. In addition, each center has a wealth of career development resources in a variety of mediums including access to the Internet. Classroom training opportunities are available through contracts with several vocational schools, technical colleges and community colleges as well as other educational providers for classroom training enrollments. Training is directed toward acquiring specific job skills in high demand occupations and will typically last six months to two years. Based on eligibility and overall need, a client may receive assistance with the cost of tuition, books, tools, uniforms and other necessary materials. To locate a service provider near you, refer to the list below or contact {e-mail: heartlandjtpa@cjnetworks.com}

Heartland Works Field Offices

- Heartland Works Topeka, 1430 SW Topeka Blvd., Topeka, KS 66614; 785-233-3131; Fax: 785-233-3433; {e-mail: heartlandwrk1@cjnetworks.com}.
- Heartland Works Lawrence, 2518 Ridge Court, Suite 105, Lawrence, KS 66049; 785-865-5463; Fax: 785-865-5465; {e-mail: heartlandwrk2@cjnetworks.com}.
- Heartland Works Manhattan, 1019B Poyntz, Manhattan, KS 66502; 785-539-0591; Fax: 785-539-1053.
- Heartland Works Satellite Office Marysville, 1021 Broadway, Marysville, KS 66508; 785-562-2238; Fax: 785-562-3036.
- Heartland Works Satellite Office, 818 Kansas Ave., Atchison, KS 66002; 785-367-0090.

- Heartland Works Satellite Office, Junction City, 136 West 3rd Street, Junction City, KS 66441; 785-762-8870.

Women Work!

Women Work! A state affiliate of the national membership organization dedicated to helping women from diverse backgrounds achieve economic self-sufficiency through job readiness, education, training and employment. Contact Kansas Women Work!, Cynthia Shanley, President, New Directions-KSU, 2323 Anderson Avenue Suite 221, Manhattan, KS 66502; 785-532-6561; {e-mail: shanley@ ksu.edu}.

Sharpen Skills

The Neosho County Community College Campus offers assistance to single parents and displaced homemakers at their Center for Academic and Vocational Excellence. It is located in the lower level of the Chapman Library on the Neosho County Community College Campus in Chanute, Kansas and is locally known as the CAVE. It consists of a computer lab, testing room, two classrooms, study areas, and offices. It is accessible to persons with physical challenges. CAVE computers provide academic tutorials to improve reading, writing, science, and math skills. In addition, word processing programs, software used in business and work settings, and programs geared toward the vocational needs of business and industry are also available. Services offered include: academic tutoring; adult basic education (ABE); computer-sided instruction; computer literacy training; developmental instruction; choices; GED preparation and testing; Internet exploration; job listings/career options; keyboarding program; problem solving skills course; resume design; seminars and workshops; and study groups. For additional information about the Center for Academic and Vocational Excellence please contact: The Panther CAVE, Neosho County Community College, 800 West 14th Street, Chanute, KS 66720; 316-431-2820, ext. 279; {www.neosho.cc.ks.us/cave.html}.

Programs For Single Parents and Displaced Homemakers

Pratt Community College has a program to assist single parents, displaced homemakers, and single pregnant women in acquiring needed education, vocational training, and marketable skills to acquire gainful employment. They can help you return to the workforce or enter the workforce for the first time by building your skills and self-confidence thus improving the your quality of life. They can also refer you to programs in local communities that can help you return to school, polish a resume, gain self-confidence, learn new skills, gain interview skills, and find rewarding work. Contact Person: Deanna Hoeme SP/DH/SPW Program, Pratt Community College & AVS, 348 NE SR 61 Pratt, KS 67124-8317; 316-672-5641, ext. 231; Fax: 316-672-5288; Attn: Deanna H; {www.pcc.cc.ks.us/Dph.htm}; {e-mail: deannah@ pcc.cc.ks.us}.

Allen County Community College has a similar program that is designed to assist single parents, displaced homemakers, and single pregnant women in acquiring needed education, vocational training, and marketable skills to acquire gainful employment. They provide the following services: outreach to potential participants; vocational assessment and advisement; career and personal counseling; academic (basic-remedial) education; vocational skill training; job search assistance; and financial assistance. Each participant will take CASAS Employability Test, and Choices Program as a career assessment. A scholarship is awarded to help pay for: child/dependent care during training/classes that are approved by the Kansas State Department of Education KSD-; transportation expenses to and from training/classes; and will pay up to 80% of tuition for one year certificates, CNA, CMA, EMT, HHA. Students may not withdraw from more that 40% of his/her credit hours for two consecutive semesters. Only serious applicants need apply. For further information, contact Michelle Harvey, Allen County Community College, Single Parent/Displaced Homemaker Program, 1801 N. Cottonwood, Iola, KS 66749; 316-65-5116, ext. 255; {www.allen.cc.ks.us/Irc/Spdh.htm}; {e-mail: harvey@acccn1.allen.cc.ks.us}.

Kentucky

One-Stop Career Centers

A network of One-Stop Career Centers throughout the state offers a wide range of employment related services including job training. Services vary by location. To find a location near you, please refer to the website {http://wtw.doleta.gov/ohrw2w/recruit/where.htm}. To learn more about the services they offer, contact your state coordinator.

Ms. Julia Gustafson, One-Stop Team Leader, Kentucky Cabinet for Workforce Development, 500 Mero Street, 12th Floor CPT, Frankfort, KY 40601; 502-564-9146; Fax: 502-564-9504.

Ms. Pam Anderson, Program Director, Career Connection, 305 West Broadway, Louisville, KY 40202; 502-574-2500; Fax: 502-574-4288.

Ms. Margaret Whittet, Commissioner, Department of Employment Services, Cabinet for Human Resources, 275 E. Main Street, Frankfort, KY 40621; 502-564-5331; Fax: 502-564-7452.

Job Service Offices

A system of Employment Service/Job Service offices is located within every state with the goal of assisting millions of job seekers and employers. While services may vary from location to location, many provide job training, skills assessment and related services. With approximately 1,800 Employment Service/Job Service offices nationwide there is bound to be one near you. To learn more about the services offered in your area, contact your state administrator. Rhonda K. Richardson, Commissioner, Department of Employment Services, 275 East Main Street, Frankfort, KY 40621; 502-564-5331; Fax: 502-564-7452.

Other State Programs

The Office of Labor Management Relations and Mediation (OLMRM) offers a variety of training programs designed to assist labor and management move toward a more cooperative and productive relationship based on trust. The training programs can be designed, based on time availability, to meet specific needs. For more information, contact Kentucky Labor Cabinet, U.S. 127S, Suite 4, Frankfort, KY 40601; 502-564 3070; Fax: 502-5645387; {www.state.ky.us/agencies/labor/labrhome.htm}.

Christian Programs

Ursuline Companions in Mission is a Christian association of lay women and men who seek to make a difference in the lives of the poor through a variety of programs including job training. They have service delivery sites in Delaware, Illinois, Kentucky, Minnesota, Missouri, New Mexico, and Ohio. Programs vary from location to location. For more information, contact Ursuline Companions In Mission, Sr. Jane Quinlan, College of New Rochelle, College Center, Room 155, New Rochelle, NY 10805; 914-654-5270; Fax: 915-654-5290; {www.theursulines.org}; {e-mail: ursulinecomp@hotmail.com}.

Louisiana

One-Stop Career Centers

A network of One-Stop Career Centers throughout the state offers a wide range of employment related services including job training. Services vary by location. To find a location near you, please refer to the website {http://wtw.doleta.gov/ohrw2w/recruit/where.htm}. To learn more about the services they offer, contact your state coordinator.

Ms. Dawn Watson, Project Administrator, Louisiana Department of Labor, 1001 N. 23rd Street (Zip 70804), P.O. Box 94094, Baton Rouge, LA 70804-9094; 504-342-7629; Fax: 504-342-7664.

Job Service Offices

A system of Employment Service/Job Service offices is located within every state with the goal of assisting millions of job seekers and employers. While services may vary from location to location, many provide job training, skills assessment and related services. With approximately 1,800 Employment Service/Job Service offices nationwide there is bound to be one near you. To learn more about the services offered in your area, contact your state administrator.

Ms. Robin Houston, Secretary, Department of Labor, P.O. Box 94094, Baton Rouge, LA 70804-9094; 504-342-3013; Fax: 504-342-3778.

Ms. Gayle Joseph, Assistant Secretary for the Office of Employment Security, Department of Labor, P.O. Box 94094, Baton Rouge, LA 70804-9094; 504-342-3013; Fax: 504-342-5208.

Occupational Information

The Louisiana Occupational Information System is a comprehensive online guide to educational/training providers in the state. You can search by geographic area, occupational training desired, or institutions. Go to {www.ldol.state.la.us/homepage.htm} and click on "training."

Women's Services

The Governor's Office of Women's Services is the official state agency legislatively charged to advocate on behalf of women. OWS coordinates public (local, state, federal), private, corporate, foundation, non-profit, volunteer, educational, and other funding sources to develop programs to address the needs of women. There are five locations: Lake Charles, Baton Rouge, New Orleans, Shreveport, and Lafayette. Depending on the location, you can receive individualized career counseling and assessment; basic skills enhancement; building and industrial trades preparatory training; clerical/medical training; job placement services; customer service training and referrals to other training opportunities. If you are interested in working at a job traditionally held by men, the Non-Traditional Training Program will be of interest. Women in this program may be economically disadvantaged, unemployed, a dislocated worker, or a Find Work participant. Training varies from 9 to 12 weeks and you can learn skills in basic electricity, industrial wiring, circuitry, AC/DC motors, mechanical devices and systems, blueprint reading and schematics, and applied mathematics including algebra, geometry, and basic computer literacy. For more information, contact Administrative Office, Governor's Office of Women's Services, 1885 Wooddale Blvd., 9th

Floor, Baton Rouge, LA 70806; P.O. Box 94095, Baton Rouge, LA 70804-9095; 504-922-0960; Fax: 504-922-0959; {e-mail: owsbrcdh@cmq.com}; {www.ows.state.la.us/}.

Local Centers

- Lafayette Displaced Homemakers Ctr., 1304 Bertrand Dr., Suite C-1, Lafayette, LA 70506; 318-262-5191; Fax: 318-262-5192.

- Lake Charles Displaced Homemakers Ctr., 2120 Hodges Street, Lake Charles, LA 70601; 318-491-2656; Fax: 318-491-6844.

- New Orleans Displaced Homemakers Ctr., 980 Navarre Ave., LA Technical College, New Orleans, LA 70124; 504-483-4664; Fax: 504-483-4664.

- Shreveport Displaced Homemakers Ctr., 752 Dalzell, Shreveport, LA 71104; 318-676-7137; Fax: 318-676-5691.

Help For Women Entrepreneurs
Women Entrepreneurs for Economic Development, Inc. (W.E.E.D.) was founded in 1989 by three businesswomen. Since its inception, W.E.E.D. has assisted over 200 women in becoming economically self-sufficient. They assist women in the Orleans Parish area of New Orleans. Contact Women Entrepreneurs for Economic Development Inc. (W.E.E.D.), Paula Pete, Executive Director, Cynthia Beaulieu, Director of Training, 1683 North Claiborne Avenue, New Orleans, LA 70116; 504-949-8885; Fax: 504-949-8885.

Back To High School
Hamilton Terrace Learning Center in Shreveport, LA, which won the Innovations in American Government award given by Harvard University and the Ford Foundation is a "second-chance" high school whose student body includes welfare recipients, working adults, and high school students who have been expelled from other schools. For more information, contact Hamilton Terrace Learning Center, c/o Caddo Parish School Board, 1105 Louisiana Ave., Shreveport, LA 71101; 318-222-4518.

Women Small Business Owners Assistance

The Women's Business Center is a program that was developed by the Southeast Louisiana Black Chamber of Commerce (SLBCC) to assist women in Jefferson Parish, but serves nine other parishes including: Orleans, St. Bernard, St. Tammany, St. James, St. John the Baptist, St. Charles, Tangipahoa, Plaquemines and Washington. The Center can provide you with training, counseling and mentoring to aid and encourage the growth and development of small businesses, owned and controlled by women. Many of the clients served through the Center have started their own businesses. The Center is located in JEDCO West, an incubator program in Harvey, LA. For more information, contact Southeast Louisiana Black Chamber of Commerce (SLBCC), Women's Business Center, Laverne Kilgore, Director, 2245 Peters Road, Suite 200, Harvey, LA 70058; 504-365-3866; Fax: 504-365-3890; {www.gnofn.org/~slbcc/wbc}; {e-mail: wbc200@bellsouth.net}.

Women Business Owners

Women Business Owners Association works to establish women business owners as an integral and influential element of the business community and promotes the success of women-owned businesses. Greater New Orleans area business owners wanting to exchange information and share experiences formed WBOA as an organization consisting of women who own businesses and associates who support women in business. In 1998, WBOA celebrated its nineteenth year. WBOA was created to: foster training, technical assistance and other learning opportunities oriented toward your needs, encourage, support, and represent women-owned businesses, cultivate economic stability of women-owned businesses, and initiate and support legislation benefiting small businesses. For more information contact WBOA, P.O. Box 8326, Metairie, LA 70011; 504-456-0505; {www.wboa.org/Default.htm}.

Help For Displaced Homemakers

The Center for Displaced Homemakers/Office of Women's Services provides services to women or men who are separated, divorced, widowed or have a handicapped spouse. If this sounds like you, you can benefit from adjustment counseling; job readiness training; weekly support group and assessment and referrals, legal assistance, resume preparation, and personal development workshops. They also act as a processing center for dislocated workers and displaced homemakers eligible for training at Women's Employment and Training Center. There are no fees for qualified clients. For more information, contact Center for Displaced Homemakers, 752 Dalzell, Shreveport LA 71104; 318-676-7137; Fax: 318-676-7149; Site Manager: Doreen McGaffey.

Job Training/Enterprise Program

The Church Army of Western Louisiana is a homeless care network based in Lafayette, LA. Projects include a day shelter, an emergency home for unaccompanied adult women, a transitional home for men, a community/activity center, and a job-training and enterprise program that is currently in development. For more information, contact Church Army of Western Louisiana, P.O. Box 2747, Lafayette, LA 70502; 318-237-7647.

Maine

One-Stop Career Centers

A network of One-Stop Career Centers throughout the state offers a wide range of employment related services including job training. Services vary by location. To find a location near you, please refer to the website {http://wtw.doleta.gov/ohrw2w/recruit/where.htm}. To learn more about the services they offer, contact your state coordinator.

Ms. Valerie Landry, Commissioner, Maine Department of Labor, 20 Union St., P.O. Box 309, Augusta, ME 04330; 207-287-3788; Fax: 207-287-5292.

Job Service Offices

A system of Employment Service/Job Service offices is located within every state with the goal of assisting millions of job seekers and employers. While services may vary from location to location, many provide job training, skills assessment and related services. With approximately 1,800 Employment Service/Job Service offices nationwide there is bound to be one near you. To learn more about the services offered in your area, contact your state administrator. Valerie

R. Landry, Commissioner of Labor, ME Department of Labor, P.O. Box 309, Augusta, ME 04330; 207-287-3788; Fax: 207-287-5292.

Help Is Just A Phone Call Away

Forced to go into the work world suddenly or do you need help getting your job skills upgraded? Women Work! is for you. They have over 1400 sites across the country to help women from diverse backgrounds achieve economic self-sufficiency through job readiness, education, training and employment. Women Work! provides these services through a network of programs in every state. Women Work! also takes on the toughest women's employment issues and fights for them in Congress and in state legislatures. For more information on Women Work! or to find a location near you contact Women Work! Regional Representative, Region I, Thia Hamilton, Maine Centers for Women, Work and Community, 200 Madison Ave., Skowhegan, ME 04976; 207-474-0788.

Training In Trade And Technical Occupations For Women

Why should a woman choose a trade or technical occupation? How about for money, satisfaction, and/or control of her life? Women Unlimited offers a program that includes basic trade and technical skills training, physical conditioning, job-based math and literacy, and personal and career development. The program is 14 weeks long, meeting 3 days per week for 8 hours a day at sites throughout Maine. Upon completion of the program, they connect you with contractors and employers hiring for entry-level and skilled positions. For more information, contact Martha Piscuskas, Executive Director, 71 Winthrop St., Augusta, ME 04330; 207-623-7576; 800-281-5259.

Help For Fledgling Women Owned Businesses

Coastal Enterprises, Inc. (CEI) is a private non-profit community development corporation that provides financing and technical assistance to Maine businesses that provide income, ownership or employment opportunities to low-income people. One of their programs is The Women's Business Development Project (WBDP) that emerged from CEI's experience in assessing women's business owners' needs, and providing women's business owners with training, technical assistance, financing and advocacy. If you have already started your own business anywhere in Maine, they can help you. You can benefit from CEI's counseling, as well as their capacity to provide access to capital through its SBA Microloan Program, the SBA Women's Pre-Qualification Loan Program and other resources. For more information, contact Coastal Enterprises Inc. (CEI), Women's Business Development Program (WBDP), Betsy Tipper, Telecommunications Business Counselor, 7 North Chestnut Street, Augusta, ME 04330; 207-621-0245; Fax: 207-622-9739; {http://eat@ceimaine.org}; {e-mail: jmr@ceimaine.org}.

Plug Into A Statewide Network of Resource Centers For Women

If you are a displaced homemaker, single parent, welfare recipient, or simply a worker in transition, Maine Centers for Women, Work, and Community can set you on the path towards self-sufficiency. This statewide women's economic development organization offers training and assistance in workforce preparation, entrepreneurship, leadership development, comprehensive assessment, referral, training, placement, and other support services through 15 resource centers and outreach sites located throughout the state. Specifically, you can benefit from workshops on employability training, career/life planning, job search skills, self-esteem, assertiveness training, self-employment issues, and personal resource management. All services are free and confidential. Note that services may vary by location. To locate a location near you, refer to the list below or contact the administrative office at Maine Centers for Women, Work, and Community, Stoddard House, University of Maine at Augusta, 46 University Drive, Augusta ME 04330-9410; 207-621-3430; 800-442-2092 (ME only); Fax: 207-621-3429; {http://mcwwc.uma.maine.edu}; {e-mail: adaigle@maine.edu}.

Maine Centers for Women, Work and Community Office Locations

- MCWWC, University College, 355 Maine Avenue, Bangor, ME 04401-6130; 800-442-2092; Fax: 207-262-7951; {e-mail: searles@maine.edu}.

- MCWWC, Bath-Brunswick Center UMS, 275 Bath Road, Brunswick, ME 04011; 207-721-8636; 800-442-2092; Fax: 207-729-8261; {e-mail: virginia.powers@maine.edu}.

- MCWWC, Mill Mall, 240 State Street, Ellsworth, ME 04605; 207-667-1834; 800-442-2092; Fax: 207-262-7951.

- MCWWC, 48-A Perham Street, Farmington, ME 04938; 207-778-2757; 800-442-2092; Fax: 207-778-2463; {e-mail: Carol.Millay@maine.edu}.

- MCWWC, PO Box 382, Located at 106 Main Street, Houlton, ME 04730; 207-532-9313; 800-442-2092 (ME only); Fax: 207-532-3639; {e-mail: audrey@maine.edu}.

- MCWWC, Lewiston-Auburn College USM/UMA, 51-55 Westminster Street, Lewiston, ME 04240; 207-753- 6622; 800-442-2092; Fax: 207-753-6658; {e-mail: daggett@maine.edu}.

- MCWWC, 28 Balsam Drive, Millinocket, ME 04462; 207-723-9331; 800-442-2092; Fax: 207-723-9128; {e-mail: evie@gwi.net}.

- MCWWC, NMTC 33 Edgemont Drive, Presque Isle, ME 04769; 207-764-0050; 800-442-2092 (ME only); Fax: 207-769-6608; {e-mail: mewilcox@ainop.com}.

- MCWWC, Saco-Biddeford Center UMS, 110 Maine Street, Suite 1101, Saco, ME 04072; 207-286-1722; Fax: 207-283-9865.

- MCWWC, St. John Valley, NMTC 33 Edgemont Drive, Presque Isle, ME 04769; 207-764-0050; 800-442-2092; (ME only); Fax: 207-769-6608; {e-mail: mewilcox@ainop.com}.

- MCWWC, 200 Madison Avenue, Skowhegan, ME 04976-1305; 207-474-0788; 207-474-7865; 207-474-0598; 800-442-2092; Fax: 207-474-3684; {e-mail: womwork@somtel.com}.

- MCWWC, 175 Main Street, South Portland, ME 04106; 207-799-5025; Fax: 207-799-5443; {e-mail: mcwwc@gwi.net}.

- MCWWC, Thomaston Center UMS, 42 Main Street, Thomaston, ME 04861; 207-354-6312; 800-442-2092; Fax: 207-354-2128; {e-mail: cogger@maine.edu}.

- MCWWC, Box 13G, 19 Hillside Avenue, Waterville, ME 04901; 207-872-9482; 800-442-2092; Fax: 207-877-8382; {e-mail: wcwwc@mint.net}.

Maine's "Parents as Scholars" Program

Maine has created a "Parents as Scholars" program in which students at two- and four-year degree-grant programs will receive a package of aid equivalent to the same cash assistance, medical coverage, and other services they would have received had they become TANF (Temporary Assistance for Needy Families) recipients. To the extent that resources permit, a TANF-eligible person must be allowed to participate if she does not have the skills needed to find work that will support a family at 85% of the median state family income; the education will improve the family's ability to be self-supporting, and she has the aptitude to complete it successfully. Contact Mary Henderson or Chris Hastedt, Maine Equal Justice Project, 71 State St., Augusta, ME 04330-5126; 207-626-7058.

Train For A New Job

Are you interested in changing your type of work? If so, and you are in Maine, an organization called the Training and Development Corporation (TDC) may be able to help you. Among other things, TDC assists eligible farm workers in obtaining free training for many types of work. TDC can help pay for a college education or other types of training. For example, learning English, construction, nursing, mechanics, child care work, and many other areas in which you may be interested. Their toll-free number is 800-371-7543. Contact the service provider nearest you.

- Training & Development Corporation, 2 Main St., Corinna, ME 04928; 207-278-5500.

- Training & Development Corporation, 1 Cumberland Pl., Bangor, ME 04401-5085; 207-945-9431.

- Training & Development Corporation, 14 High St., Ellsworth, ME 04605-1706; 207-667-7543.

- Training & Development Corporation, 18 School St., Bucksport, ME 04416; 207-469-6385.

- Training & Development Corporation, Rt. 15, Dover Foxcroft, ME 04426; 207-564-8438.

- Training & Development Corporation, 257 Harlow St. # 201, Bangor, ME 04401-4944; 207-942-9492.

Maryland

One-Stop Career Centers

A network of One-Stop Career Centers throughout the state offers a wide range of employment related services including job training. Services vary by location. To find a location near you, please refer to the website {http://wtw.doleta.gov/ohrw2w/recruit/where.htm}. To learn more about the services they offer, contact your state coordinator.

Paulette Hall, Executive Director, Office of Employment Services, 1100 Eutaw Street, Room 208, Baltimore, MD 21201; 410-767-2005; Fax: 410-767-2010; {e-mail: cwalter@careernet.state.md.us}.

John O'Connor, Assistant Secretary, Department of Labor, Licensing and Regulations, 1100 North Eutaw Street, Room 600, Baltimore, MD 21201; 410-767-2400; Fax: 410-767-2986.

Job Service Offices

A system of Employment Service/Job Service offices is located within every state with the goal of assisting millions of job seekers and employers. While services may vary from location to location, many

provide job training, skills assessment and related services. With approximately 1,800 Employment Service/Job Service offices nationwide there is bound to be one near you. To learn more about the services offered in your area, contact your state administrator. John P. O'Connor, Assistant Secretary, Division of Employment & Training Department of Labor, Licensing & Regulation, 1100 North Eutaw Street, Room 600, Baltimore, MD 21201; 410-767-2400; Fax: 410-767-2986.

Information for Women

While the Maryland Commission for Women does not directly provide job training services, they can steer you towards the right program for you. They exist to provide information and referral services to inform women about their legal rights and services available to them and provide for the increased participation of women at all levels of employment as well as voluntary and paid decision-making positions. They also maintain a list of women's organizations and a Speaker's Bureau. For more information, contact Maryland Commission for Women, 311 W. Saratoga Street, Room 232, Baltimore, MD 21201; 410-767-7137; TTY: 410-333-0017.

Help Is Just A Phone Call Away

Forced to go into the work world suddenly or do you need help getting your job skills upgraded? Women Work! is for you. They have over 1400 sites across the country to help women from diverse backgrounds achieve economic self-sufficiency through job readiness, education, training and employment. Women Work! provides these services through a network of programs in every state. Women Work! also takes on the toughest women's employment issues and fights for them in Congress and in state legislatures. For more information on Women Work! or to find a location near you contact Women Work! Regional Representative, Region III, Renew Program, Kay Shattuck, Director/ Joyce Sebian, Counselor, Carroll Community College, Room 118, 1601 Washington Road, Westminster, MD 21157; 410-876-9617; Fax: 410-876-9040; {e-mail: cglaeser@carroll.cc.md.us}.

Run Your Own Transportation Business

AdVANtage II is a van service and entrepreneurial training program sponsored by Sojourner-Douglass College and funded by a grant from the Baltimore City Department of Social Services. You can receive the training and follow-up support services needed to establish and maintain your own transportation business. They will also help you become certified as a Minority Business Enterprise. In turn, you will provide van services to up to 500 welfare-to-work customers, enabling them to commute to job assignments not served by existing transportation providers. For more information, contact AdVANtage II, Sojourner-Douglass College, 500 N. Caroline St., Baltimore, MD 21205; 410-276-9741.

Training For Low-Income People

The Center for Employment Training (CET) is a private, non-profit, community based organization that provides quality employment training for those who need it most. They offer extensive life skills and workplace know-how instruction through a program that includes job preparedness training, job development and placement. CET keeps students in training until they are placed and conducts follow-up on all placement to ensure stable employment and job growth. CET's primary activity is classroom skill training, which is provided year-round. CET does not screen applicants through testing, but accepts anyone who is willing to do the necessary work. Courses are offered on an open-entry, open-exit basis and students complete training at their own pace. CET training is intensive, with students attending 5 days and 35 to 40 hours per week for an average of seven months. CET training is competency based, highly individualized, and hands-on from day one. The average training course at CET maintains a 20-1 student/teacher ratio. CET's unique mode of training involves an integration of skill training, basic skills instruction and human development conducted in a simulated work setting. At least twenty-five job training options are offered at CET nationwide. These include automated office skills, building maintenance, electronic assembly, medical assistant, truck driving, and shipping/receiving. Skill offerings vary from one center to another. A typical CET center offers 4-5 skills and may serve up to 250 persons annually. For more information, contact their national headquarters: CET Corporate Offices, 701 Vine St., San Jose, CA

95110; 408-287-7924; 800-533-2519; {www.best.com/~cfet/main.htm}; {e-mail: cfet@best.com}. In Maryland, contact Center for Employment Training, 1100 East Baltimore St., Baltimore, MD 21202; 410-962-0238 Fax: 410-962-1558; {e-mail: c_greene@cetmail.cfet.org}.

Training For Low-Income Entrepreneurs

Women Entrepreneurs of Baltimore, Inc. (WEB), can polish your skills through an entrepreneurial training program designed to help economically disadvantaged women become self-sufficient through business development. The main components of the WEB program are: an intensive three-month business skills training course; mentoring; financing strategy development; community networking; resource sharing; and professional business consultation. For more information, contact Women Entrepreneurs of Baltimore, Inc. (WEB), Amanda Crook Zinn, Chief Executive Officer, 28 East Ostend Street, Baltimore, MD 21230; 410-727-4921; Fax: 410-727-4989.

Help For Single Parents and Displaced Homemakers

Howard Community College's New Focus program serves Howard County low-income single parents, displaced homemakers and single pregnant women in their efforts to become economically self-sufficient. They can assist in your efforts to develop marketable work skills and learn effective job search skills. The program staff will help you determine your goals and decide on the type of work you would like to do based on your interests and past experiences. They can also help you plan a program of study, provide academic advising, assist with the application for college admission and financial aid, as well as facilitate the registration process. If you are currently looking for work or a better position, the staff will provide information on resume writing, interviewing skills, the job search process and the hidden job market. The staff will also assist you with personal concerns that interfere with job or school activities. Staff members are familiar with community resources and can make referrals to community services. The New Focus Program is here to help with any difficulty you may encounter on your way to economic self-sufficiency. Interested low-income individuals who are single parents, displaced homemakers or single pregnant women residing in Howard County should contact the

Counseling and Career Services Office (Room L144 or call 410-772-4840) to schedule a New Focus orientation appointment. Howard Community College, 10901 Little Patuxent Parkway, Columbia, MD 21044; 410-772-4800; V/TDD: 410-772-4822; {www.howardcc.edu}.

Help For Homemakers

The Maryland Department of Human Resources/Displaced Homemaker Program provides funds to help individuals who have been the homemaker in a family home, and after being dependent on the income of a family member, lost part or all of that income due to separation, divorce, death or disability of the income providing family member, or loss of public assistance benefits. By participating, you will receive guidance for entering or reentering the job market, along with information and referrals to other services. You also get job-training providing opportunities to improve skills necessary for you to gain employment and support for yourself and your family. For more information about the Displaced Homemakers Program, contact Carolyn Edmonds, Department of Human Resources, 311 West Saratoga Street Baltimore, Maryland 21201; 410-767-7661; {www.dhr.state.md.us/transit/ts-dhp.htm}; {e-mail: mddhr@mail.state.md.us}.

Single Parent Program

Community College of Baltimore County has a single parent/displaced homemaker's program that may serve your needs. Through the support of the Maryland State Department of Education, the Department of Human Services, and the Community College of Baltimore County, Dundalk campus, services are provided to support single parents (both male and female), displaced homemakers and single pregnant women in their efforts to reach their academic and career goals. The Changes Program includes both credit and non-credit courses, as well as, career counseling and testing, personal counseling, and special referral services. Services also include financial support for tuition cost, GED assistance, book fees, child care and transportation. The

Program provides help with job placement needs, including resume development, employer contacts and strategies for effective job interviewing and assisting individuals to gain training leading to economic self sufficiency. For more information about these services, call the Displaced Homemaker's Program, Community College of Baltimore County, 7200 Sollers Point Road, Baltimore, MD 21222-4694; 410-285-9808; Fax: 410-285-9903; {www.dundalk.cc.md.us/}.

Help For Those In Career Changes and Life Transitions

If you are experiencing career changes or life transitions, Allegany College of Maryland/Career Transitional Services offers you the support and direction needed to become self-sufficient. Some participants are recent high school graduates preparing for entry into the workplace while others are adults ready to explore new career options as a result of changing family structure or an unstable job market. All have in common the desire for guidance, training and related services offered in an atmosphere that is designed to foster their individual success. For more specific information contact Allegany College of Maryland, Cumberland Campus, 12401 Willowbrook Road, SE, Cumberland, MD 21502-2596; Career Search/Job Placement, Ellen Durr: 301-784-5141, General: 301-784-5005; Fax: 301-724-6892; {www.ac.cc.md.us/ceps2.htm}; {e-mail: ellen@ac.cc.md.us}.

Many Direct Services For Women

While the Montgomery County Commission for Women works to bring about changes in conditions creating inequities for women, their Counseling and Career Center provides direct services to individual women. You could benefit from personal and career counseling, groups and workshops, information referral and many other services. Contact The Commission for Women, 255 North Washington Street, 4th floor, Nations Bank Building, Rockville, MD 20850-1703; 301-279-1800; TTY: 301-279-1034; Fax: 301-279-1318; {www.co.mo.md.us/cfw}.

Programs In The Baltimore Area

Mayor's Office of Employment Development is the city department responsible for effective delivery of employment and training services to the citizens of Baltimore. OED offers services to adult residents which include: career development assessment, job search assistance, employer job banks, occupational skills training, literacy & GED programs, work-experience internships, on-the-job training, and support services. Contact Office of Employment Development, 417 Fayette Street, Suite 468, Baltimore, MD 21202; 410-396-3009; (Information Line); {www.pratt.lib.md.us/slrc/job/govoff.html}.

Branch Offices

- Eastside Career Center, 3001 E. Madison Street, Baltimore, MD 21205; 410-396-9030.
- Northeast Career Center, 100 W. 23rd Street, Baltimore, MD 21218; 410-396-6580.
- Baltimore Urban League Career Center, Mondawmin Mall, Baltimore, MD 21215; 410-523-1060.
- Southwest Career Center, 201 S. Arlington Street, Baltimore, MD 21223; 410-396-3670.
- The Career Connections, 101 W. 24th Street, Baltimore, MD 21218; 410-396-6722.

Senior Training

Senior Aides Program provides part-time subsidized work experience and training for low-income Baltimore City residents 55 years or older. The goal is for individuals in the program to move from subsidized work into jobs in the community. For more information, contact Senior Aides Program, 303 E. Fayette Street, 5th Floor, Baltimore, MD 21201; 410-396-4486 or 4487.

Baltimore County Programs

Baltimore County Office of Employment and Training CareerNet provides occupational skills training and other services such as: career counseling, job search and placement assistance, and ALEX job bank listings. Their training programs include: administrative assistant, microcomputer office assistant, medical office specialist, secretary/word processing, accounting/bookkeeping, computer technology, printing technology, machine tool technology, and general office clerk. Services are free to Baltimore County residents who meet income eligibility guidelines or are dislocated workers. For more information, contact Baltimore County Office of Employment and Training CareerNet, 1 Investment Place, Suite 409, Towson, MD 21204; 410-887-4473; Fax: 410-887-5773.

Office Locations

- Catonsville, 27 Mellor Ave., Baltimore, MD 21228, 410-887-0940.
- Eastpoint, 7930 Eastern Boulevard, Baltimore, MD 21224, 410-282-4004.
- Randallstown, Liberty Family Resource Center, 3525 Resource Drive, Randallstown, MD 21133, 410-887-0630.
- Towson, 1228 E. Joppa Road, Towson, MD 21286, 410-887-4128.
- Baltimore County Reemployment Assistance Center, Dulaney Center II, 901 Dulaney Valley Road, Suite 100, Towson, MD 21204, 410-887-4400.

Massachusetts

One-Stop Career Centers

A network of One-Stop Career Centers throughout the state offers a wide range of employment related services including job training. Services vary by location. To find a location near you, please refer to the website {http://wtw.doleta.gov/ohrw2w/recruit/where.htm}. To learn more about the services they offer, contact your state coordinator.

Mr. Jonathan Raymond, One-Stop Lead, Department of Labor and Workforce Development, 1 Ashburton Place, Room 1402, Boston, MA 02108; 617-727-6573; ext. 107; Fax: 617-727-1090.

Job Service Offices

A system of Employment Service/Job Service offices is located within every state with the goal of assisting millions of job seekers and employers. While services may vary from location to location, many provide job training, skills assessment and related services. With approximately 1,800 Employment Service/Job Service offices nationwide there is bound to be one near you. To learn more about the services offered in your area, contact your state administrator. Nils Nordberg, Commissioner, Division of Employment & Training, 19 Staniford Street, 3rd Floor, Boston, MA 02114; 617-626-6600; Fax: 617-727-0315.

Career Seminars

Among their many services, FutureWorks offers the following training opportunities at no cost: career seminar - This 2-day seminar will give you information about the most effective ways to get a job in today's job market including finding job leads, developing a resume, interviewing and negotiating salary. Career specialists are on staff to serve job seekers in seminars, workshops and individual advising. A resource room includes job postings, employer directories, newspapers, information about New England employers, training institutions and community resources. Experienced staff are available to help you with questions about employers and the job market. Workshops are offered each month in one hour sessions devoted to various job search topics. You may attend as often as you wish. For more information, contact FutureWorks, One Federal Street - Bldg 103-3, Springfield, MA 01105-1160; 413-858-2800; Fax: 413-858-2810; TTY/TDD: 413-858-2800; Information & Success Hotline 413-858-2882; {www.futureworks-now.com}.

Consulting and Training

The Center for Business and Technology is part of the Division of Economic and Business Development that was created to generate and support economic growth by supporting industry and businesses in the region. They are a leading provider of training programs and consulting services that consistently meet the changing technology and workplace demands of individuals, business and industry. CBT offers a wide range of consulting and training services, as well as topics of personal interest. Courses are offered as open enrollment seminars or closed contracts with individual organizations. For more information, contact Center for Business and Technology (CBT), Springfield Technical Community College, 1 Armory Sq., Springfield, MA 01105-1204; 413-755-4225; Fax: 413-739-5066.

Computer Information

MASSCIS, for Windows is a PC based system that provides comprehensive information about the worlds of work and education for career planners of all ages. It is a product/service of the Massachusetts Occupational Information Coordinating Committee (MOICC) within the Massachusetts Division of Employment and Training (DET). You can use MASSCIS to find information about work and education, and about occupations, training programs, and financial aid. MASSCIS is available at all Division of Employment and Training (DET) Service Centers, Massachusetts Career Centers, high schools, community colleges, colleges, and various other sites. To find the address of the nearest D.E.T Employment Service Center or Massachusetts One Stop Career Center visit {www.detma.org/empserv.htm}. MASSCIS can also be tried free of charge at the Higher Education Information Center at the Boston Public Library, 700 Boylston Street, Boston, MA 02116; 617-536-0200; Information Hotline: 800-442-1171 (MA only).

Training Directory

The Employment and Training directory provides access to Internet resources where you can search for jobs or create an online resume, search for educational/training information and resources, or search a database of day care providers. To access it, visit {www.detma.org/emp_train.htm}. Remember that Internet access is often available at public libraries. The Employment and Training directory is maintained by the Massachusetts Division of Employment and Training, 19 Staniford Street, Boston, MA 02114; 617-727-6560.

Help For Minority Women

In addition to their work certifying companies as minority or women-owned or controlled, and publishing a directory listing of verified firms, the State Office of Minority and Women Business Assistance (SOMWBA) also offers technical assistance. This means you could benefit from management seminars and workshops for minority and women entrepreneurs on a wide variety of business topics. For more information, contact Business Development Office, 1 Ashburton Pl. # 2101, Boston, MA 02108-1519; 617-727-3206; 800-5-CAPITAL; {www.state.ma.us/mobd}.

Get Help With Starting Your Own Business

The Center for Women & Enterprise, Inc. (CWE) is a non-profit educational organization whose mission is to empower women to become economically self-sufficient and prosperous through entrepreneurship. The first center of its kind in Massachusetts, CWE provides courses, workshops, round tables, one-on-one consulting, and loan packaging assistance to women who seek to start and/or grow their own businesses. While services are open to everyone, scholarships target low-income women. For more information, contact Massachusetts Center for Women & Enterprise Inc., Andrea Silbert, Director, 45 Bromfield Street, 6th Floor, Boston, MA 02108; 617-423-3001, ext. 222; Fax: 617-423-2444; {http://asilbert@cweboston.org}; {e-mail: info@cweboston.org}.

Michigan

One-Stop Career Centers

A network of One-Stop Career Centers throughout the state offers a wide range of employment related services including job training. Services vary by location. To find a location near you, please refer to the website {http://wtw.doleta.gov/ohrw2w/recruit/where.htm}. To learn more about the services they offer, contact your state coordinator.

Ms. Linda Kinney, Michigan Jobs Commission, 201 N. Washington Square, Victor Office Center, 4th Floor, Lansing, MI 48913; 517-373-9616; Fax: 517-335-5945.

Economic Development Agency, 201 N. Washington Square, Victor Office Center, 4th Floor, Lansing, MI 48913; 517-373-9808; {www.state.mi.us/mjc/ceo/}; {e-mail: Customer-Assistance@ state.mi.us}.

Job Service Offices

A system of Employment Service/Job Service offices is located within every state with the goal of assisting millions of job seekers and employers. While services may vary from location to location, many provide job training, skills assessment and related services. With approximately 1,800 Employment Service/Job Service offices nationwide there is bound to be one near you. To learn more about the services offered in your area, contact your state administrator. Jack Wheatley, Acting Director, Michigan Unemployment Agency, 7310 Woodward Avenue, Detroit, MI 48202; 313-876-5901; Fax: 313-876-5587.

Resource Agency

The Michigan Jobs Commission/Michigan Works! is the state's workforce development resource agency. Through 25 local offices workforce development services are delivered close to where you live. Learn about job training opportunities and other workforce development services available in your community by contacting The Department of Career Development, 201 N. Washington Square, Victor Office Center, 1st Floor, Lansing, Michigan 48913; 517-241-4000; 800-649-3777; {www.michworks.org/}; {e-mail: Career@state.mi.us}.

All Kinds of Services for Women Seeking Self-Employment

The Women's Initiative for Self-Employment (WISE) Program provides low-income women with the tools and resources to begin and expand businesses. The WISE Program can provide you with a comprehensive package of business training, personal development workshops, credit counseling, start-up and expansion financing, business counseling, peer group support, and mentoring. The creation and expansion of businesses is only one goal of this program. The WISE Program was also designed to fight poverty, increase incomes, raise self-esteem, stabilize families, develop skills and spark a process of community renewal. For more information, contact Ann Arbor

Community Development Corporation Women's Initiative for Self Employment (WISE), Michelle Richards, Executive Director, 2008 Hogback Road, Suite 2A, Ann Arbor, MI 48105; 313-677-1400; Fax: 313-677-1465; {e-mail: mrichards@miceed.org}.

Learn A Trade

Women in Trades, in partnership with five organizations in different states, provides technical assistance to employers, contractors, and labor organizations on mega construction projects in the Midwest. They will work with contractors and apprenticeship programs meeting their goals for hiring women in job sites. These groups refer qualified tradeswomen to jobs, and most provide pre-apprenticeship programs to give women the skills needed in apprenticeship programs. They can give you information on career awareness on the range of job options for women too. For further information, contact Sharon Newton, Executive Director, Women's Resource Center, 25 Sheldon SE, Grand Rapids, MI 49503-4209; 616-458-5443.

Break Through Barriers

Grand Rapids Opportunities for Women (GROW) is a non-profit economic development organization which provides women from diverse backgrounds — many of whom are facing social or economic barriers — with opportunities to develop the skills and acquire the knowledge needed to achieve financial independence. Focusing on small businesses, GROW can provide you with entrepreneurial training needed to start a small business as well as the follow-up services needed to sustain and expand a business. Since starting a business often affects all aspects of a woman's life, GROW is committed to providing group and individual support for both business and personal development. Contact Grand Rapids Opportunities for Women (GROW), 25 Sheldon SE, Suite 210, Grand Rapids, MI 49503; 616-458-3404; Fax: 616-458-6557; {e-mail: grow@voyager.net}.

Opportunity at the Community College
Kirtland Community College has funds available for single parents, homemakers, displaced homemakers, single pregnant women, and sex equity students enrolled in approved vocational programs or courses. These funds may cover tuition, fees, books, supplies, uniforms, transportation, and/or child care. They also offer counseling, car pool list, child care exchange list, community agency liaison assistance and more. No minimum credit load is required for eligibility. Funding is also available for students who are in default on their student loans. To apply or to receive more information contact Single Parent/Displaced Homemaker and Sex Equity Programs, Kirtland Community College, 10775 North St. Helen Road, Roscommon, MI 48653; 517-275-5121, ext. 252; Administrative Center, Room 212, {www.kirtland.cc.mi.us/}.

Get Through Those Changes With Help
The Center for Women in Transition has two programs available to assist you. Women's Support Services: CWIT staff is available to help you find alternatives when going through major life changes that result from divorce, death of a spouse, unemployment/ underemployment, family dysfunction and/or conflict, and other stressful transitions. Fees for these services are based on a sliding scale. The Displaced Homemaker Program assists women who must become the family's primary provider but are underemployed or lack recent job experience. Participants must meet Department of Labor guidelines. Program offerings include the following: career coaching; communication techniques; on-the-job success strategies; interviewing techniques; referral services; "Wardrobe for Work" provides, free of charge, quality used clothing appropriate for professional employment. Funding for this program is provided by Michigan Jobs Commission. Contact 800-848-5991 or {e-mail: cfwit@macatawa.org} for general information, or contact the service providers listed below for more information. You can also visit their website {www.macatawa.org/~cfwit/} for updated information.

- Holland Center for Women in Transition, 304 Garden Avenue, Holland, MI 49424; Crisis Line 616-392-1970; Business Line 616-392-2829; Help Line 616-396-4357.

- Grand Haven Center for Women in Transition, 520 Franklin Street, Grand Haven, MI 49417; Office 616-846-0674; Help Line 616-846-4357.

- Allegan Center for Women in Transition, 231 Trowbridge Street, Suite 15B, Allegan, MI 49010; 616-673-2299.

Help For Victims

Every Woman's Place, Inc. offers services for victims of domestic violence and sexual assault. You can receive employment training, financial and housing assistance, support groups, safe shelter, legal advocacy, and counseling. They also have a displaced homemaker program. All services are free. For more information, contact Sharon Richards or Addie Randall, Every Woman's Place - Almond Center, 1221 W. Laketon, Muskegon, MI 49441; 616-759-7909; Fax: 616-759-8618.

Training For Farm workers

The Telamon Corporation has employment & training services for the farm worker population. You can receive classroom training (GED, ESL), on-the-job training, work experience, vocational training, case management, job placement, follow-up, and training-related services. For more information, contact Telamon Corporation, Ruben Santellan, Supervisor, 710 Chicago Dr., Suite 310, Holland, MI 49423; 616-396-5160.

Northern Lower Michigan

The Women's Resource Center (WRC) is a non-profit, community based membership organization dedicated to serving the women and families of northern lower Michigan. Established in 1977, the WRC serves Emmet, Charlevoix, Cheboygan, Otsego and Antrim counties. Services include: Displaced Homemaker Program and Workshops/ Special Programs/Support Groups among others. Contact 24 Hour Crisis Line 616-347-0082; 800-275-1995.

- Petoskey Office, 423 Porter Street, Petoskey, MI 49770; 616-347-0067.

- Cheboygan Office, 217 North Bailey, Cheboygan, MI 49721; 616-627-2380.

- Gaylord Office, 116 E. 5th Street, Gaylord, MI 49735; 517-731-0918.

Minnesota

One-Stop Career Centers

A network of One-Stop Career Centers throughout the state offers a wide range of employment related services including job training. Services vary by location. To find a location near you, please refer to the website {http://wtw.doleta.gov/ohrw2w/recruit/where.htm}. To learn more about the services they offer, contact your state coordinator.

Mr. Howard E. Glad, Director, Minnesota Workforce Center System, 390 North Robert Street, St. Paul, MN 55101; 651-296-7510; Fax: 651-296-0994; TTY: 651-282-5909; {e-mail: hglad@ngwmail.des.state.mn.us}.

Job Service Offices

A system of Employment Service/Job Service offices is located within every state with the goal of assisting millions of job seekers and employers. While services may vary from location to location, many provide job training, skills assessment and related services. With approximately 1,800 Employment Service/Job Service offices nationwide there is bound to be one near you. To learn more about the services offered in your area, contact your state administrator. Jane Brown, Commissioner, Minnesota Department of Economic Security, 390 North Robert Street, St. Paul, MN 55101; 651-296-3711; Fax: 651-296-0994

Help for Displaced Homemakers

The Displaced Homemaker Program provides the transitional services and vocational preparation needed to assist you in moving to training or employment. Enrollment is limited to one year and is free to those eligible. With 53 locations throughout the state, you can take advantage of workshops, support groups and networking, self-esteem building, one-to-one personal or vocational counseling, job seeking methods, employment support groups, and resume development to help you build confidence, identify skills, and seek training or employment. Other services may include referral for remedial education, child care, legal assistance, and other support services. Transportation, child care, and work or school expenses are covered as funds are available. For more information on the Displaced Homemaker Program or to find the location of your local office, contact: Susan Johnson, Minnesota Department of Economic Security/Workforce Preparation Branch, 390 North Robert Street, St. Paul, MN 55101; 651-296-6060; {e-mail: susan.m.johnson@state.mn.us}.

Here's An Example

The Central Lakes College Meta 5 is an example of a Displaced Homemaker Program mentioned above. META 5 serves Beltrami, Cass, Crow Wing, Mille Lacs, Morrison, Todd and Wadena counties. Located in Brainerd, Minnesota, they are sponsored by Central Lakes College and funded through the Department of Economic Security. Meta 5 services are offered free to those who are eligible. The mission of META 5 is to meet the specific needs of anyone attempting to make the difficult transition from home and financial dependency to the workplace and financial independence. Many people have outdated training and education, no recent work history or experience, and are often victims of age discrimination. The training and services offered provide a supportive environment designed to enhance and build self-esteem and confidence. They offer you career planning and job preparation workshops; pre-employment skills including resume writing; information and referrals to appropriate services; one-to-one guidance in making career choices; group support with others in similar situations; computerized career information programs. For more information contact META 5 at 218-828-2538; 218-825-2009, or contact Central Lakes College, 501 West College Drive, Brainerd, MN 56401;

800-933-0346, ext. 2538 or ext. 2009, {www.clc.mnscu.edu/supserv/meta5/index.html}; {e-mail: lfranz@gwmail.clc.mnscu.edu}.

Christian Programs
Ursuline Companions in Mission is a Christian association of lay women and men who seek to make a difference in the lives of the poor through a variety of programs including job training. They have service delivery sites in Delaware, Illinois, Kentucky, Minnesota, Missouri, New Mexico, and Ohio. Programs vary from location to location. For more information, contact Ursuline Companions In Mission, Sr. Jane Quinlan, College of New Rochelle, College Center, Room 155, New Rochelle, NY 10805; 914-654-5270; Fax: 915-654-5290; {www.theursulines.org}; {e-mail: ursulinecomp@hotmail.com}.

Comprehensive Career Services
The Life-Work Planning Center serves women in transition, including displaced homemakers, non-displaced homemakers, Hispanic women and youth, teen and young moms, and women transitioning from welfare to work. They provide a supportive environment where you can explore career and job options, build self-esteem, acquire confidence to make decisions, set goals, and become self-sufficient. Their services include workshops and support groups, one-to-one peer counseling, career testing and assessment. They regionally serve individuals in Blue Earth, Brown, Faribault, LeSueur, Martin, Nicollet, Sibley, Waseca and Watonwan Counties. Life-Work Planning Center has four convenient locations in four counties.

- Union Square Business Center, 201 North Broad Street, Suite 100, Mankato, MN 56001; 507-345-1577; 800-369-5166; {www.lwpc.org/}.

- New Ulm WorkForce Center, 1618 South Broadway, New Ulm, MN 56073; 507-354-3138.

- South Main St., Fairmont, MN 56031; 507-238-9361; 800-433-1706.

- Relations Center, 204 Second Street NW, Waseca, MN 56093; 507-345-1577; 800-369-5166.

Learn A Trade

Women in Trades, in partnership with five organizations in different states, will provide technical assistance to employers, contractors, and labor organizations on mega construction projects in the Midwest. They will work with contractors and apprenticeship programs meeting their goals for hiring women in job sites. These groups refer qualified tradeswomen to jobs, and most provide pre-apprenticeship programs to give women the skills needed in apprenticeship programs. They can give you information on career awareness on the range of job options for women too. For further information on programs in your state, call Pat Wagner, Minnesota Women in the Trades, Minnesota Women's Building, 550 Rice Street, St. Paul, MN 55103; 651-228-9950.

Employment and Business Services For Women

If you are looking for direction or assistance in developing your career, searching for employment, starting or expanding a business, WomenVenture is the resource for you. They can help you identify your career direction, make a career change, enter/re-enter the workforce or try for that perfect job. They can also help you get started with a new business idea or grow an existing business. Their career development services are on a sliding fee scale and include individual consulting, Myers-Briggs Type Indicator, and Strong Interest Inventory. Classes include Career & Life Planning for Women and How to Ace an Interview. There is also a Career & Employment Transition Group for Women. Specific training programs include a program geared towards challenging the boundaries of men's work through pre-apprenticeship training and placement programs in construction or printing. Another program prepares women for jobs that require minimal training or experience, but offer good pay and benefits, in such fields as banking, administrative support, food service and many other areas. They offer training in resume development; personal empowerment; sexual harassment prevention; interviewing techniques; job search strategies; job placement; job retention support; library and computer access. For more information, contact

WomenVenture, 2324 University Avenue, St. Paul, MN 55114; 651-646-3808; Fax: 651-641-7223.

Women's Business Training
If your new or existing business could benefit from expert technical assistance, Women in New Development may be right for you. They can assist you in your business goals through one-on-one counseling, classroom training (using a variety of workshop formats), an annual regional Women's Business Conference, and through several networking organizations. Since 1969, WIND has served the small business communities of Beltrami and Cass Counties in rural northwestern Minnesota. In 1995, WIND received funding to establish new sites in Hubbard and East Polk County. Services were also extended into Clearwater County. WIND provides technical assistance to new and existing businesses. In addition, WIND also provides training services to eight additional counties in northwestern Minnesota in collaboration with the Northwest Minnesota Foundation. For more information, contact Women in New Development (WIND), Susan Hoosier, WIND Coordinator, 2715 15th Street NW, P. O. Box 579, Bemidji, MN 56601; 218-751-4631; Fax: 218-751-8452; {e-mail: bicap@northernnet.com}.

Help For Women Business Owners
This site is located in rural Minnesota on the White Earth Reservation. They provide one-on-one counseling and the following training seminars: Starting a Business; Customer Service; The Business Plan; Organized Record Keeping; Entrepreneurial Peak Performance; Effective Management; The Marketing Plan; Entrepreneurial Confidence; Preparing for Financing. This site networks with the demonstration sites in Fargo, ND and Bemidji, MN to plan conferences and special programs. For more information, contact Women's Business Center, White Earth Reservation Tribal Council, Mary Turner, Director, 202 South Main Street, P.O. Box 478, Mahnomen, MN 56557; 218-935-2827; Fax: 218-935-9178.

Developing Career Skills
Mainstay Inc. Career Planning Services purpose is to provide career planning for women and men in transition and to encourage self-

reliance and independence by identifying and developing career skills. At Mainstay, they offer a relaxed, creative and confidential atmosphere where you can explore your alternatives, recognize your skills and examine your career goals. Mainstay's goal is to help people within the nine county area of southwestern Minnesota to build new lives. They achieve this goal through a variety of programs including career assessments and workshops pertaining to life and job search skills. For additional information, contact Mainstay, Inc., 308 North Third Street, P.O. Box 816, Marshall, MN 56258; 507-537-1546; 800-554-2481; {www.swmnmall.com/mainstay/}; {e-mail: mainstay@bresnanlink.net}.

Mississippi

One-Stop Career Centers

A network of One-Stop Career Centers throughout the state offers a wide range of employment related services including job training. Services vary by location. To find a location near you, please refer to the website {http://wtw.doleta.gov/ohrw2w/recruit/where.htm}. To learn more about the services they offer, contact your state coordinator.

Mr. Thomas E. Lord, Executive Director, Employment Security Commission, P.O. Box 1699, Jackson, MS 39215-1699; 601-961-7400; Fax: 601-961-7405.

Ms. Jean Denson, Director, Employment Training Division of Economic and Community Development, 301 West Pearl Street, Jackson, MS 39225-4568; 601-949-2234; Fax: 601-949-7405.

Job Service Offices

A system of Employment Service/Job Service offices is located within every state with the goal of assisting millions of job seekers and employers. While services may vary from location to location, many provide job training, skills assessment and related services. With approximately 1,800 Employment Service/Job Service offices nationwide there is bound to be one near you. To learn more about the services offered in your area, contact your state administrator. Thomas E. Lord, Executive Director, Mississippi Employment Security Commission, P.O. Box 1699, Jackson, MS 39215-1699; 601-961-7400; Fax: 601-961-7405.

Entrepreneur Training For Women of Color

If you live in Mound Bayou or Ruleville in Bolivar County and would like to become more self-sufficient, check out the economic entrepreneurial centers run by the National Council of Negro Women (NCNW) in those areas. For more information, contact Mississippi Women's Economic Entrepreneurial Project (MWEEP), Jo Thompson, Director, 106 West Green Street, Mound Bayou, MS 38762; 601-741-3342; Fax: 601-741-2195 or 601-335-3060; {www.ncnw.com}; {e-mail: jthompson@tecinfo.com}.

Women Work!

Women Work! is a state affiliate of the national membership organization dedicated to helping women from diverse backgrounds achieve economic self-sufficiency through job readiness, education, training and employment. Contact Mississippi Women Work!, Chris Tanner-Watkins, President, SP/DH Program, Hinds Community College, Utica Campus, Utica, MS 39175; 601-885-7042; 601-885-6062.

Help For Displaced Homemakers and Single Parents

Meridian Community College can boost your business skills by providing you with counseling, advocacy support and community referrals and networking with agencies. A refresher class is also offered in which single parents and/or displaced homemakers can brush up on basic skills before entering college. Seminars, support groups, and workshops are offered to refine your skills in self-confidence, time management, stress management, and money management skills, as well as working toward achieving career goals. If you are a single parent or a homemaker who needs to upgrade your skills to enter the job market, visit or call the program coordinator. The office is located in Meridian Hall on the MCC campus. Contact Meridian Community College Single Parent/Displaced Homemaker Services, 910 Highway 19 North, Meridian, MS 39307; 601-484-8836; {www.mcc.cc.ms.us/online_catalog/Single%20Parent/displace.htm}.

You Could Get A Job Usually Held By Men

Itawamba Community College has a Non-Traditional Workplace/Job Readiness Training program that provides assistance to individuals, especially women, entering non-traditional training programs. They can provide you with a broad range of services and support ranging from career orientation to mentor matching for participants in the program. The program operates concurrently or sequentially with the college's skills training activities and is free to eligible individuals. For more information, contact Itawamba Community College, 602 West Hill Street, Fulton, MS 38843; 601-862-3101; Fax: 601-862-4608; {www.icc.cc.ms.us/stu_services.htm}.

Missouri

One-Stop Career Centers

A network of One-Stop Career Centers throughout the state offers a wide range of employment related services including job training. Services vary by location. To find a location near you, please refer to the website {http://wtw.doleta.gov/ohrw2w/recruit/where.htm}. To learn more about the services they offer, contact your state coordinator.

Mr. Mike Pulliam, Director, One-Stop Lead, Division of Job Development & Training, PO Box 1087, Jefferson City, MO 65102; 573-751-7796; 888-447-2696; Fax: 573-751-6765; {e-mail: jgibson@mail.state.mo.us}.

Mr. Clinton Flowers, One-Stop Coordinator, Missouri Division of Job Development and Training, 2023 St. Mary's Boulevard, Jefferson City, MO 65109; 573-751-7897; Fax: 573-526-8204; {e-mail: cflowers@mail.state.mo.us}.

Karla McLucas, Director, Department of Labor & Industrial Relations, 3315 W. Truman Blvd., PO Box 504, Jefferson City, MO 65102-0504; 573-751-4091; Fax: 573-751-4135; {e-mail: kmclucas@mail.state.mo.us}.

Job Service Offices

A system of Employment Service/Job Service offices is located within every state with the goal of assisting millions of job seekers and employers. While services may vary from location to location, many provide job training, skills assessment and related services. With approximately 1,800 Employment Service/Job Service offices nationwide there is bound to be one near you. To learn more about the services offered in your area, contact your state administrator. David D. Mitchem, Director, Department of Labor & Industrial Relations, P.O. Box 504, Jefferson City, MO 65102-0504; 573-751-4091; Fax: 573-751-4135.

Workforce Development Services

In addition to the standard job training programs provided by One-Stop Centers, the Division of Job Development and Training offers targeted training programs. These are programs designed to provide services to enhance the employability of persons who might not otherwise qualify for help through other job training programs. There are currently four programs targeted for adults and youth in special circumstances. Non-Traditional Employment for Women programs provide wider opportunities for women and incentives to train and retain women in non-traditional jobs. School-to-Work Transition programs serve students and dropouts by providing education, counseling, assessment, and career sampling. Missouri Veterans programs help eligible veterans get job training and find employment. Food Stamp Mandatory Employment and Training Program creates increased opportunities for food stamp recipients to benefit from workforce development services. For further information contact the Missouri Division of Job Development and Training, P.O.

Box 1087, Jefferson City, MO 65102-1087; 888-447-2695; {www.ecodev.state.mo.us/jdt/}.

Re-Entry Into The Working World

The Economic Dislocation and Worker Adjustment Assistance Act provides funds for the Worker Re-entry Program. This program provides a full range of services including outreach and intake, eligibility certification, counseling and assessment, testing, job search assistance training, vocational and on-the-job training to help laid off workers secure permanent, unsubsidized employment. For further information contact the Missouri Division of Job Development and Training, P.O. Box 1087, Jefferson City, MO 65102-1087; 888-447-2695; {www.ecodev.state.mo.us/jdt/}.

Information Hotline

The Work Connections/Career Information Hotline (800-392-2949) provides dislocated workers and other individuals throughout the state of Missouri with information on occupations, education and training, financial aid, and job hunting information. The Career Information Hotline hours of operation are 9:00 a.m. to 9:00 p.m., Monday through Thursday and 9:00 a.m. to 5:00 p.m. on Friday. Individuals placing calls to the Hotline after hours will receive a voice message asking them to leave a message as their call will be returned. A career counselor is available by appointment to answer any career related questions. The Hotline is cosponsored by University Outreach and Extension and the Missouri Division of Job Development and Training. For further information contact the Missouri Division of Job Development and Training, P.O. Box 1087, Jefferson City, MO 65102-1087; 888-447-2695; {www.ecodev.state.mo.us/jdt/}.

Help For Low-Income Seniors

The Experienced Worker Program addresses the special needs of economically disadvantaged Missourians over the age of 55 who are seeking employment in growth industries by offering a variety of training services tailored to their needs. For further information contact the Missouri Division of Job Development and Training, P.O. Box 1087, Jefferson City, MO65102-1087; 888-447-2695; {www.ecodev.state.mo.us/jdt/}.

Job Training Placement

On-The-Job Training: Employment Service, through the Trade Adjustment Assistance Act and various Job Training Partnership Act contracts, assists in identifying, referring and placing eligible applicants in training positions provided by private sector employers. The employer agrees to provide the supervision and training necessary to help the trainee to become a skilled employee. During the training period, the trainee is paid relative to the occupation and the employer is reimbursed for training expenses accrued as agreed in the contract. For more information, contact Department of Labor and Industrial Relations, P.O. Box 504, 3315 West Truman Boulevard Room 213, Jefferson City, MO 65102-0504; 573-751-9691; Fax: 573-751-4135; {www.dolir.state.mo.us/dolir1a.htm}.

Training for Women

The mission of the Missouri Women's Council is to help Missouri Women achieve economic self-sufficiency by supporting education, training, and leadership opportunities. Each year the Missouri Women's Council reviews pilot program proposals across the state and selects projects to fund which promote training, employment, and support Missouri women in the workplace. As a funding source, they are aware of the newest job training programs and may be able to provide you with referrals. For more information, contact Missouri Women's Council, P.O. Box 1684, 2023 St. Mary's Blvd., Jefferson City, MO 65102; 573-751-0810; Fax: 573-751-8835; {www.womenscouncil.org/}; {e-mail: wcouncil@mail.state.mo.us}.

Workplace Readiness for Women

This program provides skills for employment in manufacturing industries for women living in Camden, Laclede, and Pulaski Counties. Training will include classroom instruction, one-on-one instruction and tutoring, computer training and work experience assignments with private employers who agree to provide the necessary supervision and work experience to assist participants with skills development and transition into employment in the manufacturing industry. For more information on this program, please contact: Trish Rogers, Central Ozarks Private Industry Council, 1202 Forum Drive, Rolla, MO 65401; 800-638-1401, ext. 153; Fax: 573-634-1865.

Workforce Preparation for Women

This program is currently served in two Missouri locations; Mineral Area College in Park Hills and Jefferson College in Hillsboro. These programs focus on self-esteem, foundation skills and competencies as identified by an assessment process, and a workforce preparation plan developed by each student. Experts from education, business, and industry serve as speakers and consultants for the training sessions. Furthermore, the program matches each student with a mentor. For more information on this program, please contact Dr. Nancy Wegge, Consortium Director, Jefferson College, Hillsboro, MO 63050; 573-431-1951; Fax: 573-431-9397.

Assess Your Skills

The St. Louis Agency on Training and Employment (SLATE) can help you assess your skills and training needs. If their assessment suggests that training is necessary, they may be able to provide tuition assistance. This training, provided at several approved public or private technical schools, colleges or universities, must be in a growth area and lead to full-time employment. They also offer the laid-off worker an opportunity for on-the-job training, if eligible. During your training period, you are employed full-time and receive normal company benefits. For providing this training, your employer is reimbursed a portion of your wage. The employer agrees to retain you full-time after training is completed. For more information, contact St. Louis Agency on Training and Employment, 317 North 11th Street, Suite 400, St. Louis, MO 63101; 314-589-8000; Fax: 314-231-7923; {www.works.state.mo.us/slate/index.html}.

Christian Programs

Ursuline Companions in Mission is a Christian association of lay women and men who seek to make a difference in the lives of the poor through a variety of programs including job training. They have service delivery sites in Delaware, Illinois, Kentucky, Minnesota, Missouri, New Mexico, and Ohio. Programs vary from location to location. For more information, contact Ursuline Companions In Mission, Sr. Jane Quinlan, College of New Rochelle, College Center, Room 155, New Rochelle, NY 10805; 914-654-5270; Fax: 915-654-5290; {www.theursulines.org}; {e-mail: ursulinecomp@hotmail.com}.

Job Training For Mothers To Be

Worldwide Love For Children has a three-fold purpose: to minister to the mother-to-be, the prospective parents, and to the child. Among their many services for expecting mothers is help with life goals, such as education and job training. These are provided by Esther's Maternity Haven, a licensed maternity home, run by Worldwide Love For Children. For more information, contact Worldwide Love For Children, E. Sunshine St., Springfield, MO 65807-2652; 417-869-3151.

Help Is Just A Phone Call Away

Forced to go into the work world suddenly or do you need help getting your job skills upgraded? Women Work! is for you. They have over 1400 sites across the country to help women from diverse backgrounds achieve economic self-sufficiency through job readiness, education, training and employment. Women Work! provides these services through a network of programs in every state. Women Work! also takes on the toughest women's employment issues and fights for them in Congress and in state legislatures. For more information on Women Work! or to find a location near you contact Women Work! Regional Representative, Region VII, Cheryl Parks Hill, 6921 N. Bales, Gladstone, MO 64119; 816-858-3723; Fax: 816-858-3278.

Support For Women Business Owners

If you are thinking of starting a business or already own one, the St. Louis chapter of the National Association of Women Business Owners (NAWBO) can help. You can benefit from one-on-one counseling, mentoring, monthly educational and networking meetings, and referrals to women-owned businesses. More importantly, they have an educational program called Success Savvy that consists of a series of classes to help women start and grow a successful business. Course topics include Do I Really Want To Be In Business, Writing a Business Plan, Basic Accounting for Your Business, Writing a Marketing Plan, and When and How to Use Professionals. The program also includes a Smart Business conference with seminars designed to educate women in the various stages of business ownership. For more information, contact NAWBO - St. Louis (National Association of Women's

Business Owners - St. Louis), Irina Bronstein, Executive Director, 7165, Suite 204, St. Louis, MO 63130; 314-863-0046; 888-560-9813; Fax: 314-863-2079; {www2.stlmo.com/nawbo/}; {e-mail: nawbostl@ ibm.net}.

Connect With Your Career

St. Charles County Community College has two programs of interest to women in transitional times. Free Adult Re-entry Workshops are held each semester to help the student who has been out of school for a number of years ease back into the classroom situation. Topics covered are goal setting and decision-making, career exploration, assertiveness training, time and stress management, college services, and study skills improvement. A Single Parent/Displaced Homemaker Program can assist you in acquiring new skills or update current skills in order to enter or re-enter the job market. All services, including seminars and individual career consultations, are provided at no charge. Persons who might benefit include single parents and/or displaced homemakers who wish to better define their career interests and/or make a career change, as well as those returning to the workforce after a brief or prolonged absence. For more information, contact the Career Connection office in 1206 ACAD or call 314-922-8248. St. Charles County Community College, 3601 Mid Rivers Mall Dr., St. Peters, MO 63376-0975; {www.stchas.edu/students/carcon.htm}.

Montana

One-Stop Career Centers

A network of One-Stop Career Centers throughout the state offers a wide range of employment related services including job training. Services vary by location. To find a location near you, please refer to the website {http://wtw.doleta.gov/ohrw2w/recruit/where.htm}. To learn more about the services they offer, contact your state coordinator.

Mr. Bob Simoneau, Director, Workforce Development Bureau, Montana Department of Labor and Industry, P.O. Box 1728, Helena, MT 59624; 406-444-2607; Fax: 406-444-3037.

Job Service Offices

A system of Employment Service/Job Service offices is located within every state with the goal of assisting millions of job seekers and employers. While services may vary from location to location, many provide job training, skills assessment and related services. With approximately 1,800 Employment Service/Job Service offices nationwide there is bound to be one near you. To learn more about the services offered in your area, contact your state administrator. Patricia Haffey, Commissioner, Department of Labor & Industry, State Capitol, Helena, MT 59624; 406-444-3555; Fax: 406-444-1394.

Help Is Just A Phone Call Away

Forced to go into the work world suddenly or do you need help getting your job skills upgraded? Women Work! is for you. They have over 1400 sites across the country to help women from diverse backgrounds achieve economic self-sufficiency through job readiness, education, training and employment. Women Work! provides these services through a network of programs in every state. Women Work! also takes on the toughest women's employment issues and fights for them in Congress and in state legislatures. For more information on Women Work! or to find a location near you contact Women Work! Regional Representative, Region VIII, Sharon Kearnes, Career Development Program, Miles Community College, 2715 Dickinson, Miles City, MT 59301; 406-232-3031, ext. 38; Fax: 406-232-5705.

Career Training in Rural Montana

The Montana Women's Capital Fund serves women's business training needs in 12 counties extending from the Helena area north to the Canadian border encompassing 30,403 square miles. Because their targeted area is large and very rural, they offer training classes in three strategically located areas; Havre, Great Falls, and Helena. To find the program nearest you, contact Montana Women's Capital Fund, Lisa Gentri, Director, 54 North Last Chance Gulch, P.O. Box 271, Helena, MT 59624; 406-443-3144; Fax: 406-442-1789.

Women's Career Development

The Career Training Institute (CTI) has many services concerned with women's career development. CTI is Montana's central Women's

Business Center and the area leader in delivery of services to women for job training, welfare-to-work, displaced homemakers, non-traditional careers, and other special target demonstration projects for women in transition to the workplace. CTI's OWBO grant targets new and expanding businesses for women in four rural counties where they maintain close contact with area employers who benefit by access to a trained workforce, and to unions, other businesses and contractors. With this many services, you know there is something there for you. CTI is located in Helena's Family Investment Center, a local one-stop education and training agency. Career Training Institute and Women's Business Center (CTI), Maureen Garrity, Director, 347 North Last Chance Gulch, Helena, MT 59601; 406-443-0800; Fax: 406-442-2745; {e-mail: mgarrity@ixi.net}.

Training For Women Business Owners

Montana Women's Economic Development Group (WEDGo) hosts business workshops that cover basic or advanced business concepts. Business owners learn from experienced trainers in a relaxed, interactive setting. The training uses real world information, featuring local business owners as speakers. Trainers emphasize practical problem solving that most business owners can carry out independently. They also help you network through marketing alliances that link similar businesses to work together on efforts, which include market research, promotion, distribution and advertising. Alliances they have developed include tourism business, child care business, arts and commercial sewing sectors. For more information, contact Women's Opportunity & Resource Development Inc., Rosalie S. Cates, Director, 127 N. Higgins Missoula, MT 59802; 406-543-3550, ext. 19; Fax: 406-721-4584; {e-mail: mcdc@montana.com}.

Get On Your Path

Whatever your career goals, Career Transitions, Inc., can help you achieve them. They want to assist you in becoming self-sufficient and strengthen your community through workforce development, education, training and employment. Find your future through their assessment tools that explore skills and interests and match to job goals, training and career paths. These include: math and English evaluation; reading evaluation (free literacy tutoring available);

interest; values, and aptitude inventories; and the Meyers-Briggs personality profile. They can also help you with programs focusing on job search, communication, and self-esteem. Then, get your business skills together through classes on interviewing, applications, resume and cover letter, computer and office skills training, computer literacy, advanced software training, computerized accounting, Internet basics, non-traditional occupations/entrepreneurship CAD, computer maintenance and repair, commercial driver's license, small business development, and much more. For more information or to sign up for their weekly orientation, contact the address and phone below, or stop by the second floor of the Bozeman Hotel on the corner of Rouse and Main. Career Transitions, Inc., 321 E. Main, Suite 215, Bozeman, MT 59715; 406-587-1721; Fax: 406-586-3249; {www.careertransitions.com/}; {e-mail: info@careertransitions.com}.

Assistance for Low-Income Entrepreneurs

The Human Resource Development Council of Bozeman (HRDC) offers microbusiness training, technical assistance, and loan funds for low-income entrepreneurs. A community action agency serving Gallatin County in southwestern Montana has developed a partnership to improve an existing microbusiness incubator program by providing crucial, but previously lacking, loan funds to low-income people seeking to pursue microbusiness enterprises. For more information, contact Jeffrey K. Rupp, Executive Director, Charles Hill, Project Director, Human Resource Development Council, 321 East Main St., Suite 300, Bozeman, MT 59715; 406-587-4486; Fax: 406-585-3538.

Nebraska

One-Stop Career Centers

A network of One-Stop Career Centers throughout the state offers a wide range of employment related services including job training. Services vary by location. To find a location near you, please refer to the website {http://wtw.doleta.gov/ohrw2w/recruit/where.htm}. To learn more about the services they offer, contact your state coordinator.

Mr. Michael J. Holland, Director, Job Service Division, Nebraska Department of Labor, P.O. Box 94600, 550 South 16th Street, Lincoln, NE 68509-4600; 402-471-3405; Fax: 402-471-2318.

Ms. Kathy Plager, One-Stop/Workforce Development Coordinator, Nebraska Department of Labor, P.O. Box 94600, 550 South 16th Street, Room 309, Lincoln, NE 68509-4600; 402-471-9928; Fax: 402-471-2318.

Mr. Fernando Lecuona, III, Commissioner of Labor, Nebraska Department of Labor, P.O. Box 94600, 550 South 16th Street, Lincoln, NE 68509-4600; 402-471-3405; Fax: 402-471-2318.

Job Service Offices

A system of Employment Service/Job Service offices is located within every state with the goal of assisting millions of job seekers and employers. While services may vary from location to location, many provide job training, skills assessment and related services. With approximately 1,800 Employment Service/Job Service offices nationwide there is bound to be one near you. To learn more about the services offered in your area, contact your state administrator. Dan Dolan, Commissioner of Labor, Department of Labor, 550 S. 16th Street, Lincoln, NE 68509-4600; 402-471-3405; Fax: 402-471-2318.

Other State Programs

Nebraska Vocational Equity Programs, located in educational sites and community based organizations, are staffed by professionals who are responsible for administering locally designed programs. Their goal is to assure access to quality vocational education programs. Programs are federally funded and are administered by the Nebraska Department of Education (NDE) with financial support from participating institutions. Below is a list of service providers. Get in touch with one near you for information about specific programs.

- Blair Community Schools, Young Women in Non-traditional Careers; Blair Community Schools, 140 S. 16, P.O. Box 288, Blair, NE 68008; 402-426-4941.

- Burke High School, Zoo and Non-traditional Career Academies, 12200 Burke Blvd., Omaha, NE 68154; 402-557-3264.

- Central Community College, Platte Campus, 4500 63rd St., P.O. Box 1027, Columbus, NE 68602-1027; 402-562-1265; 800-642-1083.

- Central Community College, Non-traditional Careers/Single Parent, Displaced Homemaker, Hastings Campus, East Highway 6, P.O. Box 1024, Hastings, NE 68902-1024; 402-461-2480; 800-742-7872.

- Central Community College, Grand Island Campus, 3134 W. Highway 34, P.O. Box 4903, Grand Island, NE 68802-4903; 308-384-5220; 800-652-9177.

- Crete PS Special Programs Office, Single Parent/Displaced Homemaker, Crete Public Schools, 920 Linden Ave., Crete, NE 68333; 402-826-5228.

- Grand Island YWCA, Single Parent/Displaced Homemaker, Incarcerated Women, Grand Island YWCA, 234 E. 3rd, Grand Island, NE 68801-5912; 402-384-0860.

- Lincoln Public Schools, Teen Parents, 5901 'O' Street, Lincoln, NE 68510: 402-436-1817.

- Lincoln YWCA, Safety Professionals, Teen Parents, 1432 'N' St., Lincoln, NE 68508: 402-434-3494.

- McCook Community College, Single Parent/ Displaced Homemaker, 1205 East Third St. McCook, NE 69001-2631; 308-345-6303; 800-658-4348.

- Metropolitan Community College, Single Parent/ Displaced Homemaker, P.O. Box 3777 Omaha, NE 68103-0777; 402-457-2319; 800-228-9553.

- Mid Plains Community College, Single Parent/Displaced Homemaker, 416 N. Jefferson, North Platte, NE 69101; 308-532-8740.

- Norfolk Public Schools, Non-traditional Careers/Teen Parent, Norfolk Public Schools, 512 Philip Ave., P.O. Box 139, Norfolk, NE 68702; 402-644-2516; 402-644-2500.

- Northeast Community College, Non-traditional Career Camp, Single Parent/Displaced Homemaker, 801 East Benjamin Ave., P.O. Box 469, Norfolk, NE 68702-0469; 402-644-0435; 402-644-0471; 800-348-9033; Direct line to Displaced Homemaker/Single Parent Program: 402-644-0471;Contact Deb Milligan; {www.wjag.com/nccstory.htm}.

- Omaha Public Schools, Teen Parent Program, 3215 Cumming St., Omaha, NE 68131; 402-557-2615.

- Omaha YWCA, 222 S. 29th, Omaha, NE 68131-3577; 402-345-6555.

- Southeast Community College, RR 2, Box 35-A, Beatrice, NE 68310-9683; 402-345-6555; 800-233-5027.

- Southeast Community College, Non-traditional Careers/Single Parent, Southeast Community College, 8800 'O' St., Lincoln, NE 68520-1299; 402-437-2629; 800-642-4075.

- Southeast Community College, Technology Careers for Women, 600 State St., Milford, NE 68405-9397; 402-761-8202.

- University of Nebraska-Lincoln, Nebraska Career Information System, Single Parent/Displaced Homemaker NH 421, Lincoln, NE 68588-0552; 402-472-2570

- Western NE Community College, Single Parent/Displaced Homemaker, 1601 East 27th St., Scottsbluff, NE 69162, 308-635-6121; 800-348-4435.

- Western NE Community College, Non-traditional Careers, 371 College Drive, Sidney, NE 69162; 308-254-7414; 800-222-9682.

Nevada

One-Stop Career Centers

A network of One-Stop Career Centers throughout the state offers a wide range of employment related services including job training. Services vary by location. To find a location near you, please refer to the website {http://wtw.doleta.gov/ohrw2w/recruit/where.htm}. To learn more about the services they offer, contact your state coordinator.

Ms. Carol A. Jackson, Director, Employment Security Division Department of Employment, Training and Rehabilitation, 500 East Third Street, Carson City, NV 89713; 702-687-4440; Fax: 702-687-3903.

Mr. George Govlick, ES Administrator, Employment Security Division Department of Employment, Training and Rehabilitation, 500 East Third Street, Carson City, NV 89713; 702-687-4630; Fax: 702-687-3903.

Job Service Offices

A system of Employment Service/Job Service offices is located within every state with the goal of assisting millions of job seekers and employers. While services may vary from location to location, many provide job training, skills assessment and related services. With approximately 1,800 Employment Service/Job Service offices nationwide there is bound to be one near you. To learn more about the services offered in your area, contact your state administrator.

Carol A. Jackson, Director, Department of Employment, Training & Rehabilitation, 1830 East Sahara, Las Vegas, NV 89104; 702-486-7923; Fax: 702-486-7924.

Stanley P. Jones, Administrator, Nevada Employment Security Division, 500 East Third Street, Carson City, NV 89713; 702-687-4635; Fax: 702-687-3903.

Self-Employment Training For Low-Income Individuals

You can participate in training programs designed to open the door to self-sufficiency through self-employment. The Nevada Self-Employment Trust serves Clark County which includes Las Vegas, North Las Vegas, Henderson, Boulder City and Mesquite. They were founded in 1991 by the Nevada Women's Fund to enhance the economic opportunities of low-income individuals. Since their classes began in January 1992, over 300 low and moderate-income individuals in Nevada have successfully participated in NSET's training programs. They can also help you capitalize your new business as NSET is a microlender under SBA's microloan program. For more information, contact Nevada Self-Employment Trust, 1600 E. Desert Inn Road, #209, E. Las Vegas, NV 89109; 702-734-3555; Fax: 702-734-3530.

Economic Self-sufficiency

Nevada MicroEnterprise Initiative is a similar program whose mission is to enhance the economic self-sufficiency and quality of life of low- to moderate-income individuals through entrepreneurial training, business technical assistance and loans for new and expanding businesses throughout the State of Nevada. These programs are designed to give you economic power by providing the most comprehensive entrepreneurial services. NMI's programs provide women and men with business skills as well as life skills. Contact Nevada MicroEnterprise Initiative (NMI), Virginia Hardman, Project Director, 1600 East Desert Inn Road, Suite 209E, Las Vegas, NV 89109; 702-734-3555; Fax: 702-734-3530; {e-mail: nmilavegas@aol.com}.

Nevada MicroEnterprise Initiative (NMI), Elizabeth Scott, Program Coordinator, 116 East 7th Street, Suite 3, Carson City, NV 89701; 702-841-1420; Fax: 702-841-2221; {e-mail: lizs@cbrcnmi.reno.nv.us}.

Training For Low-Income People

The Center for Employment Training (CET) is a private, non-profit, community based organization that provides quality employment training for those who need it most. They offer you extensive life skills and workplace know-how instruction through a program that includes job preparedness training, job development and placement. CET keeps students in training until they are placed and conducts follow-up on all placements to ensure stable employment and job growth. CET's primary activity is classroom skill training, which is provided year-round. CET does not screen applicants through testing, but accepts anyone who is willing to do the necessary work. Courses are offered on an open-entry, open-exit basis and students complete training at their own pace. CET training is intensive, with students attending 5 days and 35 to 40 hours per week for an average of seven months. CET training is competency based, highly individualized, and hands-on from day one. The average training course at CET maintains a 20-1 student/teacher ratio. CET's unique mode of training involves an integration of skill training, basic skills instruction and human development conducted in a simulated work setting. At least twenty-five job training options are offered at CET nationwide. These include automated office skills, building maintenance, electronic assembly, medical assistant, truck driving, and shipping/receiving. Skill offerings vary from one center to another. A typical CET center offers 4-5 skills and may serve up to 250 persons annually. For more information, contact their national headquarters: CET Corporate Offices, 701 Vine St., San Jose, CA 95110; 408-287-7924; 800-533-2519; {e-mail: cfet@best.com}; {www.best.com/~cfet/main.htm}; or Center for Employment Training, 520 Evans Avenue, Reno, NV 89512; 702-348-8668 Fax: 702-348-2034; {e-mail: m_smith@cetmail.cfet.org}.

Help For Displaced Homemakers

HELP of Southern Nevada offers you hands on assistance in your search for unsubsidized employment. If you have lost your sole source of income through death of a spouse, divorce, separation or disability, please call to see if you are eligible to begin the HELP of Southern Nevada week-long job seeking skills workshop for displaced homemakers and begin on the road to self-sufficiency. HELP offers you educational opportunities through the Culinary Training School, computer classes, receptionist training, medical assistant training in the dialysis field, literacy training and re-entry schooling at the community college. To see if you qualify, please contact the Displaced Homemaker Program at HELP of Southern Nevada, 953-35B East Sahara Ave., Suite 208, Las Vegas NV 89104; 702-369-4357; {www.lvrj.com/communitylink/helpofsn/dh.html}.

New Hampshire

One-Stop Career Centers

A network of One-Stop Career Centers throughout the state offers a wide range of employment related services including job training. Services vary by location. To find a location near you, please refer to the website {http://wtw.doleta.gov/ohrw2w/recruit/where.htm}. To learn more about the services they offer, contact your state coordinator.

Mr. John Ratoff, Commissioner, Department of Employment Security, 32 South Main Street, Rm. 204, Concord, NH 03301; 603-224-3311; Fax: 603-228-4145.

Ms. Doris LaChance, Chief of Operations, New Hampshire Employment Service, 32 South Main St., Concord, NH 03301; 603-228-4051; Fax: 603-229-4321.

Job Service Offices

A system of Employment Service/Job Service offices is located within every state with the goal of assisting millions of job seekers and employers. While services may vary from location to location, many provide job training, skills assessment and related services. With approximately 1,800 Employment Service/Job Service offices nationwide there is bound to be one near you. To learn more about the services offered in your area, contact your state administrator.

John J. Ratoff, Commissioner, Department of Employment Security, 32 South Main Street, Concord, NH 03301-4857; 603-228-4000; Fax: 603-228-4145.

Joseph Weisenburger, Deputy Commissioner, Department of Employment Security, 32 South Main Street, Concord, NH 03301; 603-228-4064; Fax: 603-228-4145.

Women Entrepreneurs Take Note

The Women's Business Center, Inc. is a collaborative organization designed to encourage and support women in all phases of enterprise development. They provide you with access to educational programs, financing alternatives, technical assistance, advocacy, and a network of mentors, peer advisors and business and professional consultants. They can address your women-owned business needs through several targeted programs: Seminars for Women Entrepreneurs; WBC Newsletter; Monthly Peer Advisory Meetings; Internet for Small Business Workshops; and The Entrepreneur's Network. For more information, contact Women's Business Center, Inc., Rachael Stuart, Executive Director, 150 Greenleaf Avenue, Unit 4, Portsmouth, NH 03801; 603-430-2892; Fax: 603-430-3706; {e-mail: wbc.inc@rscs.net}.

Find Job Training At An Office Near You

The New Hampshire Job Training Council is a private, non-profit organization committed to helping people learn new skills so they can begin new careers. Since 1983, they have assisted more than 25,000 state residents of all ages and backgrounds to get the training they have needed to get back to work. Their training services are available statewide and they have offices in most cities in New Hampshire. To find a location near you, contact New Hampshire Job Training Council, 64 Old Suncook Road, Concord, NH 03301; 603-228-9500; 800-772-7001 (NH only); Fax: 603-228-8557; TDD: 800-622-9180; {e-mail: nhjtc@orgtheenterprise}; {www.nhti.net/}.

Re-Training For Farm Workers

If you are a farm worker considering a different kind of work, you can get information about job training services. Workers can also visit the New England Farm Workers' Council, 44 Walnut Street, Manchester, NH 03104; 603-622-8199; 800-562-3848.

New Jersey

One-Stop Career Centers

A network of One-Stop Career Centers throughout the state offers a wide range of employment related services including job training. Services vary by location. To find a location near you, please refer to the website {http://wtw.doleta.gov/ohrw2w/recruit/where.htm}. To learn more about the services they offer, contact your state coordinator.

Ms. Connie O. Hughes, One-Stop Lead Director, Workforce New Jersey, New Jersey Department of Labor, John Fitch Plaza, CN 055, Trenton, NJ 08625; 609-292-6236; Fax: 609-777-0483; {e-mail: chughes@dol.state.nj.us}.

Mr. Melvin Gelade, Commissioner, New Jersey Department of Labor, John Fitch Plaza, CN 110, Trenton, NJ 08625-0110; 609-292-2323; Fax: 609-633-9271; {e-mail: mgelade@dol.state.nj.us}.

Job Service Offices

A system of Employment Service/Job Service offices is located within every state with the goal of assisting millions of job seekers and employers. While services may vary from location to location, many provide job training, skills assessment and related services. With approximately 1,800 Employment Service/Job Service offices nationwide there is bound to be one near you. To learn more about the services offered in your area, contact your state administrator.

Mel Gelade, Commissioner, New Jersey Department of Labor, CN 110, Trenton, NJ 08625-0110; 609-292-2323; Fax: 609-633-9271.

Frederick C. Kniesler, Deputy Commissioner, New Jersey Department of Labor, CN 110, Trenton, NJ 08625-0110; 609-292-7275; Fax: 609-777-3197.

Training For Women Business Owners

The New Jersey National Association of Women Business Owners manages the EXCEL training and counseling program. Their training programs are divided into three stages: Stage I: Thinking About Starting a Business - Are You an Entrepreneur; Stage II: Creating or Assessing Your Business Plan - Start Right, Build Right; Stage III: Looking to Grow Your Business - Grow Smart. They offer training seminars throughout the state. For more information, contact New Jersey NAWBO Excel, Harriet Scooler, Project Director, 225 Hamilton Street, Bound Brook, NJ 08805-2042; 732-560-9607; Fax: 732-560-9687; {www.njawbo.org}; {e-mail: njawbo@njawbo.org}.

Learn Basic Skills

Catholic Community Services offers training classes in basic skills as well as ABS, ESL, and GED in Elizabeth, Jersey City, Orange, Newark, and Union City. Counseling & job placement are also available with experienced instructors. For more information, contact Catholic Community Services, 494 Broad St. Fl 4, Newark, NJ 07102-3217; 973-242-1999.

Help For Displaced Homemakers

New Jersey has a network of service providers for displaced homemakers whose goals include: advocating for the needs of displaced homemakers, expanding existing services, founding centers at new sites, fundraising, and providing training to its members. To find a location near you, contact Mickie McSwieney, Displaced Homemakers Network of NJ, Inc., Circle Branch P.O. Box 5545, Trenton, NJ 08638-5545; 732-774-3363. You may also benefit from information provided by their funding source: The Women's Fund of NJ, 355 Chestnut Street, Union, NJ 07083; 908-851-7774; Fax: 908-851-7775; {www.wfnj.org/Displaced%20Homemakers.htm}.

Career Counseling and Job Placement

Take advantage of programs at the Women's Center of County College of Morris that offer individual career counseling, resume preparation, job placement, education and training referrals, career workshops, interest and aptitude testing, resources for financial assistance, child care information, support groups, computer workshops, and computer lab. Offices are located in Randolph, Morristown, Butler, and Pompton Lakes. Randolph location has free support group for working women every Thursday, 7 to 9 PM. Group emphasizes coping skills in workplace and juggling home/work environments. For more information, contact Elaine Muller, County College of Morris, 214 Center Grove Road, SCC/133, Randolph, NJ 07869-2086; 973-328-5025; Fax: 973-328-5146.

Computer Moms

Friendship Pregnancy Centers offer free training in typing and computer basics through advanced computer skills. Women who need entry level skills get help in writing resumes, advice on entering job market. All clients need to register. Other FPC's are in Wayne and Jersey City. For more information, contact Bev Frutchey, Director, 82 Speedwell Avenue, Morristown, NJ 07960; 973-538-0967; 888-324-6673; 888-3Choose; 973-644-2960.

Sheltered Employment

The Occupational Training Center can provide you with full or part time employment in a supportive setting giving you additional time to prepare for competitive employment or whose long term goal is permanent sheltered employment. Support services may include vocational and personal adjustment counseling, employability skills training, and placement assistance. For more information, contact Mary Jones, Supervising Counselor, Occupational Training Center, 10 Ridgedale Avenue, Cedar Knolls, NJ 07927; 973-538-8822.

Training and Temporary Employment For Older Workers

If you are 55 years of age and older and meet income guidelines, Green Thumb, Inc. can provide you with temporary employment and training. They offer classroom and on-the-job training in community service positions, in private sector both part-time and full-time. In particular, they target non-English speaking, handicapped, and homeless individuals. A minimum wage is provided while participant is in training or assigned to community service. Contact Richard Cooper, Morris County Office, 20 Hillside Terrace, Newton, NJ 07860; 973-383-3621.

For Career Changing And Job Seeking Women

The Women's Rights Information Center offers you seminars, job bank, workshops, resume writing, interview practice, including videotaping. Classes cover WordPerfect 5.1, Windows/Word for Windows, Lotus 123, and Intro to Computer Basics. One-on-one career and resume counseling is available for a small donation. They are open 5 days and some evenings. Call to receive their quarterly calendar. ESL classes are offered several times each week. They also offer occupational training for single parents and displaced homemakers and an annual Women's Career Expo. For more information, contact Women's Rights Information Center, 108 W. Palisade Ave., Englewood, NJ 07631; 201-568-1166.

Training, Counseling, Referrals

The Urban League for Bergen County offers you employment counseling, job referrals, employment training, mortgage counseling, and more. For more information, contact Vicky Washington, Urban League For Bergen County, 106 W Palisade Ave., Englewood, NJ 07631-2619; 201-568-4988.

Learn Food Service or Property Maintenance

Bergen County Community Action Program, Inc. offers Adult Basic Education and ESL classes, as well as, vocational training programs for entry level jobs in the food service and property maintenance fields. In addition BCCAP oversees Bergen County Head Start which provides child care for poor and low-income working families. For further information Community Action Programs, 227 E. Hanover St., Trenton, NJ 08608-1803; 609-392-1110.

Learn How To Find A Job

The Bergen Employment Action Project of the United Labor Agency, AFL-CIO offers a continual series of full day job search classes for any job seeker. Topics include attitudes, stress management, support systems, resume-polishing, locating job openings, and interviewing skills. Graduates may come in for consultations and to review job leads online and hard copy, Tuesday and Thursday from 2:00-4:00. All services are free. Contact Bergen Employment Action Project (BEAP), AFL-CIO Community Services, 214 State Street, Hackensack, NJ 07601; 201-489-7476.

All Kind Of Services For Job Seekers

The Bergen WorkForce Center unites many of the county's employment readiness programs and services needed to build the skilled labor force that will meet the rapidly changing business demands. This "One Stop" career center assists those who are eligible and most in need of employment and training services. They offer individual and group career counseling designed to assist women who are divorced, separated, widowed and/or raising children on their own to obtain high wage/high skill employment. Job search/placement assistance, resume preparation, vocational and academic assessment, academic skills refresher courses, GED preparations, ESL courses, technical and computer job skills training are also provided. Financial assistance is available for transportation, tuition and child care. Their Training for Trades Program is a free short term job training program for unemployed women and men who are interested in working in construction. The Bergen County Technical Schools, Career Life Counseling Program and the Catholic Community Services Hispanic Women's Resource Center, both well known for their services to women and minorities have formed a partnership to provide this innovative, hands-on-training, job readiness and job placement assistance to those who enroll in the program. For more information contact Jeff Sprague. They also have a program for displaced homemakers and single parents called New Beginnings. For more information contact Weptanomah Carter. Bergen Workforce Center, 540 Hudson Street, Hackensack, NJ 07601; 201-329-9600, ext. 5213; {www.users.bergen.org/~margot/}.

Get Computer Training

The JobStart Learning Center provides courses for anyone needing to know more about the computer. They focus on Word Perfect 5.1 and

Lotus 1,2,3 (No ESL classes and tutorial). They are located in the Calvary Baptist Church, 106 Central Ave., Hackensack, NJ 07601-4206; 201-646-1995.

Learn Job Search Skills

The Professional Services Group enhances job search skills in a professional environment with fax, copy and computer facilities. Meetings are held Mondays and Thursdays from 9:00-4:00 and Fridays from 9:00-12:00. They offer seminars in job search skills including resume writing, networking and interviewing, and career counseling. Members must volunteer 3 hours per week. For more information, contact Paula Wills, Bergen Workforce Center, 540 Hudson Street, Dover, NJ 07801; 201-998-8950; 201-329-9600, ext. 5410.

Employment Seminar

WISE Women's Center runs an employment seminar every Monday from 10:00-12:00 am. You can benefit from specific employment skill training and a course on how to start your own business, etc. For more information on different categories, contact WISE Women's Center, Susan MacDonnel, Assoc. Dir., Room 3276 - 3rd Level, Yellow Area, Essex County College, 303 University Ave.; Newark, NJ 07105; 973-877-3395.

Learn To Work In A Kitchen

Let's Celebrate's Job Training Program (JobPower) offers a free comprehensive 16-week program of culinary instruction and training. Your only requirements are a desire and willingness to learn, a positive attitude, and commitment to completing the program. For information contact Mr. Peacock or Mrs. Ortise, 201 Cornelison Ave., Jersey City, NJ 07304; 201-433-5438; 201-451-4049; Fax: 201-332-1728.

Help For The Worker In Transition

Passaic County Career Center offers many different re-employment services. Participants may be of many different employment and business backgrounds. They have a Career Resource Room and computer training for your benefit. For information contact Dr. Wayne Dyer, 388 Lakeview Ave., Clifton, NJ 07011; 973-340-8845; {www.netcom/~pccareer}.

Help For Displaced Homemakers

Women In Transition is a state-funded program for displaced homemakers in Passaic County. This program offers you supportive counseling, job search skills and computer training. It is open to women who need to return to work or who are underemployed because of loss of support due to death, disability of spouse, separation, divorce or abusive behavior by their spouse. They also offer individual and group counseling, typing and computer training, and an eight week job readiness class designed to enhance women's self-esteem and confidence in making career and job choices, as well as practical help in facing the job search process. No fee for qualified applicants. For more information contact Kate McAteer, Coordinator, Women in Transition, Wayne Counseling and Family Services, 1022 Hamburg Turnpike, Wayne, NJ 07470; 973-694-9215.

Sussex County Community College

Sussex County Community College offers One-Stop Career Service Center providing skill assessment, training, and job placement for unemployed residents. Contact Susan Rafter, Director of Counseling, Sussex County Community College, 1 College Hill Rd, Newton, NJ 07860-1146; 973-300-2207; 973-579-5400.

Many Job Services

The Kean Office of Continuing Education offers career counseling, vocational interest testing (Strong, Myers-Briggs), resume consultation, workshops on starting your own business, and job enhancement. Fees range from $25-75. For more information contact Kean Office of Continuing Education, 1000 Morris Ave., Union, NJ 07083; 908-527-2211.

New Mexico

One-Stop Career Centers

A network of One-Stop Career Centers throughout the state offers a wide range of employment related services including job training. Services vary by location. To find a location near you, please refer to the website {http://wtw.doleta.gov/ohrw2w/recruit/where.htm}. To learn more about the services they offer, contact your state coordinator.

Ms. Claire Lissance, One-Stop Coordinator, New Mexico Department of Labor, Tiwa Building (Zip 87102), 401 Broadway, NE, P.O. Box 1928, Albuquerque, NM 87103; 505-841-8513; {e-mail: clissance@ state.nm.us}.

Job Service Offices

A system of Employment Service/Job Service offices is located within every state with the goal of assisting millions of job seekers and employers. While services may vary from location to location, many provide job training, skills assessment and related services. With approximately 1,800 Employment Service/Job Service offices nationwide there is bound to be one near you. To learn more about the services offered in your area, contact your state administrator.

Clinton D. Harden, Jr., Secretary, New Mexico Department of Labor, P.O. Box 1928, Albuquerque, NM 87103; 505-841-8409; Fax: 505-841-8491.

Janet M. Thompson, Deputy Secretary, New Mexico Department of Labor, P.O. Box 1928, Albuquerque, NM 87103; 505-841-9042; Fax: 505-841-8491.

Other State Programs

The Job Training Division has several programs of interest. For more information on any of the following programs, contact Job Training Division, 1596 Pacheco St., Santa Fe, NM 87504; 505-827-6827; Fax: 505-827-6812; {www3.state.nm.us/dol/dol_home.html}.

- Are you looking for a job? Do you need additional training to get a job? Do you need a little help? The New Mexico Department of Labor has Employment Service Counselors (career counselors) to help you in the following areas: to make appropriate and practical career decisions; to provide you with up-to-date labor market information; to provide you with information about educational and vocational training facilities and financial aid for education; to help you develop practical action plans to achieve your career goals; to provide you with testing services to determine your career interests, aptitudes, etc. These services are available at no cost if you are looking for a job or are considering a career change. You do not have to be receiving unemployment benefits to utilize these services.

- Do you want a job but need some basic job skills? Do you want to change jobs but need some formal training to be hired? You can take advantage of a classroom training program that provides up to 104 weeks for qualifying individuals. Courses can be taken at any community college or university in New Mexico. Costs that are covered include tuition, books, fees, supplies, and may include transportation and day care. You may be eligible if you are new to the workforce or have been out of the workforce for a period of time.

- Do you have the basic skills but feel you might not be hired because you need time to learn the job duties? If so, you may be eligible for their On-The-Job Training Program. If you are eligible, the employer who hires you can be reimbursed up to 50% of your wages for up to six months. This job training service is provided for economically disadvantaged adults and youth, dislocated workers and others who face significant employment barriers.

- Have lots of skills and education but no experience? Would you like to gain work experience and basic job skills by working in a non-profit organization (public or private)? If so, here's a program for you. To be eligible you must be new to the workforce, or have been out of the workforce for a period of time and must meet certain income eligibility.

Christian Programs

Ursuline Companions in Mission is a Christian association of lay women and men who seek to make a difference in the lives of the poor through a variety of programs including job training. They have service delivery sites in Delaware, Illinois, Kentucky, Minnesota,

Missouri, New Mexico, and Ohio. Programs vary from location to location. For more information, contact Ursuline Companions In Mission, Sr. Jane Quinlan, College of New Rochelle, College Center, Room 155, New Rochelle, NY 10805; 914-654-5270; Fax: 915-654-5290; {www.theursulines.org}; {e-mail: ursulinecomp@hotmail.com}.

Learn To Be Self-Sufficient

The Women's Economic Self-Sufficiency Team (WESST Corp.) assists low-income and minority women throughout New Mexico. They can offer counseling and mentoring through professional volunteers including attorneys, accountants, insurance agents and benefits counselors. If you decide to start a new business, they can assist you in obtaining capital funds as WESST Corp. is a micro-lender under SBA's micro-loan program. Their focus encompasses the area of Las Cruces and Farmington, New Mexico, with program services provided to women in Dona, Ana, Luna, Otero and Sierra counties, with limited outreach to El Paso, Texas. Contact their main office or locate the office nearest to you listed below: New Mexico Women's Economic Self-Sufficiency Team (WESST Corp.), Agnes Noonan, Executive Director, 414 Silver Southwest, Albuquerque, NM 87102; 505-241-4760; Fax: 505-241-4766; {e-mail: wesst@swcp.com}; {Agnes Noonan's e-mail: agnes@swcp.com}.

Other Locations

- WESST Corp. - Sante Fe, NM, Marisa Del Rio, Regional Manager, 418 Cerrillos Road, Suite 26, Sante Fe, NM 87501; 505-988-5284; Fax: 505-988-5221; {e-mail: sfwesst@swcp.com}.

- WESST Corp. - Taos, NM, Dawn Redpath, Regional Manager, Box 5007 NDCBU, Taos, NM 87571; 505-758-3099; Fax: 505-751-1575; {e-mail: redpath@laplaza.org}.

- WESST Corp. - Roswell, NM, Roberta Ahlness, Regional Manager, 200 West First, Suite 324, Roswell, NM 88201; 505-624-9850; Fax: 505-622-4196; {e-mail: wesst@rt66.com}.

- WESST Corp. - Las Cruces, NM, Jennifer Craig, Regional Manager, 691 South Telshor, Las Cruces, NM 88001; 505-522-3707; Fax: 505-522-4414; {e-mail: jencraig@zianet.com}.

- WESST Corp. - Farmington, NM, Joretta Clement, Regional Manager, 500 West Main, Farmington, NM 87401; 505-325-0678; Fax: 505-325-0695; {e-mail: 4business@acrnet.com}.

New York

One-Stop Career Centers

A network of One-Stop Career Centers throughout the state offers a wide range of employment related services including job training. Services vary by location. To find a location near you, please refer to the website {http://wtw.doleta.gov/ohrw2w/recruit/where.htm}. To learn more about the services they offer, contact your state coordinator.

Ms. Fredda Peritz, Community Service Division Director, New York State Dept. of Labor, State Office Building Campus, Room 576, Albany, NY 12240-0002; 518-457-3584.

James J. McGowan, Commissioner, New York State Department of Labor, State Office Bldg., Campus Building 12, Room 500, Albany, NY 12240; 518-457-2270; Fax: 518-457-6908.

Job Service Offices

A system of Employment Service/Job Service offices is located within every state with the goal of assisting millions of job seekers and employers. While services may vary from location to location, many provide job training, skills assessment and related services. With approximately 1,800 Employment Service/Job Service offices nationwide there is bound to be one near you. To learn more about the services offered in your area, contact your state administrator.

John Sweeney, Commissioner, NYS Department of Labor, State Office Building Campus, Building 12, Room 592, Albany, NY 12240; 518-457-2741; Fax: 518-457-6908.

James Dillon, Executive Deputy Commissioner, NYS Department of Labor, State Office Building Campus, Building 12, Room 592, Albany, NY 12240; 518-457-2270; Fax: 518-485-6297.

Help In Harlem

East Harlem Partnership for Change (EHPC) is a grass roots community based membership organization. With East Harlem Employment Service/STRIVE as its managing agent, they have embarked upon a two-year employer driven community focused job training and placement initiative. The goal of this initiative is to place 400 young men and women in entry-level unsubsidized jobs. For more information, contact Robert Carmona, President & Chief Executive Officer, 1820 Lexington Avenue, New York, NY 10029; 212-828-4070; 212-360-1100; Fax: 212-360-5634, or 212-360-6225.

Help Is Just A Phone Call Away

Forced to go into the work world suddenly or do you need help getting your job skills upgraded? Women Work! is for you. They have over 1400 sites across the country to help women from diverse backgrounds achieve economic self-sufficiency through job readiness, education, training and employment. Women Work! provides these services through a network of programs in every state. Women Work! also takes on the toughest women's employment issues and fights for them in Congress and in state legislatures. For more information on Women Work! or to find a location near you contact Women Work! Regional Representative, Region II, Iren Navero Hammel, Queens Women's Network, 161-10 Jamaica Avenue, Suite 416, Jamaica, NY 11432; 718-657-6200; Fax: 718-739-6974.

You Can Learn Culinary or Health Care Skills

The Clarkson Center prepares both young people and adults to become productive, contributing members of their community's workforce is the way in which it works in partnership with area businesses to train workers that are in demand. As this area's food service and hospitality industries grow, graduates of the Clarkson Center's Culinary

Arts Institute fill jobs. The Health Care Apprenticeship Program grew out of a need for workers in the rapidly expanding health care field. For more information, contact Clarkson Center, 310 Delaware Avenue, Buffalo, NY 14202; 716-853-4500; {www.clarkson.org/jtp.html}.

Networking For Hi-Tech Women

Webgrrls International provides a forum for women in or interested in new media and technology to network, exchange job and business leads, form strategic alliances, mentor and teach, intern and learn skills needed to succeed in an increasingly technical workplace and world. They offer ongoing workshops focusing on enhancing business and communication such as refining negotiating skills. The original chapter was founded in New York City and many new branches continue to be added around the country. For more information, contact {e-mail: nyc@webgrrls.com}; {www.webgrrls.com/ny}; If you are in NYC, call 212-642-8012 and leave your name and phone number.

Training For Low-Income People

The Center for Employment Training (CET) is a private, non-profit, community based organization that provides quality employment training for those who need it most. They offer you extensive life skills and workplace know-how instruction through a program that includes job preparedness training, job development and placement. CET keeps students in training until they are placed and conducts follow-up on all placement to ensure stable employment and job growth. CET's primary activity is classroom skill training, which is provided year-round. CET does not screen applicants through testing, but accepts anyone who is willing to do the necessary work. Courses are offered on an open-entry, open-exit basis and students complete training at their own pace. CET training is intensive, with students attending 5 days and 35 to 40 hours per week for an average of seven months. CET training is competency based, highly individualized, and hands-on from day one. The average training course at CET maintains a 20-1 student/teacher ratio. CET's unique mode of training involves an integration of skill training, basic skills instruction and human development conducted in a simulated work setting. At least twenty-five job training options are offered at CET nationwide. These include automated office skills, building maintenance, electronic assembly, medical assistant, truck driving, and shipping/receiving. Skill offerings vary from one center to another. A typical CET center offers 4-5 skills and may serve up to 250 persons annually. For more information, contact their national headquarters or one of the addresses below.

CET Corporate Offices, 701 Vine St., San Jose, CA 95110; 408-287-7924; 800-533-2519; {www.best.com/~cfet/main.htm}; {e-mail: cfet@best.com}.

Center for Employment Training, East Tremont Ave., Bronx, NY 10460; 718-893-4582; Fax: 718-893-4680; {e-mail: s_coaxum@cetmail.cfet.org}

Center for Employment Training, West 17th Street, 5th Floor, New York, NY 10011; 212-924-2272; Fax: 212-924-7773; {e-mail: CETNY@aol.com}.

Get The Help You Need To Start Your Own Business

Founded in 1976, the American Woman's Economic Development Corporation is the premier national not-for-profit organization committed to helping entrepreneurial women start and grow their own businesses. Based in New York City, AWED also have offices in southern California, Connecticut and Washington, D. C. Join over 100,000 women who have benefitted from formal course instructions, one-to-one business counseling, seminars, special events and peer group support. AWED's goals is to increase the start-up, survival and expansion rates of small businesses. Contact American Woman's Economic Development Corporation (AWED), Suzanne Tufts, President and CEO, 71 Vanderbilt Avenue, Suite 320, New York, NY 10169; 212-692-9100; Fax: 212-692-9296.

Train To Start Your Own Business

The Entrepreneurial Assistance Program can provide you with classroom instruction and individual counseling, business plan development for minorities, women, dislocated workers, public assistance recipients, public housing recipients. They serve those seeking to start a new business or who have owned a business for five years or less. For more information, contact Empire State

Development Office, Entrepreneurial Assistance Program, 633 3rd Avenue, New York, NY 10017; 212-803-2410; {www.empire.state.ny.us}

Training and Loans For New Women Business Owners

The Women's Venture Fund, Inc. is based on a radically simple idea: empowering women, particularly low-income women to create new businesses by making micro-loans available to them, and then ensuring their success through their mentoring and training component. The Fund makes micro-loans to entrepreneurial women who cannot get funding through conventional sources. If you have great ideas, but desperately need small loans, business planning, and the moral support it takes to develop a business into reality, contact Women's Venture Fund, Inc., Maria Semidei-Otero, President, 155 East 42nd Street, Suite 316, New York, NY 10017; 212-972-1146; Fax: 212-972-1167.

Career and Life Planning For Women In Transition

Everywoman Opportunity Center, Inc. is a not-for-profit corporation that has served Western New York since 1977. Everywoman administers numerous programs, the largest of which is the Displaced Homemaker Program. Their mission is to help women move toward personal and economic self-sufficiency, which they accomplish by using a holistic approach to career/life planning. Women in transition often lack confidence and direction. Everywoman's individualized services are designed to bolster your self-confidence while developing the best plan for you as a participant. Participants can attend seminars and career planning classes, and/or receive one-to-one career counseling, depending on their needs. They can help you enter, re-enter or move forward in the world of paid employment by teaching job search skills, assisting with career decisions and helping to remove other barriers to career success. This often involves links with other agencies providing further education or skills training, or assistance with child care, housing, legal issues, counseling, etc. To this end, Everywoman has developed a network of referrals to meet participants' other needs. For more information, contact their main office or any of their numerous outreach locations below. State Department of Labor, Everywoman Headquarters, 237 Main St. Suite 330, Buffalo, NY 14203; 716-847-1120; Fax: 716-847-1550; {e-mail: ewocbuf@ everywoman.org}.

Outreach Locations

- Sandra Velasco, Everywoman Opportunity Center, Greenacres Blvd. Room 108, 205 Yorkshire Rd., Tonawanda, NY 14150; 716-837-2260; Fax: 716-837-0124; {www.everywoman.org}; {e-mail: ewocton@everywoman.org}.
- Susan Reilly, Everywoman Opportunity Center, 10825 Bennett Road, Dunkirk, NY 14048; 716-366-7020; Fax: 716-366-1925; {e-mail: ewocdf@everywoman.org}.
- Linda Randolph, Everywoman Opportunity Center, 800 Main Street Third Floor, Niagara Falls, NY 14301: 716-282-8472: Fax: 716-282-4868; {e-mail: ewocnf@everywoman.org}.
- Mary Snodgrass, Everywoman Opportunity Center, 265 N. Union Street, Olean, NY 14760; 716-373-4013; Fax: 716-373-7668; {e-mail: ewocol@everywoman.org}.

Beef Up Your Math, English, and Computer Skills

Here's a program that focuses on self development training with workshops and remedial classes math, English and computer training. They also offer course work in areas such as domestic violence and others. For more information, contact Iris Arroyo, Bensonhurst Displaced Homemaker Program, 1708 West 10th Street, Brooklyn, NY 11214; 718-946-8570; Fax: 718-946-8572; {e-mail: bicdhp@erols. com}.

Career Services Galore

Bronx Community College has a program that offers you career, educational, and vocational counseling and referral services; employment counseling and placement; vocational skills training in computers, customer service and office skills; job readiness cycles every month. Contact Olga Martinez, Bronx Community College DHC, 181 St. Street & University Ave., Gould Residence Hall, Room 309, Bronx, NY 10453; 718-289-5824; Fax: 718-289-6341.

Career Preparation Just For Women

The Women's Center was established in 1970 to meet the employment and training needs of women who held a marginal place in the paid labor force. Committed to the career and economic self-sufficiency of African American and other women, the Center works to provide women with the information and skills they need to obtain jobs that enable them to support themselves and their families. Specifically, they can provide you with services including a job readiness program for displaced homemakers and other women; entrepreneurial training; resume and interview assistance; job ready assessment and job development. Other individual and group support services are also provided. For more information, contact Merble Reagon, Executive Director or Carolyn Johnson, Smart DHP Director, Women's Center for Education & Career, Advancement, 45 John Street, Suite 605, New York, NY 10038; 212-964-8934; Fax: 212-964-0222.

Get Ready For Work With Computer Training Plus

F.E.G.S. Suffolk Vocational Center offers a 10-week computer training and upgrading program, a job readiness program providing life skills information, from budgeting to health issues. Additionally, the Center can offers you employment service when you are job ready. For more information, contact Faye Sutherland, Fegs DHC/Suffolk Voc. Ctr., Bailey Hall, S. Oaks Hospital, 400 Sunrise Highway, Amityville, NY 11701; 516-598-0108; Fax: 516-264-0432; {e-mail: fsutherland@fegs. org}.

Many Services For Women

This center provides training and assistance for many different needs that women like you may have. You can receive training in assertiveness, communication skills and stress management to help develop self-esteem and self-confidence. If you like, legal and financial issues can be addressed and referrals to appropriate county and community agencies are made. To assist your efforts toward self-sufficiency, job market information, job referrals, resume prep and interview strategies are stressed. An introduction to Windows and Word for Windows is provided if you need to beef up your computer skills. For more information, contact Martha Baron Kaufman, S.C. Dept. of Labor, Veterans Memorial Highway, BLDG 17, North County Complex, Hauppage, NY 11788; 516-853-6620; 516-853-6510.

A Dozen Programs For Displaced Homemakers

If you find yourself on your own without your accustomed financial support and are seeking to enter the job market, these programs are here to assist you. Find the one listed below that is nearest to you.

- *Women in SelfHelp (WISH)* has over 20 years of experience assisting displaced homemakers to enter or re-enter the job market. WISH graduates pursue careers and training in diverse fields including business, education, technical/non-traditional, health care, and human services. WISH can provide you with a 6 week course in job readiness and career exploration. Topics include: writing an effective resume; successful interview techniques; job search strategies; goals clarification; introduction to computer skills; assertiveness training; and a brush up on basic academic skills. After the program is completed, you can enter a weekly Job Club where job search strategies are put into action. For more information, contact Carol Marsh or Ingrid Niles, Women In Self Help, 503 Fifth Ave., 4th Floor, Brooklyn, NY 11215; 718-768-9700; Fax: 718-369-3192; {e-mail: CMarsh503@aol.com}.

- This program offers an eight week *Computer Based Job Readiness Program.* This program offers 80 hours of computer skills training along with business math, business English, job readiness skills and self-esteem workshops. They also offer job placement is provided along with other supportive services. Contact Displaced Homemakers Multiservice Center, E. Nadine Holsey, Economic Opportunity Commissions, DHMC, 134 Jackson Street, Hempstead, NY 11550; 516-486-2800; Fax: 516-292-3176

- A center for *Displaced Homemakers at Westchester Community College* assists women who are divorced, separated, widowed or whose spouse is unemployed or disabled to successfully re-enter the workforce. Their program offers extensive information, referral, career decisions counseling, work readiness, and employment training programs. Contact Marilyn Wald, Westchester Community College, Project Transition, 75 Grasslands Road, Valhalla, NY 10595; 914-785-6825; Fax: 914-785-6508; {e-mail: mbw@wcc.co.westchester.ny.us}

- This program offers a range of free services including: Human Potential Seminar; five session support group for active job hunters; career mentor program; self-development workshops; career information library; and employment matching service for mature workers. To participate, you must come to an informational session at 12:30 on any Wednesday or at 7:00 pm on the first Monday of the month. Contact Displaced Homemakers Women-in-Transition, Dr. Rita Lieberman, Rockland Co. Guidance Ctr., Displaced Homemaker Program, 83 Main Street, Nyack, NY 10960; 914-358-9390; Fax: 914-358-4980.

- This program runs 6-four week re-entry cycles a year. They are 40 hours of computer literacy and 40 hours of job search. Three times a year, during the cycles, they offer 1 credit college course in public speaking. For more information, contact Albany Displaced Homemaker Center, Lois Johnson, Albany DHC, 227 S. Pearl Street, Albany, NY 12202; 518-434-3103; Fax: 518-434-3211; {www.albany.net/~adhc}; {e-mail: adhc@albany.net}.

- Here's another *Displaced Homemakers Center* that serves individuals, primarily women, who are "displaced" in their lives due to loss of a job, disability, separation or divorce, death or disability of a partner, financial losses, or other changes in their economic or personal situations. DHC provides information support, and practical assistance with problem solving and decision making. Contact Displaced Homemakers Center Of Tompkins County, Dammi Herath or Sandra Hill, Tompkins County DHC,

315 N. Tioga Street, Ithaca, NY 14850; 607-272-1520; Fax: 607-272-2251; {e-mail: dhc@clarityconnect.com}.

- Providing a variety of services for the displaced homemaker of any age, this is designed to assist the person towards self-sufficiency. Offered are crisis, individual, and group counseling, information about community resources, classes in self-development and return-to-work skills, professional resumes, employment resource center and job referrals. They also present specialized workshops for public and community groups. Lifespan's Displaced Homemaker Center, Linda Lewis-Watkins, Lifespan's DH Program, 79 N. Clinton Avenue, Rochester, NY 14604; 716-454-3224, ext. 133; Fax: 716-454-3882; {e-mail: les1job@aol.com}.

- This work re-entry program offers a workshop that provides a unique intensive group experience that will enable you to clarify your goals and implement specific action plans leading to improved career opportunities. They provide both individual and group services as well as ongoing support for displaced homemakers. Clothing exchange of donated work appropriate clothing is made available free to participants, and specialized workshops for public and community groups, and workshops for the unemployed are available. There is even specialized tuition assistance. For more information, contact Greater Utica Displaced Homemaker Center, Eleanor Koslick, Utica DHC, State Office Bldg. Room 209, 207 Genesee Street, Utica, NY 13501; 315-793-2790; Fax: 315-793-2509; {e-mail: dhc207@dreamscape.com}.

- *Displaced Homemakers* have become displaced from their careers as homemakers with the loss of financial support often because of separation, divorce or death. They need job readiness training to become self-supporting. Services provided are job exploration, job market exploration, job readiness training workshops, education, and basic computer skills training. This is a grant funded program and there are no fees involved. Referral information is always available. Contact Syracuse Displaced Homemaker Program, Peggy Hanousek or Sandy Gordon, Regional Learning Service DHC, 3049 East Genesee St., Syracuse, NY 13224-1644; 315-446-0550; Fax: 315-446-5869.

- This job readiness program offers 4-six week cycles at *Schenectady County Community College* and one in *Saratoga County* annually. Workshops include key-boarding, introduction to computers skills/self assessment career exploration, applications, resume writing, interviewing skills, "Meet the Employer", job values, goal setting, job retention, and techniques for dealing with stress. The services of a job placement counselor are offered to job readiness participants. DHP - Schenectady Community Action Program, Keith Houghton, Schenectady/ Fulmont DHC, C/O SCAP, 433 State Street, Schenectady, NY 12305; 518-374-9181, Fax: 518-374-9190.

  The courses are also available at Project Lift, Fulton-Montgomery Community College, 2805 State Highway 67, Johnstown, NY 12095; 518-762-4651, ext. 346; Fax: 518-762-4334; {e-mail: dpiurek@fmcc.suny.edu}.

- The Displaced Homemaker Program offered through the *Schoharie County Community Action Program* offers women who are re-entering or entering the workforce a series of classes designed to broaden their skills. Classes are free, and are open to all women regardless of age or income. Specific job skills such as Windows 95 training are offered along with skills assessment, resume writing and interview strategies. Contact Schoharie Displaced Homemaker Program, Center Info: Barbara Rivenburgh, Cindy Massick, Diane Garufi, or Theresa Moore, 150 E. Main Street, Cobleskill, NY 12043; 518-234-2568; Fax: 518-234-3507; {e-mail: sccapinc@midtel.net}.

- *YWCA* provides free employment training for Displaced Homemakers, (widowed, divorced, separated, single parent) seeking to re-enter the workforce. Their program runs Monday - Friday, 9:00am - 4:00pm, and includes instruction in typing, business math, business correspondence, resume writing, interviewing skills, speech, ethics and morality in the workplace, and computer software. Employment seminars and group and individual counseling are also integrated part of the program. You can also participate in a mentorship program with a local corporation one day a week. As a graduate, you can receive assistance with your job search and job placement by their placement manager. The program has a 96% rating in successful placement. Contact Debra Palmieri or Susan McCarty, Senior Social Worker, YWCA - NYC DHC, 610 Lexington Ave., New York, NY 10022; 212-735-9729; Fax: 212-759-3158.

Women's Programs in NYC
The following is a list of agencies providing job, career and education information for women in NYC. Contact them directly for more information about the services they offer.

- *Access for Women*, New York City Technical College, 250 Jay Street, Brooklyn, NY 11201; 718-260-5730; Technical program for dislocated workers, divorced or separated women, and homemakers.

- *Center for Women's Development*, 1650 Bedford Avenue, Brooklyn, NY 11225; 718-270-5020; Counseling, advocacy, workshops for women. No daycare. (Free).

- *National Association for Female Executives*, 30 Irving Place, New York, NY 10003; 212-477-2200; Networking groups. (Small fee).

- Brooklyn College Women's Center, 227 New Ingersoll Hall, Brooklyn, NY 11210; 718-951-5777; workshops, speakers and legal referrals. No daycare. (Free).

- *Neighborhood Women Of Williamsburg-Greenpoint*, Maria Fava, 249 Manhattan Avenue, Brooklyn, NY 11211; 718-388-6666; offers free job training and placement, and career counseling to women. It is part of a network of service providers in the area that assist victims of domestic violence.

- *Brooklyn Public Library*, Education, Job & Computer Center, Grand Army Plaza, Brooklyn, NY 11238; 718-230-2177; various computer programs, books and other materials on careers and job hunting. No daycare. (Free).

- *New Images for the Widowed, Inc.,* 263 West End Avenue, Suite 7B, New York, NY 10023; 212-972-2084; support groups, counseling. No daycare. (Small fee).

- *YWCA*, 30 Third Avenue, Brooklyn, NY 11217; 718-875-1190; GED program, Women over 40 weekly support group; 718-875-1420 (Free).

- *Brooklyn Job Service Center*, 250 Schermerhorn Street, Brooklyn, NY 11201; 718-780-9316; group and individual counseling, support groups. (Free).

- *Careers for Women*, 80 Fifth Avenue, Suite 1104, New York, NY 10011; 212-807-7633; placement in sales, public relations, advertising & marketing. Seminars. No daycare. (Free or small fee).

- *NYS Minority & Women's Business Division Empire State Development*, 633 3rd Ave., New York, NY 10017; 212-803-2200; 212-803-2411; business assistance, financing & procurement. No daycare. (Free)

- *Carroll Gardens Neighborhood Women*, 294 Smith Street, Brooklyn, NY 11231; 718-624-3475; Non-traditional college program (Fee) ESL, GED, adult ed. (Free). No daycare.

- *NYU School of Continuing Education*, Center for Career/Life Planning, 50 West 4th Street, Shimkin Hall, Room 330, New York, NY 10012-1165; 212-998-7060; career counseling. No daycare. (Fee) Family daycare training. (Free).

- *Crystal Quilt*, 91 Franklin Street, New York, NY 10013; 212-941-4994; cultural and educational programs. (Small Fee).

- *Non-traditional Employment for Women (NEW),* 243 W. 20th Street, New York, NY 10011; 212-627-6252; training & apprenticeships for non-traditional blue collar jobs. No daycare. Women 18+ (Free)

- *Community Sponsors for Young Mothers*, 15 Claver Place, 4th Floor, Brooklyn, NY 11238; 718-857-3323; alternative high school for pregnant teens, ages 14-19. No daycare. (Free).

- *Union Center for Women*, 8101 Ridge Blvd., Brooklyn, NY 11209; 718-748-7708; support groups, classes, workshops for women of all ages. No daycare. (Small Fee).

- *Fresh Start Training Program*, 1756 Ocean Avenue, Brooklyn, NY 11230; 718-338-9200; displaced homemakers counseling, and career education workshops. No daycare. (Free).

- *Women in Community Service*, Department of Labor, Job Corps, 201 Varick St., New York, NY 10014; 212-620-3252; vocational training, and referrals. Low-income teens. Ages 16-24 (Free).

- *Hispanic American Career Education Resources (HACER),* 128 West 36 St., 3rd Floor, New York, NY 10018; 212-594-7640; job search program for women on public assistance with children. Family daycare training program. Classes in Spanish. Daycare. (Small fee).

- *Women in Need,* 115 West 31 St., New York, NY 10001; 212-695-4758; homeless women with children, and substance abusers. Provides housing, education & job assistance. Daycare.

- *La Guardia Community College*, 31-10 Thompson Avenue, L.I.C., NY 11101; 718-482-5340/5397; microcomputer assistance training program for dislocated workers collecting unemployment insurance. No daycare. (Free).

- *Women in Self-Help (WISH),* NYS Displaced Homemaker Center, 421 Fifth Ave., 2nd Floor, Brooklyn, NY 11215; 718-768-9700; re-entry program for displaced homemakers, career counseling. No daycare. (Free).

- *GED classes* for summer (July-August), Kingsborough Community College, Small Business Development Center, 2001 Oriental Blvd., Building T-4204, Brooklyn, NY 11235; 718-368-4619; Small business counseling. No daycare. (Free).

- *Women's Center for Education and Career Advancement*, 45 John Street Suite 605, New York, NY 10038; 212-964-8934; SMART Program for displaced homemakers. (Free). New Directions entrepreneur program for women who live in public housing. Career counseling, education and personal development courses. Resume workshops. No daycare. (Free).

Fresh Beginnings

If you are a displaced homemaker; have lost your source of support or must enter the job market, the Agudath Israel Fresh Start Training Program can provide you with individual counseling, career counseling, job counseling, job development, job placement and skills training to prepare you for work. They offer a unique job-readiness group that focuses on building self-esteem and setting future goals. The peer group interaction together with workshops in such areas as interview skills, resume writing, health, legal, and financial issues will help you adjust to your new situation in life. They also have on site computer training in Microsoft Word 97, to help you meet the challenges of today's job market. Contact Rachel Perl, Agudath Israel/ Fresh Start DHC, 1756 Ocean Avenue, Brooklyn, NY 11230; 718-338-9200; Fax: 718-377-3151.

Training and Job Placement Services, Agudath Israel of America Project Corp., 84 Williams Street, 16th Floor, New York, NY 10038; 212-809-5935.

Job Training For Homeless People

The Coalition For The Homeless offers a First Step Readiness Program designed to (re)integrate homeless, formerly homeless, and unemployed women into the workforce. The program provides the technical skills and emotional support they need to negotiate the arduous transition to economic independence. Often, the circumstances of homelessness result in emotional insecurity, instability, and isolation. Many of the participants are fleeing domestic violence. An eight-week class, post-graduate counseling and follow-up services and support, a mentor program, and work internships enable First Step students to overcome the barriers that prevent them from succeeding in the working world. The students also learn the concrete skills needed to set and obtain their goals. Graduates go on to employment, further education, or vocational training. For more information, contact Coalition For The Homeless, 89 Chambers Street, New York, NY 10007; 212- 964-5900, ext. 113; Fax: 212-964-1303; {e-mail: homeless@24x7.com}.

North Carolina

One-Stop Career Centers

A network of One-Stop Career Centers throughout the state offers a wide range of employment related services including job training. Services vary by location. To find a location near you, please refer to the website {http://wtw.doleta.gov/ohrw2w/recruit/where.htm}. To learn more about the services they offer, contact your state coordinator.

Mr. Michael Aheron, One-Stop Lead, Governor's Commission on Workforce Preparedness JobLink, 116 W. Jones Street, Raleigh, NC 27603-8001; 919-715-3300; Fax: 919-715-3974; {www.joblink.state.nc.us}; {e-mail: maheron@work.state.nc.us}.

Job Service Offices

A System of Employment Service/Job Service offices is located within every state with the goal of assisting millions of job seekers and employers. While services may vary from location to location, many provide job training, skills assessment and related services. With approximately 1,800 Employment Service/Job Service offices nationwide there is bound to be one near you. To learn more about the services offered in your area, contact your state administrator. Dr. J. Parker Chesson, Chairman, Employment Security Commission of North Carolina, P.O. Box 25903, Raleigh, NC 27611; 919-733-7546; Fax: 919-733-1129.

Women Work!

A state affiliate of the national membership organization dedicated to helping women from diverse backgrounds achieve economic self-sufficiency through job readiness, education, training and employment. Contact North Carolina Women Work!, Lois Cook Steele, President, YWCA of Wilmington NC, Inc., 245 South 17 Street, Wilmington, NC 28401; 910-762-7886.

Job Training in Raleigh

The Raleigh Rescue Mission seeks to meet the physical, mental and spiritual needs of men, women and children who are in crisis and homeless. In pursuit of its purpose, the Mission provides food, clothing, shelter, education, job training, rehabilitation and hope for a new life. The Mission believes that education and job training are essential if an individual is to re-enter society successfully. The Mission supports an active Learning Center that includes a variety of opportunities, including General Education Degree (GED), computer literacy training and certification, life-skill development and job training. They maintain a complete computer laboratory housing several computers all with Window-based applications and peripherals. Their Adult Basic Education includes reading, writing and public speaking, money management and budgeting, math, and employment preparation. Contact Raleigh Rescue Mission, 314 East Hargett Street, Raleigh, NC 27601; 919-828-9014; Fax: 919-833-6162; {www.raleigh-rescue.org/index.html}.

Training In Customer Service and Computer Applications

The Women's Center is a non-profit organization dedicated to the emotional, physical and financial empowerment of all women to lead self-directed lives. While the Women's Center of Wake County provides services to all women, the emphasis of their service delivery is for low-income and homeless women. The Women's Center provides job training in customer service relations and basic computer applications offering women the opportunity to join a rapidly increasing job market. They strive to offer unemployed and under-employed women the opportunity to develop skills that can begin a career with staying power and upward mobility. The Center uses an approach to job training that considers not just hard skills but soft skills such as conflict resolution at work, work ethic issues, dress codes, self-esteem, and emotional well-being. Customer Service Training includes 90 hours of classroom and hands-on computer lab training. The Center uses Customer Service software, developed by industry training professional, which offers the trainees a realistic environment in which to learn the necessary skills. For more information, contact Women's Center of Wake County, 128 E. Hargett St., Suite 10, Raleigh, NC 27601; {www.wcwc.org/}.

Training For Low-Income People

The Center for Employment Training (CET) is a private, non-profit, community based organization that provides quality employment training for those who need it most. They offer you extensive life skills and workplace know-how instruction through a program that includes job preparedness training, job development and placement. CET keeps students in training until they are placed and conducts follow-up on all placement to ensure stable employment and job growth. CET's primary activity is classroom skill training, which is provided year-round. CET does not screen applicants through testing, but accepts anyone who is willing to do the necessary work. Courses are offered on an open-entry, open-exit basis and students complete training at their own pace. CET training is intensive, with students attending 5 days and 35 to 40 hours per week for an average of seven months. CET training is competency based, highly individualized, and hands-on from day one. The average training course at CET maintains a 20-1 student/teacher ratio. CET's unique mode of training involves an integration of skill training, basic skills instruction and human development conducted in a simulated work setting. At least twenty-five job training options are offered at CET nationwide. These include automated office skills, building maintenance, electronic assembly, medical assistant, truck driving, and shipping/receiving. Skill offerings vary from one center to another. A typical CET center offers 4-5 skills and may serve up to 250 persons annually. For more information, contact their national headquarters: CET Corporate Offices, 701 Vine St., San Jose, CA 95110; 408-287-7924; 800-533-2519; {www.best.com/~cfet/main.htm}; {e-mail: cfet@best.com}.

Center for Employment Training, 4022 Stirrup Creek Drive, Suite 325, Research Triangle Park, NC 27703-9000; 919-544-7588; Fax: 919-361-1328; {e-mail: t_moore@cetmail.cfet.com}.

Help For Displaced Homemakers

If you are a woman who has lost your husband's financial support through disability, divorce or death, the North Carolina Council for Women has a special program for you. With centers throughout the state, you won't even have to travel far to take advantage of it. Each center is required to provide job counseling programs, job training and placement services, health education and counseling services, financial management services, educational services including information about secondary and post-secondary education programs beneficial to displaced homemakers seeking employment, and information about employment in the public or private sectors, education, health, public assistance, and unemployment assistance programs. For more information, contact the main office or the regional offices listed below.

North Carolina Council for Women, Merrimon-Wynne House, 526 N. Wilmington St., Raleigh, NC 27604; 919-733-2455; Fax: 919-733-2464.

- Southwestern Region, James K. Polk Bldg., 500 W. Trade St., Box 360, Charlotte, NC 28202; 704-342-6367
- Northwestern Region, 1400 Battleground Ave., Suite 202, Greensboro, NC 27408; 910-334-5094
- Western Region, 46 Haywood St., Suite 349, Asheville, NC 28801; 704-251-6169
- Southeastern Region, PO Box 595, New Bern, NC 28560; 919-514-4868
- Northeastern Region, 404 St. Andrews Dr., Greenville, NC 27834; 919-830-6595.

Displaced Homemaker Programs, Funded by the North Carolina Council for Women (Listed by County)

Alamance
Heidi Norwick, Women's Resource Center in Alamance County, 236 N. Mebane Street, Suite 128, Burlington, NC 27215; 910-227-6900; Fax: 910-227-6900.

Catawba
Wanda Horvath, Catawba Valley Community College, 2550 Highway 70 SE, Hickory, NC 28602-9699; 704-327-7000, ext. 222; Fax: 704-327-7276.

Cherokee
Robin Mauney, Reach, P.O. Box 977, Murphy, NC 29806; 704-837-8064; Fax: 704-837-2097.

Cleveland
Patty Neal Dorian, Cleveland County Abuse Prevention, PO Box 2895, Shelby, NC 28151-2895; 704-487-9325; Fax: 704-487-9325.

Columbus
Theresa Triplett, Southeastern Community College, P.O. Box 151, Whiteville, NC 28472; 910-642-7141; Fax: 910-642-5658.

Cumberland
Sylvia Ray, Women's Center, P.O. Box 2384, Fayetteville, NC 28302; 910-323-3377; 800-849-8519; Fax: 910-323-8828.

Dare
Lynn Bryant, Outer Banks Hotline Inc., P.O. Box 1417, Manteo, NC 27954; 919-473-5121; Fax: 919-473-4895.

Forsyth
Marian Ackerman, Winston-Forsyth County Council for Women, 660 West 5th Street, Winston-Salem, NC 27101; 910-727-8409; Fax: 910-727-2549.

Gates
Reba Green-Holley, NC Cooperative Extension Service, P.O. Box 46, Gatesville, NC 27938; 919-357-1400; Fax: 919-357-1167.

Guilford
Susan Sassman, Women's Resource Center, 623 Summit Avenue, Greensboro, NC 27405; 910-275-6090; Fax: 910-275-7069.

Halifax
Regina Walden, Cooperative Extension Service, P.O. Box 37, Halifax, NC 27839; 919-583-5161; Fax: 919-583-1683.

Hertford
Connie Piland, Roanoke-Chowan SAFE, P.O. Box 98, Ahoskie, NC 27910; 919-332-4047; Fax: 919-332-2155.

Jackson
Jean Bockstahler, REACH of Jackson County, P.O. Box 1828, Sylva, NC 28779; 704-586-8968; Fax: 704-586-2155.

Mecklenburg
Pat Grigg, Mecklenburg County Women's Commission, 700 N. Tryon Street, Charlotte, NC 28202; 704-336-3784; Fax: 704-336-4449.

New Hanover
Lois Cook Steele, YWCA, 22 S. 17th Street, Wilmington, NC 28401; 910-762-7886; Fax: 910-762-7885.

Orange
Diane Ranes, Orange County Women's Center, 210 Henderson Street, Chapel Hill, NC 27514; 919-968-4610, Fax: 919-932-3125.

Pamlico
John T. Jones, Pamlico Community College, P.O. Box 185, Grantsboro, NC 28529; 919-249-1851; Fax: 919-249-2377.

Pasquotank
Patricia Youngblood, Albemarle HOPELINE, P.O. Box 2064, Elizabeth City, NC 27906-2064; 919-338-5338; Fax: 919-338-1646 (call before Faxing).

Pitt
Valerie C. Thomas, Pitt County Violence Program Inc., P.O. Box 8429, Greenville, NC 27835; 919-758-4400; Fax: 919-752-4197.

Rutherford
Kim Morgan, Family Resources Center, P.O. Box 845, Spindale, NC 28160; 704-286-3411; Fax: 704-286-3417.

Surry
Helen Worrell, Tri-County Women's Resource Center, P.O. Box 1265, Mount Airy, NC 27030; 910-789-3500; Fax: 910-789-8545.

Swain
Darlene Bradley, Swain/Qualla SAFE Inc., P.O. Box 1416, Bryson City, NC 28713; 704-488-9038; Fax: 704-488-9038.

Wake
Jean Williams, The Women's Center, 128 E. Hargett Street, Raleigh, NC 27601; 919-829-3711; Fax: 919-829-9960.

North Dakota

One-Stop Career Centers

A network of One-Stop Career Centers throughout the state offers a wide range of employment related services including job training. Services vary by location. To find a location near you, please refer to the website {http://wtw.doleta.gov/ohrw2w/recruit/where.htm}. To learn more about the services they offer, contact your state coordinator.

Ms. Jennifer Gladden , Executive Director, Job Training Division, Job Service North Dakota, 1000 E. Divide Ave., P.O. Box 5507, Bismarck, ND 58506-5507; 701-328-2836; Fax: 701-328-1612; {e-mail: jgladden@pioneer.state.nd.us}.

Job Service Offices

A system of Employment Service/Job Service offices is located within every state with the goal of assisting millions of job seekers and employers. While services may vary from location to location, many provide job training, skills assessment and related services. With approximately 1,800 Employment Service/Job Service offices nationwide there is bound to be one near you. To learn more about the services offered in your area, contact your state administrator. Jennifer Gladden, Executive Director, Job Service North Dakota, P.O. Box 5507, Bismarck, ND 58506-5507; 701-328-2836; Fax: 701-328-4000.

Help For Women Entrepreneurs

Have you always wanted to start a business or are you interested in expanding your existing woman-owned business? The Women's Business Institute serves North Dakota entrepreneurs statewide. Information and counseling services are available through a toll-free Entrepreneur's Hotline. Training seminars can help you refine skills in management, marketing, financing, government contracting and entrepreneurial self-confidence. For example, past topics have included: Meet the Lenders; Communication Styles; Women & Investing - Taking Charge of Your Financial Future; How to Get Published; Retail Display; Power Networking; Analyzing Company Information Using Spreadsheets; and many others. Group mentoring is available through Business Success Teams. They offer a statewide business conference and a regionwide Women's Showcase which includes a trade show, seminars, main stage of activity and celebrity entertainment. They are also in the beginning stages of developing a kitchen incubator. For more information, contact Women's Business Institute (WBI), Penny Retzer, Director, 320 North Fifth Street, Suite 203, P. O. Box 2043, Fargo, ND 58107-2043; 701-235-6488; Fax: 701-235-8284; {www.rrtrade.org/women/wbi}; {e-mail: wbinstitute@ corpcomm.net}.

Assistance For Women Business Owners

The Women's Business Program offers a wide variety of services. They can assist you by providing counseling and technical assistance for women entrepreneurs in the following areas: maintaining a database of women-owned businesses; administering the women's incentive grant program; certifying women-owned businesses for federal and state contracting; supporting the Women's Business Leadership Council; providing information and support through trade shows and conferences; and serving as an information clearinghouse on economic development service providers. For more information about WBDP, contact Tara Holt, ND Women's Business Program, 418 East Broadway, Suite 25, Bismarck ND 58501; 701-258-2251; Fax: 701-222-8071; {e-mail: holt@btigate.com}.

Ohio

One-Stop Career Centers

A network of One-Stop Career Centers throughout the state offers a wide range of employment related services including job training. Services vary by location. To find a location near you, please refer to the website {http://wtw.doleta.gov/ohrw2w/ recruit/where.htm}. To learn more about the services they offer, contact your state coordinator.

Ms. Jean Sickles, One-Stop Project Manager, Ohio Bureau of Employment Services, 145 South Front Street, P.O. Box 1618, Columbus, OH 43216-1618; 614-728-8107; Fax: 614-728-9094; {www.obes.org/}; {e-mail: Jlsickles@obes01.a1.ohio.gov}.

Job Service Offices

A system of Employment Service/Job Service offices is located within every state with the goal of assisting millions of job seekers and employers. While services may vary from location to location, many provide job training, skills assessment and related services. With approximately 1,800 Employment Service/Job Service offices nationwide there is bound to be one near you. To learn more about the services offered in your area, contact your state administrator. Debra Bowland, Administrator, Ohio Bureau of Employment Services, 145 South Front Street, Columbus, OH 43215; 614-466-2100; Fax: 614-466-5025.

Western Reserve Business Assistance

If you are a woman business owner, the Western Reserve Business Center for Women can assist you by providing information and support to help you flourish including home-based business assistance, referrals, networking and mentoring, sources of financing, Western Business Enterprise (WBE) Certification Assistance, and government contract assistance and alternatives to assisted living. Also offered are dynamic training programs such as: Basic Business Skills; Personal Selling Skills; Promoting Self-Confidence; Time Management; Goal Setting; Developing Focus and Strategy; Evaluating Your Business Idea; Researching Your Market; Building Sales and New Businesses; Products/Services; Financial Statements; Taxes and Record-keeping; Employee/Contractor Issues; and Improving Internal Operations. The Western Reserve Business Center for Women serves Medina, Portage, Stark, Summit and Wayne Counties. Contact Western Reserve Business Center for Women, Karen Franks, Director, University of Akron, Community and Technical College, M/185V Polski Building, Room 185, Akron, OH 44325-6002; 330-972-5592; Fax: 330-972-5573; {e-mail: kdf@ uakron.edu}.

Business Support

Women's Organization for Mentoring, Entrepreneurship & Networking (WOMEN) provides training and counseling for start-up and existing small businesses. WOMEN also provides mentoring opportunities for expanding businesses. For more information, contact Women's Organization for Mentoring, Entrepreneurship & Networking (WOMEN), Carrie Herman, Acting Executive Director, 526 South Main Street, Suite 235, Akron, OH 44311-1058; 330-379-9280; 330-379-2772; Fax: 330-379-9283; {www.womennet.org}; {e-mail: cherman@womennet.org}.

Business Resources

The Women's Business Resource Program of Southeastern Ohio supports women-owned businesses through a variety of services that focus on expanding networking opportunities, including support groups, monthly networking luncheons, business classes and an annual Women in Business Trade Fair. WBRP serves a seven-county area of southeast Ohio. For more information, contact Women's Business Resource Program of Southeastern Ohio, Debra McBride, Project Director, Ohio University, 20 East Circle Drive, Suite 155, Technology and Enterprise Building, Athens, OH 45701; 740-593-1797; Fax: 740-593-1795; {e-mail: aa428@seorf.ohiou.edu}.

Business Planning Help

The Micro-Business Assistance program offers business plan development and one-on-one counseling for new and existing small businesses. Resources include technical and marketing assistance, micro loans, computer and Internet training. For more information, contact Micro-Business Assistance (MBA) Pyramid Career Services, Mary Ellen Hess, Executive Director, Elaine Sherer, MBA Program Manager, 2400 Cleveland Avenue North, Canton, OH 44709; 330-453-3767; Fax: 330-453-6079; {e-mail: pyramid@ezo.net}.

Networking For Women

Women Entrepreneurs Inc. (WEI) is a networking and membership organization for women business owners. They primarily provide specific seminars for growing and expanding businesses. They are also an SBA micro-loan technical assistance recipient. WEI provides loan packaging services and works with a variety of local lending institutions. For more information, contact Women Entrepreneurs Inc., Lyn Marsteller, Director, Sandy Evers, Program Director, Bartlett Building, 36 East 4th Street, Suite 925, Cincinnati, OH 45202; 513-684-0700; Fax: 513-665-2452; {e-mail: wei@eos.net}.

Help For Low-Income Businesswomen

Glenville Development Corporation provides long-term training to low- through moderate-income women to assist them in personal and business development. This is part of a community development corporation that provides a number of services to low-income individuals. For more information, contact Glenville Development Corporation Micro-Enterprise Program, Rosalind Brewster, Micro-Enterprise Development Officer, 10640 St. Clair Ave., Cleveland, OH 44108; 216-851-8724; Fax: 216-851-8941; {e-mail: glenville@interax.com}.

Procurement And International Trade

The Women's Business Initiative offers training for start-ups and existing women business owners. They specialize in procurement and international trade issues. They also offer the Women's Network for Entrepreneurial Training (WNET) mentoring program. For more information, contact Greater Columbus Women's Business Development Center, Linda Steward, Program Director, Dee Walker, Project Coordinator, 37 North High Street, Columbus, OH 43215-3065; 614-225-6081; 614-225-6082; Fax: 614-469-8250; {www.columbus.org/busi/sbdc/index.html}; {e-mail: linda_Steward@columbus.org}.

Business Network

The Ohio Women's Business Resource Network (OWBRN) is a statewide effort to assist women business owners. Their mission is to promote successful women's entrepreneurship. This umbrella network promotes information sharing, technical assistance and education among participating member organizations. OWBRN seeks to provide consistent baseline services to women across the state. For more information, contact Ohio Women's Business Resource Network (OWBRN), Mary Ann McClure, Director, 77 South High Street, 28th Floor, P.O. Box 1001, Columbus, OH 43215-1001; 614-466-2682; 800-848-1300, Extension 62682; Fax: 614-466-0829; {www.ohiobiz.com}; {e-mail: msacct@eurekanet.com}; {e-mail: lsaikas@odod.ohio.gov}.

Low-Income Women Assistance

The Women's Development Center provides a long-term training program. This program focuses first on personal development and then on entrepreneurship. They target primarily low-income women. The Center assists women with packaging their loans. For more information, contact Women's Development Center, Evelyn France, Executive Director, 42101 Griswold Road, Elyria, OH 44035; 216-324-3688; Fax: 216-324-3689.

Business Center

The Women's Business Center is part of an Enterprise Center sponsored by Ohio State University Extension. The Women's Business

Center focuses on rural transition issues and alternative income sources. In the statewide network, this Center is one of the international trade assistance centers. For more information, contact Enterprise Center / Women's Business Center, Dr. Don McFeeters, Executive Director, Kendra Conley, Coordinator, Women's Business Center, Ohio State University, 1864 Shyville Road, Piketon, OH 45661; 614-289-3727; 800-860-7232; Fax: 614-292-1953; {www.ag.ohio-state.edu/~prec/}; {e-mail: enterprise@agvax2.ag.osu.edu}.

Northwest Women Business Support

The Northwest Ohio Women's Entrepreneurial Network sponsors training for start-up businesses and seminars for existing women business owners. They are developing an "Expert Team Review" program that allows women-owned businesses to meet with a panel of successful women business owners to discuss problems with their business plans. For more information, contact Northwest Ohio Women's Entrepreneurial Network, Linda Fayerweather, Director, 5555 Airport Highway, Suite 210, Toledo, OH 43615; 419-381-7555; Fax: 419-381-7573; {e-mail: lindafay@primenet.com}.

Empower Women

EMPOWER primarily works with start-up women business owners on one-on-one counseling and business plan development. They have developed a mentoring program, using SBA's WNET Program as a model. They also assist women-owned businesses with loan packaging. For more information, contact EMPOWER Pyramid Career Services, Mary Ellen Hess, Director, 2400 Cleveland Avenue NW, Canton, OH 44709; 330-453-3767; Fax: 330-453-6079.

Women Work!

Women Work! is a state affiliate of the national membership organization dedicated to helping women from diverse backgrounds achieve economic self-sufficiency through job readiness, education, training and employment. Contact: Ohio Women Work!, Marilyn

Mead, President, Awareness 101, Advantage Vocational School, 818 N. Franklin Street, Van Wert, OH 45891; 419-238-5411.

Christian Programs

Ursuline Companions in Mission is a Christian association of lay women and men who seek to make a difference in the lives of the poor through a variety of programs including job training. They have service delivery sites in Delaware, Illinois, Kentucky, Minnesota, Missouri, New Mexico, and Ohio. Programs vary from location to location. For more information, contact Ursuline Companions In Mission, Sr. Jane Quinlan, College of New Rochelle, College Center, Room 155, New Rochelle, NY 10805; 914-654-5270; Fax: 915-654-5290; {www.theursulines.org}; {e-mail: ursulinecomp@hotmail.com}.

Learn A Trade

Women in Trades, in partnership with five organizations in different states, can provide technical assistance to employers, contractors, and labor organizations on mega construction projects in the Midwest. They help contractors and apprenticeship programs meet their goals for hiring women in job sites. These groups refer qualified tradeswomen to jobs, and most provide pre-apprenticeship programs to give women the skills needed in apprenticeship programs. They can give you information on career awareness on the range of job options for women too. For further information on programs in your state call Kathy Augustine, Executive Director, Hard Hatted Women, 4207 Lorain, Cleveland, OH 44113; 216-961-4449.

Help For Displaced Homemakers

This program enables individuals who have been dependent on a spouse for financial support to become financially self sufficient. Once you have attended an orientation and have been accepted to Project Succeed, you will sign up for their support group titled Personal Enrichment and Career Development. You must pre-register for these groups. Call The Center for Women at 419-530-8570 to sign up. They also have a program called Project Succeed which offers you support groups; workshops on stress management, assertiveness, and self-esteem; career development workshops; job seeking skills assistance; assistance in returning to college as an adult student; scholarships for credit and non-credit courses at the University of Toledo. For more information, contact The University of Toledo, Catharine S. Eberly Center for Women, Tucker Hall 0168, Toledo, OH 43606-3390; 419-530-8570; Fax: 419-530-8575; {www.student-affairs.utoledo.edu/eberly-ctr/index.html}; {e-mail: ecwomen@utnet.utoledo.edu}.

Oklahoma

One-Stop Career Centers

A network of One-Stop Career Centers throughout the state offers a wide range of employment related services including job training. Services vary by location. To find a location near you, please refer to the website {http://wtw.doleta.gov/ohrw2w/recruit/where.htm}. To learn more about the services they offer, contact your state coordinator.

Mr. Glen E. Robards, Jr., Director of JTPA, Employment Security Commission, 2401 North Lincoln, Will Rogers Bldg., Rm. 408, Oklahoma City, OK 73152; 405-557-5329; Fax: 405-557-7256.

Job Service Offices

A system of Employment Service/Job Service offices is located within every state with the goal of assisting millions of job seekers and employers. While services may vary from location to location, many provide job training, skills assessment and related services. With approximately 1,800 Employment Service/Job Service offices nationwide there is bound to be one near you. To learn more about the services offered in your area, contact your state administrator. Jon Brock, Executive Director, Employment Security Commission, 2401 North Lincoln, 215 Will Rogers Memorial Office Building, Oklahoma City, OK 73105; 405-557-7201; Fax: 405-557-7256.

Help Is Just A Phone Call Away

Forced to go into the work world suddenly or do you need help getting your job skills upgraded? Women Work! is for you. They have over 1400 sites across the country to help women from diverse backgrounds achieve economic self-sufficiency through job readiness, education, training and employment. Women Work! provides these services through a network of programs in every state. Women Work! also takes on the toughest women's employment issues and fights for them in Congress and in state legislatures. For more information on Women Work! or to find a location near you contact Women Work! Regional Representative, Region VI, Patty McGuire, Displaced Homemaker Program, High Plains AVTS, 3921 34th Street, Woodward, OK 73801-0009; 405-571-6149; Fax: 405-571-6190.

Entrepreneur Camp

The Women's Business Center is an "entrepreneurial training camp" where a team of small business supporters are committed to help those who want to help themselves and their businesses. They offer you a complete one-stop resource toolbox. Entrepreneur-led educational experiences will empower you with knowledge and develop every aspect of your small business skills. They create opportunities to build business-support networks and connect their community's entrepreneurs with one another. Through their alliance with the Small Business Administration and the First National Bank of Bethany, they can provide you with access to capital once you are in their program. Other monthly programs include: Connections - Building Business Networks; Quest for Capital; Intro. to the Internet and Entrepreneur 101. Bi-monthly programs offered are Camp Cash Flow and Jungle Marketing. Each Fall and Spring semester, they offer Premier FastTrac I and Premier FastTrac II. For more information, contact Women's Business Center, Working Women's Money University (WWMU), Lori Smith, Director, 234 Quadrum Drive, Oklahoma City, OK 73108; 405-232-8257; Fax: 405-947-5388; 405-842-5067; {e-mail: lori@wbc-okc.org}; {e-mail: charlotte@wbc-okc.org}.

Help For Displaced Homemakers

Are you making the transition from homemaker to provider because your spouse has died or is disabled, you are divorced or separated, you are single and pregnant, or you are a single parent? The responsibility of making ends meet all by yourself is difficult and can reduce or take away your self-esteem. With your added responsibilities, the thought of also returning to school, especially if you've been out for a while, can be overwhelming. The Displaced Homemaker/Single Parent Program at Canadian Valley Vo-Tech helps students adjust to a changing lifestyle while offering valuable support. Counselors will offer support groups to talk about problems and gain new coping skills; coordinate employment assistance and provide job readiness skills through their job placement office; provide information about community and state agencies; enhance your personal growth and development with life skill programs such as parenting, co-dependency, assertiveness training; and lead workshops on professional image, money management, health and nutrition. There is no charge for any of the services provided. Limited reimbursement for mileage, child care and emergency situations are available on a case-by-case basis. For more information, contact El Reno Center, Beth Kouba, 6505 East Highway 66, El Reno, OK 73036; 405-262-2629.

Vocational Technology

Mid-America Vo-Tech Displaced Homemaker/Single Parent/Single Pregnant Woman Program is available to qualified students to assist them in reaching their professional and career goals. Mid-America Vo-Tech is located approximately 20 miles south of Norman, Oklahoma at Wayne America. For additional information Chickasha Center, Marge Albin-Walker, 1401 N. Michigan Avenue, Chickasha, OK 73018; 405-224-7220; or Mid-America Vo-Tech, Counseling Office, Box H, Wayne, OK 73095; 405-49-3391; Fax: 405-449-3395; {http://cust.iamerica.net/mavotech/service.html}.

Program for Displaced Homemakers

Metro Tech's Displaced Homemaker/Single Parent/Single Pregnant Woman offers retraining in a vocation that offers more opportunity and better pay. The staff also supports the student's efforts through individual counseling and referral to community and state agencies as needed. Many qualify for career assessment and financial and employment assistance. The program is open entry/open exit, and completion is determined by the individual. Services include: career counseling; job readiness classes; assessment; newsletters; monthly support group meetings; referrals to social service agencies as needed; workshops and seminars; GED preparation classes; job search assistance; clothes closet; emergency fund; financial assistance. Clients should call 405-424-8324 for the next Displaced Homemaker/Single Parent and Single Pregnant Women's program Orientation date and location. Applications are completed during a 2-hour session. Coordinator's office is located at 1600 Springlake Drive, Oklahoma City, in the Assessment and Employment Services (AES) building. The telephone extension is 432. Program secretary is located at 1700 Springlake Drive, Oklahoma City, in the Adult and Continuing Education (ACE) building. The telephone extension is 430. General contact information is Metro Tech, 1900 Springlake Dr., Oklahoma City, OK 73111; 405-424-8324; Fax: 405-424-7815; {www. metrotech.org}.

Oregon

One-Stop Career Centers

A network of One-Stop Career Centers throughout the state offers a wide range of employment related services including job training. Services vary by location. To find a location near you, please refer to the website {http://wtw.doleta.gov/ohrw2w/recruit/where.htm}. To learn more about the services they offer, contact your state coordinator.

Marc Overbeck, Governor's Office of Education and Workforce Policy State One-Stop Office, 255 Capitol Street NE, Suite 126, Salem, OR 97310; 503-378-3921, ext. 33; Fax: 503-378-4789; {e-mail: marc.overbeck@state.or.us}.

Job Service Offices

A system of Employment Service/Job Service offices is located within every state with the goal of assisting millions of job seekers and employers. While services may vary from location to location, many provide job training, skills assessment and related services. With approximately 1,800 Employment Service/Job Service offices nationwide, there is bound to be one near you. To learn more about the services offered in your area, contact your state administrator. Virlena Crosley, Director, Employment Department, 875 Union Street, NE, Salem, OR 97311; 503-378-3208; Fax: 503-373-7298.

Self-Sufficiency Programs

The Department of Human Resources works to help Oregonians achieve a maximum level of independence through their employment and self-sufficiency programs. This means reducing or eliminating barriers to employment, achieving and maintaining employment and increasing income levels. They can offer you a broad range of career opportunities, as well as training to gain and improve skills. Some of their occupational oriented training programs include: alcohol and drug training; child protective services; emergency medical technicians training, including the mobile training unit; long-term care; adult foster care training; training for nursing facility staff and elder abuse. For more information, contact Oregon Department of Human Resources, 500 Summer Street, NE - Salem, OR 97310-1012; 503-945-5944; Fax: 503-378-2897; TTY: 503-945-5928; {www.hr.state.or.us/}.

Help Is Just A Phone Call Away

Forced to go into the work world suddenly or do you need help getting your job skills upgraded? Women Work! is for you. They have over 1400 sites across the country to help women from diverse backgrounds achieve economic self-sufficiency through job readiness, education, training and employment. Women Work! provides these services through a network of programs in every state. Women Work! also takes on the toughest women's employment issues and fights for them in Congress and in state legislatures. For more information on Women Work! or to find a location near you contact Women Work! Regional Representative, Region X, Sandy Nelson, The New Workforce, Chemeketa Community College, Building 20, 4000 Lancaster Drive, NE, Salem, OR 97305-1453; 503-399-6554; Fax: 503-399-2580.

Break Through Barriers

SOWAC provides business training, mentoring and financing services for women and men with barriers including low-income Hispanic entrepreneurs and very rural entrepreneurs. Join more than 288 students who have participated in their training program or 65

businesses which they have helped start-up or expand in Jackson and Josephine counties. As a training graduate, you may apply to SOWAC's Mentor Program to receive assistance from an experienced person who volunteers expertise over a six month period, and/or for a SOWAC business loan of up to $25,000. SOWAC is funded by the SBA Office of Women Business Ownership, private foundations, client fees, interest income and local contributions. For more information, contact Southern Oregon Women's Access to Credit (SOWAC), Mary O'Kief, Director, 33 North Central, Suite 209, Medford, OR 97501; 541-779-3992; Fax: 541-779-5195; {www.sowac.org}; {e-mail: jasmith@sowac.org }; {e-mail: geninf@sowac.org}.

Business Assistance for Native Americans By Native Americans

Organization of Native American Business & Entrepreneurial Network (ONABEN) is a non-profit public benefit corporation created by Northwest Indian Tribes to increase the number and profitability of private enterprises owned by Native Americans. ONABEN offers training, individual counseling, assisted access to markets and facilitated access to capital for its clients. Each of the ten tribes hosting an ONABEN Service Center pays annual dues of $2,500 plus 40% of the cost of operating their site. The sites, located on reservations in Oregon, Washington and California, deliver services to all citizens regardless of tribal affiliation. Some have up to 40% of users coming from the surrounding non-Native community. For more information, contact ONABEN - A Native American Business Network, Patrick Borunda, Director, 520 Southwest 6th Avenue, Suite 930, Portland, OR 97204; 503-243-5015; Fax: 503-243-5028; {www.onaben.org}; {e-mail: borunda@onaben.org}.

Help For Displaced Homemakers and Single Parents

Whether a single parent or displaced homemaker, if your interest is preparing immediately for the job market or exploring the possibility of returning to school, the Newmark Center has the staff and support to assist you. They offer an innovative approach to student and client services because they share a building and a philosophy of seamless service with community agencies like Adult and Family Services, Consumer Credit Counseling, and the Small Business Development Center. As a student, you can choose from a menu of classes including life skills, academic skill enhancement, career and job development, and introduction to computers and word processing. Students eligible for the Single Parent/Displaced Homemaker program benefit from a free clothing closet, transportation vouchers, and use of the lending library, as well as access to all adult basic education classes available at Southwestern Oregon Community College. Services are free of charge. Contact Newmark Center: Adult Learning Skills Program, Southwestern Oregon Community College, 1988 Newmark, Coos Bay, OR 97420; 503-888-7121; Fax: 503-888-7120; {www.teleport.com/~ctrc2004/oww/newmar.htm}.

Pennsylvania

One-Stop Career Centers

A network of One-Stop Career Centers throughout the state offers a wide range of employment related services including job training. Services vary by location. To find a location near you, please refer to the website {http://wtw.doleta.gov/ohrw2w/recruit/where.htm}. To learn more about the services they offer, contact your state coordinator.

Linda Trimpey, Chief Operating Officer, Career Development Marketplace System, 1723 Labor and Industry Building, Seventh and Forster Streets, Harrisburg, PA 17120; 717-787-7184; Fax: 717-772-1461.

Mr. Michael J. Acker, Deputy Secretary for Workforce Development and Safety, Department of Labor and Industry, 1720 Labor and Industry Building, Seventh and Forster Streets, Harrisburg, PA 17120; 717-787-8665; Fax: 717-772-1461.

Job Service Offices

A system of Employment Service/Job Service offices is located within every state with the goal of assisting millions of job seekers and employers. While services may vary from location to location, many

provide job training, skills assessment and related services. With approximately 1,800 Employment Service/Job Service offices nationwide there is bound to be one near you. To learn more about the services offered in your area, contact your state administrator.

Johnny J. Butler, Secretary, Department of Labor & Industry, Labor & Industry Building, Room 1700, Harrisburg, PA 17121; 717-787-3756; Fax: 717-783-5225.

Alan Williamson, Deputy Secretary, Employment Security & Job Training Department of Labor & Employment Security, Labor & Industry Building, Room 1700, Harrisburg, PA 17121; 717-787-3907; Fax: 717-787-8826.

Job Training Assistance

The Delaware County Office of Employment & Training is interested in supporting you in your quest to achieve your career goals. They can help you assess your skill level and determine occupational needs. Then they can provide any of the following: basic education skills, including ABE/GED/ESL training; occupational skills training; referrals to supportive services; employer interview referrals. In addition, the office participates in regional cooperative efforts with private industry councils, community colleges, job centers, assistance offices, chambers of commerce, and commerce departments implementing regional strategies for developing the workforce as a tool for economic development in southeastern Pennsylvania. The staff also works with local school districts and employers to develop concrete school-to-work strategies, again with the focus on workforce development. For more information, contact Delaware County Office of Employment & Training, 20 S. 69th Street, Upper Darby, PA 19082-2521; 610-713-2200; Fax: 610-713-2224; {www.delcopa.org/training.html}.

Women Work!

Women Work! is a state affiliate of the national membership organization dedicated to helping women from diverse backgrounds achieve economic self-sufficiency through job readiness, education, training and employment. Contact Pennsylvania Women Work!, Janice

Himes, New Options, Bradford High School, 81 Interstate Parkway, Bradford, PA 16701; 814-362-6188; {e-mail: jmhst88@pop.pitt.edu}.

Job Training For Adults And Teens
Aliquippa Alliance for Unity and Development, Inc. is a private non-profit corporation providing service in business development, commercial development, education and social services. AAUD service area is Aliquippa, Center and Hopewell. Education services include summer programs for teens through 21 years old, computer classes in computer basics, WordPerfect and Lotus, low or no cost desktop publishing services, GED preparation program for AFDC parents and a variety of job training and career development services for adults and teens. For more information, contact Aliquippa Alliance for Unity and Development, Inc. (AAUD), Pauline Cooper, Executive Director, 300 Main Avenue, Aliquippa, PA 15001; 412-378-7422; Fax: 412-378-9809.

Learn Professional Horticultural Skills
Awbury Arboretum is a unique cultural and historic landscape that offers horticultural job training for adults as well as educational programs to school children, families and others. For more information, contact Awbury Arboretum Association, The Francis Cope House, 1 Awbury Rd., Philadelphia, PA 19138; 215-849-2855; Fax 215-849-0213; {http://awbury.org/}.

Puerto Rican Human Services
Congreso de Latinos Unidos is a multicultural, human services agency based in the Puerto Rican and Latino community of North Philadelphia. Congreso has a range of health, education, employment, and social services. In addition to a job training program, they also offer emergency housing assistance, a community Learning Center that offers continuing adult education and job training, HIV/AIDS program, drug and alcohol treatment, maternal and child health education, Latina domestic violence program, youth programs, prevention of child abuse and neglect, and a Women's Center. Contact Congreso, 719 W. Girard Avenue, Philadelphia, PA 19123; 215-763-8870; {www.libertynet.org/cdlu/}.

Training Programs For Women and Minorities

The Workforce 2000 Advisory Council designs and implements training programs to prepare minorities and women for the workplace of the future. Their programs include computer and Internet training, and a year-round education and training program to prepare youth for careers in the health industry among others. For more information, contact The Workforce 2000 Advisory Council, 1207 Chestnut Street, 3rd Fl., Philadelphia, PA 19107; 215-851-1848; Fax: 215-665-9886; {www.libertynet.org/wf2000/}; {e-mail: wf2000@libertynet.org}.

Learn To Manage Parks

Organized in 1991, the Cobbs Creek Community Environmental Education Center (CCCEEC) is designed to institutionalize the practice of Urban Environmental Education. Their Park Management Program is a career path for participants to learn and become trained in preserving and protecting neighborhoods. For more information, contact Cobbs Creek Community Environmental Center, Carole Chew-Williams, c/o Penn State Cooperative Extension, 4601 Market Street, 2nd floor, Philadelphia, PA 19139; 215-471-2223; Fax: 215-471-2231; {e-mail: Rednet44@aol.com}; (When sending e-mail, please use "Cobbs Creek" in the title of your message); {http://users.ntr.net/~reddin/CobbsCreek.html}.

Training For Home Health Care

HomeCare Associates provides 6 to 12 weeks of job readiness and skills training for entry level home health-care jobs. Training is followed by a paid 90-day placement in a private company, during which time HomeCare Associates provides job coaching, peer mentoring, and counseling support. The private company agrees to hire the trainee in a permanent job if she proves satisfactory. For more information, contact HomeCare Associates, 1314 Chestnut Street, Philadelphia, PA 19107; 215-735-0677.

Get Paid To Take Notes

The Court Reporting Institute offers courses in court reporting, scoping (court reporting editing), medical transcription, administrative assisting, and office technology. Contact Court Reporting Institute (CRI), 1845 Walnut Street, 7th floor, Philadelphia, PA 19103; 215-854-1854.

Jewish Career Assistance

The Jewish Employment and Vocational Service (JEVS) provides Philadelphia-area residents with employment assistance, educational programs, and health-related services. They offer a range of services and programs for career changers, the unemployed, those seeking to improve their careers, high school and college students, and senior citizens. For more information, contact Jewish Employment & Vocational Service, 1845 Walnut St., Philadelphia, PA 19103-4708; 215-854-1853; {www.libertynet.org/jevs/}.

Empowering Women Entrepreneurs

The Women's Business Development Center (WBDC) is dedicated to the economic empowerment of women. The Center enables women to launch new businesses and to more successfully run their existing businesses. If you are a start-up, emerging or established woman entrepreneur, they offer you a unique continuum of supportive services including: Premier FastTrac I & II, comprehensive course work culminating in the development of a viable business plan for each entrepreneur; individualized business consulting in management, marketing, and financial matters; loan packaging; procurement and certification assistance. By offering a full range of services and utilizing the expertise of successful women business owners to deliver its programs, the Women's Business Development Center will be the Greater Philadelphia Region's focal point for women's economic empowerment opportunities. For more information, contact Women's Business Development Center (WBDC), Geri Swift, President, 1315 Walnut Street, Suite 1116, Philadelphia, PA 19107-4711; 215-790-9232; Fax: 215-790-9231; {e-mail: wbdc@erols.com}.

Job Assistance For Low-income Women

Community Women's Education Project provides secondary and post-secondary education, educational support systems, and connections to the workplace for low-income women and their families in their community. You can join more than 13,000 adults and children who have benefitted from CWEP's programs, developing the educational skills they need to move into economic self-sufficiency. Contact Community Women's Education Project, 2801 Frankford Avenue, Philadelphia, PA 19134; 215-426-2200; Fax: 215-426-3284; {http://users.nni.com/cwep}; {e-mail: CWEP@nni.com}.

Find Satisfying Work
OPTIONS is dedicated to empowering individuals to achieve satisfaction throughout each stage of their working lives and to expand options within the workplace for diverse individuals. They can offer you assistance with your job search, career change, or career management. Their services are offered with reduced fees available for low-income clients. Other organizational training and consulting includes career management, diversity and sexual harassment prevention. For more information, contact OPTIONS, 225 S. 15th Street, Suite 1635, Philadelphia, PA 19102-3916; 215-735-2202; Fax: 215-735-8097; {www.optionscareers.org}; {e-mail: Info@ optionscareers.com}.

Work At A Job Traditionally Held By Men
Tradeswomen of Purpose/Women in Non-Traditional Work facilitates a nationally recognized job training program that prepares low-income women for non-traditional occupations. As a graduate of the program, you can expect to begin a new job at an average hourly wage of $12 per hour. TOP/WIN can also provide technical assistance to employers, labor unions and other job training providers on issues such as recruitment and retention of women in non-traditional work and on managing a diverse workforce. For more information, contact TOP/WIN, 2300 Alter Street, Philadelphia, PA 19146, 215-545-3700 (PA); 609-728-5931 (NJ); Fax: 215-545-8713.

Puerto Rico

Help For Women Entrepreneurs
The Women's Business Institute (WBI) at University of the Sacred Heart, Center for Women's Entrepreneurial Development (CWED) offers technical assistance to women interested in establishing a business. If you are a woman business owner, they provide a place to expose and share ideas, objectives and experiences. The WBI will contribute to the social and economic development of women through training on empowerment and business ownership as an alternative in attaining economic independence. For more information, contact Women's Business Institute (WBI), Universidad Del Sagrado Corazon,

(The University of the Sacred Heart), Joy Vilardi de Camacho, Director, Center for Women's Entrepreneurial Development, P.O. Box 12383, San Juan, PR 00914-0383; 787-728-1515, ext. 2560 ; 787-726-7045; Fax: 787-726-7077; {e-mail: womenbiz@caribe.net or carms@caribe.net}.

Job Service Offices

A system of Employment Service/Job Service offices is located within every state with the goal of assisting millions of job seekers and employers. While services may vary from location to location, many provide job training, skills assessment and related services. With approximately 1,800 Employment Service/Job Service offices nationwide there is bound to be one near you. To learn more about the services offered in your area, contact your state administrator. Carmen McCulloch, Assistant Secretary, Human Resources, 505 Munoz Rivera Avenue, Hato Rey, PR 00918; 787-754-2132; Fax: 787-756-1070.

Rhode Island

One-Stop Career Centers

A network of One-Stop Career Centers throughout the state offers a wide range of employment related services including job training. Services vary by location. To find a location near you, please refer to the website {http://wtw.doleta.gov/ohrw2w/recruit/where.htm}. To learn more about the services they offer, contact your state coordinator.

Dr. Lee Arnold, Director, Department of Labor and Training, 101 Friendship St., Providence, RI 02903; 401-222-3600; Fax: 401-222-2731; {e-mail: larnold@dlt.state.ri.us}.

Mr. Robert Palumbo, Associate Director of Program Operations, Department of Labor and Training, 101 Friendship St., Providence, RI 02903; 401-222-2092; Fax: 401-222-1807.

Ms. Wendi Miller, One-Stop Project Manager, Department of Employment and Training, 101 Friendship St., Providence, RI 02903; 401-222-1133; Fax 401-222-1136; {e-mail: wmiller@dit.state.ri.us}.

Job Service Offices

A system of Employment Service/Job Service offices is located within every state with the goal of assisting millions of job seekers and employers. While services may vary from location to location, many provide job training, skills assessment and related services. With approximately 1,800 Employment Service/Job Service offices nationwide there is bound to be one near you. To learn more about the services offered in your area, contact your state administrator. Dr. Lee Arnold, Director, Department of Employment & Training, 101 Friendship Street, Providence, RI 02903-3740; 401-277-3732; Fax: 401-277-1473; {e-mail: larnold@dlt.state.ri.us}.

South Carolina

One-Stop Career Centers

A network of One-Stop Career Centers throughout the state offers a wide range of employment related services including job training. Services vary by location. To find a location near you, please refer to the website {http://wtw.doleta.gov/ohrw2w/recruit/where.htm}. To learn more about the services they offer, contact your state coordinator.

Mr. Joel T. Cassidy, Executive Director, Employment Security Commission, 1550 Gadsden Street, P.O. Box 995, Columbia, SC 29202; 803-737-2617; Fax: 803-737-2642.

Job Service Offices

A system of Employment Service/Job Service offices is located within every state with the goal of assisting millions of job seekers and employers. While services may vary from location to location, many provide job training, skills assessment and related services. With approximately 1,800 Employment Service/Job Service offices nationwide there is bound to be one near you. To learn more about the services offered in your area, contact your state administrator. Joel Cassidy, Executive Director, SC Employment Security Commission, P.O. Box 995, Columbia, SC 29202; 803-737-2617; Fax: 803-737-2642.

Women Work!

Women Work! is a state affiliate of the national membership organization dedicated to helping women from diverse backgrounds achieve economic self-sufficiency through job readiness, education, training and employment. Contact: South Carolina Women Work!, Gilda Kennedy, President, South Carolina Department Of Social Services, 3150 Harden Street, Columbia, SC 29204; 803-737-4430.

Help For Women Entrepreneurs

The mission of the Center for Women Entrepreneurs at Columbia College of South Carolina is to expand economic opportunities for women by advancing entrepreneurship and providing resources to assist in successful business start-ups, maintenance of growth, and exploration of new business opportunities. You could benefit from services that include individual consultations, management and technical assistance, annual women's conference, round table luncheon series, resource guides, seminars and workshops, and internships. The focus on communications through the Online Women's Business Center enables the project to serve not only mature women ready to start businesses or women already in business, but young female entrepreneurs in high schools. As local support for this project can attest, the Center for Women Entrepreneurs is an active advocate of collaborative ventures among resources that support women entrepreneurs. For more information, contact Center for Women Entrepreneurs, Columbia College of South Carolina, Susan Davis, Project Director, Ms. Sam McKee, Director of Grants, 1301 Columbia College Drive, Columbia, SC 29203; 803-786-3582; Fax: 803-786-3804; {www.colacoll.edu}; {e-mail: susdavis@colacoll.edu or smckee@colacoll.edu}.

South Dakota

One-Stop Career Centers

A network of One-Stop Career Centers throughout the state offers a wide range of employment related services including job training. Services vary by location. To find a location near you, please refer to the website {http://wtw.doleta.gov/ohrw2w/recruit/where.htm}. To learn more about the services they offer, contact your state coordinator.

Mr. Lloyd Schipper, Deputy Secretary, South Dakota Department of Labor, 700 Governors Drive, Pierre, SD 57501-2291; 605-773-3101; Fax: 605-773-4211.

Job Service Offices

A system of Employment Service/Job Service offices is located within every state with the goal of assisting millions of job seekers and employers. While services may vary from location to location, many provide job training, skills assessment and related services. With approximately 1,800 Employment Service/Job Service offices nationwide there is bound to be one near you. To learn more about the services offered in your area, contact your state administrator. Craig Johnson, Secretary, South Dakota Department of Labor, 700 Governors Drive, Pierre, SD 57501-2277; 605-773-3101; Fax: 605-773-4211.

Help For The Homeless

The Good Shepherd Center offers job, lifestyle and computer training, laundry and shower facilities, children's center and free counseling for homeless individuals. For more information, contact Good Shepherd Center - Family Center, Jim Walden Director, 300 N. Main Avenue, Sioux Falls, SD 57104; 605-335-3321.

Entrepreneur Training For Women

If you are or would like to be an entrepreneur in South Dakota, the Entrepreneur's Network for Women may be just what you are looking for. The program offers you toll-free phone counseling, training seminars in management, marketing, financing, government contracting and entrepreneurial confidence. Networking sessions, a group mentoring program and Business Success Teams are offered at many locations in the state. The Network publishes a quarterly newsletter and holds an annual spring conference. The Network works in cooperation with the Women's Business Institute in North Dakota and is a division of the Watertown Area Career Learning Center, which is further described below. For more information, contact The Entrepreneur's Network for Women (ENW), Pat Helgeland, Direct or Becky Doerr, Kay Tschakert, 100 South Maple, P.O. Box 81, Watertown, SD 57201; 605-882-5080; Fax: 605-882-5069.

Help For Women In Transition

The Watertown Area Career Learning Center has assisted single parents, displaced homemakers, dislocated workers and economically disadvantaged persons since the late 1980s. The Career Learning Center offers job search workshops, counseling, resume development and more. For more information, contact Sandy Albertsen, Director, Watertown Area Career Learning Center or The Entrepreneur Network for Women (ENW), Kay Solberg, Director or Becky Doerr, Business Specialist, 100 South Maple, P.O. Box 1505, Watertown, SD 57201-0081; 605-882-5080; Fax: 605-882-5069; {www.network4women.com}; {e-mail: network4women@basec.net}.

Women Work!

Women Work! is a state affiliate of the national membership organization dedicated to helping women from diverse backgrounds achieve economic self-sufficiency through job readiness, education, training and employment. Contact South Dakota Women Work!, Connie Hermann, President, SP/DH Program, Northwest Area Schools Multi-District, 100 E. Utah Street, P.O. Box 35, Isabel, SD 57633-0035; 605-466-2206; {e-mail: conniehermann@hotmail.com}.

Vocational Services in Sioux Falls

Proteus, Inc. offers eligible applicants, depending upon availability of funds, assistance with financial aid for vocational schools and colleges, subsidized on-site training programs, employment counseling, job placement, testing and evaluation, financial assistance in relocating for education training and job placement, and emergency financial services such as, but not limited to, emergency food, shelter, and transportation costs. Proteus serves Sioux Falls and surrounding communities in Minnehaha County. For more information, contact Proteus, Inc., Kathy Knudson Career Development Coordinator, 301 S. Garfield Avenue Suite 6D, Sioux Falls, SD 57104-3140; 605-338-4352; Fax: 605-338-4396.

Tennessee

One-Stop Career Centers

A network of One-Stop Career Centers throughout the state offers a wide range of employment related services including job training. Services vary by location. To find a location near you, please refer to the website {http://wtw.doleta.gov/ohrw2w/recruit/where.htm}. To learn more about the services they offer, contact your state coordinator.

Mr. Michael E. Magill, Special Assistant to the Governor, Workforce Development Office, 400 Deaderick Street, Citizens Plaza Building, Ste. 200, Nashville, TN 37243; 615-253-1324; Fax: 615-253-1329.

Ms. Jocelyn E. Fraizer, Director, Tennessee One-Stop Career Development Centers, 400 Deaderick Street, Citizens Plaza Building, Ste. 200, Nashville, TN 37243; 615-253-1324; Fax: 615-253-1329.

Job Service Offices

A system of Employment Service/Job Service offices is located within every state with the goal of assisting millions of job seekers and employers. While services may vary from location to location, many provide job training, skills assessment and related services. With approximately 1,800 Employment Service/Job Service offices nationwide there is bound to be one near you. To learn more about the services offered in your area, contact your state administrator. Hazel Albert, Acting Commissioner, TN Department of Employment Security, 12th Floor - Volunteer Plaza, 500 James Robertson Parkway, Nashville, TN 37245-0001; 615-741-2131; Fax: 615-741-3203.

Empowering Women Business Owners Statewide

The National Association of Women Business Owners (NAWBO) is a membership-based organization that informs, empowers and promotes women business owners and invites its members to impact the social, political and economic communities. In Tennessee, they have established chapters in Chattanooga, Memphis and Tri-Cities, thus creating a statewide partnership of women business owners. The Nashville NAWBO has established the first, SBA-funded women's business center in Tennessee known as the Women's Resource Center. They offer you on-site business counseling services, training programs and technical assistance if you are a woman business owner in Middle Tennessee, which includes 21 counties. Through the consortium of Sister NAWBO Chapters and a corporate partnership with Bell South and the Tennessee Economic Development Center, the Women's Resource Center can also provide training programs statewide through satellite, two-way interactive videoconferences and the Internet. Contact The National Assn. for Women Business Owners - Nashville Chapter (NAWBO), Janice S., Thomas, Executive Director, P.O. Box 101024, Nashville, TN 37224; 615-248-3474; Fax: 615-256-2706; {e-mail: tnwrc@bellsouth.net}.

Training For Low-Income People

The YWCA of Greater Memphis/Women in Trades Project trains low-income people to be certified lead abatement workers and supervisors. And they work with low-income and minority contractors, non-profits, and CBO's who want to get into the field of lead abatement. For further information on the workshops and other activities, call YWCA of Greater Memphis, 1044 Mississippi Blvd., Memphis, TN 38126; 901-948-8899.

Women Work!

Women Work! is a state affiliate of the national membership organization dedicated to helping women from diverse backgrounds achieve economic self-sufficiency through job readiness, education, training and employment. Contact Tennessee Women Work!, LaSherrie McKinnie, President, West Tennessee Area Health Education Center, 295 S. Belle View, Memphis, TN 38104; 901-274-9009.

Help For Single Parents and Others

Shelby State Community College has a New Horizons Program that can help in a number of ways. They conduct workshops on job training, interviewing techniques, stress management, and coping with single parenting. They offer career planning as well as information and referral to job training. They can assist you in preparing for college entrance tests and/or in applying for and obtaining Pell Grants for full-time student enrollment. They even provide a stipend for child care or transportation for those who qualify. For more information, contact Shelby State Community College New Horizons Program, Brenda Smith, Director, Building F, Room 309, 737 Beale St., P.O. Box 40568, Memphis, TN 38174-0568; 901-544-5063; Fax: 901-544-5480; {www.jericho.org/_sscc_nh.html}.

Texas

One-Stop Career Centers

A network of One-Stop Career Centers throughout the state offers a wide range of employment related services including job training. Services vary by location. To find a location near you, please refer to the website {http://wtw.doleta.gov/ohrw2w/recruit/where.htm}. To learn more about the services they offer, contact your state coordinator.

Ms. Ruth Burrell, One-Stop Project Director, Texas Workforce Commission, 101 E. 15th Street, Room 526T, Austin, TX 78201; 512-463-6438; Fax: 512-463-8547; {e-mail: ruth.burrell@twc.state.tx.us}.

Job Service Offices

A system of Employment Service/Job Service offices is located within every state with the goal of assisting millions of job seekers and employers. While services may vary from location to location, many provide job training, skills assessment and related services. With approximately 1,800 Employment Service/Job Service offices nationwide there is bound to be one near you. To learn more about the services offered in your area, contact your state administrator. Mike Sheridan, Acting Executive Director, Texas Workforce Commission, 101 E. 15th St., Austin, TX 78778; 512-475-2216; Fax: 512-475-1133.

Assistance For Women Business Owners

The Texas Center for Women's Business Enterprise is a public/private initiative dedicated to the entrepreneurial success of Texas women. If you are thinking about starting a business or already own one and would like to expand it, TxCWBE can help you. As a member of this new generation of entrepreneurial women, they will prepare you for business success by dealing with topics including: certification information; Internet training for small businesses; business plans; loan assistance referral program; women's construction network; and consortium and contributing partners. Conveniently located in the capital city, TxCWBE has served Texas women for over six years. In 1996, Texas ranked 2nd out of the 50 states with 552,000 women-owned businesses, employing over 1 million people and generating $129.6 billion in sales. In addition to providing current training for today's businesses, the TxCWBE has also assisted in capitalizing women-owned businesses with $13 million in bank loans. For more information, contact Texas Center for Women's Business Enterprise (TXCWBE), Susan Spencer, Executive Director and Contract Administrator, Michele Pettes, Senior Advisor/Trainer, Joy Williamson, Training Assistant, Two Commodore Plaza, 13th Floor, 206 East 9th Street, Suite 13.140, Austin, TX 78701; Mailing Address: P.O. Box 340219, Austin, TX 78734-0219; 512-261-8525; 512-499-3083; Fax: 512-261-8525; {www.onr.com/CWE}; {e-mail: txcwbe@onr.com}.

Christian Job Training

Mission Waco offers the Wings Job Training Program. In their words, "Mission Waco has long acknowledged the importance of helping the poor secure jobs as part of its ministry toward Christian discipleship. Dealing with the root causes of poverty requires serious involvement in the marketplace. Due to years of welfare entrapment and a lost work ethic, many of the poor became dependent on a system which stole their personal pride and responsibility. Now, through various changes, those who can work are returning to the community to find work. But for many, basic job getting and keeping skills are difficult. With "Wings", there is the freedom to "fly" from the nest of that cycle." For more information, contact Mark Pearson & Matt Sciba, Mission Waco, 628 N.15th Street, Waco, TX 76707; 254-753-4900; {www.missionwaco.org/}.

Training For Low-Income People

The Center for Employment Training (CET) is a private, non-profit, community based organization that provides quality employment training for those who need it most. They offer you extensive life skills and workplace know-how instruction through a program that includes job preparedness training, job development and placement. CET keeps students in training until they are placed and conducts follow-up on all placement to ensure stable employment and job growth. CET's primary activity is classroom skill training, which is provided year-round. CET does not screen applicants through testing, but accepts anyone who is willing to do the necessary work. Courses are offered on an open-entry, open-exit basis and students complete training at their own pace. CET training is intensive, with students attending 5 days and 35 to 40 hours per week for an average of seven months. CET training is competency based, highly individualized, and hands-on from day one. The average training course at CET maintains a 20-1 student/teacher ratio. CET's unique mode of training involves an integration of skill training, basic skills instruction and human development conducted in a simulated work setting. At least twenty-five job training options are offered at CET nationwide. These include automated office skills, building maintenance, electronic assembly, medical assistant, truck driving, and shipping/receiving. Skill offerings vary from one center to another. A typical CET center offers 4-5 skills and may serve up to 250 persons annually. For more information, contact their national headquarters: CET Corporate Offices, 701 Vine St., San Jose, CA 95110; 408-287-7924; 800-533-2519; {www.best.com/~cfet/main.htm}; {e-mail: cfet@best.com}.

Center for Employment Training, 10102 North Loop Dr., Socorro, TX 79927; 915-859-1070; Fax: 915-860-9089; {e-mail: s_avila@cetmail.cfet.org}.

Learn About Procurement and More

The North Texas Women's Business Development Center, Inc. (NTWBDC) is a collective effort of the National Association of Women Business Owners (NAWBO), the Greater Dallas Chamber of Commerce Women's Business Issues Division, the North Texas Women's Business Council, and the Bill Priest Institute for Economic

Development. One area of focus is women's government contracting opportunities in addition to long-term training, counseling and mentoring. North Texas Women's Business Development Center Inc. For more information, contact North Texas Women's Business Development Center Inc., Branda Williams, Technical Counseling and Programs, Bill J. Priest Institute for Economic Development, 1402 Corinth Street, Suite 1536, Dallas, TX 75215-2111; 214-428-1177; Fax: 214-428-4633; {e-mail: women@onramp.net}.

Women Work!

Women Work! is a state affiliate of the national membership organization dedicated to helping women from diverse backgrounds achieve economic self-sufficiency through job readiness, education, training and employment. Contact Texas Women Work!, Mary C. Levandovsky, President, Student Support Services, Central Texas College, P.O. Box 1800, Killeen, TX 76540; 254-526-1291; {e-mail: mlevando@ctcd.cc.tx.us}.

Help For Displaced Homemakers and Single Parents

The Richland College Working Wonders Program is designed to prepare and support single parents/displaced homemakers in preparing for new careers. You too can have an exciting new career! Are you a single parent or displaced homemaker in transition looking for change? You'd like a new career with opportunities, but, you say, "I haven't worked in years," "I have no skills," "I can't afford to go back to school," and "What about the kids?" The Working Wonders Program is here to help you meet the challenges of entering or re-entering the workforce by providing you with the support and encouragement you need to get started and succeed. Services provided include: enrollment/registration assistance; academic advising; financial aid assistance; crisis intervention; personal counseling; community referrals; career exploration; textbook loans; child care referrals; and more. For more information, please contact Carol Castillo, Coordinator at 972-238-6972, room C157. Mailing address: Richland College, Adult Resource Center, Dallas County Community College District, 12800 Abrams Road, Dallas, TX 75243-2199; 972-238-6106; {www.rlc.dcccd.edu/ce/ARC/WorkWon.html}.

Community College Program
Single Parent / Displaced Homemaker Services at McLennan Community College can provide you with special services to help you achieve your goals at MCC. Services include counseling, mentoring, funds to assist with child care or transportation, and community referral service. For more information, contact McLennan Community College, Career Development Office, 1400 College Drive, Waco, TX 76708; 254-299-8614; 254-299-8414.

Utah

One-Stop Career Centers
A network of One-Stop Career Centers throughout the state offers a wide range of employment related services including job training. Services vary by location. To find a location near you, please refer to the website {http://wtw.doleta.gov/ohrw2w/recruit/where.htm}. To learn more about the services they offer, contact your state coordinator.

Mr. James Whitaker, One-Stop Coordinator, Utah Department of Workforce Services, 1385 S. State Street, Salt Lake City, UT 84115; 801-468-0265; Fax: 801-468-0160; {e-mail: wscfam.jwhitak@state.ut.us}.

Job Service Offices
A system of Employment Service/Job Service offices is located within every state with the goal of assisting millions of job seekers and employers. While services may vary from location to location, many provide job training, skills assessment and related services. With approximately 1,800 Employment Service/Job Service offices nationwide there is bound to be one near you. To learn more about the services offered in your area, contact your state administrator.

Robert C. Gross, Executive Director, Department of Workforce Services, 140 East 300 South, P.O. Box 143001, Salt Lake City, UT 84114-3001; 801-531-3780; Fax: 801-536-7500.

Curtis Johnson, Administrator, Department of Employment Security, 140 East 300 South, P.O. Box 45249, Salt Lake City, UT 84145-0249; 801-536-7401; Fax: 801-536-7420.

Training for Women Business Owners

You can receive training to help you establish or expand your business in a program established by the Utah Technology Finance Corporation (UTFC) dubbed the Utah Office of Women's Business Ownership. Training is available both in Salt Lake City and in outlying areas of the state. In addition, they maintain a database of women business owners in the state of Utah. UTFC administers the SBA microloan program for Utah. For more information or to locate a service provider near you, contact Utah Technology Finance Corporation, Kathy Thompson, 177 East 100 South, Salt Lake City, UT 84111; 801-364-1521, ext. 3; Fax: 801-364-4361.

High Tech Business Center

The Women's Business Center at the Chamber supports the success of women business owners throughout Utah with counseling, training and loan packaging assistance. With more than 30 committees and task forces, the Chamber provides you with unique networking opportunities as well as a full service export assistance program. Their onsite high-tech center offers access to the Internet and all types of business software. Women business owners can access help with marketing, management, finance and procurement. There is a modest fee for some services, but scholarships and specialized training are available for socially or economically disadvantaged women. Contact the Women's Business Center at the Chamber, Salt Lake Area Chamber of Commerce, Ramona Rudert, Director, 175 East 400 South, Suite 600, Salt Lake City, UT 84111; 801-328-5051; Fax: 801-328-5098; {www.slachamber.com}; {e-mail: ramona@slachamber.com}.

Short-Term Intensive Training

In today's job market, technical skills are critical to both new and experienced workers. Mountainland Applied Technology Center short-term, non-credit, competency based training is important to adults preparing for competitive jobs in the Mountainland region communities. This program offers you training in a wide variety of employable skills including: accounting, basic office skills, boiler operation & maintenance, building construction, certified nurse aide, commercial drivers license, computer programming, computer repair, computer training, critical work skills, customer service, data entry, dispatch academy, electrical repair/maintenance, electronic assembly, emission failure diagnosis & repair, entrepreneurship, first aide and CPR, flagging, forklift safety, home health aide, home health aide for certified nurse aides, Internet, major appliance repair, medical terminology, coding and insurance billing, network management, pilot/escort certification, small business tax education, speedbuilding, statistical process control and quality management, typing/keyboarding, and vehicle safety inspection. For more information, contact Information, Utah Valley State College, 800 West 1200 South, Orem, UT 84058; 801-222-8000; {www.uvsc.edu/depts/matc/}; {e-mail: info@uvsc.edu}.

Vermont

One-Stop Career Centers

A network of One-Stop Career Centers throughout the state offers a wide range of employment related services including job training. Services vary by location. To find a location near you, please refer to the website {http://wtw.doleta.gov/ohrw2w/recruit/where.htm}. To learn more about the services they offer, contact your state coordinator.

Mr. Robert Ware, Director of Jobs & Training, Department of Employment & Training, 5 Green Mountain Drive, P.O. Box 488, Montpelier, VT 05602; 802-828-4151; Fax: 802-828-4374; {e-mail: bware@pop.det.state.vt.us}.

Job Service Offices

A system of Employment Service/Job Service offices is located within every state with the goal of assisting millions of job seekers and employers. While services may vary from location to location, many provide job training, skills assessment and related services. With approximately 1,800 Employment Service/Job Service offices nationwide there is bound to be one near you. To learn more about the services offered in your area, contact your state administrator. Susan D. Auld, Commissioner, Department of Employment & Training, P.O. Box 88, Montpelier, VT 05601-0488; 802-828-4300; Fax: 802-828-4022.

Training For New And Existing Women Business Owners

The Women's Small Business Program offers a continuum of services to women seeking to identify, start, stabilize and expand a small business. You could benefit from services that include: Getting Serious, a workshop to determine a business idea and whether business meets personal goals; Start-Up, a 15 week intensive course to develop a business plan and business management skills; Working Solution, topic specific workshops for micro-business owner; and a graduate association to foster ongoing networking and access to information. They also offer comprehensive skills training and the opportunity to connect with other women entrepreneurs. Grants and scholarships for training are available to income eligible women. For more information, contact Economic Development Department, National Life Dr., Montpelier, VT 05602; 802-828-3211, 800-341-2211; Fax: 802-828-3258; {www.state.vt.us/dca/economic/developm.htm}.

Entrepreneurial Training

Northeast Employment and Training Program was incorporated in 1978 as a non-profit agency for the purpose of delivering educational and charitable programs to low-income Vermonters. One of their offerings is the Vermont Entrepreneurial Training Program, a classroom-training program providing an in-depth look at starting and operating a business. It is taught over Vermont Interactive Television and in individual classrooms. The program is regularly scheduled in September, January and April, but can and will be taught on demand. The program is divided into modules of which students may take all or any one. The cost of individual modules range from $25 to $200. The course information is project based along the creation of a business plan. Students are not graded on work performance but do a self analysis of learning. For more information, contact Northeast Employment and Training Program, P.O. Box 186, Johnsbury, VT 05819-0186; 802-748-8935; Fax: 802-748-8936; {www.vt-neto.org/index.html}.

Virginia

One-Stop Career Centers

A network of One-Stop Career Centers throughout the state offers a wide range of employment related services including job training. Services vary by location. To find a location near you, please refer to the website {http://wtw.doleta.gov/ohrw2w/recruit/where.htm}. To learn more about the services they offer, contact your state coordinator.

Dr. William L. Carlson, Governor's Employment and Training Department, Theatre Row Building, 9th Floor, 730 E. Broad Street, Richmond, VA 23219; 804-786-2270; Fax: 804-786-2340; {e-mail: wlc@richmond.infi.net}.

Job Service Offices

A system of Employment Service/Job Service offices is located within every state with the goal of assisting millions of job seekers and employers. While services may vary from location to location, many provide job training, skills assessment and related services. With approximately 1,800 Employment Service/Job Service offices nationwide there is bound to be one near you. To learn more about the services offered in your area, contact your state administrator. Dr. Thomas J. Towberman, Commissioner, VA Employment Commission, 703 East Main Street, Richmond, VA 23219; 804-786-3001; Fax: 804-225-3923.

Financial Assistance For Job Training

If you need more job skills to become self-sufficient or to make it in this job market, then the Piedmont Works Education for Independence Program may be able to help you. They can provide you with financial assistance for tuition and books as well as child care and transportation reimbursements while you attend school or job training. Participants typically attend PVCC, CATEC or local adult education programs with the goal of obtaining a GED, Career Studies Certificate, or an Associate of Applied Science degree. Making decisions about your career that will affect your family and your future can be confusing and overwhelming. They can help you set goals and make a plan of action through a variety of services including the following listings.

- Career Exploration for Women - This is a special one credit Student Development course at PVCC designed especially for your needs. Examine your interests, abilities, circumstances, and needs in the context of the job market, available training programs, and non-traditional career opportunities. Personal and Career Counseling; Gender Equity Education; Tuition Assistance; Textbooks and Class Materials; GED Preparation.

- Training on the Job - Provides information to help you find internships, cooperative education placements and work-study jobs, volunteer and work experience opportunities in the community to learn skills outside the classroom; Professional Development; Job Search Assistance; Child care - The Education for Independence Program can assist with child care expenses while you attend school; Transportation - Education for Independence can assist with transportation expenses so that you can attend school; Tutoring and Study Skills; Information and Referral; Career Development.

They have two locations to serve you:

PVCC, 501 College Drive, Room 206, Charlottesville, VA 22902; 804-961-5228; Fax: 804-961-5224.

FOCUS, 1508 Grady Avenue, Charlottesville, VA 22903; 804-977-5627; 804-977-2662; Fax: 804-977-3495; {piedmontworks.org/women.htm}; {e-mail: cpg20d@pvcc.cc.va.us}.

Training for Those Under 22

Teensight offers a variety of services for men and women under the age of 22. All assistance and services are provided free of charge. The Teensight program is part of Focus: A Women's Resource Center, a non-profit organization. Teensight is composed of several programs. Each of these programs works to overlap with the others. The mission of Teensight is to offer a holistic, complete and comprehensive service for the young adults in their area. For more information, find the location nearest you from the list below or contact Teensight, 1508 Grady Avenue, Charlottesville, VA 22903; 804-295-8336; Fax: 804-

295-8336; {http://monticello.avenue.gen.va.us/Community/Agencies/Teensight/home.html}.

The following Teensight regions offer job training

- Region IX - For men and women (teens or older) who reside in the counties of Orange, Culpeper, Madison, Faquier or Rappanhannock, Teensight provides employment assistance free of charge to those that qualify. Employment assistance includes Pre-Employment and Work Maturity training, employment skills training, job development, and employment placement assistance. Teensight can provide financial assistance for tuition, child care, transportation, and other items on a needs-based basis. For more information, please call Teensight Plus, 634 Schoolhouse Rd., Madison, VA 22727; 540-948-3562.

- Region X - Teensight can provide employment assistance for men and women under the age of 22 who reside in the City of Charlottesville, or in the counties of Albemarle, Greene, Fluvanna, Louisa or Nelson, as long as they qualify under federal guidelines. Employment assistance includes Pre-Employment and Work Maturity training, employment skills training, job development, and employment placement assistance. Teensight can provide financial assistance for tuition, child care, transportation, and other items on a needs-based basis. For more information, please call Teensight, 1508 Grady Avenue, Charlottesville, VA 22903; 804-295-8336; Fax: 804-295-8336; {http://monticello.avenue.gen.va.us/Community/Agencies/Teensight/home.html}.

Training For Low-Income People

The Center for Employment Training (CET) is a private, non-profit, community based organization that provides quality employment training for those who need it most. They offer you extensive life skills and workplace know-how instruction through a program that includes job preparedness training, job development and placement. CET keeps students in training until they are placed and conducts follow-up on all placements to ensure stable employment and job growth. CET's primary activity is classroom skill training, which is provided year-round. CET does not screen applicants through testing, but accepts anyone who is willing to do the necessary work. Courses are offered on an open-entry, open-exit basis and students complete training at their own pace. CET training is intensive, with students attending 5 days and 35 to 40 hours per week for an average of seven months. CET training is competency based, highly individualized, and hands-on from day one. The average training course at CET maintains a 20-1 student/teacher ratio. CET's unique mode of training involves an integration of skill training, basic skill instruction and human development conducted in a simulated work setting. At least twenty-five job training options are offered at CET nationwide. These include automated office skills, building maintenance, electronic assembly, medical assistant, truck driving, and shipping/receiving. Skill offerings vary from one center to another. A typical CET center offers 4-5 skills and may serve up to 250 persons annually. For more information, contact their national headquarters: CET Corporate Offices, 701 Vine St., San Jose, CA 95110; 408-287-7924; 800-533-2519; {www.best.com/~cfet/main.htm}; {e-mail: cfet@best.com}.

Center for Employment Training, 2762 Duke St., Alexandria, VA 22314; 703-461-9767 Fax: 703-461-9761 {e-mail: d_jroosa@cetmail.cfet.org}.

Work In Politics

If you are a young Republican woman who is interested in the political process, this program could provide you with some valuable experience when you enter the workforce. The Dorothy Andrews Kabis Memorial Internship is a program offered to four undergraduate women each year. The interns have a one-month experience at NFRW headquarters in Alexandria, VA, and they are housed at Georgetown University. No monetary allowance is given, but round trip airfare is provided. Applicants must be 21 years of age or older, and should have a general knowledge of government, a keen interest in Republican politics, campaign experience, as well as some clerical office skills. For more information, contact National Federation Of Republican Women, 124

North Alfred Street, Alexandria, VA 22314; 703-548-9688; Fax: 703-548-9836; {www.nfrw.org/internships.htm}; {e-mail: (membership) joinnfrw@worldweb.net}; {e-mail: (events) nfrwevents@worldweb.net}.

Job Training For The Economically Disadvantaged

The Job Training Agency provides help with job training and employment. Eligible job seekers must be economically disadvantaged. For more information, contact Job Training Agency, 102 Heritage Way, NE, Suite 202, Leesburg, VA 22075; 703-777-0540.

Washington

One-Stop Career Centers

A network of One-Stop Career Centers throughout the state offers a wide range of employment related services including job training. Services vary by location. To find a location near you, please refer to the website {http://wtw.doleta.gov/ohrw2w/recruit/where.htm}. To learn more about the services they offer, contact your state coordinator.

Mr. Gary E. Gallwas, Deputy Assistant Commissioner, Washington State Employment Security Department, 605 Woodland Square Loop, P.O. Box 9046 MS/6000, Olympia, WA 98507-9046; 360-438-4614; Fax: 360-438-4014.

Mr. Dennis Cole, One Stop Lead, Washington State Employment Security Department, 605 Woodland Square Loop, P.O. Box 9046 MS/600, Olympia, WA 98507-9046; 360-438-3258; Fax 360-438-4041; {e-mail: dcole@win.com}.

Job Service Offices

A system of Employment Service/Job Service offices is located within every state with the goal of assisting millions of job seekers and employers. While services may vary from location to location, many provide job-training, skills assessment and related services. With approximately 1,800 Employment Service/Job Service offices nationwide there is bound to be one near you. To learn more about the services offered in your area, contact your state administrator. Carver C. Gayton, Commissioner, Employment Security Department, P.O. Box 9046, Olympia, WA 98507-9046; 360-902-9301; Fax: 360-902-9383.

Training Assistance For Women and Minority Business Owners

You can access resources and technical assistance to start or expand your business through the Minority & Women Business Development program. MWBD can provide you with entrepreneurial training, contract opportunities, bonding assistance, export assistance, and access to capital for start-ups or expanding businesses in the minority and women's business community. For more information, contact Minority & Women's Business, 406 Water St. SW, Olympia, WA 98501-1047; 360-753-9693 or Community Trade & Economic Development, 906 Columbia St. SW, Olympia, WA 98501-1216; 360-753-4900; {http://access.wa.gov}.

Business Assistance For Native Americans and Others

ONABEN - A Native American Business Network, is a non-profit public benefit corporation created by Northwest Indian Tribes to increase the number and profitability of private enterprises owned by Native Americans. ONABEN offers training, individual counseling, assisted access to markets and facilitated access to capital for its clients. Each of the ten tribes hosting an ONABEN Service Center pays annual dues of $2,500 plus 40% of the cost of operating their site. The sites, located on reservations in Oregon, Washington and California, deliver services to all citizens regardless of tribal affiliation. Some have up to 40% of users coming from the surrounding non-Native community. For more information, contact ONABEN - A Native American Business Network, Sonya Tetnowski, OWBO Coordinator, 3201 Broadway, Suite C, Everett, WA 98201; 425-339-6226; Fax: 425-339-9171; {www.onaben.org}; {e-mail: sonya@onaben.org}.

Help For Displaced Homemakers

If you have lost your source of support through divorce or the loss of a spouse, you can take advantage of several programs throughout the state designed to help you gain self-sufficiency. These programs are coordinated by the Higher Education Coordinating Board of Washington State/Displaced Homemaker Program whose aim is to provide "real solutions to those who face barriers to education, training, and employment." You can access overall information about these programs at {www.hecb.wa.gov/college/homemaker/#definition} or refer to the list below to locate a service center near you. Specific information is provided wherever it was available.

Displaced Homemaker Program Locations by County

Asotin/Columbia/Garfield
Impact!, Walla Walla Community College/Clarkston Center, 1470 Bridge Street, Clarkston, WA 99403; 509-758-1716; Fax: 509-758-9512.

Benton/Franklin
Columbia Basin College, 2600 North 20th Avenue, Pasco, WA 99301; 509-547-0511, ext. 357; Fax: 509-546-0401; {www.cbc2.org/}.

Chelan/Douglas
Lifestyles Displaced Homemaker Program, YWCA of Wenatchee Valley, 212 First Street, Wenatchee, WA 98801; 509-662-3531; Fax: 509-663-7721.

Clark
The Southwest Washington Regional Displaced Homemaker Center can give you the tools to get back on your feet and provide for yourself and your family. They have centers open in Clark and Cowlitz counties and offer free services to displaced homemakers who live in the four county region covering Clark, Cowlitz, Skamania and Wahkiakum counties. Information and referrals are provided to local and regional organizations and agencies that can help you during the transition between unemployment and employment. They offer Job Readiness Classes, four-week/60 hour sessions, that address: discovering hidden

job skills; dealing with stress, anger, and health issues; how to stretch your current income; legal assistance; learning about the jobs that are available in the area; how to fill out job applications and write resumes; personal and group counseling; support groups; educational advising. One-day outreach workshops are held throughout the four county region to provide information on employment and educational opportunities, building self-esteem, and networking with others in the same situation. For more information, please contact Becky Merritt, Southwest Washington Regional Displaced Homemaker Center, Clark College, 1800 East McLoughlin Blvd., Vancouver, WA 98663; 360-992-2321; 360-992-2366; Fax: 360-992-2878; {www.clark.edu/StudentServices/StudentSupportServices/Displaced/}; {e-mail: bmerritt@gaiser.clark.edu}.

YWCA of Clark County
YWCA of Clark County, 3609 Main St., Vancouver WA 98663-2225; 360-696-0167; Fax: 360-693-1864.

Cowlitz
Lower Columbia College, 1600 Maple Street, P.O .Box 3010, Longview, WA 98632-0310; 360-577-3429; Fax: 360-578-5470; {http://lcc.ctc.edu/}.

Lower Columbia Community Action Council, 1526 Commerce Avenue, Longview WA 98632; 360-425-3430; Fax: 360-425-6657.

Kittitas
Yakima Valley Community College, PO Box 1647 (16th and Nob Hill), Yakima, WA 98907; 509-574-4976; Fax: 509-574-4731; {www.yvcc.cc.wa.us/}.

Pierce
The Women's Center offers a large range of services to Pierce College students, employees, and community members. Some of those services include: information resources; workshops special events; women's library; women's lounge; support groups; individual counseling; student leadership; scholarship information. The Displaced Homemaker Program is also located in the Women's Center. This program is free

and offers 160 hours of classroom instruction, 6 hours of support groups, and 2 hours of individual counseling for eligible displaced homemakers. Workshop exercises and topics include: computer training; aptitude testing; interests testing; career exploration; dependable strengths articulation process; developing a vocational plan; job search skills, resume writing and interviews; putting plans into action. For more information, contact Pierce College Women's Center, Fort Steilacoom Campus, Room 300J, 9401 Farwest Drive SW, Lakewood, WA 98498-1999; 253-964-6298; {www.pierce.ctc.edu/Users/Depts/Womenctr/main.htm}

Skagit
Turning Point, Skagit Valley College, 2405 East College Way, Mount Vernon, WA 98273; 360-416-7762; Fax: 360-416-7890.

Snohomish
The cornerstone of the Pathways for Women YWCA employment program is their Displaced Homemaker Program, which provides comprehensive instruction and assistance with job placement for women entering or re-entering the workforce. They work creatively with women who are displaced homemakers to ease the transition they must make as they become wholly self-supported. Participants then take part in a comprehensive instruction workshop that allows 58 hours of self-assessment, job readiness training, assistance with career decisions and job placement. During the intensive workshops, women learn how to identify their marketable skills, how to network, and how to access the hidden job market. The women participating in the program also enjoy supportive services through the counseling staff who teach women skills in coping with stress, with anger, and with going through transitions. Also, women can participate in assertiveness training and self-esteem building programs. Contact Pathways for Women YWCA, 6027-208th St. SW, Lynnwood, WA 98036; 425-774-9843, ext. 223; Fax: 425-670-8510; {www.ywcaworks.org/snohomish.html} and {www.housinglink.com/}.

Edmonds Community College Women's Programs offer workshops, support groups, women's studies and agency sponsored groups. Contact Edmonds Community College, 20000 68th Ave. West, Lynnwood, WA 98036-5999; 425-640-1309; Fax: 425-771-3366; {www.edcc.edu/WomensPrograms.htm}.

Spokane
ChangePoint, Community Colleges of Spokane, 3305 W. Ft. George Wright Drive, Spokane, WA 99224-5228; 509-533-3760; Fax: 509-533-3226.

Whatcom
The Northwest Washington Displaced Homemaker Center has a program called Turning Point that can help you start on the road to discovery. In friendly, supportive surroundings you can explore your personal strengths and interests, and you can learn ways to present your skills to prospective employers. Turning Point is a program of the Northwest Displaced Homemaker Center. It offers free workshops on building self-esteem and assertive communication skills for individuals needing to earn a livable wage. It also offers free classes that help with: career and life planning; personal skills; assessments; job search skills (resume writing and interview techniques); job market trends; and exploring career, training, and employment opportunities. Classes are small and confidential, with numerous opportunities for self-growth. Graduates report long-lasting increases in their self-esteem. The majority of individuals who attend are either working or enrolled in a training program within 60 days of class completion. They represent a wide variety of interests, programs and careers. Contact Turning Point at Whatcom Community College, 237 West Kellogg Road, Bellingham, WA 98226; 360-676-2170, ext. 3416; Fax: 360-676-2171; {www.whatcom.ctc.edu/servs/turning.htm}; {e-mail: rbailey@ whatcom.ctc.edu}.

Yakima
WA State Migrant Council, 301 N. 1st Street, Sunnyside, WA 98944; 509-544-0904; 800-234-4615; Fax: 509-544-0922.

Meeting Basic Needs in Seattle

Seattle is blessed with many programs that address job training and career development. Contact any of the service providers listed below for more information. Updated contact information can be found at {www.metrokc.gov/dad/guide/jobs.htm}

- *Asian Counseling and Referral Services*: Vocational and employment training, and job placement. 1032 South Jackson, Suite 200, Seattle, WA 98104; 206-720-5374.

- *Central Area Motivation Program*: Must be clean and sober; offer ex-offender program. 722 18th Ave., Seattle, WA 98122; 206-329-4114, ext. 305.

- *Downtown Human Services Council*: Job readiness, placement; bilingual Spanish. 115 Prefontaine Pl. South, Seattle, WA 98104; 206-461-3865.

- *DSHS*, Dept. of Vocational Rehabilitation: Help for people with disabilities (including alcohol/drug dependence or mental illness) to re-enter employment. Call for appointment. 1700 East Cherry St., Seattle, WA 98122; 206-720-3200.

- *El Centro de la Raza*: Training and placements; call for appointment; bilingual. 2524 16th Ave. South, Seattle, WA 98144; 206-329-7960.

- *Interaction Transition*: Employment assistance, referrals; work with recent releases from jails. 16th Ave., Seattle, WA 98122; 206-324-3932.

Job Service Centers

- Belltown: 2106 2nd Ave., Seattle, WA 98121; 206-464-6449.

- North Seattle: 12550 Aurora N., Seattle, WA 98133; 206-440-2500.

- Rainier: 2531 Rainier South, Seattle, WA 98122; 206-721-6000.

- Urban League of Metropolitan Seattle: Job bank; limited support. 105 14th Ave., Seattle, WA 98116; 206-461-3792.

- United Indians of All Tribes Foundation: Employment referral and placement. 1945 Yale Pl. SE, Seattle, WA 98102; 206-325-0070.

- Women & Family Center, Millionaire Club: Day jobs available, must be sober; job referral and employment training. 113 1st Ave. North, Seattle, WA 98109; 206-301-0833.

- YWCA, Employment Service: Job preparation, referral and placement. 118 5th Ave., Seattle, WA 98101; 206-461-4448 (voice mail).

- YWCA, West Seattle Center: Job preparation, referral and placement. 4800 40th SW, Seattle, WA 98116; 206-461-4485.

- YWCA, East Cherry, Employment Services: Job boards, readiness, placement help for low-income women. 2820 East Cherry, Seattle, WA 98112; 206-461-4882.

- ANEW, Apprenticeship and Non-Traditional Employment for Women: Employment training in trades and industry; income eligibility applies. P.O. Box 2490, 3000 NE 4th Street, Renton, WA 98056; 206-235-2212.

- Center for Career Alternatives (CCA): Various training courses; help with job search and placement. Must call for appointment. 901 Rainier Ave. South, Seattle, WA 98144; 206-322-9080.

- Pacific Associates: Training, job search and placement. 6 months sobriety. 2200 6th Ave., Suite 260, Seattle, WA 98121; 206-728-8826.

- Pioneer Human Services, Pioneer Industries: Paid training, then placement. Call by Wednesday for intake appointment Friday.

Need clean UA at intake. 7000 Highland Parkway SW, Seattle, WA 98106; 206-762-7737.

- Seattle Indian Center: Employment training and referrals. 611 12th Ave. South, Suite 300, Seattle, WA 98144; 206-329-8700.

- Washington Works: Job training; job search support; most clients on AFDC. 616 1st Ave., Fifth Floor, Seattle, WA 98104; 206-343-9731.

West Virginia

One-Stop Career Centers

A network of One-Stop Career Centers throughout the state offers a wide range of employment related services including job training. Services vary by location. To find a location near you, please refer to the website {http://wtw.doleta.gov/ohrw2w/recruit/where.htm}. To learn more about the services they offer, contact your state coordinator.

Ms. Quetta Muzzle , Director, Employment Service and JTPA Division Bureau of Employment Programs, 112 California Ave., Rm. 616, Charleston, WV 25305; 304-558-1138; Fax: 304-558-1136.

Ms. Lisa Wells, One-Stop Project Manager, WV Bureau of Employment Programs, 112 California Avenue - 5204, Charleston, WV 25305; 304-558-3461; 304-558-3470; {e-mail: st1597@stmail.wvnet.edu}.

Job Service Offices

A System of Employment Service/Job Service offices is located within every state with the goal of assisting millions of job seekers and employers. While services may vary from location to location, many provide job training, skills assessment and related services. With approximately 1,800 Employment Service/Job Service offices nationwide there is bound to be one near you. To learn more about the services offered in your area, contact your state administrator. Andrew

Richardson, Commissioner, WV Bureau of Employment Programs, 112 California Avenue, Charleston, WV 25305-0112; 304-558-2630; Fax: 304-558-2992.

Other State Programs

- The Northern Panhandle Private Industry Council can provide you with a list of job search and training service providers by contacting 2003 Warwood Avenue Wheeling, WV 26003-7103; Fax: 304/277-2013; {www.state.wv.us/bep/jobs/JTP/default.htm}.

- The Private Industry Council of Kanawha County can both provide and refer you to a list of job search and training service providers by contacting 405 Capitol Street, Suite 506, Charleston WV 25301; 304-344-5760; Fax: 304-344-5762; {www.state.wv.us/bep/jobs/JTP/pickan.htm}.

The following is a list of the Governor's Program Subcontractors compiled from the website {www.state.wv.us/bep/jobs/JTP/govpsubs.htm}. These service providers offer a variety of programs that are briefly described below.

- Huntington Housing offers on-the-job training, classroom training in various occupations. First phase provides six months of classroom training in occupations such as carpentry, painting, electrical work, landscaping and lead-based paint abatement. After completion of classroom training, second phase involves on-the-job training. 30 Northcott Court, P.O. Box 2183, Huntington, WV 25722; 304-526-4400; Fax 304-526-4427.

- Mid-Ohio Valley Regional Council offers an older worker program that includes classroom training for a certified nursing assistant. Contact P.O. Box 247, 531 Market Street, Parkersburg, WV 26101; 304-422-4993; Fax 304-422-4998.

- North Central OIC provides classroom training for business education, nurse's aide and child care provider. Contact 120 Jackson Street, Fairmont, WV 26554; 304-366-8142; Fax 304-366-8143.

- NAACP Jobs Program offers on-the-job training and life skills. Contact Suite 206, 910 4th Avenue, P.O. Box 1611, Huntington, WV 25717; 304-523-7819; Fax 304-523-1266.

- Wyoming County Opportunity Council, Inc. offers on-the-job training, basic skills and life skills. Contact Box 1509, Oceana, WV 24870; 304-682-8271; Fax 304-682-8274.

- Division Of Technical & Adult Education Services provides classroom training in various occupations such as pre-employment skills training/working maturing skills; skills cluster; work experience; limited use of advanced learning technology for education, job preparation and skills training; remedial education and basic skills training; internship training; and vocational training-institutional skills training. Contact Building 6, Room B-044, Capitol Complex, Charleston, WV 25305; 304-558-2681; Fax 304-558-1055.

- Construction Trades, Training & Advancement Program (CTTAP) provides occupational skills training serving participants in various construction trades and advancement programs. Contact 2301 Seventh Avenue, Charleston, WV 25312; 304-346-3863; Fax: 304-346-3862.

- Mercer County EOC offers on-the-job training; life skills; and basic skills. Contact 212 Federal Street, Bluefield, WV 24701; 304-324-0450; Fax: 304-324-8822.

- Potomac Highlands Support Services offers training in culinary arts. Contact P.O. Box 869, Airport Road, Petersburg, WV 26847; 304-257-1221; Fax: 304-257-4958.

- Potomac Highlands Support Services provides training for home health aide/certified nursing assistant. Contact PO Box 869, Airport Road, Petersburg WV 26847; 304-257-1221; Fax: 304-257-4958

- Career Works Associates Ltd. offers career transition and outplacement services. Contact 1207 Quarrier Street, Suite 304, Charleston, WV 25301; 304-344-2273; 800-718-5941; Fax: 304-343-0328.

- Charleston OIC provides feeder programs, nursing assistant and clerical/word processing. Contact 737 Virginia Street West, Charleston, WV 25302; 304-344-9681; Fax: 304-344-5965.

- Potomac Highlands Support Services offers on-the-job training (OJT) with life management skills/workforce development or basic education skills. Contact P.O. Box 869, Airport Road, Petersburg, WV 26847; 304-257-1221: Fax: 304-257-4958.

- MULTI-CAP, INC. provides work experience, on-the-job training, and occupational skills. Contact P.O. Box 3228, Charleston, WV 2 5332; 304-342-1300; Fax: 304-344-1098.

- The J.O.B.S. Company provides classroom training in retail and consumer sales. Remediation and basic skills training are also available. Contact 411 Capital Street, P.O. Box 3763, Charleston, WV 25337; 304-344-0048; Fax: 304-345-3295.

You Can Work At Home

If you live in rural West Virginia and would like to learn about alternative approaches to economic development such as networks of home-based business entrepreneurs, the Center for Economic Options can help. This is a non-profit, statewide, community-based organization that promotes opportunities to develop the economic capacity of West Virginia's rural citizens, particularly women, and communities. The Center creates unusual approaches to economic development including home-based business support and works with communities to help build support for small and micro-businesses. For more information, contact Center for Economic Options, Inc., Pam Curry, Executive Director, 601 Delaware Avenue, Charleston, WV 25302; 304-345-1298; Fax: 304-342-0641; {www. centerforeconoptions.org/}; {e-mail: wvmcoptns@citynet.net}.

Training In Technology

The Multi-County Community Action Against Poverty, Inc. brings together human, financial and material resources of the public and private sectors of Kanawha, Putnam, Boone, Clay, and Fayette counties to remove the causes of poverty, and to assist the poor in lifting themselves from poverty. Among a large variety of programs and services designed to help disadvantaged people, their job training services include Women in Non-Traditional Jobs, Welfare-To-Work, Single Parent/Displaced Homemaker programs, and Training in Technology Center. For more information, contact Multi-County Community Action Against Poverty, Inc., 1007 Bigley Ave., Charleston, WV 25302; 304-342-1300 Fax: 304-344-1166; {www.multi-cap.org/}.

Help For Single Parents and Displaced Homemakers

The primary goal of the Bluefield State College Single Parent/Displaced Homemaker Program is to assist single parents, single pregnant women and displaced homemakers in acquiring marketable educational and occupational skills that will enable them to support themselves and their families. They can provide you with: scholarship information; a mentor (through INSPIRE); support and encouragement; special workshops and seminars; information about daycare and daycare financial support; assist with admissions and financial aid paperwork; make referrals to community agencies, as appropriate; and more. You can obtain more information by contacting: Robin Dishner, Educational Outreach Counselor, Bluefield State College - Conley Hall Room 307, 219 Rock Street, Bluefield, WV 24701; 304-327-4500; {www.bluefield.wvnet.edu/}; {e-mail: rdishner@bscvax.wvnet.edu }.

Wisconsin

One-Stop Career Centers

A network of One-Stop Career Centers throughout the state offers a wide range of employment related services including job training. Services vary by location. To find a location near you, please refer to the website {wtw.doleta.gov/ohrw2w/recruit/where.htm} or refer to the website {www.dwd.state.wi.us/careers/} for more complete and updated information. Mr. Ron Hunt, Director, One-Stop Lead, Job Center Bureau Department of Workforce Development, P.O. Box 7972, 201 E. Washington Avenue, Room 231X, Madison, WI 53702; 608-266-2687; Fax: 608-267-0330.

Job Service Offices

A System of Employment Service/Job Service offices is located within every state with the goal of assisting millions of job seekers and employers. While services may vary from location to location, many provide job training, skills assessment and related services. With approximately 1,800 Employment Service/Job Service offices nationwide there is bound to be one near you. To learn more about the services offered in your area, contact your state administrator. Linda Stewart, Secretary, Department of Workforce Development, 201 E. Washington Avenue, P.O. Box 7946, Madison, WI 53707-7946; 608-266-7552; Fax: 608-266-1784.

Women Work!

Women Work! is a state affiliate of the national membership organization dedicated to helping women from diverse backgrounds achieve economic self-sufficiency through job readiness, education, training and employment. Contact Wisconsin Women Work!, Barbara Schall, President, Moraine Park Technical College, 2151 North Main Street, West Bend, WI 53090; 414-335-5770; {e-mail: bschall@moraine.tec.wi.us}.

Learn A Trade

Women in Trades, in partnership with five organizations in different states, will provide technical assistance to employers, contractors, and labor organizations on mega construction projects in the Midwest. They will work with contractors and apprenticeship programs meeting their goals for hiring women in job sites. These groups refer qualified tradeswomen to jobs, and most provide pre-apprenticeship programs to give women the skills needed in apprenticeship programs. They can give you information on career awareness on the range of job options for women too. For further information on programs in your state call:

Nancy Nakkoul, Projects Coordinator, Employment Options, Inc., 2095 Winnebago Street, Madison, WI 53704; 608-244-5181.

Nancy Hoffman, Director, Non-traditional Employment Training Program, YWCA of Greater Milwaukee, 101 E. Pleasant, Milwaukee, WI 53212; 414-224-9080.

Access Business Education Programs and/or Business Lending Programs

The Wisconsin Women's Business Initiative Corporation is an economic development corporation providing quality business education, technical assistance and access to capital. They consult, educate and mentor small and micro-businesses throughout Wisconsin. You could benefit from approximately 200 business courses and workshops offered in Milwaukee, Madison, Racine/Kenosha, Green Bay/Fox Valley, Beloit/Janesville annually. Topics include business planning, entrepreneurship, management, marketing, finances, and the Internet. In addition, if you are a woman, person of color, or low-income individual who owns or can demonstrate the ability to operate a small business, they can provide access to loans of $100-$25,000 to help you along.

Wisconsin Women's Business Initiative Corporation, 2821 N. Fourth Street, Milwaukee, WI 53212; 414-263-5450; Fax: 414-263-5456.

WWBIC - Madison Office, 217 S. Hamilton Street, Suite 201, Madison, WI 53703; 608-257-7409; Fax: 608-257-7429; {www.wwbic.com} and {www.onlinewbc.org}; {e-mail: info@wwbic.com}.

Help For Displaced Homemakers and Single Parents

Mid-State Technical College Displaced Homemaker and Single Parent Programs provides services to help you regain a sense of balance in your life. Their goal is to assist you in gaining confidence so you may evaluate your abilities, establish goals, and choose appropriate training or employment to eventually become emotionally and economically self-sufficient. Guidance is given through both individual and group advising in areas such as self-concept, career exploration, job seeking strategies and self-management skills. Support group activities are offered to all participants. For further information, refer to {www.midstate.tec.wi.us/} or contact the Mid-State Technical College campus closest to you from the list below and request the Students Services Department.

- Mid-State Technical College, 500 32nd St., NE, Wisconsin Rapids, WI 54494; 715-423-5650.
- Mid-State Technical College, 2600 W. 5th St., Marshfield, WI 54449; 715-387-2538.
- Mid-State Technical College, 933 Michigan Ave., Stevens Point, WI 54481; 715-344-3063.
- Mid-State Technical College, 401 N. Main St., Adams, WI 53910; 608-339-3379.

Wyoming

One-Stop Career Centers

A network of One-Stop Career Centers throughout the state offers a wide range of employment related services including job training. Services vary by location. To find a location near you, please refer to the website {http://wtw.doleta.gov/ohrw2w/recruit/where.htm}. To learn more about the services they offer, contact your state coordinator.

Ms. Beth Nelson, Administrator, Employment Resources Division, P.O. Box 2760, 100 West Midwest, Casper, WY 82602-2760; 307-235-3254; Fax: 307-235-3278.

Job Service Offices

A System of Employment Service/Job Service offices is located within every state with the goal of assisting millions of job seekers and employers. While services may vary from location to location, many provide job training, skills assessment and related services. With approximately 1,800 Employment Service/Job Service offices nationwide there is bound to be one near you. To learn more about the services offered in your area, contact your state administrator.

Frank S. Galeotos, Director, Department of Employment, 122 West 25th Street, Herschler Building, 2nd Floor East, Cheyenne, WY 82002; 307-777-6402; Fax: 307-777-5805.

Beth Nelson, Administrator, Department of Employment, Division of Employment Resources, P.O. Box 2760, Casper, WY 82620; 307-235-3254; Fax: 307-235-3278.

A Good Resource

The Wyoming Commission for Women can assist you with a number of employment issues as well as offer you referrals. Their mission is to work to improve the quality and equality of life for Wyoming's women. The Commission For Women focuses its actions on the needs and concerns of Wyoming women in the following areas: educational opportunities, employment, family and community, public policy, legal rights and responsibilities. For more information, contact Wyoming Women's Center, 1000 West Griffith, P.O. Box 20, Lusk, WI 82225; 307-334-3693; Fax: 307-334-2254; {http://{wydoe.state.wy.us/wcwi/}.

General Career Sites

ADAMS JOBBANK ONLINE

www.careercity.com

Explore current career possibilities in the fields of computer, finance, management, healthcare, sales, and lots more. Adams Jobbank Online offers an excellent job search engine to facilitate your research. Corporations will be glad to discover that this service offers free job posting. The Career Center offers links especially dedicated to graduating students.

ADGUIDE

www.adguide.com

Even though they call themselves a "College Recruiter Employment Site," these job listings are for entry level and experienced employees. Each job has a link to the potential employer through e-mail and/or a company web page. Check out a prospective employer before even submitting your resume. By entering your e-mail address, you will be notified of the new help wanted ads immediately. They also have an expansive list of articles and links to free information on financial aid if you want to further your education.

ALLIED TECHNOLOGY INTERNATIONAL, INC. (ATI)

www.mindspring.com/~mcafee/ATI/index.html

Allied Technology International, Inc., provides a multitude of services related to employment of personnel and submission of proposals for work. Their database contains a wide variety of positions that range from medical, engineering and technical fields in a number of locations. It is an excellent place to begin your job search.

AMERICA JOB BANK

www.ajb.dni.us

Quite likely the most successful job search site on the Net, America Job Bank has been recognized by PC Magazine as one of the top 100 sites. In other words, this is a great place to start your search for employment. Three options are available: you can perform a nationwide search, link to state search engines, or link to employer maintained job listings. The nationwide listings include opportunities for people looking for federal or military employment. Be forewarned that not all states have developed a website to go along with its other employment services. According to the Job Bank however, most states are in the process of putting up a site.

AMERICAN FEDERAL JOBS DIGEST

www.jobsfed.com

Working in the Federal Government offers paid training, tuition reimbursement, accrued sick days, job security and a host of other benefits. This site offers you a place to look for those jobs. You can either search the Live Jobs section or use the Job Matching service to find the job right for you. These sections have detailed information on what type of person they want to hire and how you can advance to a higher level. Also, check out the Federal Hiring News, which has information on job leads.

AMERICA'S EMPLOYERS

www.americasemployers.com

Developed by professional career consultants to help you complete an easy and successful electronic job search,

America's Employers is at your service. New employment opportunities are added continually and company databases are updated weekly to help job seekers tap into the "hidden" job market, and the site also offers a discreet and confidential resume bank for hundreds of hiring employers to see. With America's Employers, you have nothing to lose.

AMERICA'S EMPLOYERS COMPANY DATABASES

www.americasemployers.com/database.html

This site concentrates on the "hidden job market" and lets the job seeker contact potential employers directly. According to the site, "the hidden job market is responsible for the bulk of hiring that goes on in companies." You may search for companies in several states and industries of your choice. Once you submit your criteria, the search engine returns the names, addresses, and phone numbers of companies that match your request. This site is updated almost daily, so it pays to check in often!

America's Help Wanted!

www.jobquest.com

This diversified site has a lot of tools to help you with your job hunt. After you create your free personal account, you will create an online resume which potential employers will be able to browse. Once the profile forms are filled out, you will be able to access the job search tools and try to find the perfect job. This service takes the job seeker very seriously, so stop by!

Best Jobs In The USA Today

www.bestjobsusa.com

Through this outstanding site, you can search employment ads from USA TODAY and have access to a free resume depository that's searched by thousands of companies worldwide. In addition to providing lists of national career events and a career store that features books, audio tapes and videos designed to maximize the effectiveness of your job search, Best Jobs In The USA Today also allows you to keep up with new positions and new employment trends through the online employment review magazine. Best Jobs

In The USA Today surely has something for anyone seeking a career.

BRAVE NEW WORK WORLD

www.newwork.com:80

There are those who prophesy the coming of a great revolution. And then there are those who claim that the revolution is already here. This site would agree with the latter at least as far as world economics and employment are concerned. Brave New Work World, a site that represents many academic, professional, and practical experience fields, conducts daily surveys of worldwide press reports and is committed to informing you about what you can do to succeed in the revolutionary new world economy. As the site itself claims, it consists of "information, ideas, opinions, advice, continuing work education, and a range of interesting, entertaining content through a variety of media, helping you prepare for the new millennium. " Along with links to many other resources and archives of articles, this interesting and empowering site is a must to check out.

BRIDGEPATH.COM

www.bridgepath.com

At Bridgepath, you receive job announcements by e-mail. After filling out a questionnaire about your skills, job preferences and background, employers will contact you directly. This is all confidential, too. If you use Resume Review, your resume will be critiqued by professionals and colleagues when it is posted. There also is a newsletter published weekly which you can view. You will find suggested publications, links to the hottest sites and some fun ones too!

Business Job Finder

www.cob.ohio-state.edu/~fin/osufobs.htm

This site is a great place to visit to identify which business career is right for you. It will help to determine how to start in a career, what it takes to do the job, and what skills are needed for the work. They also include recommendations on books with topics such as Self-Exploration and Careers, and Jobs in Business. It has information on an array of business career areas and other reference material. This is an excellent site for those wanting a career in the business world.

Candidate Pool

www.candidatepool.com

Although they specialize in the areas of technology, they also offer a broad range of job listings. They have over 2,000 jobs to search listed through 500 hiring companies. Your resume will be sent to companies looking for an employee with your skills once it is posted. The potential employer will contact you personally to set up an interview. You can also check out the company profiles so that you know who it is you will be dealing with.

Career and Resume Management for the 21st Century

http://crm21.com

Through Career and Resume Management for the 21st Century, job seekers can post their resumes electronically onto a listing of resume databases on the net, browse through available job opportunities and have access to other free employment related resources such as resume review and evaluation, articles on interviewing, resumes, networking, hot tips on interviewing and listing of career-advancement books. Check it out.

Career Avenue

www.careeravenue.com

With this free service, job-seekers can search for all types of positions. All it takes is a job description and a location to begin! After that, you can receive help to create a resume before posting it. The Human Resource Team is available for questions concerning employment issues. They also have advice and job columns available that contain additional information.

Career Builder

www.careerbuilder.com

Career Builder has a Personal Search Agent! With this free service you will be e-mailed when your "dream" job is located. You can also research any company in their database or use the links provided to search other companies. Also included are guides titled, *Getting Hired*, *How to Succeed at Work* and *Managing Your Career*. This site offers a lot of information!

CareerCast

www.careercast.com

This easy to search site offers numerous jobs to review. You can search all of the jobs posted in UseNet Groups, or directly from the employer's web site. It can even be narrowed down as far as the specific city you would like to work in! You will also be able to link to different career sites that contain information that will aid you in finding a great job and how to get it.

Career Expo

www.careerexpo.com

Career Expo calls themselves a "Virtual Job Fair." They have a job search, company directory and company search just to start. There are over 300,000 jobs listed that are updated daily. Career Index allows you to search specific job databases such as High-Tech Employment, Company Pages, and Business/Financial. Through the Human Resource Center you can submit your resume and use the Salary Calculator. Be sure to check the Job Fair Schedule for an event in your area.

CAREERFILE

www.careerfile.com

CareerFile is a free and confidential resume referral service for executive, managerial and technical talent, specifically designed for busy professionals like you seeking a new step in your career. The services are simple, efficient and free. When there is a job match to your credentials and interest, one of CareerFile's recruiters will let you know and you can decide where your resume will go and who will see it. What could be better?

CAREER INFORMATION ACCESS

www.jobservices.com

This free service will link you to employment agencies and recruiters nationwide. Instead of a resume, you will fill out a job search profile containing the most important information needed as an initial qualifier for a job. It includes career objectives, qualifications and other information. To keep your information private, agencies and recruiters that specialize in your job area will only access your profile.

CAREERMART

www.careermart.com

CareerMart offers a wide variety of employment information and resources, including an extensive jobs database, information on recruitment specialists, and general career reference materials. By entering "the one stop Internet marketplace for worldwide employment information" job shoppers can browse through a variety of job listings, learn about employers, view company home pages, and have access to pertinent information useful to a job seeker.

CareerMosaic

www.careermosaic.com/cm

A job search site that has been recognized by many Internet ratings as one of the best of its kind, CareerMosaic has a lot to offer. The CareerMosaic J.O.B.S. database offers "thousands of up-to-date opportunities from hundreds of employers." Here you'll find a search engine that covers all regional and national job listings on the Usenet. You may want to take advantage of CareerMosaic ResumeCM service and post your resume online for employers to browse. Also available here are entry-level job opportunities, as well as detailed profiles of potential employers.

Career Park

www.careerpark.com

Use the quick links to featured jobs or search the databases by job category. Also, check Hot Jobs to see what the most popular career is, and who is offering work at this time. The employer list shows a little about a specific company and if there are any current job openings. There are also updates on the time and place of current job fairs being put on. Connect to Professional organizations, employers and career information sites through the Resource Center for help with your career. You can submit a resume either by using the available form or follow the guidelines for your own scannable or electronic resume.

CAREERPATH.COM

www.careerpath.com/infoseek/index3.html

If you live anywhere in the vicinity of Boston, Chicago, Los Angeles, New York, San Jose, or Washington, DC, or simply would like to find out what jobs are available in these areas, visit CareerPath.com. This site lets you search for job classifieds from major newspapers in those cities. The search engine is very well designed, letting you browse through one or all of the newspapers, and as many job categories as you wish. If you wish to take advantage of all the features at CareerPath.com, you may register online and gain instant access. The service is completely free.

CAREER PLANNING PROCESS

www.bgsu.edu/offices/careers/process/process.html

This site, providing you with self assessment tools necessary to execute a successful career search, "encourages individuals to explore and gather information which enables them to synthesize, gain competencies, make decisions, set goals and take action." Career Planning Process, offering the job seeker many interesting exercises, definition and informative resources along with information concerning internships and employment, is a truly wonderful site that you shouldn't pass by.

CAREER SEARCH LAUNCH PAD

www.pantos.org/cslp

The Career Search Launch Pad is a comprehensive guide to keyword searchable career databases on the Net. Use the help of this service and the job of your dreams may be only a click away.

CAREER SHOP'S RESUME, JOB AND EMPLOYMENT SITE

www.careershop.com

Designed for professionals seeking careers in fields of their choosing, this online database for resume profiles and employment opportunities is designed to assist job seekers just like you. Free of any charge, you can post resume profiles on the resume database and perform job searches of the online database by city, state, company name, category or any combination. The Career Shop also features tips for conducting a successful interview and links to other career related sites.

CAREERS.WSJ.COM

www.careers.wsj.com

This site is from the Wall Street Journal Interactive Edition. There is so much information to check out at this site! The question and answer, career columnists, salaries and profiles sections are just the beginning of what is available. Of course, there is a job seeker section. You can look for jobs by category and area, or check out a specific company for a job. Read up on what the experts have to say about sending out a resume after locating the job you want. So, whether you are just starting your career search, or are ready to get that job, this is the site to look at!

CareerWEB

www.cweb.com

CareerWeb is much more than a simple collection of job opportunities. Visiting this site will enable you to get on track for a new career, or enhance your current one. A number of tools are available. The Resource Center offers sure-fire ways to present yourself or discover the perfect career. Also here is a listing of advertising agencies, books, and publications, that might help you along the way. A monthly newspaper is released by CareerWeb with some of the latest information from this agency. Of course, those who are looking for a job will be happy to know that CareerWeb offers a premier job search service.

The Catapult on JobWeb

www.jobweb.org/catapult/catapult.htm

The Catapult lives up to its name: it is among the choice places on the Net to launch your new career. The Catapult does not list job openings, it is rather a site that organizes links to over 200 career sites on the Web into categories. Plenty of resources are available for career practitioners, as well as novices in the labor force. Other sites are listed under Help Guides and Career Library Resources and

Professional Development Opportunities. The Catapult is updated very often, so it's a must site for your bookmark file!

CENTER ON EDUCATION AND WORK

www.cew.wisc.edu

Maintained by the University of Wisconsin-Madison, this site "conducts research development and capacity building technical assistance designed to improve the connections for youth and adults between places of education and places of work." In other words, the Center on Education and Work is concerned with improving the links between education and work to help people engage in meaningful and productive careers. The site provides information concerning education-related publications and software, conferences, seminars and workshops and consulting and technical assistance. It can be a useful resource to help keep you at the top of the job market.

Cool Jobs

www.cooljobs.com

Have you ever wanted a career in the rescue field, electronic game design, or a space job? Well, you can find all of them and many other "cool" jobs at this site. You will be connected to many different companies that have these job openings and are just waiting for the right person to fill them!

Direct Marketing World

www.dmworld.com

Direct Marketing World is a site that can prove to be useful both to the employer and the employee, and the best part is that most of the services offered here are free! The job hunter will be delighted to find a sophisticated search engine that allows searches by region and nature of the job. Also, DM World allows its visitors to post their

resume, discover information on mailing lists and databases available on the Net, and even browse the library which contains helpful online documents designed to help anyone in the job market.

EAGLEVIEW

www.eagleview.com

Whether you are looking for your first job or are a seasoned employee, Eagleview has numerous opportunities for the jobseeker. After the brief registration process, your resume will be posted. After that, hiring managers from leading companies will be able to view you credentials. Take advantage of the opportunities that are available at this free site.

E-SPAN

www.espan.com/

E-SPAN claims to be your online employment connection, and it really does offer many tools to help you find a job. Two databases are available for the job seeker, as well as a variety of "job tools", which include tips on how to create a resume, how to conduct yourself in your next interview, and even help you get job ads in your virtual mailbox! You can also check out profiles of several employers featured at E-SPAN, and read some useful related articles.

4WORK.COM

www.4work.com/

A simple and concise job search site, 4Work.Com lets seekers across the country look for openings in their area. It is also possible to search for internship and volunteer openings here, and employers may find out how to post on this server.

Go Jobs

www.gojob.com

Start your job search off at the Career Center! Besides having great advice, it also has links to major jobs boards by region or occupation. You will be able to pinpoint what it is you want! You can conduct a job search locally or nationwide with the parameters that you choose. They offer a lot of resources for someone looking for employment.

HeadHunter.NET

www.HeadHunter.NET

This site boasts that thousands of professionals have found new careers using its services. You can search professional categories such as computer jobs, engineering jobs, accounting, work from home and so many more. Your resume will be posted for free, or upgraded for a small fee so that it is at the top of a search. You also have the option to keep it private at VIP resume services, where only the most serious employers will view it.

HEART/CAREER CONNECTIONSE

www.carrer.com/HCC/hcc.html

Would you like to find out about the hottest job openings in over 35 companies? How about joining a CyberFair hosted by an employer in your area? If these prospects interest you, or you simply want to explore other features offered by this service, then point your browser HEART's way. This site is under development at the moment, but has big plans for the future, so check in often to see what's new.

HOT JOBS

www.hotjobs.com

Have the Personal Search find the job you want and e-mail it to you. Submit your resume and control which of the member companies can see it. You will also be able to track how many times it has been accessed! The Message Board can be used to contact staff for assistance or to talk to fellow job seekers. Check out all this site has to offer!

INPURSUIT'S EMPLOYMENT NETWORK

www.inpursuit.com/e-network

InPursuit's Employment Network offers a wide range of products and services that could help you, the job seeker. The site's best features include a resume center, career related articles and a professional career center. To find out about their other superb ways to assist you in finding the career of your dreams, simply check out their site.

Integro Temporary Staffing Services

www.integrostaffing.com

This temporary and permanent placement service specializes in strategic staffing solutions. Integro places professionals in four areas: office, legal, scientific and accounting and financial services. Unlike many other staffing service providers, Integro offers professional personnel through its special services divisions so that it can provide the personal attention necessary to fully understand and work in specific markets. If you are interested in working in one of the fields mentioned above, check out this site. You won't regret it.

Internet Professional Association

www.ipa.com/

This site is a successful virtual employment association with over 1800 members. Through Internet Professional Association, you can search exhaustive job banks featuring numerous available job openings, post your resume or consult the career center for career advice. It is the purpose of this site to help employment professionals and those looking for contacts to find each other and pave ways to successful and long lasting careers.

IPA, Recruiter Online Network

www.ipa.com

The Internet Professional Association offers the job seeker career advice, a facility for resume postings and valuable connections to employment professionals, including recruiting firms. With over 1,800 members and associate firms linked together, IPA claims to be the world's largest virtual association of employment professionals. All you have to do is apply for free membership, browse through the current job listings and find the one that suits you best. Nothing could be easier.

JobCenter

www.mindspring.com/~cultech/jobc.htm

Tired of searching through thousands of job ads, day after day, week after week? Tired of constantly wondering which ads are new and which ones you've seen before? Have you asked yourself if there's an easier way? There is. Finding a job has never been simpler than through this site. Post your resume on the Employment Services Section of JobCenter and let them conduct your job search for you! JobCenter maintains a database of resumes from prospective employees and compares them with job descriptions from hiring employers. When a match is found, the copy of your resume is sent directly to the employer. You also receive a message to inform you of the status of your resume, and copy of the job description so that you know exactly what the employers are seeking. Instead of searching for new job ads in papers, through JobCenter, you'll receive new matching ads right in your electronic mail box each day! In addition, this site includes a special feature for the recent graduates to ensure that they'll have positions immediately after their graduation and an online search engine to browse through the job ads posted in JobCenter's databases.

The JobExchange

www.jobexchange.com

The JobExchange claims to match the talents of individuals seeking employment opportunities with the specific requirements of companies wishing to fill available positions. It offers two different searchable databases, one for part and full time employment and one for work on a contract basis. Accessible 24 hours a day, seven days a week, the site is updated daily and operates in an efficient, easy to use manner.

JobHunt: OnLine Job Meta-List

www.job-hunt.org

If you're not certain where to begin your job search, check out this extensive, well-maintained and current site. It is the purpose of JobHunt to provide you with a listing of useful accessible job-search resources and services on the Internet and it's sure to include something for everyone.

JobNet: Human Resources Online

www.jobnet.com

This is far from being a passive Internet resume listing service. JobNet is, on the contrary, an active database linking employers with prospective employees through lists of available opportunities and a resume service. It guarantees that you will receive the best services to aid and empower you in finding the job of your dreams, so you should definitely give their services a shot.

Job Resources by U.S. Region

www.wm.edu/csrv/career/stualum/jregion.html

This site links the job seeker to regional sites where they then choose a specific state. From that, pick from local sites that offer work in their area. Besides connecting to local communities, Job Resources, also offers Help Guides. The information can be used to help to create better resumes and interview skills. Access to national sites and short-term work is also included.

Jobs on the Web

www.jobontheweb.com

This is an excellent site with precise job listings. Each field is broken down into separate occupational categories. After you have made your job choice you pick which state that you would like to work in. Each listing has job requirements, descriptions and salary ranges. They are updated a couple of times a week. After visiting the Help/Writing section, submit your resume for free by e-mail, fax, or mail. There are job hunting and interviewing tips, as well as links to many professional organizations. There is an enormous amount of information here!

JobSAT

www.jobsat.com

This free site, designed to help you better execute your job search, features thousands of currently available job opportunities from across Canada and United States. Their database is easy to use and can quickly help you find the career that you've always desired.

JobWeb

www.jobweb.org

JobWeb is very likely America's most effective and efficient link to assist students, recent graduates and experienced professionals in their career search. Owned and maintained by the National Association of Colleges and Employers, this site is an up-to-date info source of salaries, legal issues, diversity recruitment, internships, college relations and general employment/ labor statistics relating to professional staffing and college-educated work force. JobWeb has 40 years of experience, an established reputation and a solid brand image as the leading publisher of career information for graduating college students and experienced alumni. Most importantly, it's here to help you find a career and you shouldn't miss out on its excellent services.

THE JOBZONE

www.thezones.com/jobzone

Are you frustrated with seeking employment through newspapers and bulletin boards? If so, there are sites on the Internet that can make your job search a whole lot easier. This free search engine, for example, is devoted to helping those seeking employment by providing thousands of job listings from private sector and government employers. You can simply search through their database and find a job that suits you best. The JobZone is updated weekly so keep checking back for updates.

MBA PLACEMENT PROGRAM

http://phoenix.placement.oakland.edu/career/emplist.htm

This direct and comprehensive site offers an alphabetical list of employers currently hiring MBA's and other professional disciplines. All you have to do is browse through the categories, find the ones that suit your interests and you will have already taken the first step toward a successful career.

THE MONSTER BOARD

www.monster.com

This is by far the best place the place to begin your search for a fulfilling career. The Monster Board offers free access to over 55,000 job opportunities worldwide in all levels and fields. Whether you hunt for a job, post your resume to their national database or conduct extensive research on employers worldwide, you won't be disappointed with the results from this superb site.

Nation Job Network

www.nationjob.com

Search for a job or a company that meets your wants. Their flagship service, PJ Scout, sends the job seeker any new jobs that fall into the category that they are looking in. The Specialty Pages list a variety of job types available and links to the job openings in that field. Check out the Community Sponsorship Program that has up-to-date openings and profiles of selected communities.

National Business Employment Weekly

www.nbew.com

Maintained by the National Business Employment Weekly, this site claims to be the nation's preeminent career guidance and job-search publication. The page's best features include profitable tips related to self-employment, job interviews and resumes, truths about job hunting and a savvy buyers guide to advance-fee job search to help you choose among career marketing firms.

National Employment Job Bank

www.nlbbs.com/~najoban

This great site offers the browser lists of current career opportunities that range from accounting to human resources. All offers come from some of the finest employers and employment services in the country and what's more, the service is completely free to you.

NetJobs

www.netjobs.com/index.html

This informative sight is a job seeker's dream. In addition to browsing through the employment listings, resume online services, job related newsgroups, resume writing tips from the experts, job interview tactics, unemployment insurance information and a training resource inventory, you can initiate your own search by company name and job location or find links to complimenting employment searches. This site also has bonuses for the recent graduate and the self-employed: NetJobs maintains a special service designed for the college graduate's first job hunt and a consultant's corner through which individuals working for themselves can utilize the Internet to improve their businesses.

Net-Temps

www.net-temps.com

Whether you're seeking temporary or permanent work, this in an ideal location to begin your quest. Through this free service, your resume information is taken via an online form and placed directly into the resume bank to be accessed by hiring employers looking for qualified candidates. You can also access Net-Temps' powerful job search engine that links you to a career magazine downloading and indexing all of the job postings from the major Internet job newsgroups and making them searchable by location, job title and/or skills required. Or you can browse through Net-Temps' archive of articles about job fairs, interviewing and personal networking. And if that isn't enough, this comprehensive site also maintains access to a directory of employer profiles where you will find detailed information on employers of your interest around the world.

NCS Career Magazine

www.careermag.com

This site is bound to be useful to anyone who is currently in the job market. The most impressive feature of this service is the job search engine, which uses data from all the Usenet job announcement groups. You may also want to browse the numerous employer profiles, discover the products and services available from Career Magazine, and even catch up on the latest news in the labor market! Also available here is a career links section and a World Wide Web resume bank.

123 Careers

www.123Careers.com

123 Careers features sections of new available job listings in various fields of employment and offers a free and effective way to forward your resume online to major companies and leading recruiters. Whatever you are looking for, this site will surely answer your needs in job search.

Opportunity Knocks

www.oppknocks.com

At this site they will walk you through creating a multimedia resume. They believe adding an audio or video presentation will set you apart from a paper only resume. It will be active for as long as you want it accessed by employers. After finishing that, start your search for jobs using the custom keyword, position and salary range options. They also have a great list of links to sites that include maps, moving calculators, labor statistics and a lot more.

Passport Access Employment Network

www.passportaccess.com

Whether you currently have a job and are looking for a better one or you are seeking a brand new opportunity , by placing your resume on this site, you can easily keep your options open. In addition to free resume posting, The Passport Access Employment Network also offers links to recruiting services and additional employment information. When you utilize their services, you have easily obtained the passport to a new, successful career.

PROFESSIONS

www.jobsarus.com

Take advantage of this site's no fee, no obligation services that include information concerning specific career fields and hot resume tips and networking tips. What better way to find a way to the profession of your choice than through PROFESSIONS?

RECRUITING-LINKS.COM

www.recruiting-links.com/job_search.asp

Recruiting-links.com is a free, comprehensive search engine with links to employers' recruiting pages. The database can be searched, for free, through over 700 combinations of geographic, industry and occupational employment preferences. If simplicity, accuracy, swiftness and good results is what you desire in your job search, recruiting-links.com can provide all of that and more.

SearchEase

www.searchease.com

SearchEase advertises that they have much more to offer in a search for a career. They have a job search where you can apply immediately or use the Job Search Agent to look for you. They also offer a Jobs In-Box in which you can keep job postings that are appealing, view interview requests submitted to you and even enter notes of previous interviews. You will be able to post a resume and add pictures, hyperlinks, and more creative features. All of this is free too!

USA Jobz

www.adgrafix.com/jobz/index.html

USA Jobz is a free, comprehensive database of vacant job opportunities offered across the United States. You can search by categories whether it be professional, medical, sales, retail, business or general information you require as well as by location. USA Jobz has got you covered all across the nation.

Usenet Jobs List

www.careermosaic.com/cm/usenet.html

This site is a well-designed, free search engine that can easily locate your dream job for you. All you have to do is type in a job description, and the search begins. You can also narrow the search by specifying a particular field, company, city etc, that suits your interests best. In addition, Usernet Jobs List has an index of thousands of postings from newsgroups with career opportunities that can match the ones appropriate for you. Try it, it's simple to use and produces immediate results.

Virtual Job Fair

www.vjf.com

The Virtual Job Fair claims to be the fastest growing career site on the Web. An easy-to-follow and direct place to begin your job search, this site has links to bulletin boards that provide information about the job of your choice, helpful ways to search for employers and career opportunities by title, technology, location or company and chances to send your resume directly to employers online. It claims to have connections throughout America and with such an exhaustive database, it is hard to doubt. This site offers a quick and easy way to begin your job search and the effective results are bound to follow.

WinWay

www.winway.com

Utilize this site and you'll surely win your way into a new successful career. WinWay is most helpful in assisting you to discover strategies for resume writing, interviewing and salary negotiations. In addition, it offers connections to online job finding resources, places to post your resume, and links to seek out hiring employers on the Web. WinWay also has an added bonus. If you're bored with your job hunt and need a refresher break, WinWay offers links to cool sites on the Web that range from helpful to humorous. This site is a friendly and empowering place to start your job search.

Work-Web

www.work-web.com

This educational and informative site provides a database of jobs and resume banks to assist people who need to brush up on classroom and/or job skills, or who otherwise need assistance in gaining employment. If you are looking for a job or just want to change your current position, this site is for you. You can search through available job openings and create your own resume and display it at no charge. Either way, your dream job could be only a click away through Work-Web.

Career Planning

Equal Opportunity Publications

www.eop.com

This empowering website specializes in affirmative action and workforce diversity recruitment for minorities, women and people with disabilities. Equal Opportunity Publications is dedicated to connecting employers committed to the recruitment of a diversified work force with qualified career seekers. The site links to five career magazines to help you land the job you want, a career center with a listing of career opportunities offered by leading companies, government agencies, schools and hospitals, information on upcoming career fairs and a fact center with tips for a better career search. What more could you ask for?

1ST STEPS IN THE HUNT
www.interbiznet.com/hunt

This newsletter for the job seeker is updated almost daily, and contains a lot of useful information. Discover great online points to start your job hunt, design and distribute your resume, and lots more! The best starting point for your hunt, this site has been named "Hot Site" by USA Today.

GOOD THINKING CO.
www.dnai.com/g-think

This is without a doubt one of the more interesting career related sites the Net has to offer. The Good Thinking Co. features articles on college success, career planning, and personal development, a list of websites with similar foci, success stories about profitable career moves and inspiring people, and a list of hot success books and inspirational movies. As a bonus, the site also features a collection of cool, interesting quotes. The best thing to demonstrate your good thinking power would be to sign on to this list for free and receive the frequently updated list of hot tips, success suggestions, and inspirational quotes directly in your e-mail box.

JOB OPTIONS
www.joboptions.com/esp/plsql/espan_enter.sepan_home

Job Options is a job database, private resume builder and recruitment resource for anyone looking for employment. You can search a job by category, location in the country, or by a keyword. You can send your resume e-mail with a single click of a button.

Outsource 2000 Handbook

www.outsource2000.com/?id+917364159

The Outsource 2000 Handbook offers a listing of sources that provide specific career information, an archive of articles about finding jobs and evaluating a job offer, and other occupational information valuable to any job seeker. The site also links to other occupational publications that can help you during your search for a better career.

Relocation Salary Calculator

www.homefair.com/homefair/cmr/salcalc.html

Are you planning to relocate but are unsure about what you are getting yourself into? The Relocation Salary Calculator can at least help you out in some aspects. It provides a living index for over 450 cities in the US which allows you to figure out the income you will need to maintain your current living standard when you move to a new city. Maintained by the Center For Mobility Resources, this effective tool thus allows you to determine the salary you would need to make in a new city, based on cost of living differences with your current location. This is a truly useful and necessary sight for anyone planning a move.

Specialized Career Sites

Academic Career Sites

ACADEMIC EMPLOYMENT NETWORK

www.academploy.com

If you're looking for a job in teaching or seeking other academic positions, this is an educational must. AEN contains a comprehensive listing of educational employment opportunities for teachers and other school-related positions at all academic levels, categorized in alphabetical order by state, educational institutions and positions. All position listings include info about inquiries, resume submissions, contact person, and best ways to submit your application. The Academic Employment Network also provides relocation services that present data concerning salary differentials, rental rates, demographic comparisons and various other statistics.

ACADEMIC PHYSICIAN AND SCIENTIST

www.acphysci.com

"Academic Physician and Scientist is the centralized resource for positions in academic medicine," claim the founders of this site. Indeed this site has listings of current administrative, basic science, and clinical science openings. Also here you will find job announcements from the National Institute of Health, and the FDA.

THE ACADEMIC POSITION NETWORK

Location (via gopher): wcni.cis.umn.edu:11111

This gopher site is dedicated to posting job announcements from colleges and universities throughout the world. From Alabama to Sri Lanka to Wyoming, this site covers more ground that most WWW sites of the same nature. You don't need to have a Ph.D. to find a job at the Academic Position Network. Plenty of administrative and research positions are available for the taking all around the globe.

AGORA EMPLOYMENT LISTINGS

http://agoralang.com:2410/agora/employment.html

If you are interested in teaching a language, check out this site. Agora Employment Listings provides current nationwide job listings in the field of language instruction. The openings range from administrative positions to jobs as ESL and specific foreign language teachers.

American Mathematical Society

www.ams.org

Is your job search in the field of mathematics not adding up to success? Let The American Mathematical Society help you find the job that you've been seeking. Their informative and daily updated site presents an impressive list of employment opportunities for those with an advanced degree in mathematics. Included are many positions in academia as well as in business and nonprofit organizations. Employing this site to help you can equal success in your career search.

EDUCAUSE Job Posting Service

www.educause.edu

Maintained by the association for managing and using information resources in higher education, EDUCAUSE Job Posting Service is dedicated to providing a career searching service for professionals interested in the field of information resources. The site lists a number of information resource related positions, available for your search as well as links to other informative and helpful sites on the Net. Furthermore, EDUCAUSE is completely free to you.

JOB OPENINGS IN ACADEMY (FROM ACADEME THIS WEEK PUBLICATION)

www.chronicle.com/jobs

This site is dedicated wholly to the job opportunities in academia. Listings are usually available in the fields of humanities, social sciences, science and technology, and professional fields. A section of this site has been apportioned for administrative and executive openings. The ads are updated very often, so this is a good site to bookmark.

JOB OPENINGS FOR ECONOMISTS (JOE)

http://vuinfo.vanderbilt.edu:70/11/employment/joe

This site is right on the money in assisting the job seeker in his job search. JOE features a large collection of employment postings, most of that are faculty positions in academe, but also carries information about job opportunities in businesses and nonprofit organizations. Featuring both browsable and searchable listings, JOE makes the job search easy and economical.

National Information on Software and Services (NISS)

www.niss.ac.uk/noticeboard/index.html#jobs

This career related site features available job vacancies in the worldwide academic community. Arranged by discipline, the listings are easy to choose from and browse. NISS's overseas job vacancies contain career opportunities in universities in the UK and Associations of Commonwealth Universities in Africa, the Caribbean, Australia, Hong Kong, New Zealand and Canada.

Telejob

www.telejob.ethz.ch

Telejob is an electronic job exchange board, maintained by the associations of assistants and doctoral students from the technological institutes of Zurich and Lausanne. If you've always wished to work in Europe, this site contains plenty of interesting jobs for young professionals from the academic or business worlds. Through an easily accessible directory, all that you have to do is choose the area of interest and read all the erudite offers that range from positions in architecture to law.

Arts and Design

ARTJOB

www.webart.com/artjob

Are you having difficulty finding employment as an artist? This bi-monthly newsletter can come to your rescue. ARTJOB, an elegantly created site, presents comprehensive, up-to-date national and international listings of arts employment, including information regarding academic agencies, internships, presenting and producing organizations and publications. It also features areas of specific interest concerning artistic performances, conferences and related opportunities. Any way you view it, ARTJOB is your source of opportunities in the arts.

DesignSphere Online Job Hunt

www.dsphere.net/comm/jobs.html

Are you looking for a new position in the field of art and design? Here is a place to let the community know that you're available as well as conduct a search of your own. DesignSphere provides job opportunities and jobs wanted listings for everyone involved in the communication arts, including designers, illustrators, photographers and software and print experts!

INTERNET FASHION EXCHANGE

www.fashionexch.com

Has it always been your dream to work as a designer or be involved in the fashion industry? Let this site help you find a position that you're looking for. Internet Fashion Exchange claims to be the only Website exclusively dedicated to providing centralized employment marketplace for the fashion and retail industry. Here is your opportunity to make your unique qualifications known to thousands of companies by utilizing IFE's resume bank where they can be accessed by people who are seriously looking for qualified industry professionals. Confidentiality is assured, and moreover, the services provided by this site are absolutely free.

Careers For Minorities and Women

SALUDOS: NATIONAL JOB LISTINGS

www.saludos.com

As part of their service to the Hispanic community, this website is a home to job listings from employers who are actively recruiting qualified Hispanics for positions in their companies. Whether you are seeking a career in administration, computers, engineering, finance, human resources, management, marketing, entertainment industry, sales, telecommunications or therapy, Saludos can offer you a helping hand. You can browse a list of all current job openings, arranged by state, view their tips on creating effective resumes or visit other career and employment sites on the Net, all for no charge whatsoever. This is a truly empowering and informative site.

WOMEN'S STUDIES EMPLOYMENT OPPORTUNITIES

www.inform.umd.edu/WomensStudies/Employment

Designed as a straightforward bulletin board, this site presents connections to job offers specifically for women and concerning women, along with direct contacts and dates the offers expire. The selection of opportunities is wide and ranges from careers in teaching and leadership to legal studies, counseling and research. In addition, this site offers excellent information about grants aimed to help those interested in the field of women's studies. No woman searching for employment should let this site pass by.

WOMEN'S WEAR DAILY

www.wwd.com/classified/classified.htm

Looking for a more attractive career move? Let this site help you. If you are a woman interested in working in the field of fashion, apparel, cosmetics or retail, Women's Wear Daily lists many vogue opportunities that range from sales to management and could get you the job of your dreams. Check it out.

Computers and Technology

AD&A Software Jobs Home Page

www.softwarejobs.com

With a network of over 600 recruiting affiliates, in almost every state, AD&A has access to career opportunities from coast to coast and you shouldn't miss out on their services. Their Software Jobs Home Page lists over 100 software job openings featuring many permanent, full time positions offering full benefits. You can search this database, access information on how to apply for the positions that interest you as well as link to other useful career related resources. In addition to providing general recruitment and placement services, AD&A also provides guidance on the job market for candidates in specialized areas. This is an excellent free and up to date service.

Computer Consultant Job Board and Resource Center

http://computerwork.com

Computer Consultant Job Board and Resource Center, a NACBB sponsored site, displays a broad job board for computer consultants in search of their next contracting opportunity. If you choose this site to search for current opportunities and submit your resume to the resume bank for companies to see, you can pick your dream career from the best technical job and contract employment opportunities currently available.

Computer Software/Systems Job Openings

www.nationjob.com/computers

This virtual bulletin board is updated almost as often as a real one (once a week), and holds even more information. Services obtainable from this location include P. J. Scout, a search engine that will e-mail any new openings that fit criteria you specify (it's free!), a list of featured employers and links to their websites, and, of course, job announcements from all over the country! This is a five-star site and a definite must for your bookmark file if you are in the computer industry.

Computerworld

http://careers.computerworld.com/jobs/jobs.html

Are you seeking employment in the world of computers? Check out this site. Computerworld can help you search current jobs through the automated career system called

CareerMail, a special agent that enables the careers you desire find you. All you have to do is register for free to have relevant career opportunities automatically arrive at your electronic mail box. Through this service, you can also skim through the corporate profiles and review descriptions of the employers who have posted their career opportunities on Computerworld.

Contract Employment Weekly Online

www.ceweekly.wa.com

Contract Employment Weekly claims to have "more job listings for contract technical employment than any other publication in the world." Unfortunately, the full database is only accessible to subscribers, who pay a moderate fee. Non-subscribers can also access this site and even browse some job announcements. There are plenty of other resources this site offers, such as a list of other related career sites, and interesting online articles. But to get the full benefit from Contract Employment Weekly, make sure you have a recent browser that supports Java, and be prepared to dish out a little money.

Cyberspace Jobs

www.careersbest.com

If you've ever wondered what kinds of jobs are out there in cyberspace, this is the place to check out all the various opportunities. Each of the 17 job descriptions that range from interactive actor to online researcher and cyberjournalist, link to related web sites, and news groups to provide you with more info if you are interested. Check it out — you won't regret it.

Data Processing Independent Consultants Exchange (DICE)

www.dice.dlinc.com

This site offers a high-tech job search engine for high-tech professionals. Free of charge, you may browse the index of companies currently offering jobs. You may also perform a search by keyword, state, area code, job type, and term. At the time of this review, the site had 4,802 job announcements. DICE claims that they renew the site every week, so this one is a must for your bookmark file!

Get A Job!

http://sensemedia.net/getajob

Get A Job will post your HTML format resume for no charge and will then promote their site as a place to find hypermedia professionals so that hiring companies may hire you directly. Get A Job also offers links to other job search engines that you shouldn't miss in your career search.

HUMMER WINBLAD VENTURE PARTNERS

www.humwin.com

Looking for a new job or a more exciting career? This site is ready to assist people from programmers to vice presidents in winning positions in the software industry's fastest growing companies. If you're searching for a cool job in a hot company, this site is for you.

INDUSTRYNET

www.industry.net

Along with bringing you the latest in engineering design, automation and manufacturing news that includes information concerning new products and online tradeshows, the IndustryNET also provides job postings from nearly 3000 top technological companies. Search their vast database and discover the ultimate business connections through this impressive site.

JOB MARKETPLACE

www.scrip.org/jobmrkt.html

This straightforward bulletin board of job listings can be of help to those seeking employment in the field of computers and technology. The Job Marketplace provides a list of browsable job descriptions complete with contact info and job requirements. This may well be the place through which you will find the perfect career for you.

JOB.NET

www.vnu.co.uk

There are a lot of solutions to job hunting, and a lot of answers as well. This site provides all of the good aspects of job searching in one location to help you find exactly what you're looking for. If you are searching for a career in computer technology, Job.Net features listings of the latest contract opportunities to computing professionals as well as an inventory of companies looking for employees. If you are a newcomer into the field, let this site offer you a helping hand through the informative guide for first time contractors.

PENCOM CAREER CENTER

www.pencomsi.com/careerhome.html

If you're seeking new career opportunities and possess technical or managerial expertise in today's computer technology, this is the right place for you to begin your search. PCC's well organized site's features include an interactive salary guide, nationwide job listings and in-depth articles covering both career and technology issues in the field of your choice. Check it out today and find a hiring company in need of your skills.

TRAINING AND DEVELOPMENT JOB MART

www.tcm.com/ht-careers/career

This is a job market site designed especially for training and development and multimedia positions. It offers a listing of the top US and Canadian companies in the field, access to full information of the available positions, and an opportunity to e-mail your resume directly to the hiring organizations. If after browsing through their data, you still haven't found what you're looking for and are open to a career in a foreign country, the site also offers a link to the Hong Kong job market.

UNIXIS SOLUTIONS

www.it-connect.com

This UK based recruitment consultancy focuses on employment in the client server, open systems, and technical computing arenas. Providing information about permanent, contract and graduate vacancies as well as opportunities for computing researchers, Unixis Solutions' quick and simple listings make it easy to find the job you're looking for in the United Kingdom.

VIRTUAL SEARCH

www.vsearch.com

Virtual Search provides listings of positions in the interactive multimedia and game development field. It focuses on the interactive multimedia talent pool that specializes in highly qualified technical, creative and marketing professionals for companies involved in advanced technology and next generation applications and products.

WESTECH CAREER EXPOS

www.vjf.com/jobsearch.html

In addition to Westech's specialty career expos, where companies and their potential employees can get acquainted, this site also offers a multitude of other free services. Along with listing the participating exhibitors and locations for the expos (complete with directions and maps), Westech has links to employer homepages, chances to post your resume and an online job search for those interested in a technological profession. A bulletin board is available, boasting over 15,000 possible high-tech career opportunities. This site has links to archived articles that enable you to research companies and technologies that match your interest. This site is a must see, packed tightly with helpful, high quality information.

ZDNET JOB DATABASE

www.jobengine.com

ZDNet Job Database is a comprehensive, nationwide listing of employment opportunities for professionals in high technology field. Whether you wish to search for a job or post your resume, this is a site that can help you in an efficient and orderly manner.

Education Related Career Sites

USJOBNET

www.usjobnet.com

The creators of this site have succeeded in centralizing all the US school districts' employment opportunities into one Internet location. It offers a list of jobs available in K-12 that range from administration to teaching and counseling, as well as links to other education related jobs, individual schools and school districts with a homepage on the Internet, education related associations and lists of upcoming job fairs for educators. Through this masterfully organized site, anyone looking for a career in the field of education can place an ad on the Internet and be on the way to a challenging and rewarding job.

Entertainment, Sports and Recreation Industries

Carbonate Your Brain: Job Pool

www.7up.com/html/nonflash/sindex.html

This 7UP sponsored site is a truly cool spot, particularly for students interested in the music industry. Carbonate Your Brain: Job Pool is serving up a new world of music and fun, fizzing job opportunities (some of which include additional information concerning salary, housing allotment and travel costs) and political expressions. Drink up!

CPB Jobline

www.cpb.org/jobline/index.html

If it's always been your dream to work either in the radio or television industry, this site offers a perfect opportunity. Provided by the Corporation for Public Broadcasting, job announcements from all over the country are posted on this Web server. Each job opening post includes the requirements to qualify for the position, the starting salary, the address to direct your resume, and the deadline for the application.

EMAP Media Web

www.emap.co.uk/jobs

This straightforward bulletin board features jobs in the fields of advertising and journalism as well as the radio and television industries. Clearly organized listings make it easy to browse through the available opportunities to search for the job of your choice and directly contact the hiring employers. If it has always been your dream to work in the entertainment industry, visiting this site is a definite must.

Online Sports Career Center

www.onlinesports.com/pages/CareerCenter.html

If you've always wished for a career in the sports or recreation industry, you can begin scoring points in your job search by checking out this site. Maintained by Sports Management Enterprises, a professional search firm for the sporting goods industry, the site is complete with resources on sports-related career opportunities, and a resume bank where potential employers within the many segments of the sports and recreation industries can have access to your qualifications. The online career center also provides links to other invaluable job search resources on the Net. Surely, this site can put you ahead of the game in your pursuit for employment.

Entry Level Jobs

COLLEGE GRAD JOB HUNTER

www.collegegrad.com

The one thing that is on the mind of most recent college graduates is getting a good job. This site offers numerous tips and strategies to find that job. Look into the step-by-step guide on how to look for the job, write your resume, plan for interviewing success, behave during the negotiation period, and even prepare for the first day on the job!

JOBDIRECT

www.jobdirect.com

Whether you are a graduating senior worried about what's awaiting you after college or a motivated undergrad trying to find internships, you have come to the right place to find assistance. JobDirect specializes in entry level positions for students and recent grads, especially non-technical jobs. JobDirect is the most effective way to obtain current information on entry level job market, internship opportunities, student related nonprofit organizations and international employment. Once you've registered, the site's services conduct a constant job hunting process which notifies you of any new posted jobs which match your interests. JobDirect is free, fast, and easy to use.

JOBTRAK

www.jobtrak.com

Yes, there is indeed life after college, and this site is proof of it. JOBTRACK, a college recruiting database, maintains partnerships with over 300 college and university career centers to provide a resume bank, list of top recruiters and a search engine for job listings to assist recent college graduates to look for their first jobs. This comprehensive and organized site also includes job search and resume writing tips and a guide to graduate.

SEACNET

www.seacnet.org

Seacnet, also known as the Southeastern-Atlantic Coast Career Network, is dedicated to helping students find their way in the "real world" of employment opportunities. The job seeker can search hundreds of job postings at participating universities in southeast United States, visit the links to employment centers, graduate and professional schools and potential employers. Though still in development, Seacnet already provides promising services for the college job seeker, and will surely have more to offer in the near future.

STUDENT CENTER

www.studentcenter.com

Are you a recent graduate in search of a job and having a little trouble out there in the "real world'? Visit the Student Center and all your troubles may be over. This site offers the latest in career-related information for entry-level job seekers just like you, including a 35,000 company searchable database and resume, interview, and job hunting tips. The Student Center is here to help you identify your personal strengths, define your career goals, and learn about the companies that best match your interests. Among other useful tools, their services enable you to take a self-diagnostic test to determine the right career for you and explore employment opportunities in major cities in all 50 states, as well as familiarize yourself with the international career market. In every way, this excellent site truly aspires to "help job seekers develop the sophisticated job search skills they need in today's competitive environment."

Environmental Careers

The Environmental Careers Organization

www.eco.org

The Environmental Careers Organization is a national nonprofit company dedicated to promoting careers in the environment. Their homepage specializes in services related to environmental internships, career counseling, employment resources, conferences, and job listings. By supporting "the development of environmental professionals and citizens who will make effective, balanced, and responsible decisions", this site can assist you in making environmentally responsible and successful career moves. The site also offers a link to a hot list of other ecological employment related websites to assist you in your search for an environmental career.

Environmental Careers World Online

www.infi.net

To check out this semi-monthly listing of job opportunities and career information published in Hampton, VA is the best way to start your environmental job search. Environmental Careers World Online helps people work for the environment by improving access to and awareness of environmental career information. Their consolidated and comprehensive information exchange fosters greater environmental workforce diversity and offers available employment listings in the fields of ecology, biology, forestry, natural resources, environmental education, policy, advocacy, law, science and engineering. Don't miss out on this great opportunity to start your job search.

JobBoard

http://fscnet.tamu.edu/jobs.htm

There are many ways to search for jobs and the Internet can prove an effective tool in this quest. This site, maintained by the Department of Wildlife and Fisheries Sciences of Texas A&M University, includes job postings that range from entry-level to professional, in the field of natural resources. Along with info on internships, seasonal employment and volunteer opportunities, this site also features links to other mechanisms to search for employment via Internet. Don't miss out.

UWIN
www.uwin.siu.edu/announce/jobs

UWIN is designated to serve as a clearinghouse of jobs and related opportunities in various water resources fields. The positions categorized into academic and student opportunities and are complete with contact information. If you think this is a field of your interest, check it out to begin in a winning career.

The Finance Market

ACCOUNTING NET
www.accountingnet.com/index.html

The Accounting Net features a job search database for accountants and auditors along with an area designed for the posting of resumes. It is user-friendly and free of charge, an excellent utility to the accounting professional seeking a new career move.

THE BUSINESS JOB FINDER

www.cob.ohio-state.edu/dept/fin/osujobs.htm

Want to get into the business industry? Check this site for the current job opportunities in the areas of finance, accounting, and management. You may also browse the list of sites maintained by individual employers, find information on several MBA programs, and link to other career sites on the Net.

FINANCIAL/ACCOUNTING/INSURANCE JOB OPENINGS

www.nationjob.com/financial

If your expertise lies in the field of finance, accounting, or insurance, this site will help you find a way to apply your knowledge. New job announcements from all over the country are added every week to an already extensive database of openings. Companies from all over the country post on this site, although most of the job openings seem to center around the mid-US region. Nevertheless, this is a good site to visit regularly regardless of your current location.

MARKETING CLASSIFIEDS

www.marketingjobs.com

This is a carefully designed site dedicated to helping professionals find a career in their chosen field of marketing, sales or advertising. The featured online resume database is divided into two sections: the executive resumes division for professionals with over 10 years of marketing, sales or advertising experience, and a general marketing resume division for job seekers with less exposure in these fields. Both sections are password protected and confidential. The site also features a list of current employment opportunities from across the United States, links to company web pages, a resume shop where you can tune up your resume, an address book where you can find addresses, phone and fax numbers for companies of your interest and links to other employment related sites on the Internet. And, of course, the best feature of all these services is that they are absolutely free to you, the job seeker.

Marketing and Sales Jobs Page

www.nationjob.com/marketing

This weekly updated site features hundreds of marketing and sales jobs. All you have to do is click on the job you would like to view and the information you need to begin a new career is at your fingertips. Moreover, you can just enter your job preferences and your e-mail address, and they'll send you any new jobs that match your choices each week, all through a free and confidential service. What more could you ask for?

Top Jobs on the Net

www.topjobs.co.uk

If you are looking for a job in information technology, sales, finance, marketing or consulting, Top Jobs on the Net is the best place for you to begin your search. This sophisticated site provides services to some of the most prestigious companies in the world and is dedicated to match the best candidates with the best companies. Complete with a career index of available positions listings and links to companies that range from Lotus to Kellogg, this display might ensure you either a contract or permanent career opportunity in the UK or the rest of Europe. Check it out.

100 Careers in Wall Street

www.globalvillager.com/villager/wsc.html

If you've been searching for a profitable career in the investment business, this website is well worth your time. You may browse job opening ads placed by the most prestigious companies all around the U.S. You may also submit a "job wanted" ad of your own and read the online pamphlet *Career Guide To Wall Street*. This site is aimed at the novice as well as the Wall Street shark.

Government/Federal Jobs

Department of the Interior Automated Vacancy Announcement System (AVAILS)

www.doi.gov/doi_empl.html

This authoritative and direct site announces job announcements with the US Department of the Interior. You can limit your search to different bureaus of the department and begin searching for a career that fits your interest best. Job search through this site is easy — specific contact addresses needed for you to take the necessary measures toward advancing your career are included in each announcement.

FEDERAL JOBS CENTRAL

www.fedjobs.com

Dedicated to matching people with jobs in the federal government, Federal Job Central has put together a toolbox specifically targeted for federal job hunters, helpful to both first time applicants as well as those already employed in the field. Their listings include various types of federal employment white or blue collar, full-time or temporary, in every possible location throughout the United States, and their services give job seekers the advice and how-to information they need to land the jobs they want and tips on how to make the most of their career investment. Updated every workday, the listings provide all the information needed to apply for the jobs, including a contact person and a telephone number. Current, comprehensive and accurate, this site is an authoritative database for federal job openings.

U.S. OFFICE OF PERSONNEL MANAGEMENT

http://usajobs.opm.gov

This is the complete listing of all government jobs available. You can search from A to Z or by agency. You can also look at the types of jobs available. Online applications are accessible with the click of the mouse.

Health Care Industry

MedSearch America

http://medsearch.com

It is the purpose of this site to assist professionals in the field of health care search for employment. MedSearch can aid you whether you are seeking permanent, temporary, internship, contract, or volunteer positions and the fields range from pharmaceuticals to sports medicine and health insurance. You can search for opportunities by job category, organization, title, or location and there are never any fees for the services.

NURSINGNET

http://nationjob.com/nursingnet

If you are a nurse seeking employment, the NursingNet can put you on the right track in your search for successful employment. The site can attend to your concerns regarding domestic, foreign, and overseas careers and also in resume preparation and offer you a helping hand in any other employment related issue you may have.

Military Positions

NAVY JOBS

www.navyjobs.com

The United States Navy is in need of a few good men and women. Whether you're a high school or a college graduate, the Navy has great opportunities for your career moves by offering employment in fleet or in the medical field and you can find out all about it through this site. If you're a recent college-bound high school graduate, be sure to check out the details of the Navy's many programs, which could help you pay for your college education.

U.S.Army
www.goarmy.com

Be all that you can be and check out this site. The U.S.Army homepage informs you of the opportunities in the United States Army for high school graduates as well as those with college experience. There are nearly 250 military occupational specialties that range from positions in accounting to medical services, and if you are interested, it is easy to find a fitting place in the Army through this site.

Sciences

AAS Job Register - American Astronomical Society
www.aas.org/JobRegister/aasjobs.html

This site is a straightforward bulletin board for those with careers in the field of astronomy. Available positions range from astrophysicists to research associates and are complete with a brief job description and contact information.

ACADEMIC CHEMISTRY EMPLOYMENT CLEARINGHOUSE

http://hackberry.chem.niu.edu:70/1/ChemJob

Academic Chemistry Employment Clearinghouse provides information concerning vacancies in the fields of analytical, inorganic, organic, physical and biochemistry. Positions are supplied from universities and other academic institutions across United States and can be searched by location or job description.

AMERICAN INSTITUTE OF PHYSICS

www.aip.org/aip/careers/careers.html

Have you ever asked yourself what to do with your physics major now that you're out of college or wondered what the next step in your physics vocation should be? With a weekly updated database of over 200 physics related job listings in academia, government and industry, this site can come to your rescue. The American Institute of Physics' services informs students about various careers in physical sciences as well as assist individuals with experience in the field search for new chances.

American Physiologist Society

http://oac.hsc.uth.tmc.edu:3300/00/employ/list

If you are looking for employment in the field of physiology, this site, maintained by the American Physiologist Society can help you search for new career options. The frequently updated entries are listed with the recently submitted options on top for your convenience, and the positions range from postdoctoral research to avail physiologists and department chairs in America's universities. Without a doubt, a good place to begin your job search.

Biomedical Positions

www.informatik.uni-rostock.de/HUM-MOLGEN/positions

This server contains job opening announcements for research associates, professors, as well as clinical, higher academic, and non-academic positions. Interested parties may post an ad of their own for free.

BIO ONLINE CAREER CENTER

www.bio.com/hr/hr_index.html

The BIO Online Career Center lists a number of resources related to careers in the biological sciences. Their listing of job opportunities includes positions from companies such as Genetech, Cell Therapeutics and Icos and the site contains links to other field related sites as well as an archive of biology related articles. It is a comprehensive and orderly site created for your convenience when searching for a job in the field of biology.

BIOSPACE CAREER CENTER

www.biospace.com/b2/job_index.cfm

Are you seeking a job in the field of biosciences? By checking out this frequently updated site, you can materialize in the best place to begin your job search. The BioSpace Career Center features a vast body of information concerning employment in the bioscience industries. The positions are grouped by region, category, and company and include employment in companies such as Bio-Rad Laboratories and Roche Molecular Systems. The site also links to other biotechnology resources that can assist you during your job search.

BIOTECHNOLOGY JOB BANK

www.labmart.com/employ

Maintained by Delco Scientific, this site "helps individuals seek high quality employment in sales, management, administration and technology in the fields of biotechnology, biopharmaceutical and laboratory products." If interested in any ad posted here, you will have the opportunity to e-mail the employer your resume right away.

Career Connection

www.ebi.ac.uk/htbin/biojobs.pl

Maintained by the European Bioinformatics Institute, this straightforward classifieds site lists numerous job opportunities in the fields of bioinformation, biochemistry, and molecular biology. You can execute your search by entering keywords or categories and find positions that suit you best in the category of your choice, whether it be in government, academia, or industry related occupations.

Cell Positions Available

http://jobs.cell.com

If you are a professional in the life sciences, you might want to point your browser to this address. Job announcements are listed in a very straightforward fashion, and there are plenty of them. Hyperlinks are available to classifieds from Neuron and Immunity publications. The site is updated regularly.

EMPLOYMENT LINKS FOR THE BIOMEDICAL SCIENTIST

www.his.com/~graeme/employ.html

As we all know, it is difficult to gain access to favorable positions in the field of sciences. The Internet can offer a particularly useful medium for exchange of employment related information, but not everybody has the time to sort through the wide variety of material out there. This site makes the search a whole lot simpler by offering links to employment related sites in the fields of biomedics, as well as other sciences.

EXPERIMENTAL MEDICINE: JOB LISTINGS

www.medcor.mcgill.ca/EXPMED/DOCS/jobs.html

If you are interested in experimental medicine, this site can help you find the perfect job. Experimental Medicine: Job Listings offers a bulletin board of post doctorate and university placement job listings in United States and Canada, along with links to many other field related resources. It's efficient and resourceful.

FASEB CAREERS ONLINE

www.faseb.org/careers

Maintained by the Federation of American Societies for Experimental Biology, this career resources site specializes in biomedical career advancement services. FASEB Careers OnLine confidentially matches applicants at all career levels with employers who need biomedical scientists and technicians. The site also provides information regarding national and international job fairs.

Franklin Search Group

www.medmarket.com/employ/empall.html

This free online career service is particularly helpful to those with interest in employment in the bio-technical and medical industries. You can post your resume, search for jobs or check out salary surveys and articles about employment, all at no charge whatsoever.

FSG Online Jobs in Biotechnology, Pharmaceuticals and Medicine

www.medzilla.com

This site provides a forum where employers and candidates can easily find each other and explore new job opportunities. Through FSG, you can easily find a new job in the field of biotechnology, pharmaceuticals, and medicine through their accessible database. Among other services, this site also allows you to post your resume, browse articles concerning employment, and current salaries in the field of science, and access an online book store featuring books and publications about working and finding jobs.

Job Opportunities in Entomology

www.colostate.edu/Depts/Entomology/jobs/jobs.html

Are you getting bogged down by the job search that seems to get you nowhere? This site may hold the answer for you. Stop the rest of your search now and browse through Job Opportunities in Entomology — a comprehensive listing of hiring research centers, universities and colleges around the country that could make your career search fly faster than before. You won't regret it.

Jobs In Physics, Astronomy and Other Fields

http://yorty.sonoma.edu/people/faculty/tenn/Jobs.html

This comprehensive site provides useful links to any young scientist looking for a job. It features a career planning center for beginning scientists and engineers, a student planning guide to grad school and beyond as well as a listing of part-time, temporary and summer jobs for students and a complete collection of links to other field related job pages. If you are just beginning your career in the field of science, this is a site you shouldn't miss.

Journal of Minerals, Metals, and Materials Classifieds

www.tms.org

This site lists all the ads that appeared in the last three issues of JOM. The JOM page is a perfect place to visit whether you are looking to start a new career in the metallurgy and minerals field or are a bona-fide specialist in those areas.

Medical Ad Mart

www.medical-admart.com

Medical Ad Mart is a compilation of current classified advertising of positions from widely read medical journals. It includes a listing of over 330 positions intended for physicians, pharmacists, laboratorians, life scientists, veterinarians, physician assistants, and nurses and provides messages from companies that specialize in servicing the medical community's needs for products, equipment, supplies, and continuing educational opportunities.

MedSearch America

www.medsearch.com

This site is a database of jobs in the medical and healthcare industries. You can either submit your resume into their database via an online form, execute an individual job search, or browse through health career forums and employers profiles. All the services are free and offer a complete coverage of the medical and healthcare fields that can help you during your job search.

National Physician Job Listing - EMBBS

www.embbs.com

The National Physician Job Listing - EMBBS contributes practice opportunities through North America for all medical specialties with a focus on emergency, internal and family medicine and pediatrics. This is the place to find the ideal practice opportunity for you and the site also offers a variety of other information related to the field, such as radiology, library, and clinical photos.

NIH Senior Job Opportunities

http://helix.nih.gov:8001/jobs

The NIH Senior Job Opportunities site offers a comprehensive listing of senior scientific, medical, and administrative job openings at the National Institutes of Health. As the foremost biomedical research organization in the world, they constantly seek candidates of the highest caliber to fill these senior leadership positions. To find the opportunity that suits you best, you can browse through the hypertext job announcements, submit your resume online or jump to related sites.

Physics Jobs online

http://physicsweb.org/TIPTOP

This is a dynamic job list for physicists, through which one can both search for and submit jobs in the physics field. The services are absolutely free of charge and up-to-date, since the old announcements are removed automatically after a week from the application deadline. Though the site offers mostly Ph.D. studentships, there are plenty of other opportunities as well for the job seeker in the field of physics.

Physics World Jobs Online

www.iop.org

If you are looking for a job in physics, you need to look no further. There is no more need to scan other different publications. You can see the latest opportunities directly on Physics World Jobs Online. Here are new job vacancies in the physics field as published in the *Physics World* magazine, or if you prefer, you can receive notification of new vacancies by e-mail directly to your mailbox. It is an efficient and wonderful site.

Poly-Links

www.polymers.com/polylink/jobank.html

Poly-Links presents job listings in the plastic and polymers industries. Whether you wish to browse the help wanted ads, create and post a resume or view the other field related sites, Poly-Links is flexible and can fit all of your job seeking needs.

R.Ph On The Go

www.rphonthego.com

R.Ph On The Go is an efficient pharmacy employment service placing pharmacists in pharmacies both as relief and full-time placements. On this site, the new job postings are updated regularly and the creators of the site are "committed to making a significant contribution with the rapidly changing health care industry". They also offer a growing menu of products and services designed to meet the changing needs of pharmacies and pharmacists.

Science's Next Wave

www.edoc.com

Science's Next Wave, "an electronic network for the next generation of scientists" displays a series of forums on science careers, a section focused on alternative scientific careers, a network of correspondents and data on the latest trends in science related careers. If you still haven't found what you are looking for, the site also offers hot links to other science related fields in funding, academia and other similar topics.

Sonus Technical Search

www.starnetinc.com

Sonus Technical Search provides engineers and scientists with listings of outstanding jobs in the fields of electronics, acoustics, physics, mechanical and electrical engineering and computer science. The listings are complete with a location, brief job description, summary of qualifications and contact information. In addition, Sonus allows you to submit your resume directly to the company of your choice. This is a thorough and excellent service. Check it out.

YSN Jobs Page

www.physics.uiuc.edu

Are you a scientist looking for a job? YSN Jobs Page offers a listing of jobs posted to the Young Scientists' Network. In addition to a number of links to other related resources, the site also provides hints of interviews, tips on interviewing in industry, job hotlines of various sorts and information about job fairs and regional meetings of the scientific community.

Transportation Industry

AIRLINE EMPLOYEE PLACEMENT SERVICE

www.aeps.com/aeps/aepshm.html

This site is the online source for professionals looking for employment in the aviation industry. You may browse the latest job postings, add your resume to the listing of available employees, and even ask a question in the Aviation Information Exchange forum. Employers can post a job opening without paying a penny. Also available here is a site newsletter, and a hot link to the main aviation site on the Internet. Happy flying!

DIRECT TRANSIT JOB OPENINGS

www.nationjob.com

This weekly updated site is a list of current job openings with Direct Transit. Whether you are looking for a job as a long haul driver, operator or team driver, this site provides you with a list of nationwide and regional opportunities. All you have to do is simply click on the job title to view a more detailed description of the offered opportunity and you can be steering directly toward the job you've been searching for.

FLIGHT INSTRUCTOR

www.cogweb.com/chode

You have just landed on a site dedicated to finding employment for pilots and flight instructors around the world. If you're seeking employment in the aviation industry, this is the place to launch your new career. Flight Instructor provides lists of commercial pilots around the world as well as aviation classifieds and links to other cool, aviation related sites. With a little help from this site, your career could soar to new heights.

Working At Home

NATIONAL HOME WORKERS ASSOCIATION

www.homeworkers.com

As this site claims, "if you work at home, you are one of more than 300 million home employees, united by a common need for comprehensive insurance, technology assistance, and practical services for the home work place." And if, as home worker, you are in need of a new job or simply considering the possibility of home employment, check out this highly comprehensive site. The National Home Workers Association lists more than 125,000 work-from-home positions open across North America, positions that range from typing, jewelry making and sewing, proofreading, writing, and much, much more. Their broad listings allow you to pick from thousands of legitimate home income opportunities and save time and money by doing so. Check it out and you won't regret it.

Miscellaneous

Au Pair

AUPAIR JOBMATCH

www.aupairs.co.uk

Located in the United Kingdom, this service matches nannies and families from all over the world. If you think you have what it takes to be a professional au pair, visit this site and find the perfect job/travel opportunity! If you are looking for an au pair, you may find out how to advertise on this server.

Building Industry

BUILDING INDUSTRY EXCHANGE

www.building.org/index.html

If you are currently seeking a career in the building industry, let this site help you with your search. Building Industry Exchange is a lofty resource for career info, job listings and other services for building industry professionals. Complete with an online database, lists of upcoming events, building industry related newsgroups and services, this site is a great place to begin assembling the career of your dreams.

Journalism

National Diversity Journalism Job Bank

www.newsjobs.com

This comprehensive list of job openings in the field of journalism should be an essential source for any journalist. Not an employment agency or a representative of any one newspaper, this ample job bank helps newspapers link up with potential applicants and encourages the participation of minorities and women. Complete with a list of job openings and a place to post your resumes, the site also links to other job banks and journalism related sites. Check back often for updates and new career opportunities hot off the press!

Landscaping

Landnet Job Listing

www.asla.org

Maintained by American Society for Landscape Architects, this site is allotted especially for the benefit of those who seek employment in the field of landscaping. The site features numerous postings of positions in landscape architecture and ecology and in other related fields along with a resume bank. It is an easy to access, resourceful, and well-maintained spot on the Net.

Law

LAW EMPLOYMENT CENTER

www.lawjobs.com

Finding a job that's just right for you may be a hard case to crack, but there's no need to lose hope. The Law Employment Center is here to assist you. If you're an attorney seeking employment, this is an excellent place to check out some new opportunities. The Law Employment Center's site contains hundreds of legal employment listings from the National Law Journal, New York Law Journal, and the Law Technology Product News along with an index of legal recruiting firms in states all over America, answers to your questions regarding the law employment marketplace and national salary survey. This is a truly superb site.

Library and Informational Sciences

LIBRARY AND INFORMATION SCIENCE JOBSEARCH

http://carousel.lis.uiuc.edu/~jobs

Are you interested in library and information services related employment? Maintained by the University of Illinois, this site may have just what you're looking for. With as many as 180 new records added each month, Library and Information Science JobSearch allows you to view notices by experience level, employer, keywords, library type or region, and links to library jobs from other online sources. Let your search begin here.

Seasonal Employment

Summer Jobs Web
www.summerjobs.com

Out of school for the summer and looking for a job? Let this site clue you in to the hottest summer opportunities around the country and abroad. The opportunities are organized by country, state or province, region, city or town and encompass all fields possible from retail to childcare. While the primary focus is summer employment for students and educational professionals, other jobs may be posted here as well, so it's worth a look.

Senior Citizens

The Senior Staff Home Page
www.srstaff.com

Designed exclusively for the job seeker over 50 years of age, The Senior Staff Home Page collects, categorizes, and markets current job information reserved particularly for that age group. If this category applies to you, you're in luck, for this site offers some of the best information around.

PopJobs
www.popjobs.com

This career site is designed specifically for the point of purchase advertising industry and is thus particularly useful for P-O-P professionals seeking careers in account management, merchandising, design, engineering or production. Popjobs' page also offers details on the latest technological developments and applications in the field, along with profiles of merchandising professionals and departments at leading consumer product companies.

Regional Employment in the United States

Alaska

ALASKA JOBS CENTER

www.ilovealaska.com/alaskajobs

The Alaska Job Center, job seekers resource page from the Alaska Department of Labor, is well equipped in providing the best resources to assist Alaskans seeking employment. The site's services include Alaska's economic indicators, relocation information and listings of government, seasonal employment, and volunteer positions. If you are seeking employment in Alaska, this site is a helpful tool.

Arizona

ARIZONA CAREERS ONLINE

www.arizonajobs.com

If you are seeking employment or relocation in the state of Arizona, check out this site. With diverse and up-to-date resources, ACO provides access to community, academic, and professional links, over 10,000 weekly updated position announcements, and comprehensive lists of job hotlines. Your resume is simply forwarded to employers and recruiters for no charge and you will be personally contacted if there are matches for your qualifications. What could be more convenient?

Arkansas

ARKANSAS CAREERS ONLINE

www.arkansas.com/relocation/index.html

Arkansas Careers Online is the premier, cost free location for local employment information in Arkansas, dedicated to electronically linking employers to employees. As the site itself claims, it is "a valuable resource center for people seeking a wide range of information concerning employment, entrepreneurial, career and education related issues". For best results, you can execute a keyword search for a position of your choice or electronically post your resume to their database. Check it out! You won't regret it.

Atlanta and the Southwest

ATLANTA'S COMPUTERJOBS STORE

www.computerjobs.com

This is the premier site, updated and validated every day, for available high tech and computer related job openings in Atlanta and the Southwest. Designed to inform professionals seeking contracting, consulting, or permanent jobs, the ComputerJobs store offers a variety of available job opportunities, links to other job centers in the Southwest and Dallas area, a list of 100+ Atlanta computer firms, along with brief descriptions and information on high tech careers fairs in Atlanta and the Southwest. All you have to do to make your job search even more effective is enter your resume online and wait for recruiters to contact you when appropriate jobs become available. Through this site, you can also learn more about Atlanta's computer market and advance your career with training and certification.

Baltimore and Washington

Global Commerce and Information

www.globalci.com

Global Commerce provides permanent and contracting employment information located in the Baltimore and Washington area. Updated weekly, this well maintained site seeks top individuals in a variety of technical areas, from client server to mainframe to multi platform environments, and aspires to help them find the jobs for which they are best suited.

California, Northern

Opportunity NOCs

www.tmcenter.org

This weekly updated listing of paid positions in Northern California nonprofit agencies can be of help to everybody seeking employment in the area. The job opportunities range from entry level to executive positions and are categorized conveniently for your benefit. Most positions are located primarily in the SF Bay Area and Sacramento. If this is what you are looking for, your dream career could be only a click away.

California, Southern

JOB SEARCH

www.ventura.com/jsearch/jshome1.html

The so called "hidden job market" comes from successful, dynamic and growing companies that seldom publicize their job openings. In such a case, relying on help wanted ads, computer postings, agencies, recruiters, or even networking contacts gets you nowhere. There is hope, however, through Job Search. It is the aim of this site to help you get your foot in the door of the hidden job market. With exclusive databases of 40,000 companies and over 100,000 continually updated news stories that identify the "hidden job market" in Southern California, Job Search is a job seeker's dream. Through their services, you can target

companies for potential employment, prepare job winning resumes and cover letters and even mail them to decision makers of companies of your choice so that you can be directly contacted by the company for an interview. In addition, Job Search's powerful search engine allows quick access to over 100,000 revealing and continually updated news stories and editorials regarding the job market in Southern California.

Colorado

Colorado Online Job Connection

www.peakweb.com/index.html

If you are ready for an office with a Rocky Mountain view, check out the current job openings through this site. The Colorado Online Job Connection is the best access to the Rocky Mountain region's job market, providing you with a listing of job openings, salary info and other useful resources that can help you locate a career in Colorado. In fact, you can even send them your resume and let their database search for the perfect job match for you.

District of Columbia (Washington, DC)

CareerBuilder

www.careerbuilder.com

CareerBuilder allows you to search for jobs in a number of companies in the Washington, DC area. You can immediately launch your search by selecting from a variety of limitations including location, job category and salary, or register with a free personal search agent who will search the site each day and e-mail you new positions that meet your search criteria. Either way, CareerBuilder can be your path to a new successful career in Washington, DC.

Florida, Southern

Career Spot, The

www.careerspot.com

If you live in Southern Florida or are planning to move there and are in need of employment, this is the site for you. The Career Spot, an easy to use job search database, provides current job listings, industry profiles and insightful articles that can assist you in executing a successful job search. Through their services, you can learn about top companies, search for a specific job or browse through all the available opportunities. This is a great place to begin the search that will lead to that perfect job.

Nebraska

OMAHA CAREER LINK

www.omaha.org/careerlink.html

If you are interested in employment in Nebraska, you need to look no further. The Cornhusker state needs workers, especially in the information technology, telecommunication and engineering sectors and the Omaha Career Link is your "one-stop shopping center for professional staff opportunities in Nebraska." Maintained by the Applied Information Management Institute, this site provides efficient career search facilities to match qualified professionals with available opportunities. You can explore the available job and internship positions, as well as search through company profiles and be on the way to the career of your dreams in Nebraska.

New England and New York

ADEPT, INC.

www.adeptinc.com

ADEPT, Inc. is an Information Services consulting firm located in Massachusetts with many openings in the New England and the New York area. It claims to be "the absolute choice in information technology consulting" and assists you by enabling you to submit your resume for employers to view and to view corporate job openings. If you're looking for a job in the field of information technology consulting, this site can offer excellent help.

New Jersey

Workforce New Jersey Public Information Network

www.wnjpin.state.nj.us

Are you interested in being employed in New Jersey? If the answer is yes, check out this superb site. The goal of Workforce New Jersey Public Information Network is to enable workers, students and those seeking employment to access a rich variety of information including education, employment and training opportunities, labor market info, job search tools and social services. It certainly lives up to its promise, providing job listings, demographic and economic information about New Jersey and its counties and information about services available from the NJ Departments of Labor, Human Services and Commerce and Economic Development. What more do you need?

NYWorks

www.nyworks.com

Through this fascinating web site, you can find information and links to nearly anything that concerns employment in the Big Apple. NYWorks can help you define your professional skills and help you search for customers, people or companies that will pay you for your product, service, or ability. In addition, it provides lists of available offers, links to job search and networking resources, a resume bank, tips and tactics of a successful job search as well as lists of alternative job opportunities in freelance, temp or telecommute. In short, this is everything you could ever ask for and more. Don't miss out!

North Carolina

CHARLOTTE'S WEB JOBPAGE

www.charweb.org/job/jobpage.html

This North Carolina based site features listings of available job opportunities, job banks, government agencies, educational institutions and nonprofit organizations in North and South Carolina. Charlotte's Web, a community network, also offers a link to a job hunters support group that may be of help to the frustrated career seeker.

Northwest United States

JOBSNORTHWEST

www.jobsnorthwest.com

Serving software companies, consulting firms, and MIS departments all over the northwestern United States, JobsNorthwest guarantees to match quality people with the quality positions they deserve. If you're a high tech specialist from the Northwest in need of a new job, check out this site for the job openings in your area of interest and you won't be disappointed.

Oregon

Oregon Employment Department

www.emp.state.or.us

Are you seeking employment in Oregon? Check out this site maintained by the Oregon Employment Department. Their homepage features information concerning jobs available throughout Oregon, resources concerning quality child care, and lists of local entities that can provide you with the career information that you need. Research and labor market statistics along with recent news releases and fact sheets on the Oregon economy are also included. And if that isn't enough, the site also provides links to local unemployment insurance services and other employment related state agencies.

Seattle

Seattle Employment Opportunities

www.pan.ci.seattle.wa.us

Are you seeking employment in the rainy city? Close your umbrella and look no further. The Seattle Employment Opportunities website can offer you all the information you need. Whether you need to browse through current city jobs and internships or are inquiring about information regarding women's employment and employment related newsgroups, this site provides everything you need to find a great job.

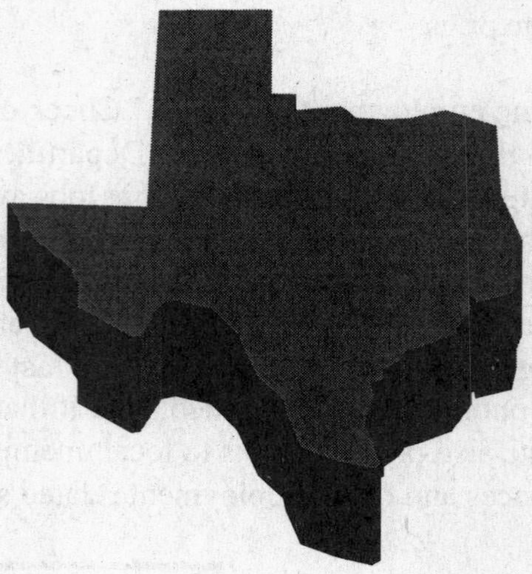

Texas

TEXAS PARKS AND WILDLIFE DEPARTMENT

www.tpwd.state.tx.us/involved/jobvac/job.htm

This site is a statewide listing of jobs available at the Texas Parks and Wildlife Department. The job info is sorted conveniently into departments such as human resources, wildlife, fisheries, public lands, law enforcement, conservation communications and resource protection. If this is the field you've always wished to work in, there is no better place to begin your search for employment.

Vermont

VERMONT DEPARTMENT OF EMPLOYMENT AND TRAINING

www.det.state.vt.us

If you're seeking employment information about the State of Vermont, this site can really help you. The Vermont Department of Employment and Training provides ample info concerning Vermont's labor market, job listings for both full and part time employment, resumes, and the latest unemployment rates. If you're thinking about working in Vermont, this site can find you the job that you desire.

International Employment

Asia

DAEDAL INTERNATIONAL

www.ozemail.com.au/~daedal

If you are an international student returning home to Asia and need a job, Daedal can help you locate a career in an easy and quick manner. They specialize in assisting overseas trained graduates just like you, and the employment offers can range from engineering to teaching located in a wide variety of countries from Thailand to Vietnam.

Australia

THE AGE CLASSIFIED ADS

www.theage.com.au:80/class

Interested in a career Down Under? This site brings you classified ads from The Age, the biggest daily newspaper in Melbourne, Australia. The Age Classified Ads, updated weekly, lists top jobs in information technology, higher education, health, and hospitals. Whether you wish to execute a specific job search or browse through all the ads, you can benefit from The Age.

JOBNET AUSTRALIA

www.jobnet.com.au/index.html

If you are seeking employment in the field of computers and technology and would be interested in working in Australia or Asia, this site is a must to check out. JOBNET Australia, updated daily, enables you to browse through a list of current job vacancies that include skills specification and contact details, or use the JOBNet Daily Email service to receive announcements of suitable job opportunities directly in your e-mail box. This site claims to be the best source of IT employment opportunities in Australia and Asia.

Canada

RESUME CANADA

www.bconnex.net/~resume

If you are seeking employment in Canada, Resume Canada can help you both post your resume and search through available career opportunities. This service is simple to use and free to the job seeker.

Central America

GREEN ARROW'S GUIDE TO VOLUNTEER WORK

www.greenarrow.com/nature/work.htm

If you're looking for information on voluntary work, research opportunities and courses in tropical agriculture, forestry and sustainable development, this is the site for you. Green Arrow's Guide to Volunteer Work, the largest Central American website in the world, provides information on tourism and conservation to an international market of over 40 million and works closely with environmental organizations, universities and ecotourism projects which enable it to develop and maintain a comprehensive database of opportunities in the field. Their site offers access to a large database and can help applicants find jobs in the areas of ecotourism, forestry, conservation, tropical agriculture and others. It is well maintained, informative and fascinating. A definite must for any job seeker.

Japan

O-Hayo Sensei, English Teaching Jobs in Japan

www.wco.com/~ohayo

Have you always wanted to teach English abroad but didn't know how to go about scoring a job overseas? Have you considered a teaching position in Japan? If so, O-Hayo Sensei can help you find suitable employment anywhere in Japan. Its extensive lists feature teaching positions at conversation and public schools, colleges and universities as well as survival tips, articles and information about contacting schools by phone or mail. This excellent site will also inform you in detail about the qualifications that will get you hired, current salaries, benefits, specific schools, housing, transportation, and contracts; help you search for jobs by city or region and network by mail, e-mail or fax.

O-Hayo Sensei can save you time and money by allowing you to place your job search in their hands and helping you find the job that you really want.

New Zealand

CV-Web

www.stimulus.co.nz

Has it always been your dream to be employed in New Zealand? This site may help make your dream come true. CV-Web is a New Zealand based job site through which you can write about yourself and your qualifications and submit it into the database or search for a suitable position from the classified ads. Either way, after checking out this site, you may be on your way to an exciting new career in New Zealand.

United Kingdom and Europe

JobServe - The Job Server

www.jobserve.com

Updated every weekday, JobServe features thousands of contract and permanent vacancies from hundreds of IT recruitment agencies in the United Kingdom and Europe. If you specify your needs and skills, JobServe will send you information from the wide range of job openings that apply specifically to your needs. Their services are fast, reliable, friendly, and free, and aimed to help you find the career that you desire.

Index

A

B

C

I

J

K

L

M

P

R

S

T

U

V

W

Y